THE BEST OF THE
REJECTION
COLLECTION

297 Cartoons That Were
Too Dark, Too Weird, or Too Dirty
for *The New Yorker*

Rescued by **MATTHEW DIFFEE**

Foreword by Emma Allen

WORKMAN PUBLISHING · NEW YORK

DEDICATION

In memory of the cartoonists we've lost along the course of this journey:
Handelsman, Cullum, Crawford, Weber, Ziegler, Wilson, Shanahan, and Darbyshire.
The world will miss their brilliant work, and we will miss their friendship.

This book is neither authorized nor sponsored by *The New Yorker*.

Copyright © 2011, 2022 by Matthew Diffee

Library of Congress Cataloging-in-Publication Data is available.

ISBN 978-1-5235-1239-3

Design by Galen Smith

This book is a revised second edition of *The Best of the Rejection Collection* by Matthew Diffee, first published in 2011 by Workman. Much of the material in this book originally appeared in *The Rejection Collection* and *The Rejection Collection, Vol. 2* by Matthew Diffee (published by Simon Spotlight Entertainment, a division of Simon & Schuster, in 2006 and 2007, respectively).

Page 375 constitutes an extension of the copyright page.

Workman books are available at special discounts when purchased in bulk for premiums and sales promotions as well as for fundraising or educational use. Special editions or book excerpts can also be created to specification. For details, contact the Special Sales Director at specialmarkets@workman.com.

Workman Publishing Co., Inc.
225 Varick Street
New York, NY 10014-4381

workman.com

WORKMAN is a registered trademark of Workman Publishing Co., Inc.

Printed in the United States of America on responsibly sourced paper.

First printing April 2022

10 9 8 7 6 5 4 3 2 1

THE BEST OF THE
REJECTION
COLLECTION

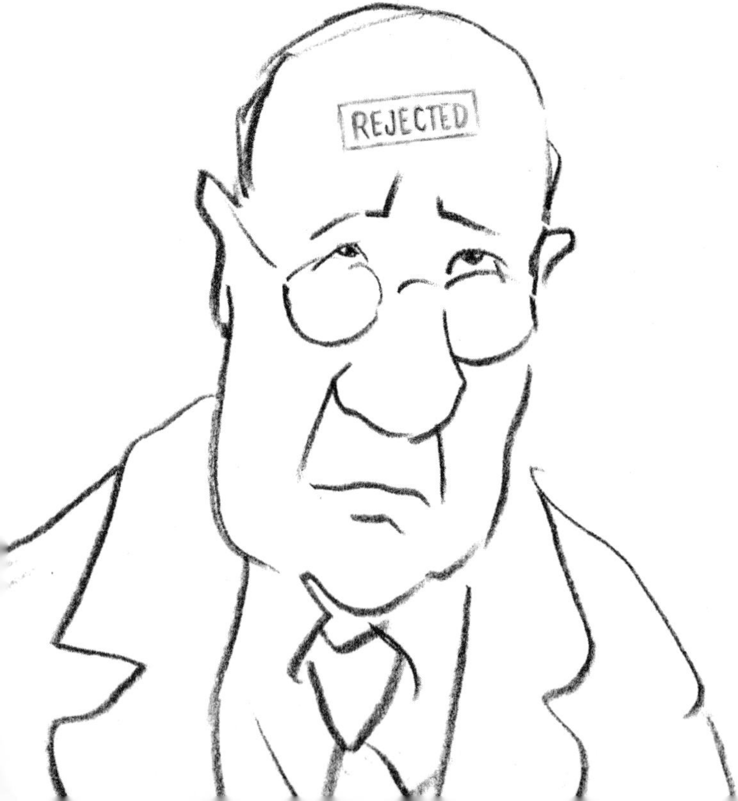
REJECTED

CONTENTS

FOREWORD BY EMMA ALLEN VII

INTRODUCTION 1

10 POSSIBLE REASONS WHY CARTOONS
GET REJECTED BY *THE NEW YORKER* 9

THE REJECTS

    Robert Leighton 22

    Jack Ziegler 26

    Roz Chast 34

    David Sipress 38

    Felipe Galindo 46

    Harry Bliss 52

    Leo Cullum 58

    Sara Lautman 68

    Mary Lawton 76

    Gahan Wilson 82

    P. C. Vey 88

    Jason Patterson 96

    Navied Mahdavian 100

    Carolita Johnson 106

    Michael Shaw 116

    Alex Gregory 124

    Teresa Burns Parkhurst 132

    Robert Weber 138

    Pat Byrnes 142

    Barbara Smaller 148

    Rich Sparks 154

    Drew Dernavich 160

    Mort Gerberg 168

    Julia Suits 174

Jon Adams..178

C. Covert Darbyshire...184

Marshall Hopkins...192

John O'Brien...196

Zachary Kanin...204

Emily Flake..208

Juan Astasio Soriano...214

J. B. Handelsman...220

Michael Crawford...224

Marisa Acocella Marchetto..230

William Haefeli...236

Nick Downes..242

Ellis Rosen..246

Ariel Molvig...252

Arnie Levin..262

Kim Warp..268

Eric Lewis...274

Maddie Dai...282

Sidney Harris...288

J. C. Duffy..292

Mike Twohy...300

Glen Le Lievre..306

Mick Stevens...316

Ed Steed..324

P. S. Mueller..332

Tom Cheney..340

Paul Noth...346

Lars Kenseth...352

Sam Gross...358

Christopher Weyant..366

ACKNOWLEDGMENTS..374

COPYRIGHT INFORMATION...375

BY EMMA ALLEN

cartoon editor for *The New Yorker*

Rejection is the pits. Disagree? Let me illustrate my point. Once, I was out on a date (yes, yes, please hold your applause). We were way uptown, and, as we prepared to board the subway we'd both be riding back to Brooklyn, my erstwhile beau said that he'd taken stock, and I wasn't for him, but no hard feelings. Reader, I'll admit, there were some hard feelings. Into a crowded subway car we went, together, making the awkward small talk of the never-going-to-see-you-again-so-why-do-I-care variety. Then the train stopped, between stations, for *forty-five* minutes.

Sometimes I run into cartoonists on the street and they give me that recently dumped, trapped in a subterranean tin can look, and while they may not believe me (even after my painful confession above), I get it. When I took the job of Cartoon Editor at *The New Yorker*, I mistakenly thought that I was signing on for a lifetime of nonstop laughter and witticisms lobbed back and forth over lunchtime martinis. About one week into the gig—and one misguided day-drinking foray later—I came to see that I'd actually assumed the mantle of Grim Reaper of Jokes.

Earlier volumes of *The Rejection Collection* describe the fifty-odd cartoonists who would submit weekly batches of ten gags. These days, I'm fielding batches from a hundred-plus regulars—not to mention the unsolicited stuff. And yet we're still only running around fifteen to twenty cartoons in each print issue. (I'm bad at math, but I can tell you, that math is bad.) This means that every Tuesday, I'm basically taking my scythe and slashing and burning my way through a lush jungle of more than a thousand submissions—most not-terrible, some pretty awful, and occasionally some truly unprintable ones. But you bought the book.

Thank goodness, come Friday, I get to buy a couple dozen brilliant, original cartoons. (For the interested, *The Acceptance Collection* is delivered to your mailbox each week, and comes with a free tote bag.) Only then, for a brief moment, can I drop the hooded cape and feel a bit more like a different cartoon trope—the fairy godmother, maybe, or at least something slightly less horrifying to run into on the street than the specter of death (perhaps guy with a hot-dog cart?). Anyway, *that's* when I get my martini. Then it's back to the weekly grind of breaking hearts and providing Matt Diffee with fodder for his next volume.

It's been ten years since I pulled together the original edition of the book you're holding in your hands. Bob Mankoff was the cartoon editor then, and was responsible for rejecting much of the material in these pages, along with Editor-in-Chief David Remnick, who of course makes the final call. Now it's Emma Allen keeping those rejection fires burning, keeping that big soul-crushing wheel turning, keeping us slippery scribblers firmly pinned under the heavy thumb of political (and most other kinds of) correctness. Meh, the truth is everyone gets it, the cartoonists as well as the editors, as Emma so charmingly laid out in her foreword. Mankoff got it too: "Funny isn't about beauty—" he wrote, "it's about freedom. Sometimes that freedom leads to disrespect, ridicule, and outright offensiveness."

Yep. Welcome to *The Best of the Rejection Collection*. In this book, you'll find a bunch of wonderfully awful and some awfully wonderful rejected *New Yorker* cartoons. They're not really *New Yorker* cartoons (after all, *The New Yorker* rejected them), but they are cartoons by *The New Yorker* cartoonists. I'm one of those cartoonists. My job is to come up with cartoons and pitch them to the magazine. The magazine's job is to reject almost all of those cartoons. Including this classy gem . . .

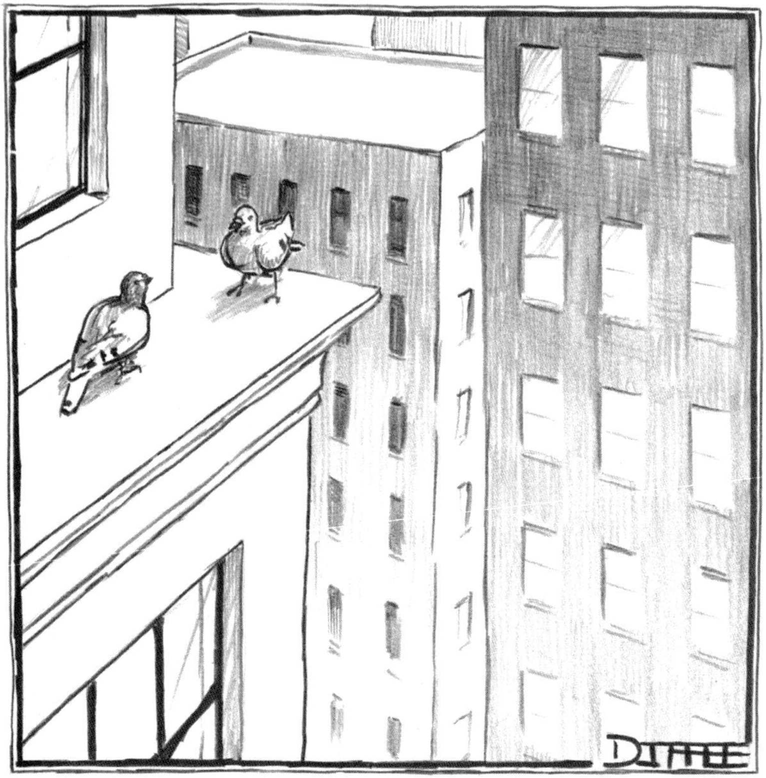
DIFFEE

"I'd say my biggest influence is probably Pollock."

You might think, like I did when I submitted it, that a gag like this could totally be in *The New Yorker,* but you, like I, would be wrong. Sure, it makes an erudite reference to an abstract expressionist painter whose work you have to know in order to get the joke, but it's also a cartoon about bird poop. Oddly, *The New Yorker* doesn't seem to go for that kind of thing. I assume that's why the editors passed on it. (Of course I don't really know for sure why this or any of the cartoons in this book were rejected. I have only my hunches. I've made a list of those and illustrated each with an example from my own healthy stack of rejects. You'll find them at the end of this introduction.)

At any rate, that's what you'll find here in this book: good cartoons that were bad for *The New Yorker,* the best of the worst, the rowdy, raunchy rejects, the ones that we the cartoonists kind of like best.

Let me take just a second here and put all this rejection business into perspective for you. The cartoons you actually see printed in *The New Yorker* are only a small percentage—the tip of the iceberg. We cartoonists are lucky if the magazine takes one of the ten ideas we pitch each week. It's a 90 percent rejection rate, but it's actually worse than that because our final ten, the ones we deem good enough to sketch up and pitch, are the tip of an even bigger iceberg. Well, it's the same iceberg, and I guess it can't technically be the tip because I just called the other part the tip. It's the next part below the tip. If it were a piece of candy corn, it would be the dark orange part. (And speaking of that, why would anyone name candy after a vegetable? Makes no sense.) Tell you what. Forget the candy corn. Stay with me on the iceberg. In fact, let me draw it. . . .

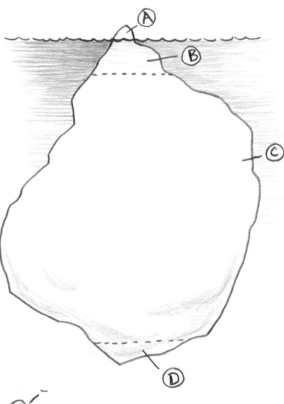

A. Tip of the Iceberg. The cartoons *not* rejected by *The New Yorker.* You can see these by getting yourself a subscription.

B. Top of the Iceberg. These are the cartoons that are rejected by *The New Yorker,* but not rejected by the cartoonist. See what I'm saying? These are his or her ten best ideas from a week's worth of work, what we call the *batch.* You can see the best of these in the pages of this book.

C. Bulk of the Iceberg. These are cartoon ideas that the cartoonist rejected. See, in order to get ten good gags for the batch, the cartoonist comes up with a whole lot more. Probably close to 90 percent more. The theory being that the more ideas generated, the better the quality will be of the final ten that are drawn up and pitched. These are probably not good ideas. Where can you see them? Well, you're not supposed to see them. In a way, they don't even exist because they weren't good enough to draw. However, in the interest of science, I'll give you a glimpse of these on the following pages of this introduction.

D. Butt of the Iceberg. A special classification of the above category, these are cartoon ideas that the cartoonist has rejected from other people. They can come from family members, former friends, psychiatric professionals, and even complete strangers. In most cases these are the worst cartoon ideas EVER. We showed some of these in a previous volume but decided against it this time. You're welcome.

E. A Blue Whale.

So that's the cold hard truth about cartoon ideas. Get it? Huh? Get it? Sorry. Now, as promised, in the interest of science, I'm going to give you a look at some of my ideas that would fall into the "bulk of the iceberg" category. Again, these are the surplus ideas that I didn't think were strong enough to get into the final ten that I sketched and sent to the magazine. Hopefully, this will also take us a few steps toward answering the question cartoonists get asked more than any other: *How do you come up with your ideas?* The honest but not very satisfying answer is, *We think of them.* It's unsatisfying because people want to know *how* we think of them, and that's tough to answer and impossible to demonstrate because it happens in our heads—but I'll give it a try here.

What you're about to see on the following page is the closest I can come to showing what happens in my brain, bad ideas and all. It's a piece of paper that I used to jot down my thoughts during an idea-getting brainstorm session many years ago. I can't pinpoint the date, but I think it must have been sometime in 2005.

See, every day, I make a pot of coffee and then sit down with a pen in front of a blank sheet of paper and think. If things are working correctly, by the time the pot's empty, the page will be full. What it's full of is scribbling. There'll be a bunch of half ideas, false starts, and then a few actual cartoon ideas. Almost all of these, however, will be "bulk of the iceberg" ideas. I think this is what some people call a mind map. Most of the work happens in my head of course, but the notes here provide a sort of dotted line of where my mind wandered. It might not look like much, but it represents a day's work for me. And of course, when I say a day, I'm really talking about a few hours—I'm a cartoonist not a coal miner.

A DAY IN THE BRAIN OF A CARTOONIST

A
TACKLE BOX
boxing
football

wiffle ——
nerf

just because you/I —— doesn't mean
let's just keep this between me and you and the internet
and our facebook friends

A restaurant That serves airplane food D
called ——

B Fear of flying

picket line
picket fence — fencing
dont picket fence me in
protestors strike
say no to protests
stop the picketing

Beware of dog
Cat crap

sign next to hot dog vendor ?

RobinHood steal from the rich and give to middleclass the wife

(a penny saved is a penny earned
but which is
a penny who has accepted Jesus as his personal savior ?

its all in the wrist

offensive driving

drivers Ed guy: make sure you keep both knee one on the wheel

Student Driver

C Sign on air plane
tractor bicycle
zamboni

I'm trapped in an effusive relationship

this might be the most important fig newton of my life.

E

some guy in a bar: you want a piece of me??

medal
metal Detector = tin man
man in suit of armor "maybe its your keys."
Super man: Oh I know what it is. I'm the man of steel."

or should be clark Kent.

I'm just going thru a hard time right now
said by a guy missing an arm and leg or just a head?

cubical on fire

looking in window at a bird in a cage

Reality TV
literature

H I need to join a gym but I want to get in shape first.

The real you/me
I want to know the real you unless the real you is ——
isnt rich

PIGEONS on a Wire
can you feel the electricity
we met online
target practice
bomb

take a page from my book
on the same page

Workaholic

kick the tires.
rotate.
burnrubber

need a bigger bucket
Bucket
kick the bucket
KFC
L list

floating belly up
little castle

Gold fish in a bowl
bronze
silver

GRim Reaper
raking leaves

I as artist: right now I'm working on a bus sort of an homage to Pollock

F fish sticks
fish out of water
luck
gas
money
filet o' fish phish
filet o' ——

pillow case
guitar case
detective

kick it again

cowboy hat how big is it in liters?

LOST AND Found
I lost my Lunch.
at zoo?
at ——
at Amusement park

If it aint broke...
If it aint Baroque
broken leg?

man trying on hats
— beret
do you have this in ——
do you have anything more pretentious
I want a beret that says I wannabe an artist
does it make me look like an artist

Shallow girl: I just dont want to be alone for the rest of my week weekend
G
Sometimes I'm afraid I'll end up...

hm, what should I do with this
eating lunch
extra boiled egg?

Construction workers
up on an i beam
dropped tool?

sign: men working on their tans
mentalking
scared of Heights (widths)

Here's a guide to a few points of interest:

A. This is a topic. Nothing going on with it really, but when I first sit down, I often start by just scribbling any and every random thing that comes to me. It helps to get rid of some of the scary white space. You gotta start somewhere.

B. This is a topic too, but not as random as the other. It's a topic that I had a funny feeling about. A topic I thought I'd be able to wring some humor from. As you can see by the lack of additional notes, I was mistaken.

C. "The old switcheroo." Here, I started with a thing, in this case a "student driver" sign that you'd see on top of a driver's ed car. Then I just tried to come up with a funny alternative vehicle to replace the car. Sometimes this works. Here it didn't. Clearly, the funniest vehicle option is a Zamboni. There's just something funny about a Zamboni, but that by itself isn't an idea. It needed more, and apparently I didn't come up with anything to nudge that notion into an actual cartoon idea. Thinking now, the obvious thing would be to have the Zamboni with the student driver sign in some sort of bad situation: The driver's rammed it into the wall, or he's running over figure

skaters, but that's not anything really. You could go absurd with it and have him driving it out in the middle of a desert. Or, I don't know. . . . See? This is what happens. If those are ideas at all, they're easily rejected ones.

D. This is a setup that didn't lead anywhere. Hence the blank. I'm sure I thought of stuff, but nothing worth writing down. Either that or I got distracted and didn't come back to it.

E. This is just a phrase I was hearing at the time. From there I try to think of a surprising image to use with it, or some way of manipulating the phrase into a joke. You can see some of that process here. Sometimes something comes from it, but usually not.

F. This fish business is just a little riff that I got into. Trying to generate something by jotting down a bunch of things around a single topic. I'm "fishing" for ideas here. Get it? Sorry. The closest thing to an idea here is taking the phrase "fish out of water" and changing it to "fish out of money." You can imagine a few ways that one could turn that into a cartoon, but can you think of any way to turn it into a good cartoon? I couldn't. Probably wasted eleven minutes of my life trying.

G. This is an idea. It's not that great. I rejected it.

H. This is also an idea: It's circled, so I guess I thought it was okay. Good enough to consider sketching up. I don't remember how the idea came to me, and you don't see any of the process here. I do remember drawing it, and I remember it getting rejected, which surprises me. Not that it was rejected, but that I remember it, because the idea itself isn't very memorable.

I. This is another idea, and this is the reason I chose this sheet to show you instead of all the others. This is the germ of the idea for that Pollock pigeon cartoon I showed you a couple pages back. It looks like I got to the idea from the seemingly random starting point of "pigeons on a wire" a few lines above. You'll notice I streamlined the caption later, making it better, but this is the initial spark. At this point, I was thinking the idea would work only if the reader pictured the pigeon "splatter" landing on something Pollock-size and rectangular, thus the bus reference. Going back through the week's idea sheets a few days later and selecting this one to draw, I had a better perspective on it and realized the bus wasn't necessary.

So there you go. That pigeon idea was a "top of the iceberg" idea. Not even a "tip of the iceberg" idea. It was good enough for me but not for *The New Yorker*. I don't know if I sold a cartoon at all that week, but I know I didn't sell that one. Sad, huh? If you multiply this sheet times six or seven, depending on whether I took a day off or not, and then add 50 percent for the ideas that didn't even make it to the page, you'll get a ballpark idea of how big the "bulk of the iceberg" was for me that week. Multiply that times the number of cartoonists in this book and then times the number of weeks in a year and suddenly we're talking about a pretty big ball of ice.

I hope you also get from this a sense of how a cartoonist—at least this one—thinks. You'll get a whole lot more of that in the following pages. Particularly in the sections between the cartoons, where I asked (okay, forced) my cartooning colleagues to answer some ridiculous questions in hopes of offering you a peek at their personalities and revealing just how endlessly creative and occasionally twisted they really are.

But first, as I mentioned earlier, here's a batch of some of my own rejected cartoons along with my best guess as to why they might have been rejected. Consider this a "what not to do" list if you want to get your cartoons into a sophisticated literary magazine.

WHY CARTOONS GET REJECTED BY

The New Yorker

··········

*As Exemplified by Some of
My Own Favorite Rejects*

REASON #1:

PLEASE DO NOT
FEED THE ANIMALS
CHILI.

The New Yorker shies away from anything of this sort. No poop jokes, no projectile vomiting, and certainly nothing coming in or out of noses. (I know . . . what else is there?) I, for one, have done scores of scatological jokes over the years and never sold one. But what are you gonna do? Stop doing 'em? The funny thing is, when you spend all day trying in vain to create little diamond-cut tidbits of sophisticated, intellectual humor, nothing makes you giggle at the drawing board like a good old-fashioned flatulent pachyderm gag. Alas.

REASON #2:

TOO POLITICALLY INCORRECT

GO INDIANS

I don't know. To me this cartoon is less about Native Americans and more about people who paint their faces at ball games. And besides, you can't say the gentleman on the right isn't wholeheartedly pro-Indian. Crap, I'm gonna get letters.

REASON #3:

"Come on in. The kids are in the backyard bobbing for pinkeye."

By "too dark" I mean cartoons that are too morbid, too creepy, too sick, or twisted—cartoons that are a little too "real" about dying, disease, dismemberment, drug use, bad things happening to animals or children. Surprisingly, I can't think of anything funny to say about those things.

REASON #4:

"Kids at school call us 'eight eyes.'"

I told you, it's weird.

Here's another:

"She's a weiner cat."

For some reason a lot of my rejects fall into this category. It's the flip side of having complete creative freedom. Occasionally, I'm gonna do stuff that's a little too "me." I can't really explain why, but to me these are funny. I am apparently alone in that opinion, and I'm surprisingly okay with that.

REASON #5:

I actually don't have any examples for this one. I'm just not very political. And it used to be that *The New Yorker* wouldn't run overtly political cartoons, at least not about specifics, so all that material got rejected. That has changed. They seem to actively seek out political stuff now, but the problem is that my own political views are extremely unpopular these days.

I'm in the middle somewhere: reasonable, balanced, open-minded, and nobody wants to hear that crap. I grew up in Texas, but I've spent most of my adulthood in New York City and Los Angeles. Splitting your time between the reddest and the bluest corners of the country gives you some perspective. I know it's not true, but it can make you think sometimes that people on both sides are equally intelligent and good-hearted.

Well, maybe I am political. I'm part of the impassioned middle. We're planning a rally next month. In a phone booth.

REASON #6:

(And when readers do get it, it isn't funny enough to justify the effort, prompting the thought, "Is there something more here that I'm missing?")

"Sellouts."

It's a Nike symbol . . . and therefore hilarious, and no, there isn't anything else that you're missing. It's just not that funny. A swing and a miss. Or, at best, a foul ball. Get it? Foul ball—as in fowl? Which leads us nicely into the next reason. . . .

REASON #7:

HORSE-DRAWN CARRIAGE

This is one of my favorites. I'm goofy.

REASON #8:

"It's from my Swiss account."

This is a bad cartoon. Just terrible. It's a pun, the domain of amateurs. Puns are to cartooning what lip-synching into a hairbrush is to show business. I can only say that when I did this, it must have been a really slow week in my head. Notice that I didn't even bother to do a finished drawing of this one. What you see here is the "rough" used to pitch the idea to the magazine.

REASON #9:

"You say sex pervert. I say horse enthusiast."

The New Yorker does plenty of sex-related cartoons, but there are some things the magazine won't touch—mostly things that are illegal. I guess there's a good reason why you've never seen *The New Yorker Book of Bestiality Cartoons.*

REASON #10:

ALL OF THE ABOVE

BALLOON GENITALS!
$5
DIFFEE

Sorry, Mom.

THE

REJECTS

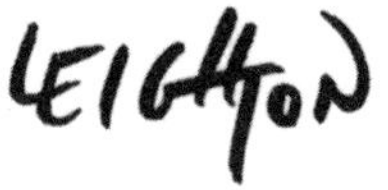
LEIGHTON

Robert Leighton

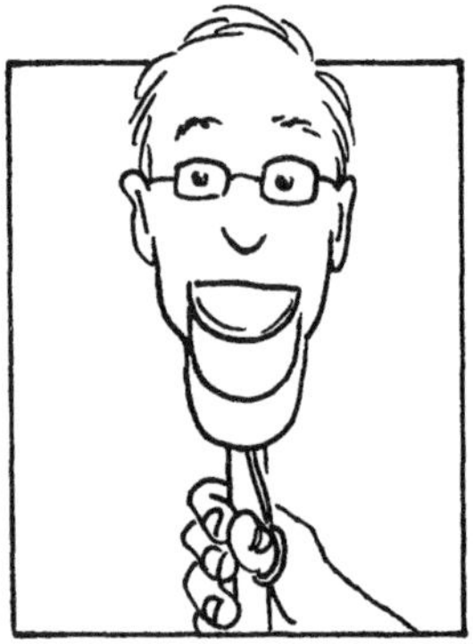

Frequently Asked Questions

- *Where do you get your ideas?*
  Happy Dragon Cartoon Mill, Hong Kong (trade secret).

- *Which comes first, the picture or the caption?*
  Usually, I draw a sketch that suggests an idea/cartoon . . . which then suggests a different picture.

- *How'd you get started?*
  R. L. Stine published my work when he was an editor at Scholastic.

- *I admire . . .*
  Ayad Meyer. (Complete coincidence.)

- *How do you deal with rejection?*
  As a *New Yorker* cartoonist, I thrive on rejection. Imagine my disappointment on those fortunately rare occasions when they buy one of my cartoons.

- *What are some things that make you laugh and why?*
  Buster Keaton's *One Week*, Harvey Kurtzman's *Starchie*, *Calvin and Hobbes* Sunday strips, *The Onion's Our Dumb Century*. In each case, the humor is in the details.

- *I've got a great idea for a cartoon—wanna hear it?*
  Not unless you want to hear my great idea for investment banking.

Infrequently Asked Questions

- *Have you mooned or been mooned more often in your life?*
  Been mooned (1), Mooned (0).

- *What would make a terrible pizza topping?*
  Those stringy things you peel off bananas.

- *What might one expect to find at a really low-budget amusement park?*
  Bring-your-own safety bar/Walk-up Ferris wheel.

- *What did the shepherd say to the three-legged sheepdog?*
  It's kind of slow around here. I'm going to have to let another one of your legs go.

Draw Some Sort of Doodle

. . . using the random lines below as a starting point.

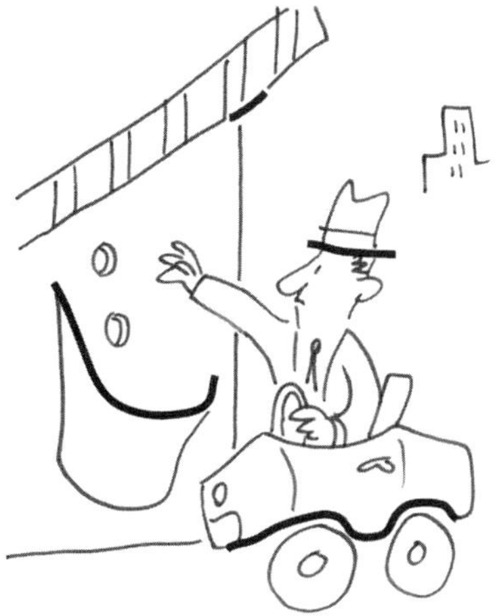

And Now for a Few More Questions . . .

- *What do you hate drawing?*
  Mansion interiors, crowd scenes, cars.

- *Being as accurate as possible, how many desert island cartoons do you think you've come up with and submitted to* The New Yorker*?*
  Sixteen. (None sold.)

- *What's the funniest thing that you witnessed, overheard, or came up with that you couldn't figure out how to use in a cartoon?*
  Being indiscreet/Peeing in the street.

Naming Names

- *What name might you give to a mild-mannered, middle-aged, bespectacled dental assistant in one of your cartoons?*
  Peg or Josie. (I have Steely Dan playing in the background.)

- *Other than Lance, what name would you give to a twenty-eight-year-old entertainment lawyer with a blue-dyed fauxhawk who cycles on weekends?*
  Billy-Bob. (Playing against stereotypes here.)

- *Come up with a name for an unpleasant medical procedure.*
  The Paine-Hertz procedure.

- *If you used a pen name, what would it be?*
  Who says I don't?

Complete the Pie Chart Below

. . . in a way that tells us something about your life or how you think.

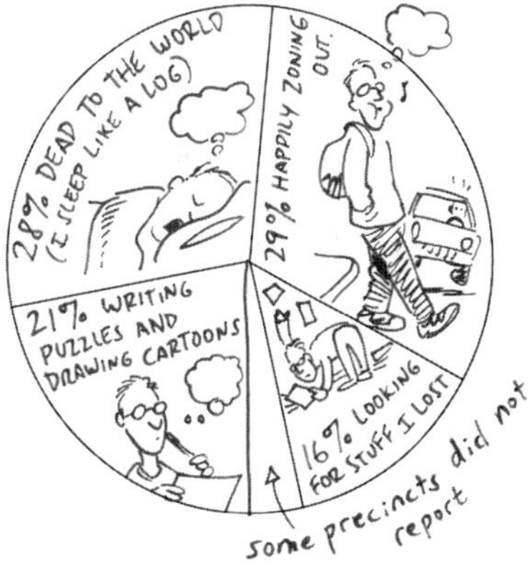
28% DEAD TO THE WORLD (I SLEEP LIKE A LOG)
29% HAPPILY ZONING OUT.
21% WRITING PUZZLES AND DRAWING CARTOONS
16% LOOKING FOR STUFF I LOST
some precincts did not report

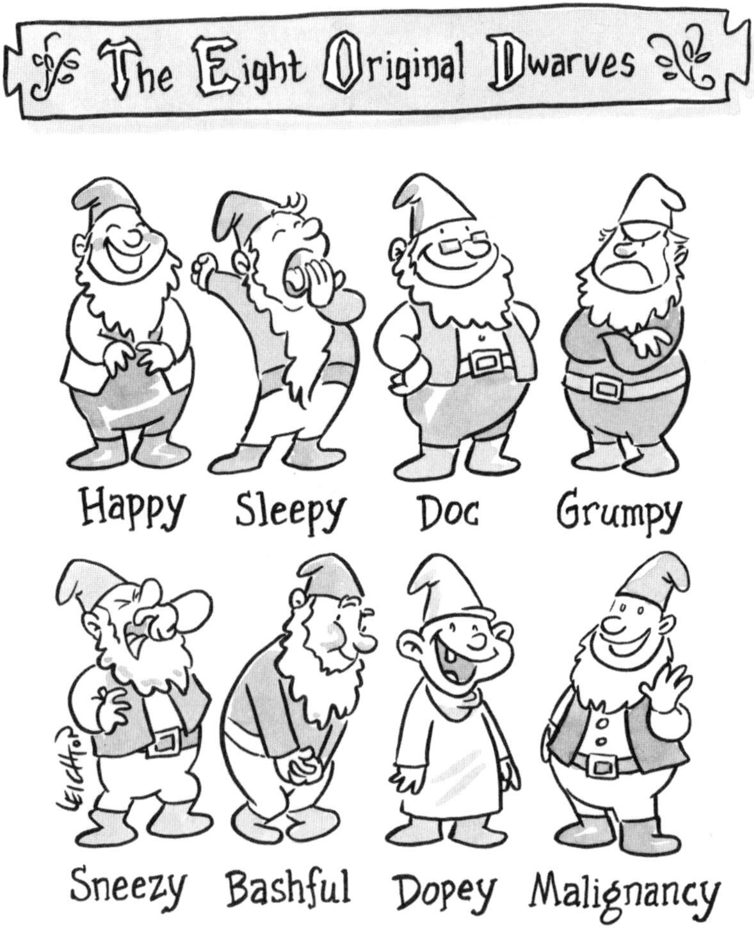
The Eight Original Dwarves
Happy
Sleepy
Doc
Grumpy
Sneezy
Bashful
Dopey
Malignancy
LEIGHTON

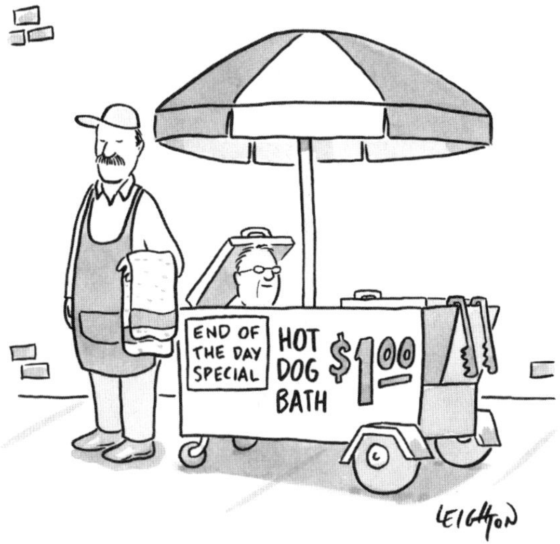
END OF THE DAY SPECIAL
HOT DOG BATH
$1.00
LEIGHTON

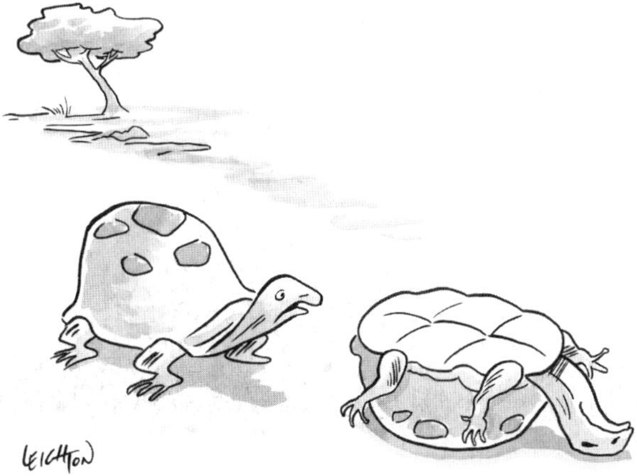
LEIGHTON

"I came as soon as I heard."

ZIEGLER

Jack Ziegler

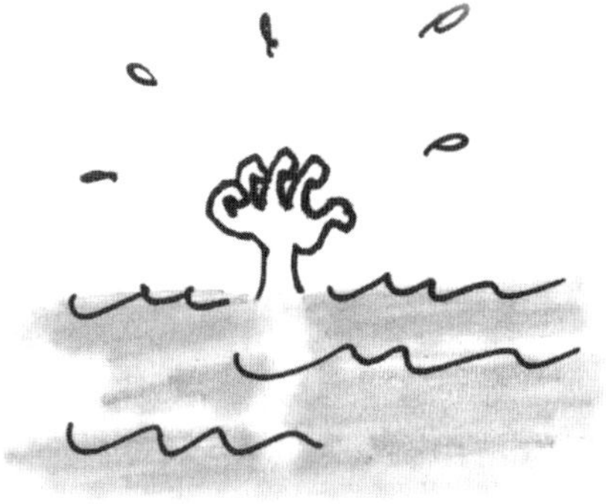

Frequently Asked Questions

- *Where do you get your ideas?*
  Macy's.
- *Which comes first, the picture or the caption?*
  Neither. Breakfast comes first.
- *How'~~d~~* DO *you get started?*
  With lots of baby oil—and then WATCH OUT!!
- *I admire . . .*
  Steinberg, Picasso, Steig, Henry Miller, George Booth, Alan Dunn, B. Kliban, M. K. Brown, André Francois, Wayne Thiebaud, Rick Griffin, Harvey Kurtzman, Mobius, etc.
- *How do you deal with rejection?*
  I go out and hunt down small creatures in the forest.
- *What are some things that make you laugh and why?*
  David Caruso in any episode of *CSI: Miami*, any *Seinfeld* rerun featuring Jerry Stiller, Dane Cook, certain friends who shall be unnamed. Why? Because they're funny.
- *I've got a great idea for a cartoon—wanna hear it?*
  I'm all ears.

Infrequently Asked Questions

- *Have you mooned or been mooned more often in your life?*
  Neither.
- *What would make a terrible pizza topping?*
  Iron filings.
- *What might one expect to find at a really low-budget amusement park?*
  David Caruso.
- *What did the shepherd say to the three-legged sheepdog?*
  Fetch! And this time more quickly please.

Draw Some Sort of Doodle

. . . using the random lines below as a starting point.

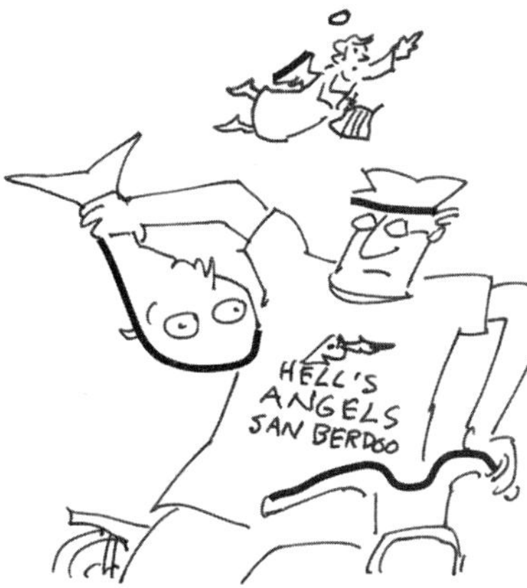
HELL'S ANGELS SAN BERDOO

And Now for a Few More Questions . . .

- *What do you hate drawing?*
  Tall people.
- *Being as accurate as possible, how many desert island cartoons do you think you've come up with and submitted to* The New Yorker*?*
  Hundreds. (Rejection rate: 97 percent.)
- *What's the funniest thing that you witnessed, overheard, or came up with that you couldn't figure out how to use in a cartoon?*
  My first lobotomy.

Naming Names

- *What name might you give to a mild-mannered, middle-aged, bespectacled dental assistant in one of your cartoons?*
  Bob.
- *Other than Lance, what name would you give to a twenty-eight-year-old entertainment lawyer with a blue-dyed fauxhawk who cycles on weekends?*
  Bob.
- *What would be a good name for a new, commercially unviable breakfast cereal?*
  Fibrous Bob-o-Links.
- *Come up with a name for an unpleasant medical procedure.*
  The Bob Reduction.
- *If you used a pen name, what would it be?*
  Bob.

Complete the Pie Chart Below

. . . in a way that tells us something about your life or how you think.

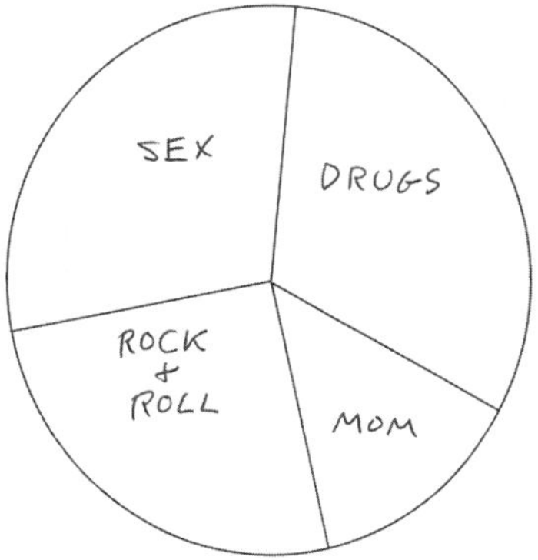
SEX
DRUGS
ROCK + ROLL
MOM

"Sorry, Ted. Generally, what happens in the pants stays in the pants."

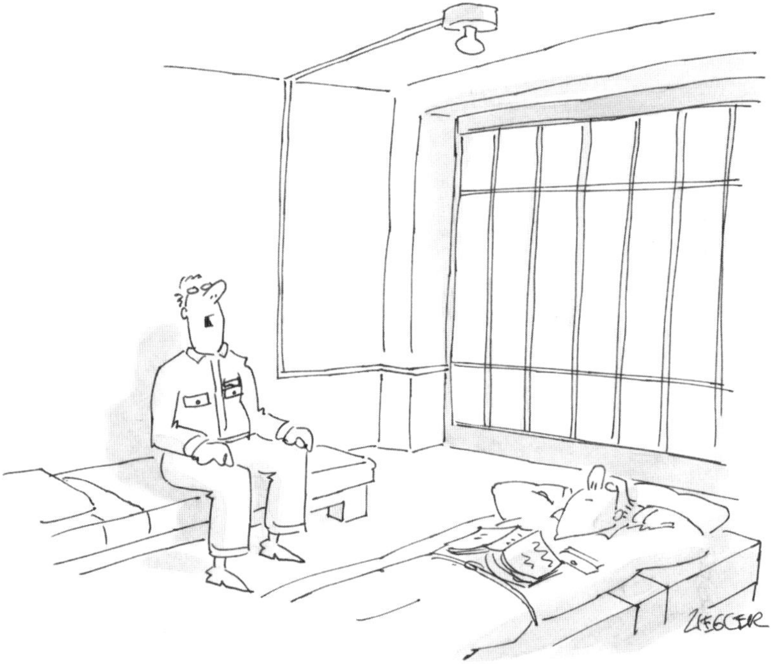
ZIEGLER

"As an ex-priest, I'm having a hard time adjusting to these noncathedral ceilings."

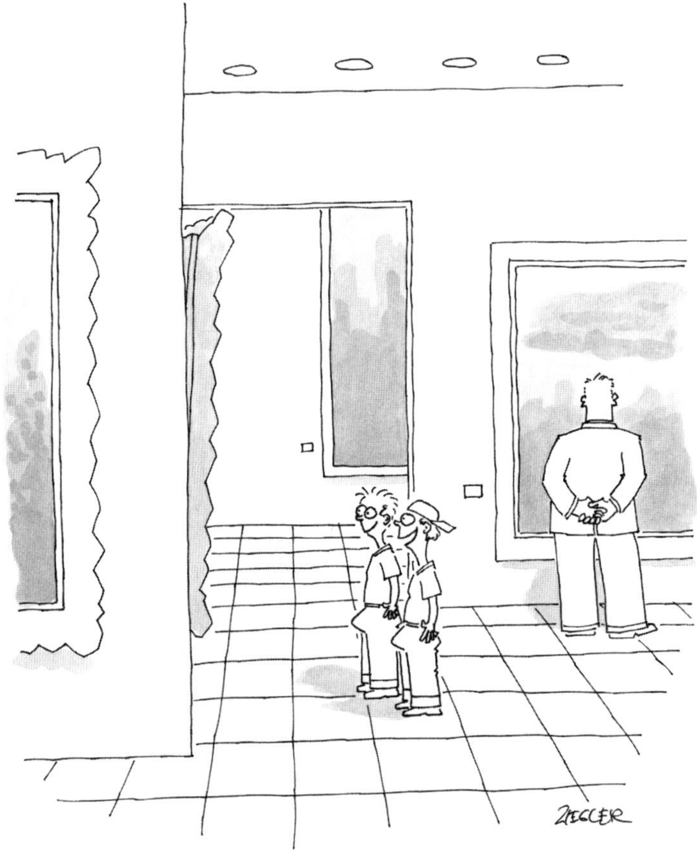
ZIEGLER

"Wow! Great Nude!"

"What's the deal, Gramps? You couldn't get any color film at Auschwitz?"

"I'm afraid I made quite a nuisance of myself in here last night."

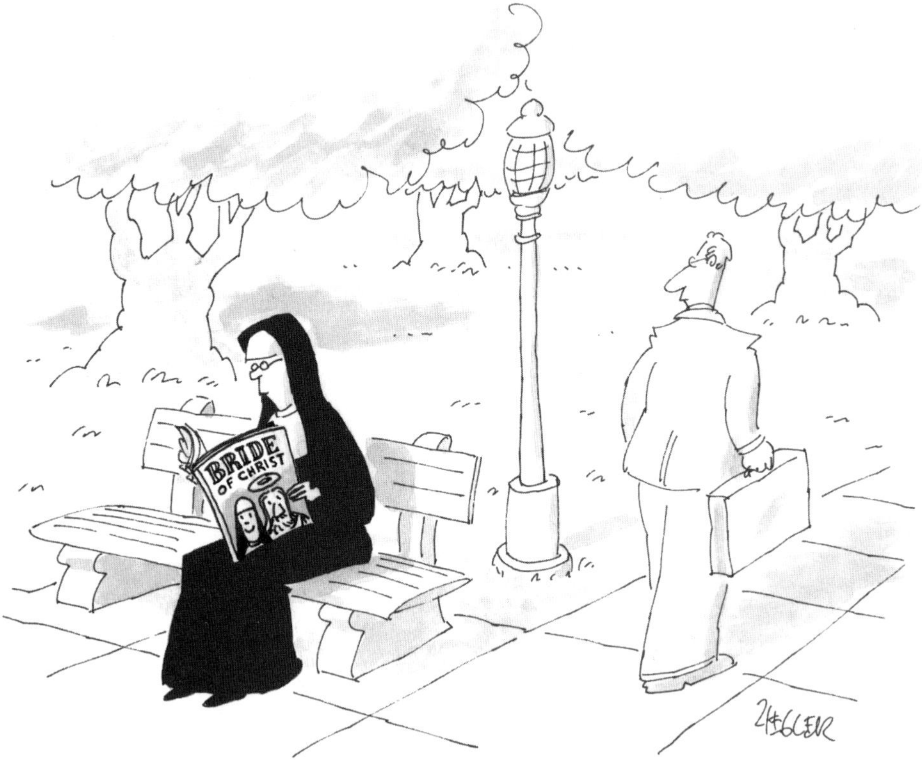
BRIDE
OF CHRIST
ZIEGLER

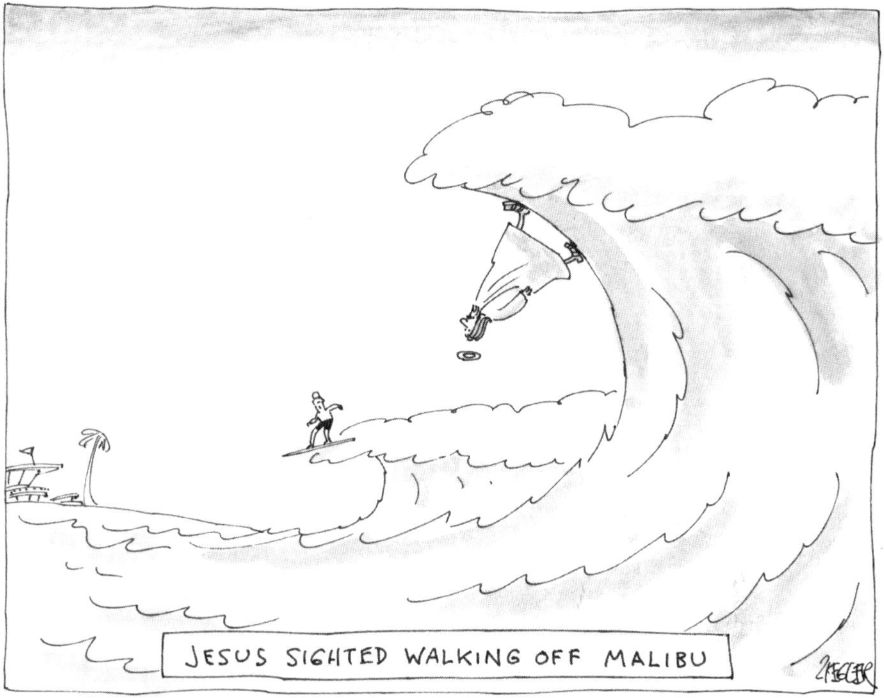
JESUS SIGHTED WALKING OFF MALIBU
ZIEGLER

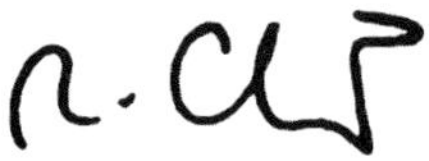

Roz Chast

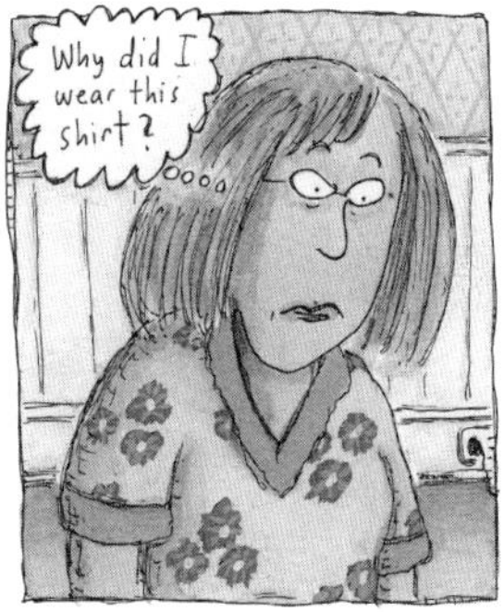
Why did I wear this shirt?
Oooo

Frequently Asked Questions

- *Where do you get your ideas?*
  No.
- *Which comes first, the picture or the caption?*
  Yes.
- *How'd you get started?*
  Sometimes.
- *I admire . . .*
  Bruce Jay Friedman, Charles Portis, Thomas Mann, Charles Addams, Mary Petty, Sue Coe, Jack Ziegler, Gahan Wilson, Stephin Merritt, and about a million others. It would sicken you if I listed all of them.
- *How do you deal with rejection?*
  I feel very sorry for myself and sometimes get into a panic. Then I do my best to get back to work because what else is there to do? There's only so much origami a person can fold.
- *What are some things that make you laugh and why?*
  Once I was at lunch with a group of cartoonists and the word *bolus* came up. A bolus is a lump of chewed food. That made me really laugh, but I don't know why. I also find *It's a Gift*, an old W. C. Fields movie, very hilarious, especially that scene when the mother and the daughter are discussing whether to buy something called Syrup of Squill. Weird, unexpected things set me off way more than scripted jokes, which sometimes just make me depressed.
- *I've got a great idea for a cartoon—wanna hear it?*
  Rarely.

Infrequently Asked Questions

- *Have you mooned or been mooned more often in your life?*
  Neither.
- *What would make a terrible pizza topping?*
  Stye ointment.
- *What might one expect to find at a really low-budget amusement park?*
  My family.
- *What did the shepherd say to the three-legged sheepdog?*
  How did you lose your leg?

Draw Some Sort of Doodle

. . . using the random lines below as a starting point.

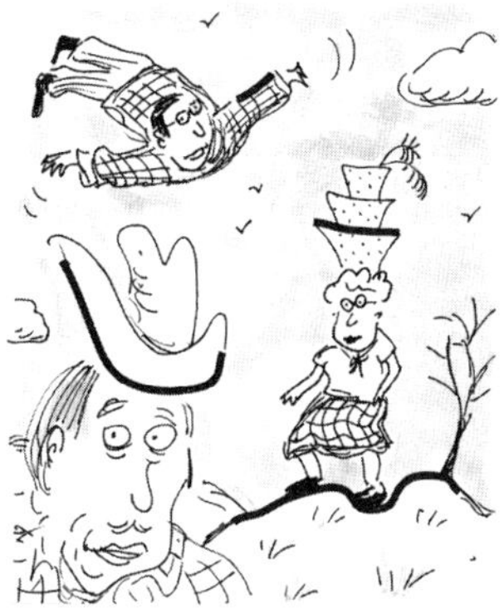

And Now for a Few More Questions . . .

- *What do you hate drawing?*
  Forests.

- *Being as accurate as possible, how many desert island cartoons do you think you've come up with and submitted to* The New Yorker*?*
  Four.

- *What's the funniest thing that you witnessed, overheard, or came up with that you couldn't figure out how to use in a cartoon?*
  My husband told a highway tollbooth clerk that soon her job would be done by a robot.

Naming Names

- *What name might you give to a mild-mannered, middle-aged, bespectacled dental assistant in one of your cartoons?*
  Trixi.

- *Other than Lance, what name would you give to a twenty-eight-year-old entertainment lawyer with a blue-dyed fauxhawk who cycles on weekends?*
  Mance.

- *What would be a good name for a new, commercially unviable breakfast cereal?*
  Kidney Chex.

- *Come up with a name for an unpleasant medical procedure.*
  Eyeball 'Splodofication.

- *If you used a pen name, what would it be?*
  Penny McPen.

Complete the Pie Chart Below

. . . in a way that tells us something about your life or how you think.

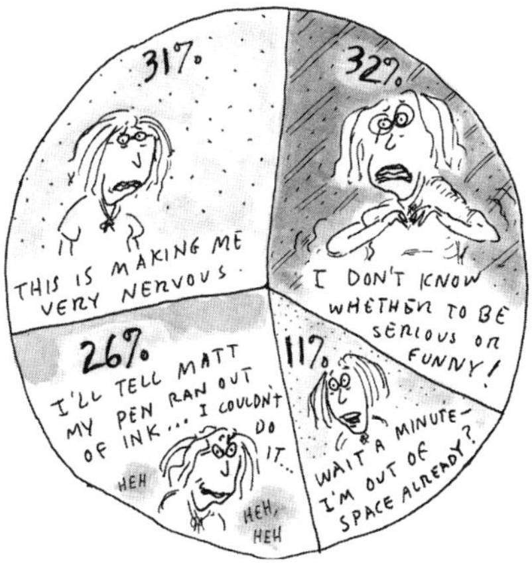
31%
THIS IS MAKING ME VERY NERVOUS
32%
I DON'T KNOW WHETHER TO BE SERIOUS OR FUNNY!
26%
I'LL TELL MATT MY PEN RAN OUT OF INK... I COULDN'T DO IT...
HEH
HEH, HEH
11%
WAIT A MINUTE- I'M OUT OF SPACE ALREADY?

THE HORN OF BY-PRODUCTS

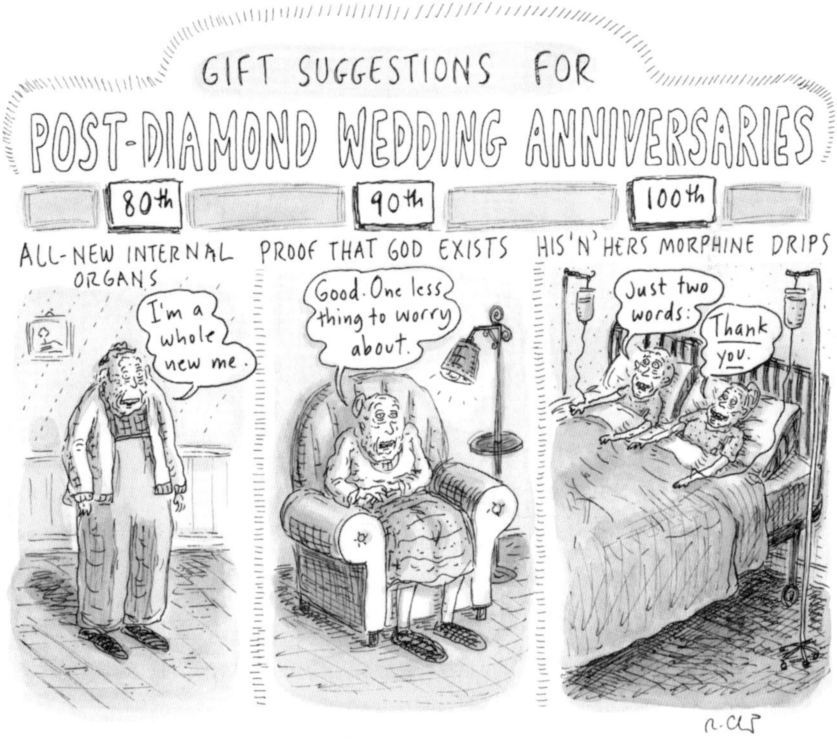
GIFT SUGGESTIONS FOR
POST-DIAMOND WEDDING ANNIVERSARIES
80th
90th
100th
ALL-NEW INTERNAL ORGANS
I'm a whole new me.
PROOF THAT GOD EXISTS
Good. One less thing to worry about.
HIS'N'HERS MORPHINE DRIPS
Just two words:
Thank you.
R. Chast

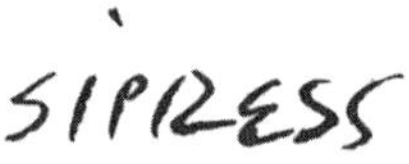

SIPRESS

David Sipress

Frequently Asked Questions

- *Where do you get your ideas?*
  Barcelona.

- *How do you deal with rejection?*

- *What are some things that make you laugh and why?*

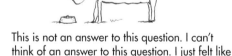

This is not an answer to this question. I can't think of an answer to this question. I just felt like drawing a dog with a guy's head.

- *Which comes first, the picture or the caption?*
  The egg.

- *How'd you get started?*
  God appeared to me in a vision and handed me crow quill pen points and a Bristol pad.

- *I admire . . .*
  Anyone who has a regular job—how the hell do they do it?

- *I've got a great idea for a cartoon—wanna hear it?*
  Are you from Barcelona?

Infrequently Asked Questions

- *Have you mooned or been mooned more often in your life?*
  This question is asinine.

- *What would make a terrible pizza topping?*
  Stool softener.

- *What might one expect to find at a really low-budget amusement park?*
  Poor children.

- *What did the shepherd say to the three-legged sheepdog?*
  Yum—that was delicious. I think I'll go ahead and eat the other three.

Draw Something in This Space

. . . that will help us understand your childhood.

"You're a loser."
"You're a failure."
"You'll never amount to anything."
"It's a motivational technique I learned from my father."

And Now for a Few More Questions . . .

- *What do you hate drawing?*
  Anything complicated.

- *Being as accurate as possible, how many desert island cartoons do you think you've come up with and submitted to* The New Yorker*?*
  Ten thousand.

- *What's the funniest thing that you witnessed, overheard, or came up with that you couldn't figure out how to use in a cartoon?*
  Two people stuck on a desert island.

Naming Names

- *What name might you give to a mild-mannered, middle-aged, bespectacled dental assistant in one of your cartoons?*
  I don't give people in my cartoons names. They come up with them themselves.

- *Other than Lance, what name would you give to a twenty-eight-year-old entertainment lawyer with a blue-dyed fauxhawk who cycles on weekends?*
  See above.

- *What would be a good name for a new, commercially unviable breakfast cereal?*
  Nukes.

- *Come up with a name for an unpleasant medical procedure.*
  Checkup.

- *If you used a pen name, what would it be?*
  Bic.

Complete the Pie Chart Below

. . . in a way that tells us something about your life or how you think.

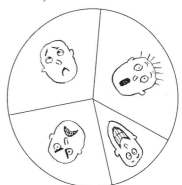

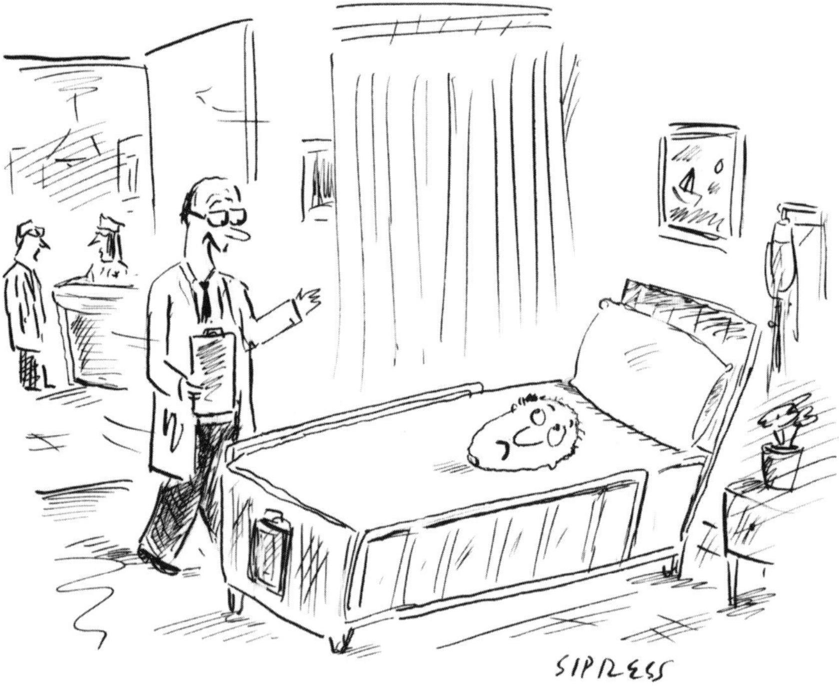
SIPRESS

"Congratulations! I think we got it all."

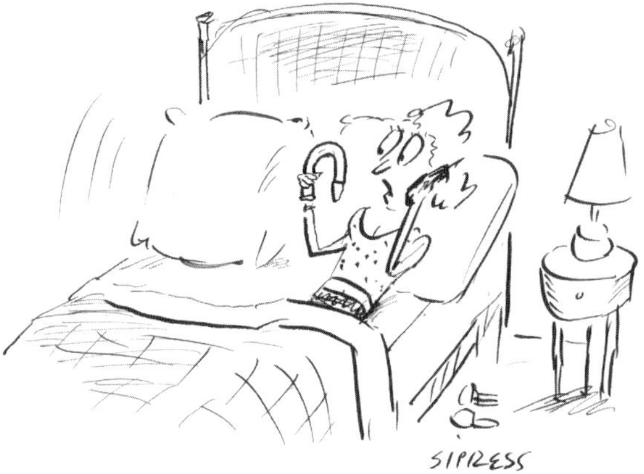
SIPRESS

"Hello . . . technical support?"

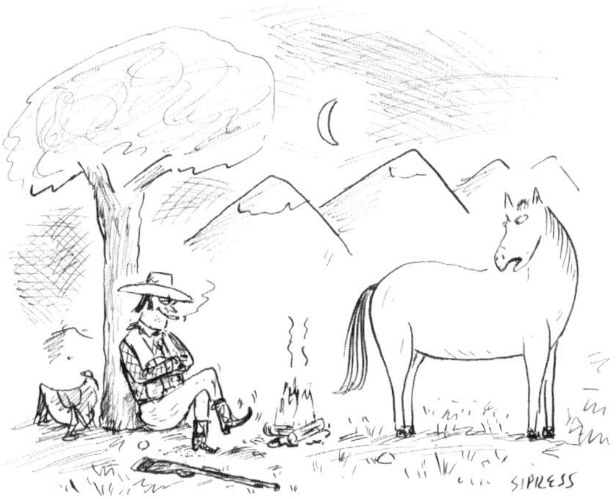
SIPRESS

"Don't even think about it, cowboy."

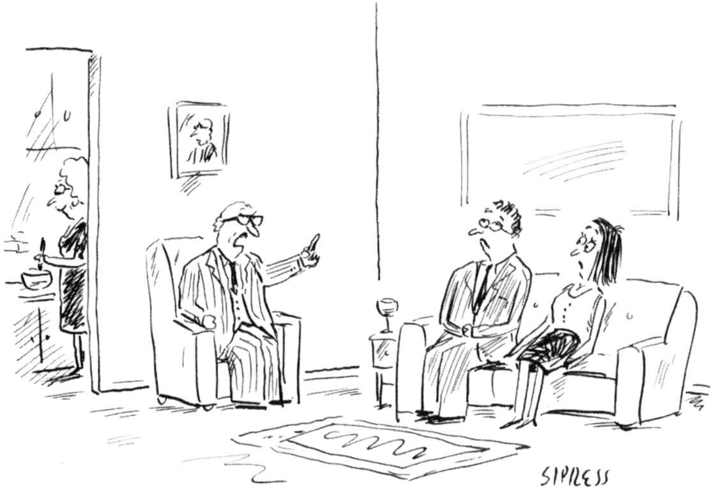
SIPRESS

"I came to this country with nothing but the hair on my back."

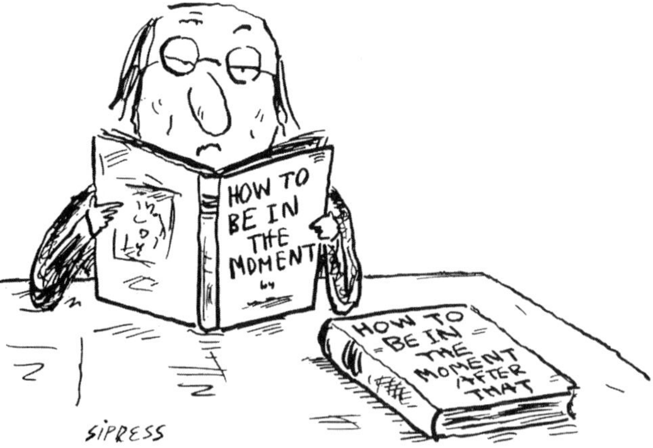
HOW TO BE IN THE MOMENT
HOW TO BE IN THE MOMENT AFTER THAT
SIPRESS

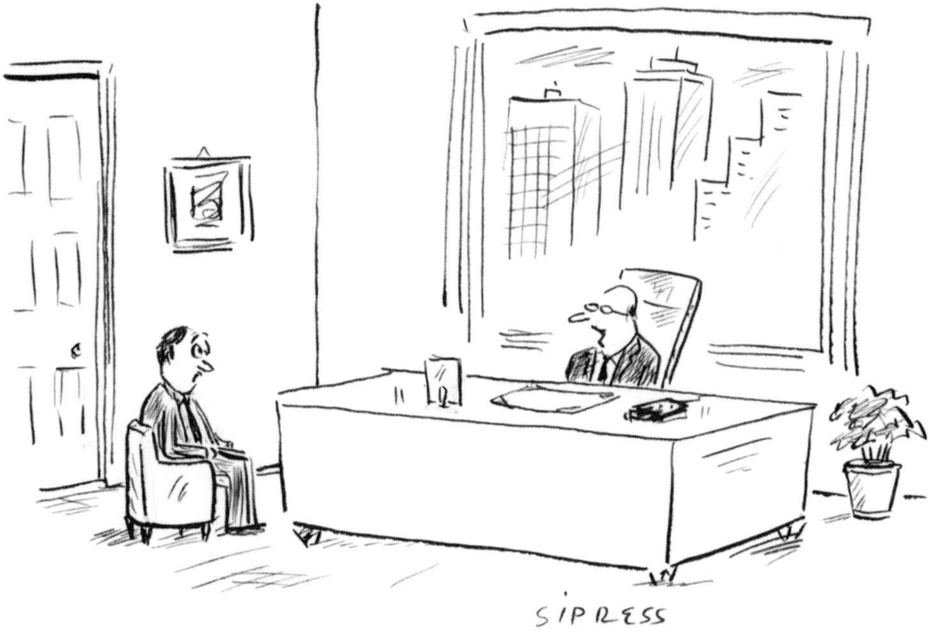
SIPRESS

"Corporate Diversity would like you to get a sex change."

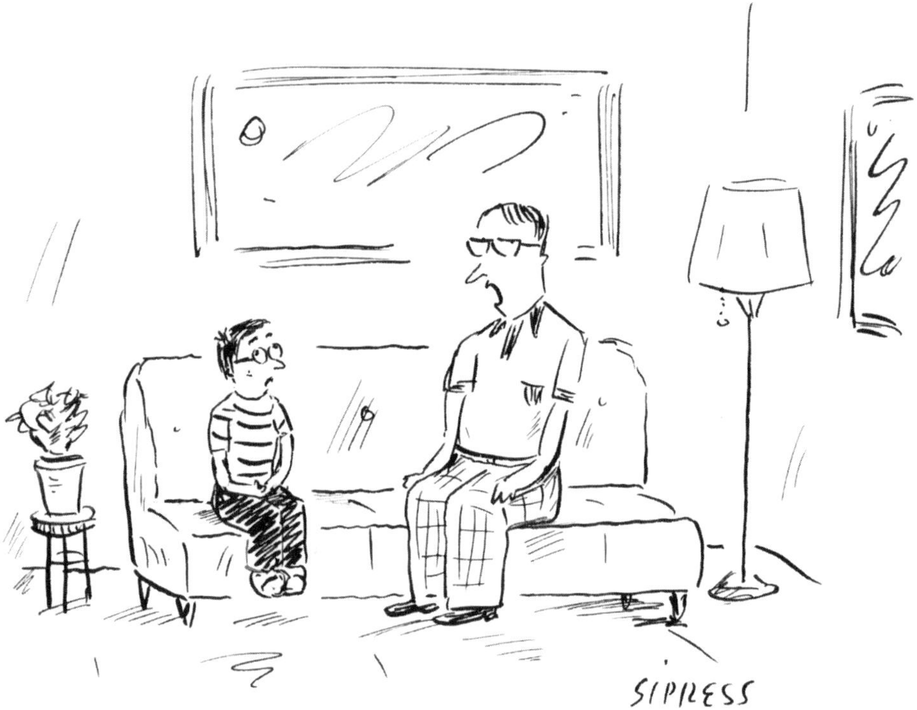
SIPRESS

"From everything you're describing, son, it sounds to me like you've just had your first boner."

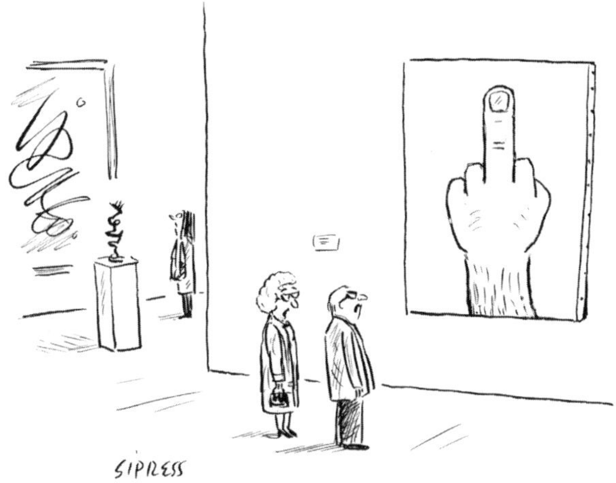
SIPRESS

"I don't think you're supposed to like it."

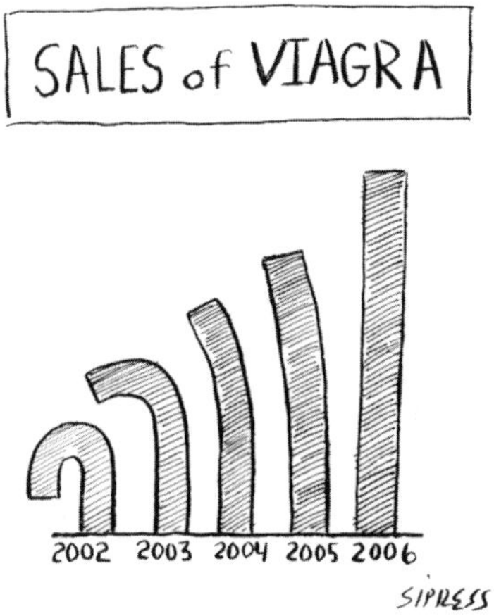
SALES of VIAGRA
2002 2003 2004 2005 2006
SIPRESS

Felipe Galindo

feggo

Frequently Asked Questions

- *Where do you get your ideas?*
  From my past lives.

- *Which comes first, the picture or the caption?*
  A mix of both, trying to turn the charcoals into diamonds although a lot of cubic zirconias are obtained in the process.

- *How'd you get started?*
  Coffee with a good dose of procrastination.

- *I admire . . .*
  Pablo Picasso. When he was dead poor, he got an offer to do cartoons for lots of money! He rejected the job to stick to art. And the rest is history! I did the opposite, and my history still hasn't rest.

- *How do you deal with rejection?*
  Taking a deep breath and chanting "OM, another test from the universe."

- *What are some things that make you laugh and why?*
  Everything, because I think there's laughable material in everything. But you have to choose when to laugh and when to keep it to yourself.

- *I've got a great idea for a cartoon—wanna hear it?*
  Anytime. For a fee, of course.

Infrequently Asked Questions

- *Have you mooned or been mooned more often in your life?*
  Both, by accident, I guess.

- *What would make a terrible pizza topping?*
  Enchiladas.

- *What might one expect to find at a really low-budget amusement park?*
  A Misfortune Wheel.

- *What did the shepherd say to the three-legged sheepdog?*
  Do you know Paul McCartney did a song about a dog like you, but never one abut three-legged shepherds!

Draw Something in This Space

. . . that will help us understand your childhood.

Draw Some Sort of Doodle

. . . using the random lines below as a starting point.

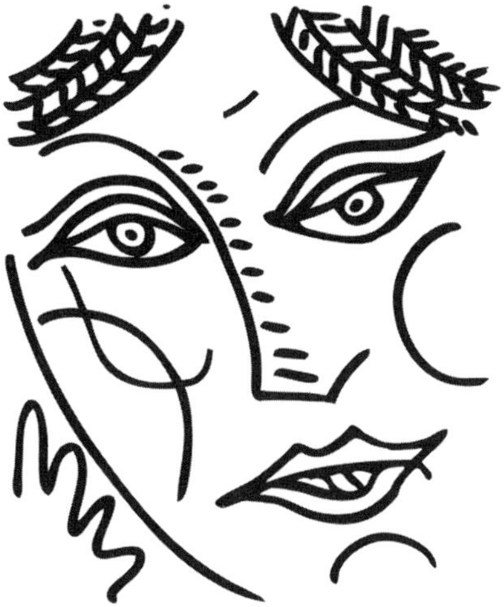

And Now for a Few More Questions . . .

- *What do you hate drawing?*
  Feet, politicians, crowds.
- *Being as accurate as possible, how many desert island cartoons do you think you've come up with and submitted to* The New Yorker*?*
  Probably around a hundred; I have submitted most of them and sold one to *TNY* (and many to other publications).
- *What's the funniest thing that you witnessed, overheard, or came up with that you couldn't figure out how to use in a cartoon?*
  All that religious preachers say.

Naming Names

- *What name might you give to a mild-mannered, middle-aged, bespectacled dental assistant in one of your cartoons?*
  Paquito.
- *Other than Lance, what name would you give to a twenty-eight-year-old entertainment lawyer with a blue-dyed fauxhawk who cycles on weekends?*
  Gonzalito.
- *What would be a good name for a new, commercially unviable breakfast cereal?*
  Taquitos.

Complete the Pie Chart Below

. . . in a way that tells us something about your life or how you think.

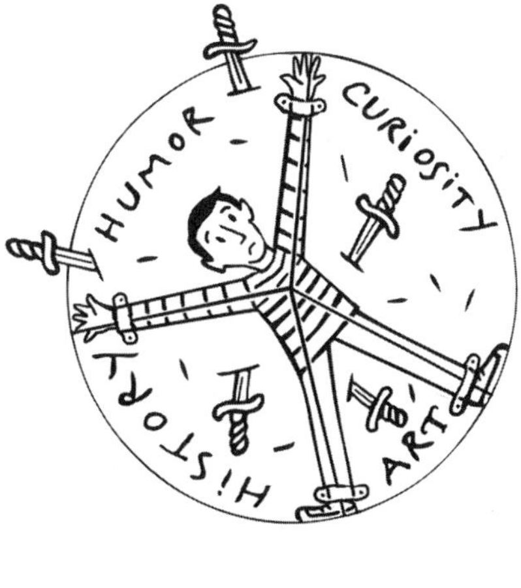
HUMOR
CURIOSITY
HISTORY
ART

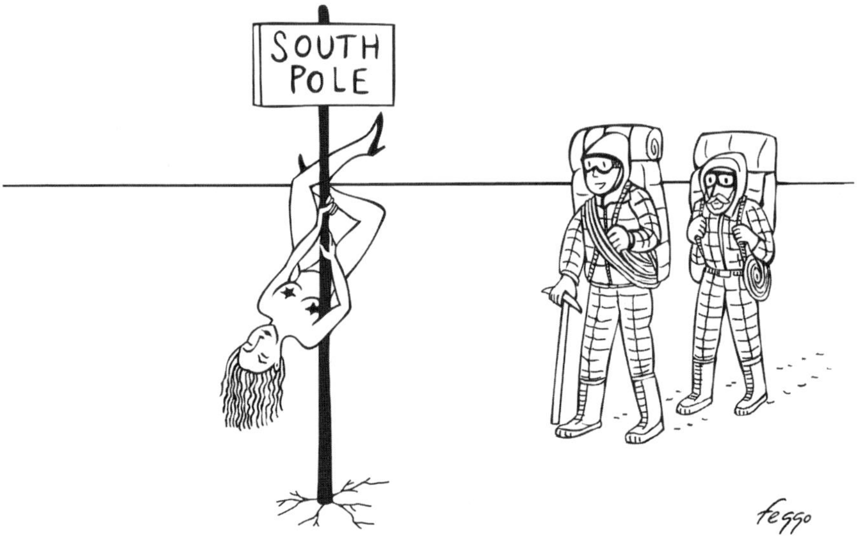
SOUTH POLE
feggo

"Dude, you gotta love global warming!"

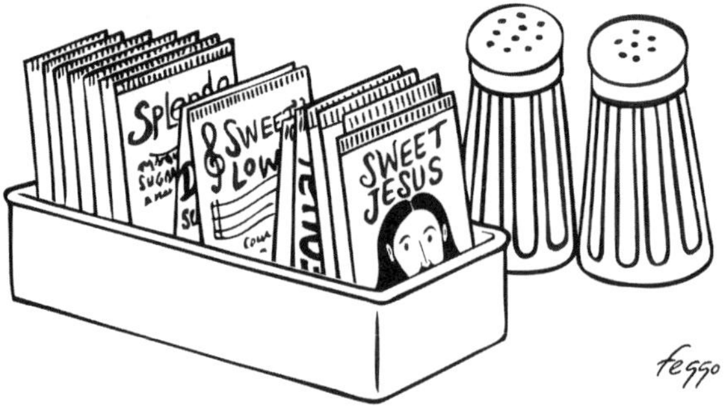
SWEET JESUS
feggo

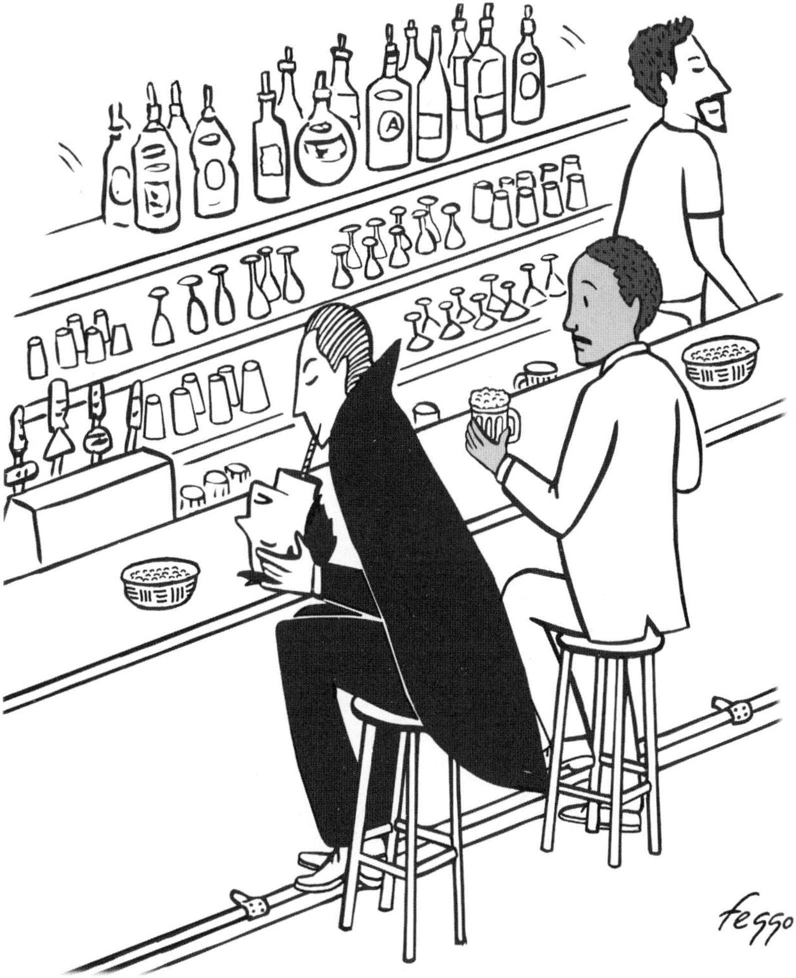
feggo

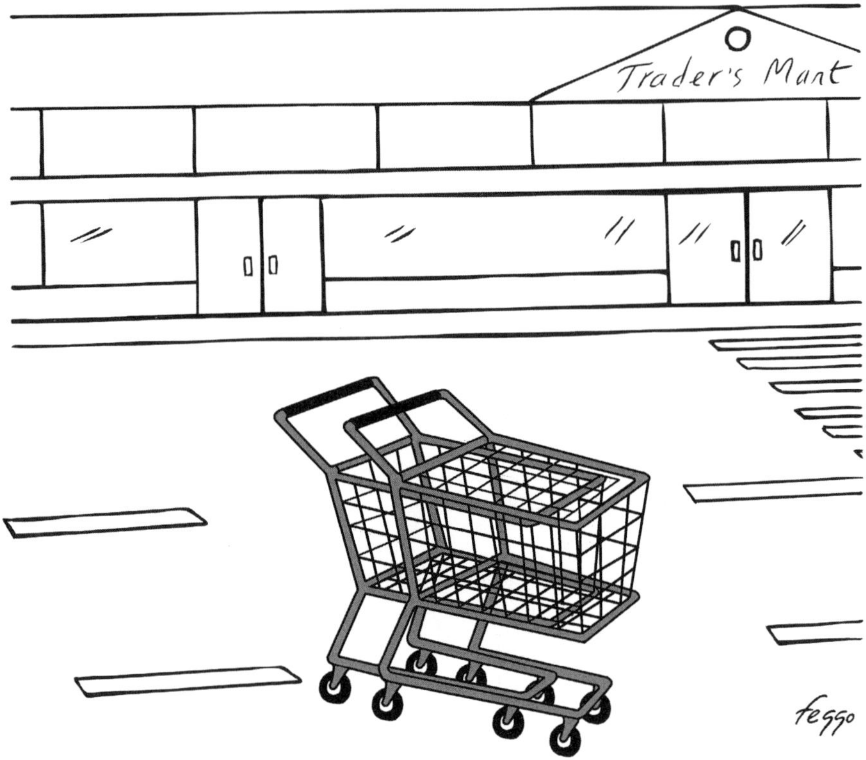
Trader's Mart
feggo

"Tony, stop it! Not in public!"

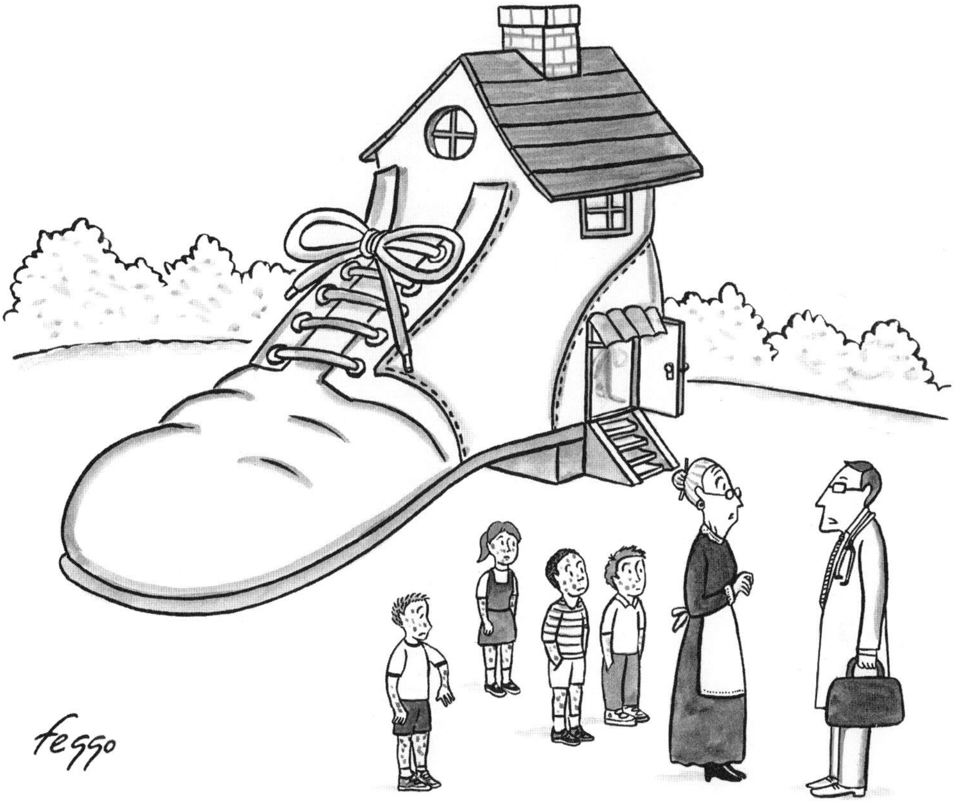
feggo

"Your kids don't have measles, they have athlete's foot."

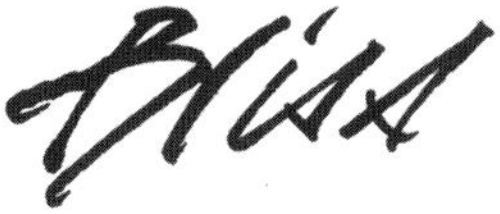
Bliss

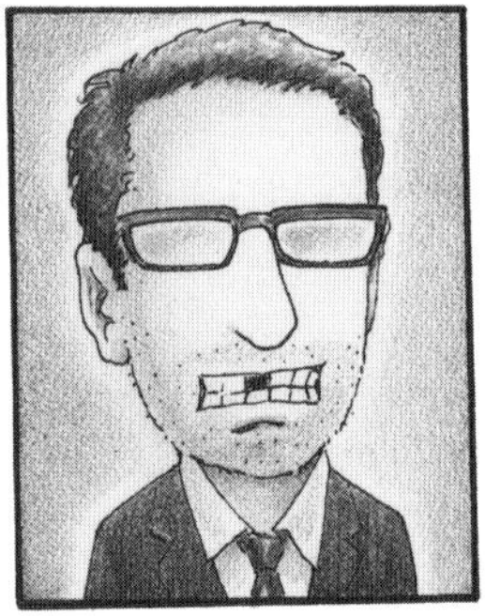

Harry Bliss

Frequently Asked Questions

- *Where do you get your ideas?*
  I get most of my ideas from all the great dead cartoonists who can no longer sue me for stealing their ideas. Also, my pals say funny stuff, and I just draw it.

- *Which comes first, the picture or the caption?*
  Neither, see above.

- *How'd you get started?*
  How did we all "get started"? The sperm fertilizes the egg. . . .

- *I admire . . .*
  I admire my dog, Penny, specifically the way she's able to catch and release squirrels—amazing. Oh, and I also admire a million dollars.

- *How do you deal with rejection?*
  Are you kidding? I'm constantly reflecting. I'm the most self-reflect—what's that? Rejection? Oh, I thought you said reflection—my bad. Does this mean I'm not going to be included in the book?! What, just because I screwed up on one of your stupid questions?! Do you know who the _uck you're dealing with?! How dare you! I know where you live, mother_ucker!

- *What are some things that make you laugh and why?*
  One thing that really cracks me up is stalking kiss-ass interviewers who think they have the balls to not publish my work because of one misunderstanding. I laugh so freaking hard when I secretly watch them at home with their family, like the serial killer in Red Dragon or like Robert De Niro in Cape Fear . . . or what about Glenn Close when she cooked the family's fluffy new bunny in the soup pot . . . hilarious!

- *I've got a great idea for a cartoon—wanna hear it?*
  Sure, go ahead. I'm just gonna leaf blow my yard, but you go ahead. I'm listening.

Infrequently Asked Questions

- *Have you mooned or been mooned more often in your life?*
  Nope, never mooned or been mooned . . . nor have I streaked since the '80s.

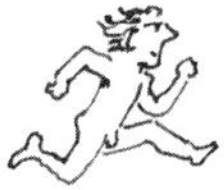

- *What would make a terrible pizza topping?*
  Shredded kitten cartilage.

- *What might one expect to find at a really low-budget amusement park?*
  Dead children.

- *What did the shepherd say to the three-legged sheepdog?*
  Okay, forget corralling the sheep, how proficient are you with PowerPoint?

And Now for a Few More Questions . . .

- *What do you hate drawing?*
  English muffins, tempeh, midwife toads, cassowaries, the Sistine Chapel, galvanic tractors, and venereal disease.

- *Being as accurate as possible, how many desert island cartoons do you think you've come up with and submitted to* The New Yorker*?*
  Roughly, twenty-seven and two-thirds.

- *What's the funniest thing that you witnessed, overheard, or came up with that you couldn't figure out how to use in a cartoon?*
  I once dreamed that Adolf Hitler and Anne Frank were on *The Brady Bunch*, except Hitler was Marsha and Anne was Peter and she hit Hitler in the nose with a football and Hitler yelled in German, "Ich vun du shleip von deuth!"

Naming Names

- *What name might you give to a mild-mannered, middle-aged, bespectacled dental assistant in one of your cartoons?*
  Lorthrope.

- *Other than Lance, what name would you give to a twenty-eight-year-old entertainment lawyer with a blue-dyed fauxhawk who cycles on weekends?*
  Wanker.

- *Come up with a name for an unpleasant medical procedure.*
  Testicular Removaloscopy.

- *If you used a pen name, what would it be?*
  Funny Mother_ucker.

Complete the Pie Chart Below

. . . in a way that tells us something about your life or how you think.

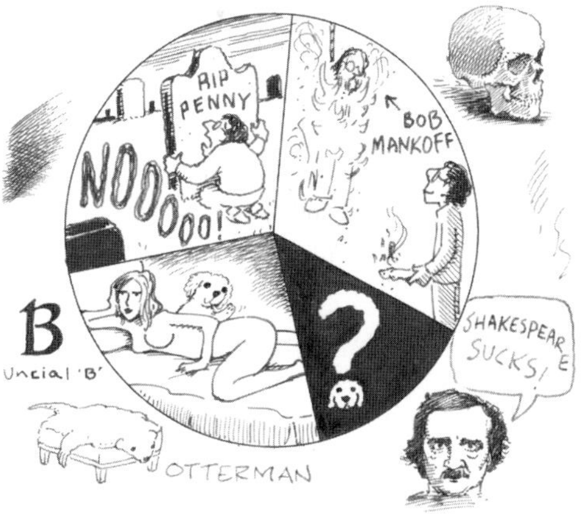
RIP
PENNY
NOOOooo!
BOB
MANKOFF
?
B
Uncial 'B'
SHAKESPEARE
SUCKS!
OTTERMAN

"I'd invite you in, but my crap is all over the place."

"*That's it, mister. You just lost your 'free range' status.*"

"I have an enormous favor to ask you."

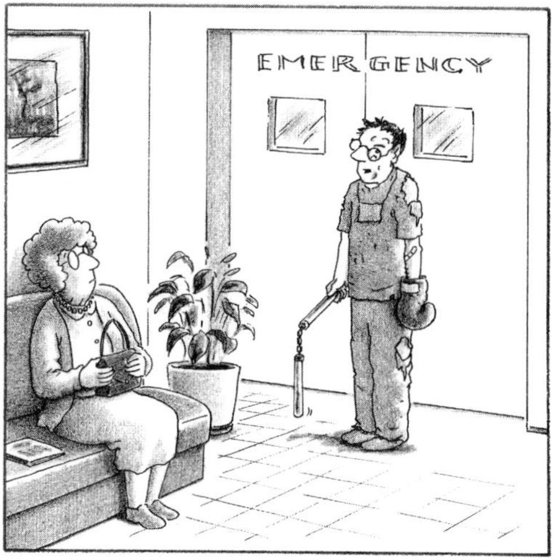
EMERGENCY

"He fought like hell."

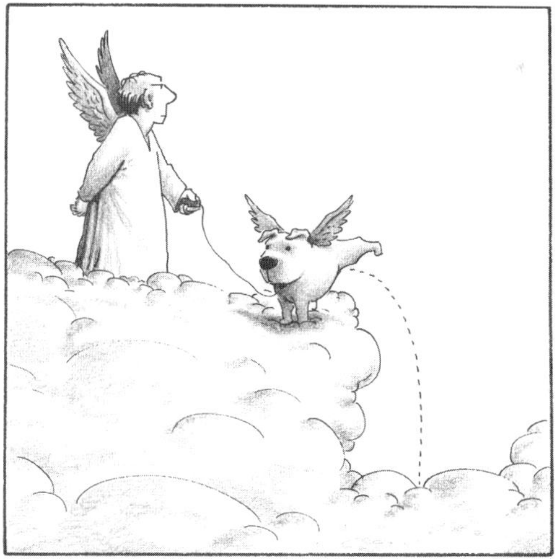

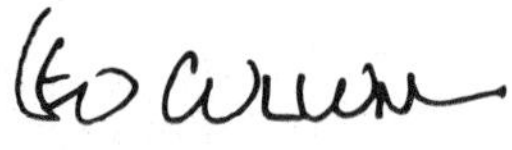

Leo Cullum

Frequently Asked Questions

- *Where do you get your ideas?*
  I find them under my pillow when I wake up.
- *Which comes first, the picture or the caption?*
  The caption, which then smokes a cigarette . . . oh please!
- *How'd you get started?*
  In the child cartoon factories of Korea.
- *I admire . . .*
  Things from a distance. Usually with binoculars.
- *How do you deal with rejection?*
  I find someone to publish a book of rejected cartoons. Hey, it's working!
- *What are some things that make you laugh and why?*
  Being tickled. I guess it's because of sensitive skin or something? Also a good cartoon will occasionally make me laugh out loud and exclaim, "Why, in the name of cosmic justice, didn't I think of that!"
- *I've got a great idea for a cartoon—wanna hear it?*
  Is it in any way hurtful or insensitive?

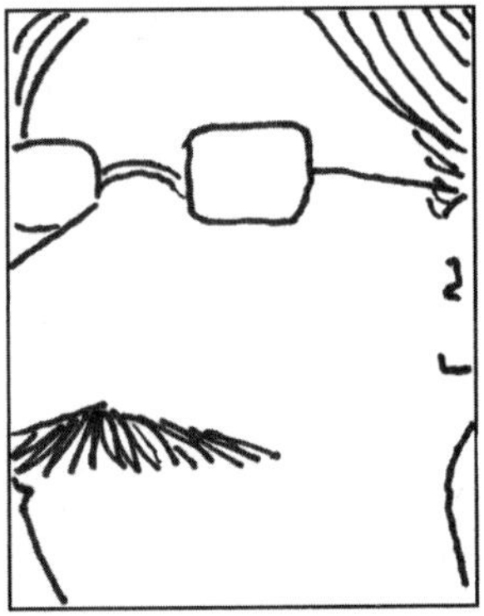

Draw Something in This Space

. . . that will help us understand your childhood.

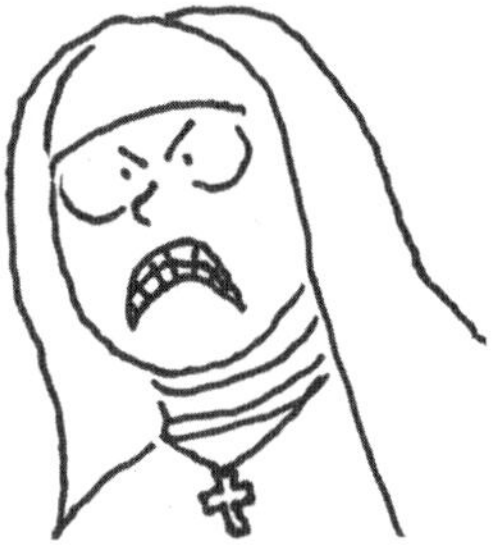

Infrequently Asked Questions

- *Have you mooned or been mooned more often in your life?*
  Been mooned, usually by clergy.
- *What would make a terrible pizza topping?*
  The leg of a sheepdog.
- *What might one expect to find at a really low-budget amusement park?*
  Me, having a fabulous time.

- *What did the shepherd say to the three-legged sheepdog?*
  What *could* he say? It was all very sad.

Draw Some Sort of Doodle

. . . *using the random lines below as a starting point.*

And Now for a Few More Questions . . .

- *What do you hate drawing?*
  Most outdoor scenes.

- *Being as accurate as possible, how many desert island cartoons do you think you've come up with and submitted to* The New Yorker?
  227, and sold every one.

- *What's the funniest thing that you witnessed, overheard, or came up with that you couldn't figure out how to use in a cartoon?*
  Sandals with black socks.

Naming Names

- *What name might you give to a mild-mannered, middle-aged, bespectacled dental assistant in one of your cartoons?*
  Roger.

- *Other than Lance, what name would you give to a twenty-eight-year-old entertainment lawyer with a blue-dyed fauxhawk who cycles on weekends?*
  I'd give him my daughter's name.

- *What would be a good name for a new, commercially unviable breakfast cereal?*
  Roto Rooties.

- *Come up with a name for an unpleasant medical procedure.*
  Cassandra.

- *If you used a pen name, what would it be?*
  Sharpie.

Complete the Pie Chart Below

. . . *in a way that tells us something about your life or how you think.*

"Now I think of Mom whenever it's cold."

"What did Jesus order?"

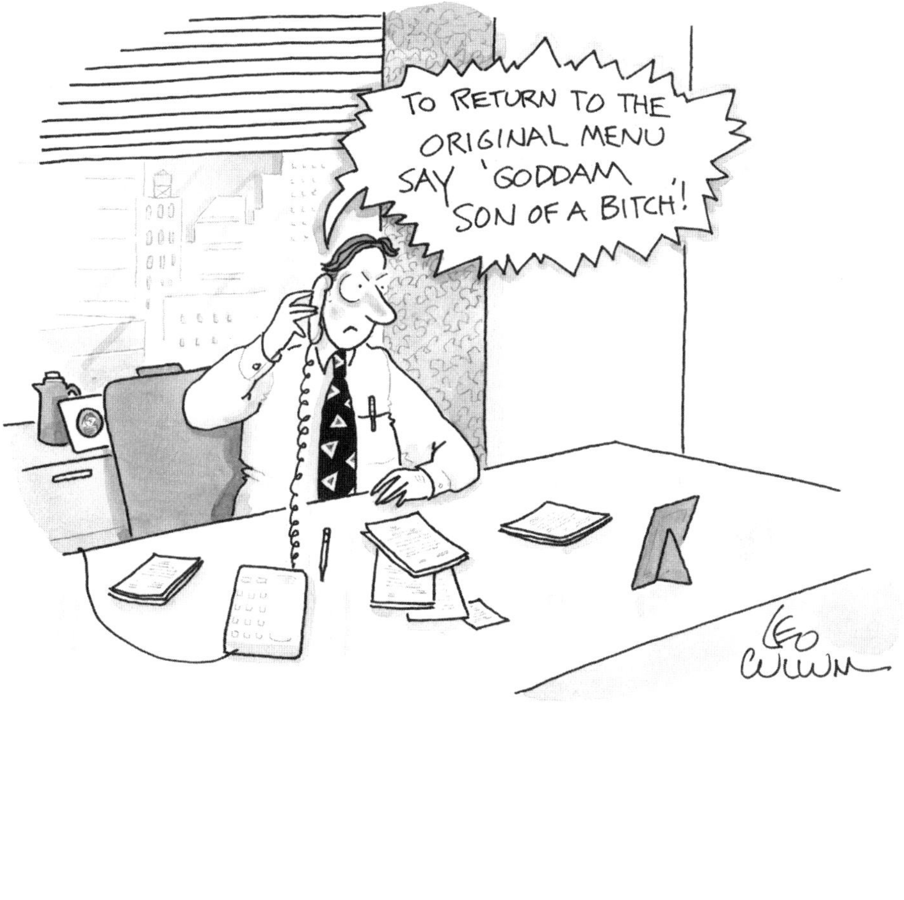
TO RETURN TO THE ORIGINAL MENU SAY 'GODDAM SON OF A BITCH'!
LEO CULLUM

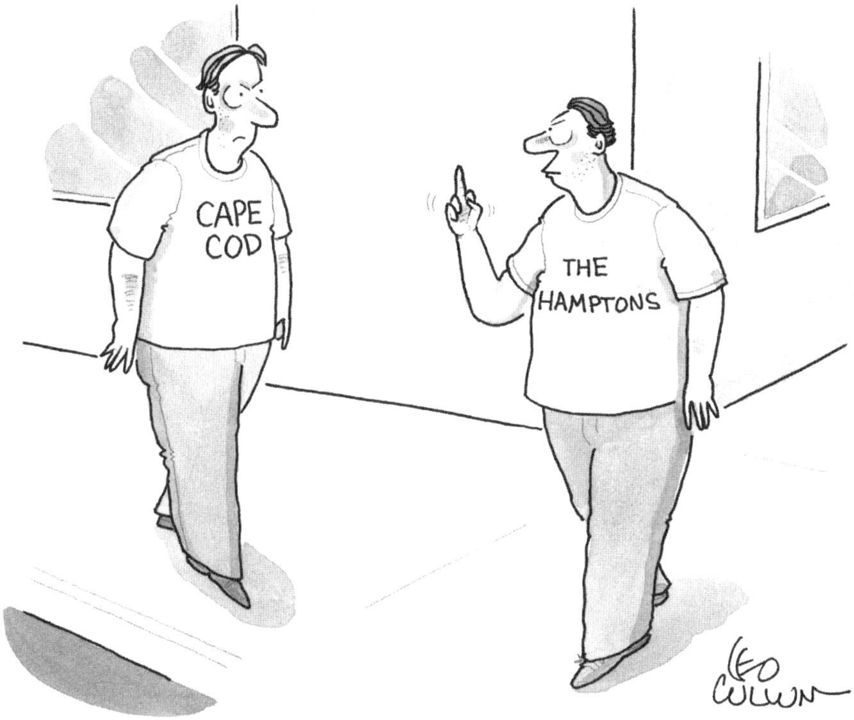
CAPE
COD
THE
HAMPTONS
LEO
CULLUM

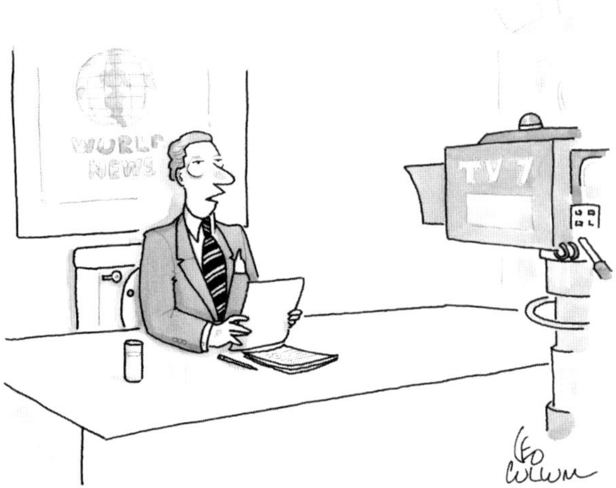
WORLD
NEWS
TV 7

"Good evening, ladies and gentlemen, this is Jack Kruthers on the toilet."

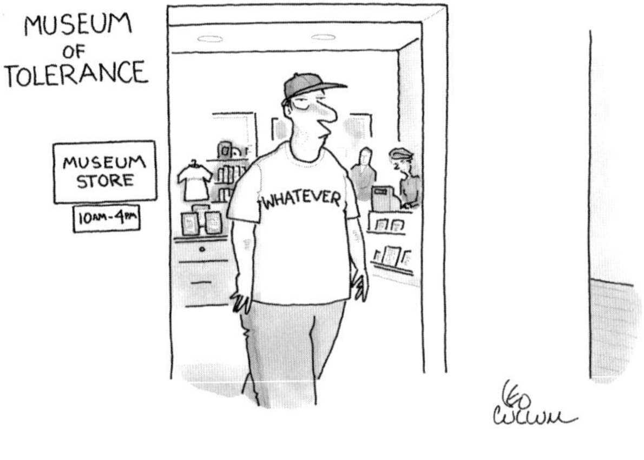
MUSEUM
OF
TOLERANCE
MUSEUM
STORE
10AM-4PM
WHATEVER

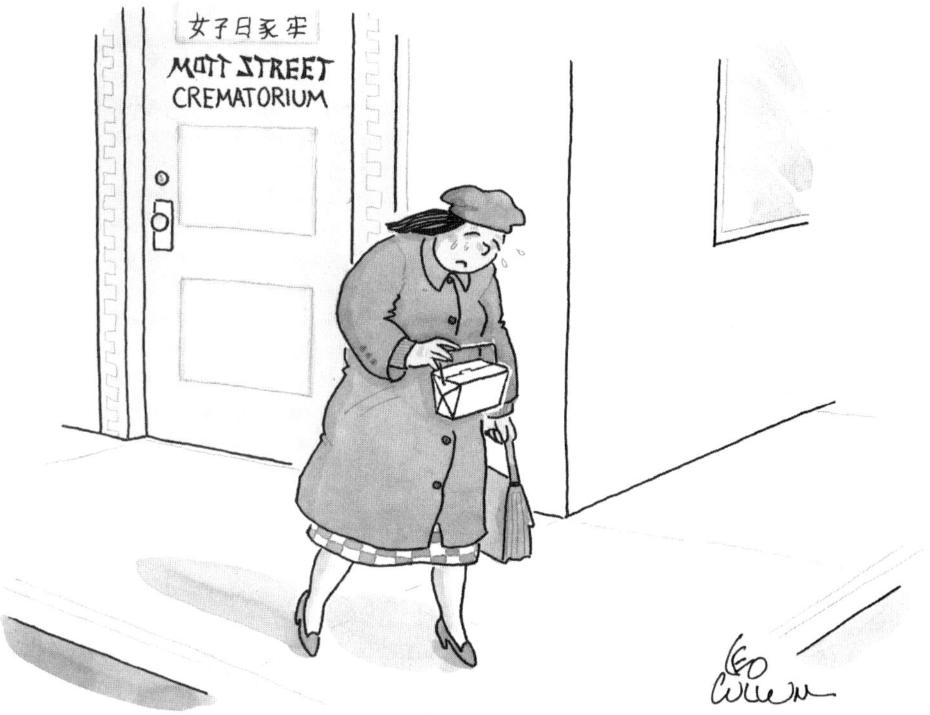
MOTT STREET
CREMATORIUM
LEO CULLUM

"And if we start televising the executions we can also market a hilarious bloopers tape."

"He's going to be even more of a vegetable."

SLAVT

Sara Lautman

Frequently Asked Questions

- *Where do you get your ideas?*
  Usually from other people (reading books, watching movies, talking to friends). This answer is boring but true.

- *Which comes first, the picture or the caption?*
  The caption or a concept. Sometimes both. Rarely an image. It's a process with a lot of variation, which is why it's fun.

- *How'd you get started?*
  I turned to drawing in my early twenties because I had put too much pressure on myself to "be a writer" in college. I was way too self-conscious to give myself a chance at having fun with writing. Drawing, on the other hand, was great because I could just fail and fail at it, and have a great time failing. I was relaxed enough to put drawings on Tumblr. Then I bagged a little job drawing cartoons for a local weekly. There is no "and the rest was history" but I did finally feel happy in a creative practice, and secure enough to show people. That was a really big deal.

- *I admire . . .*
  Teenagers.

- *How do you deal with rejection?*
  Go running or swimming about it. And make sure I'm doing enough creative work and play that pleases me, and that I have agency in. Of course everyone needs some positive reinforcement from the outside world. Working on projects with friends and comics peers brings me a lot of those vitamins.

- *What are some things that make you laugh and why?*
  Old *Simpsons* episodes. Inside jokes. The funniest things in the world to me are hard to translate into single-panel cartoons. Right now the funniest thing is a video of my two friends singing the song "Confrontation" from Les Misérables together. They are very, very skilled at singing it, and it's a challenging song to sing. The reason it's funny to me is that they are TOO good at it. They each made time to learn these complex singing parts, with extreme gravitas. That makes me laugh endlessly, but it probably won't translate into a cartoon.

- *I've got a great idea for a cartoon—wanna hear it?*
  Sure, but I have to like you already.

Infrequently Asked Questions

- *Have you mooned or been mooned more often in your life?*
  Uhm . . . both?

- *What would make a terrible pizza topping?*
Poison!

- *What might one expect to find at a really low-budget amusement park?*
A quarry.

- *What did the shepherd say to the three-legged sheepdog?*
"You are cute! Here, I'll give you to a local shelter because, even though I like you personally, I cannot afford to keep a non-working dog. Farewell, my friend."

Draw Something in This Space

. . . *that will help us understand your childhood.*

(ACTUAL FAVE/KIN = RAPHAEL)

And Now for a Few More Questions . . .

- *What do you hate drawing?*
Dogs, shadows, bushes, offices, money, scissors, Ancient Egypt, fire, snails, hands, sand, oranges, glass, fish, crowds, heights, enclosed spaces, snakes, flying, meeting new people, blood.

- *Being as accurate as possible, how many desert island cartoons do you think you've come up with and submitted to* The New Yorker?
About ten.

Naming Names

- *What name might you give to a mild-mannered, middle-aged, bespectacled dental assistant in one of your cartoons?*
Beebo.

- *Other than Lance, what name would you give to a twenty-eight-year-old entertainment lawyer with a blue-dyed fauxhawk who cycles on weekends?*
Clive.

- *What would be a good name for a new, commercially unviable breakfast cereal?*
Butt Tarts Cereal.

- *Come up with a name for an unpleasant medical procedure.*
Torso Reversal (Physical Therapy).

- *If you used a pen name, what would it be?*
Something as boring and forgettable as possible . . . Rebecca Weiss. Rachel Schwartz. B. Dalton.

Complete the Pie Chart Below

. . . *in a way that tells us something about your life or how you think.*

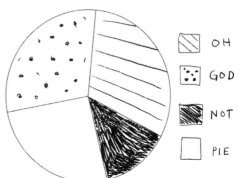

OH
GOD
NOT
PIE

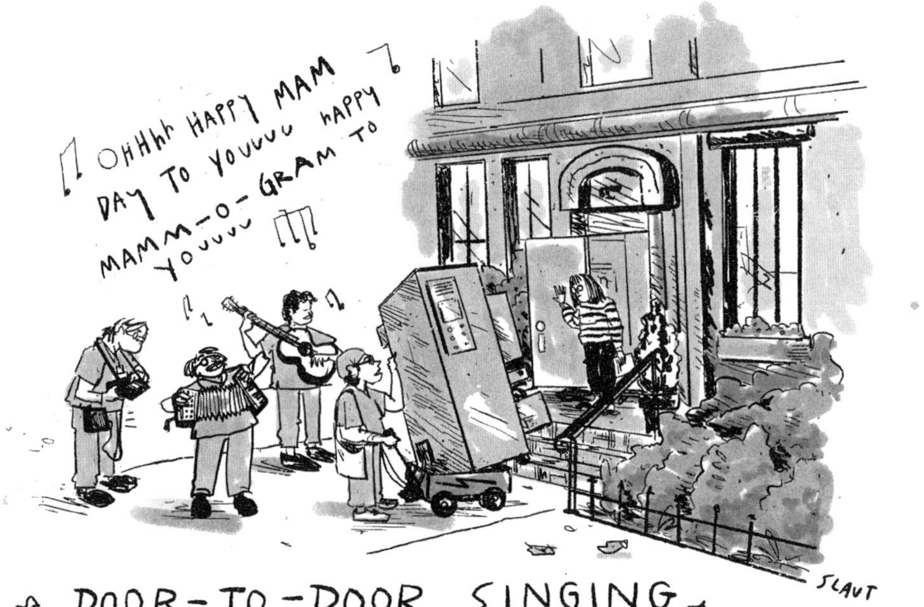
OHHHh HAPPY MAM
DAY TO YOUUUU HAPPY
MAMM-O-GRAM TO
YOUUUU
SLAUT

DOOR-TO-DOOR SINGING MAMMOGRAM

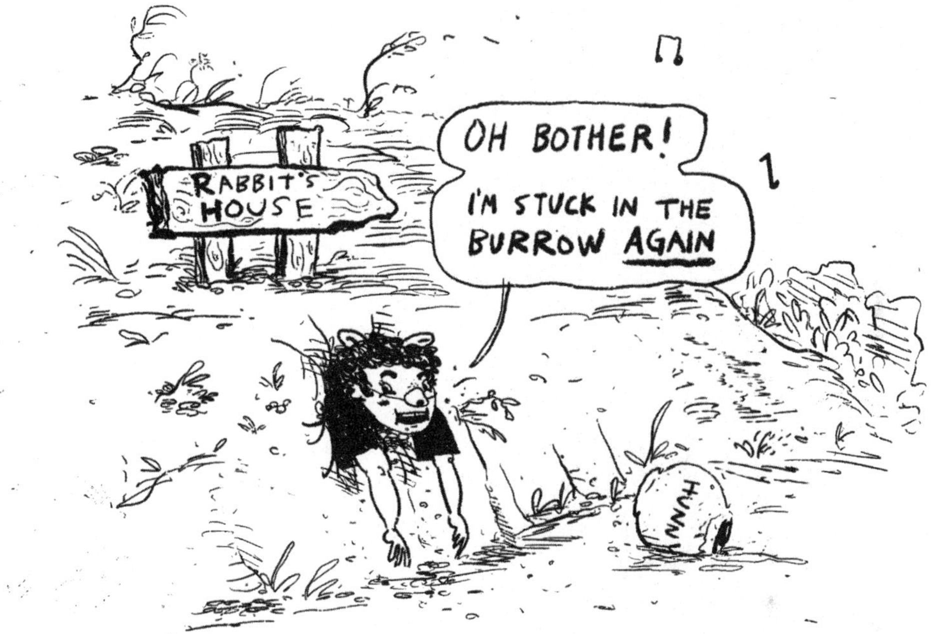
RABBIT'S HOUSE
OH BOTHER!
I'M STUCK IN THE BURROW AGAIN
HUNNY

DESPITE WEEKS of PLANNING, VAL'S CHILDRENS'-LITERATURE-THEMED SEX PARTY WAS A DISAPPOINTMENT

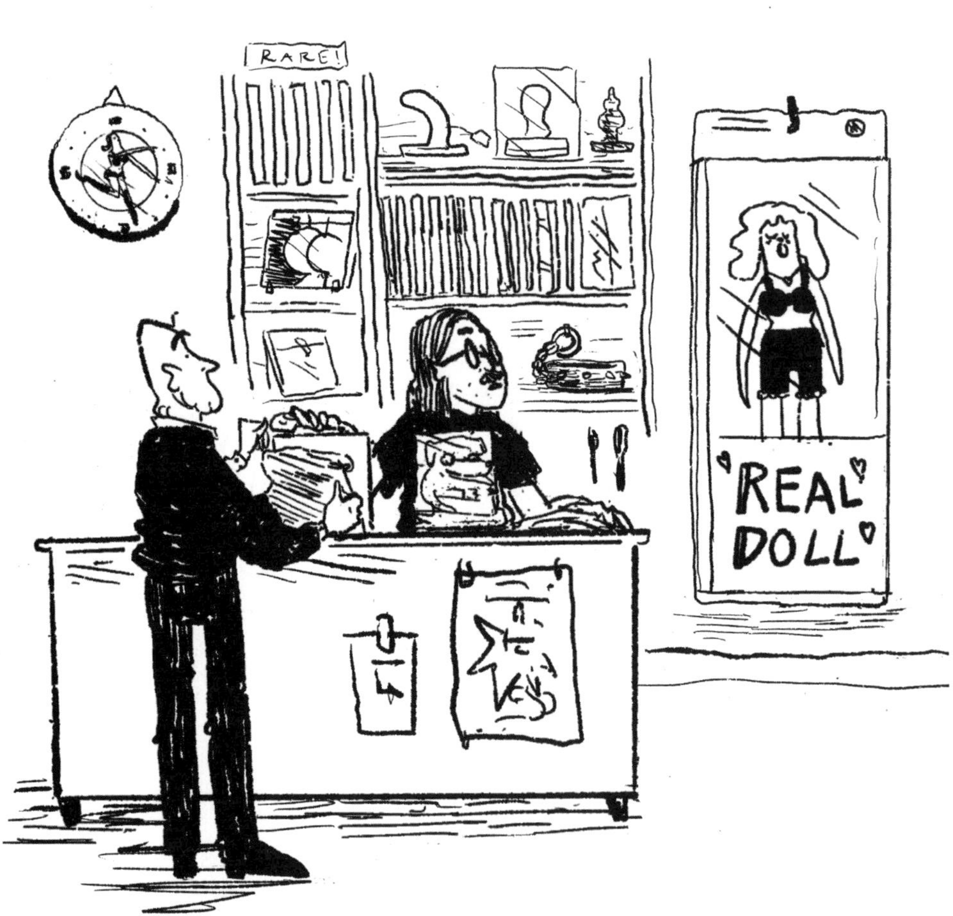
RARE!
REAL DOLL

"Y'know what, you'd be surprised."

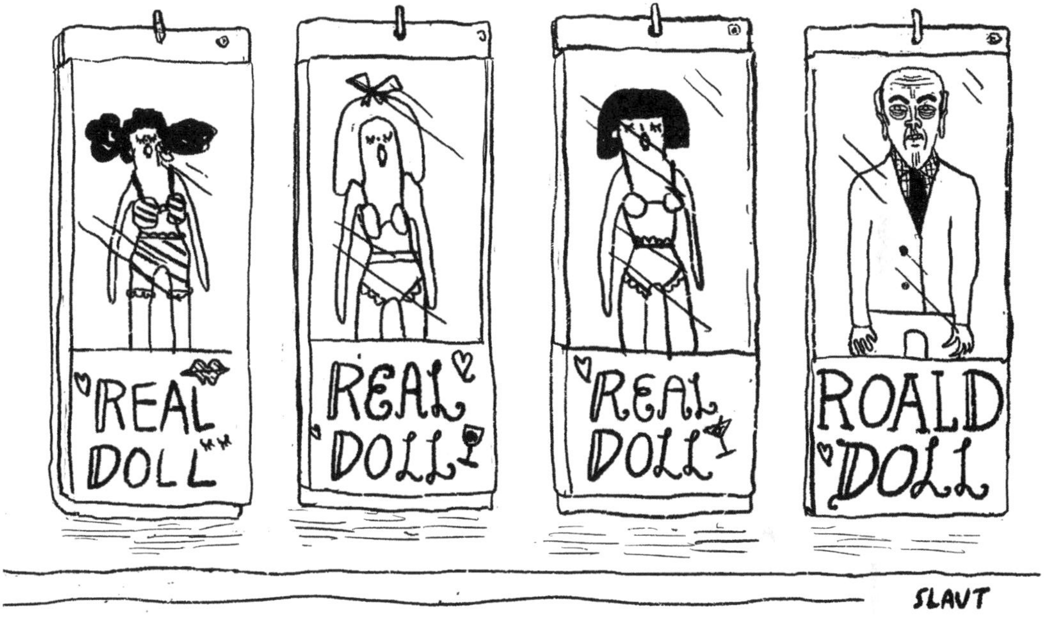
REAL DOLL
REAL DOLL
REAL DOLL
ROALD DOLL
SLAUT

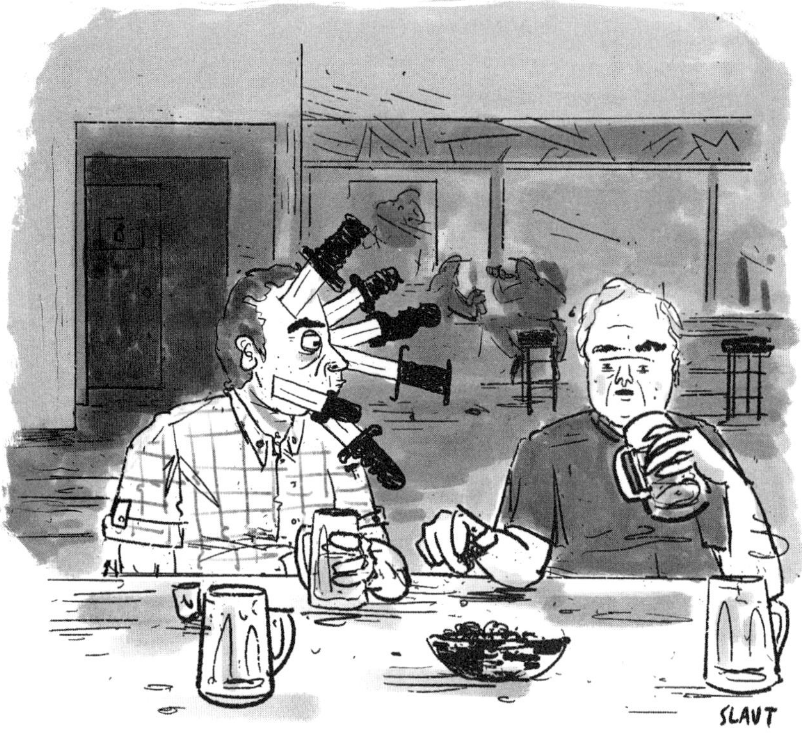
SLAVT

"Well . . . they say by fifty, everyone has the face they deserve."

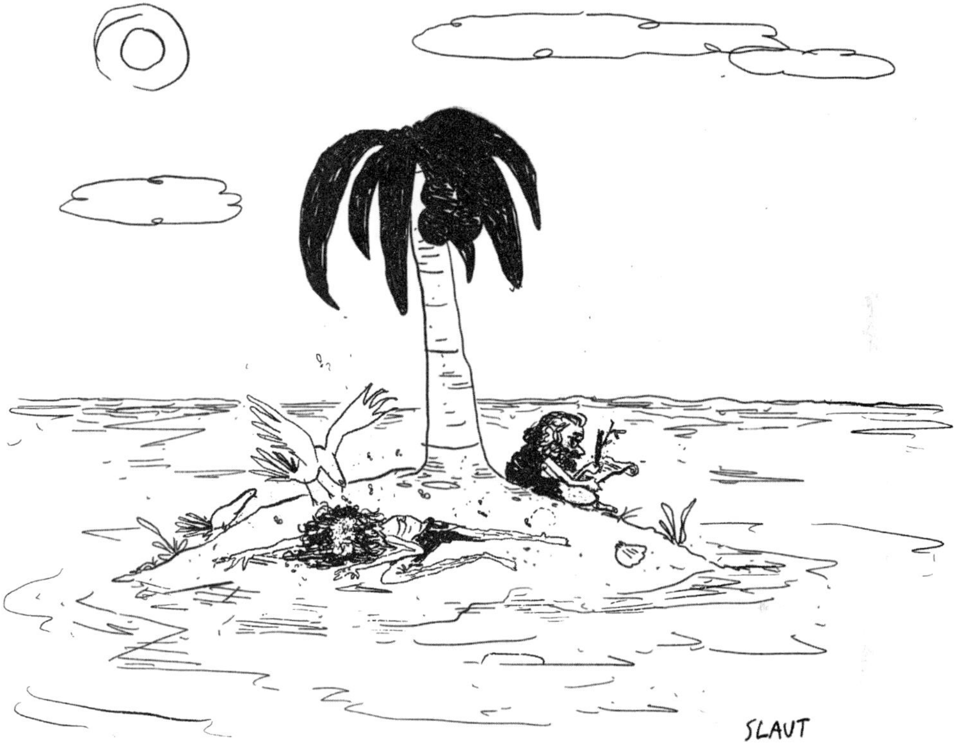
SLAUT

*"'We made love again this morning.
As usual, I had to initiate.'"*

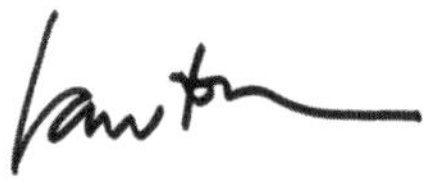

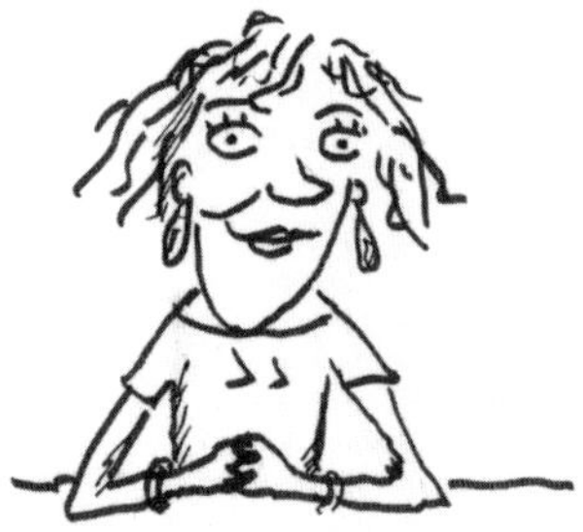

Mary Lawton

Frequently Asked Questions

- *Where do you get your ideas?*
  Under my dog's upper lip.

- *Which comes first, the picture or the caption?*
  I think they both appear and play together, not always nicely.

- *How'd you get started?*
  I drew cartoons in elementary school that made my friends and family laugh, which of course felt good. The addiction continues to this day.

- *I admire . . .*
  Truth tellers.

- *How do you deal with rejection?*
  I dislike it but I don't take it personally.

- *What are some things that make you laugh and why?*
  The Fish Slapping Dance by the Monty Pythons. Cartoons. Stand-up comedy. My cousin Eva.

- *I've got a great idea for a cartoon—wanna hear it?*
  Yes I'll listen!

Infrequently Asked Questions

- *Have you mooned or been mooned more often in your life?*
  I never joined the moonies or any cult.

- *What would make a terrible pizza topping?*
  Any topping that is angry and abusive to the pizza.

- *What did the shepherd say to the three-legged sheepdog?*
  "Who's a good Tripedal? Who's a good Tripedal?"

Draw Something in This Space

. . . that will help us understand your childhood.

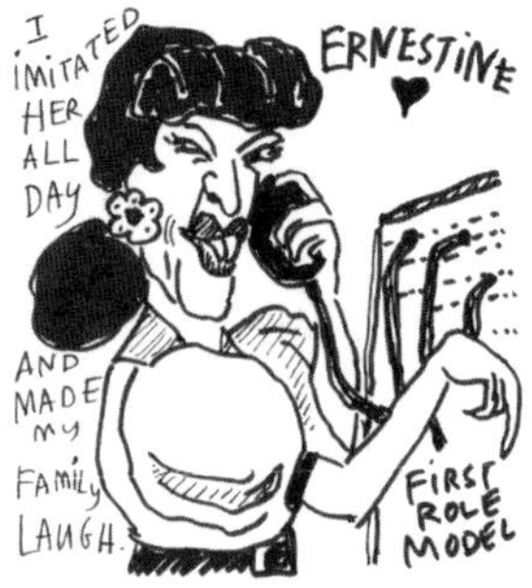
I IMITATED HER ALL DAY
ERNESTINE
AND MADE MY FAMILY LAUGH.
FIRST ROLE MODEL

Draw Some Sort of Doodle

. . . using the random lines below as a starting point.

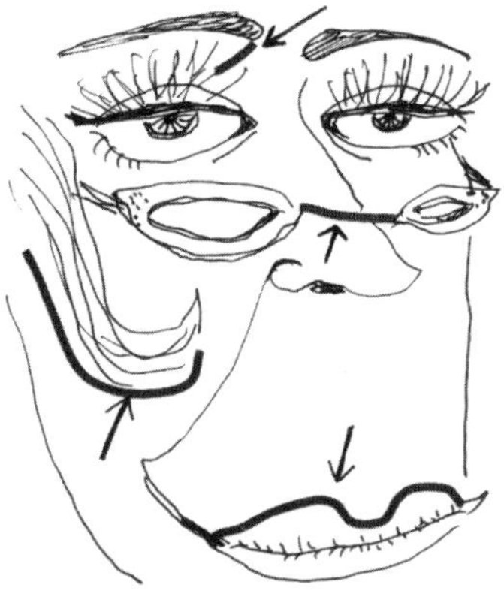

And Now for a Few More Questions . . .

- *What do you hate drawing?*
  Interiors of cathedrals.

- *Being as accurate as possible, how many desert island cartoons do you think you've come up with and submitted to* The New Yorker*?*
  I need HELP remembering. . . .

- *What's the funniest thing that you witnessed, overheard, or came up with that you couldn't figure out how to use in a cartoon?*
  I've been wanting to do a cartoon about a really filthy keyboard I keep seeing.

Naming Names

- *What name might you give to a mild-mannered, middle-aged, bespectacled dental assistant in one of your cartoons?*
  Bruiser McPick.

- *Other than Lance, what name would you give to a twenty-eight-year-old entertainment lawyer with a blue-dyed fauxhawk who cycles on weekends?*
  The Annoyer.

- *What would be a good name for a new, commercially unviable breakfast cereal?*
  Crispy Cramps.

- *Come up with a name for an unpleasant medical procedure.*
  Cosmetic umami removal.

- *If you used a pen name, what would it be?*
  Penny.

Complete the Pie Chart Below

. . . in a way that tells us something about your life or how you think.

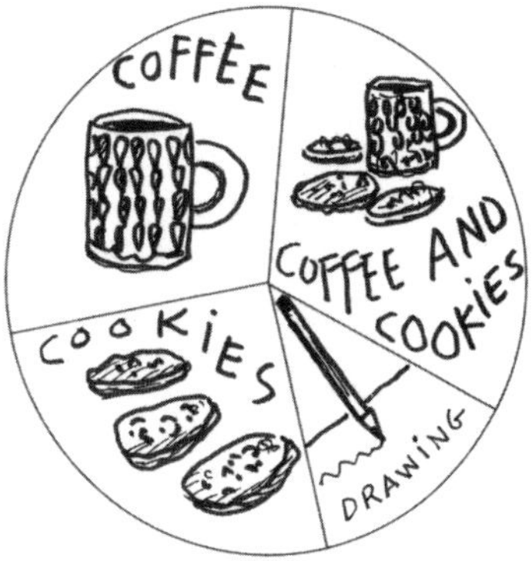
COFFEE
COFFEE AND COOKIES
COOKIES
DRAWING

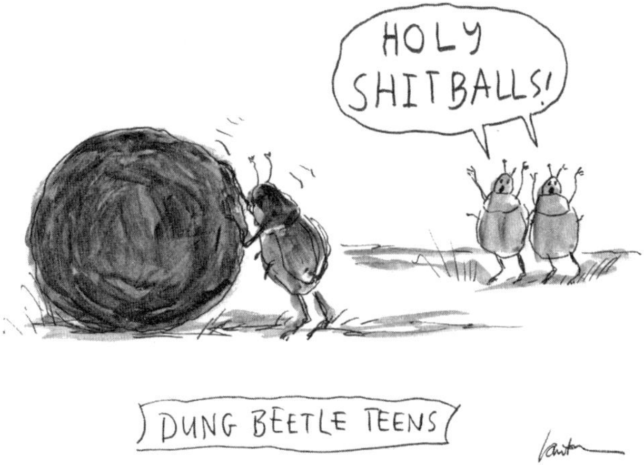
HOLY SHITBALLS!
DUNG BEETLE TEENS

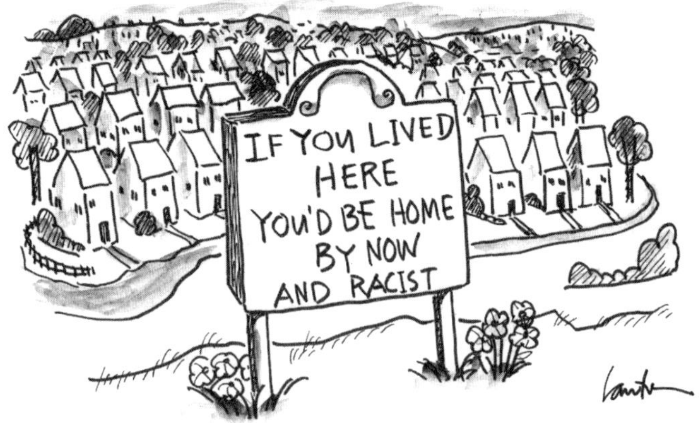
IF YOU LIVED HERE YOU'D BE HOME BY NOW AND RACIST

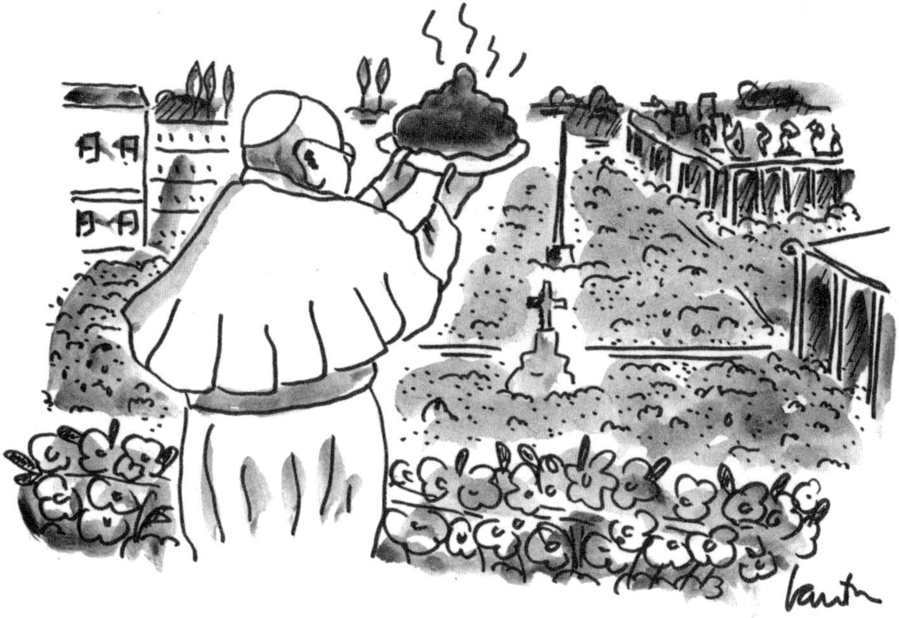

POPE DELIVERS MASS
{OF STEAMING BULLSHIT}

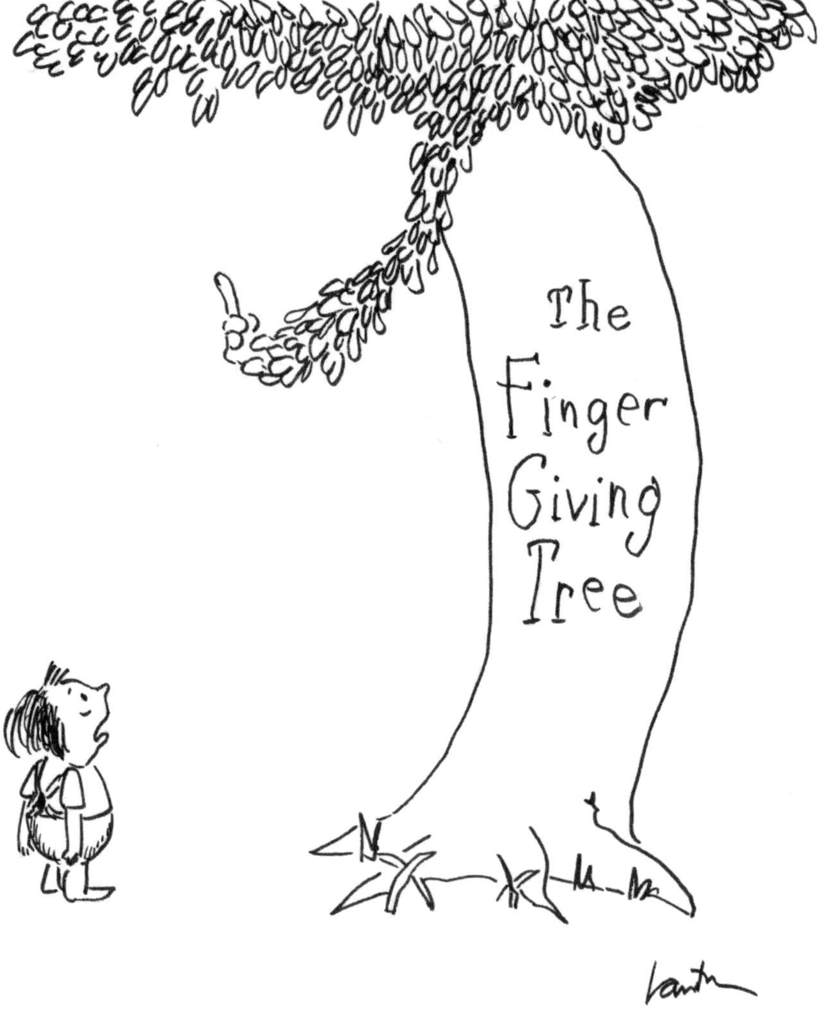
The
Finger
Giving
Tree

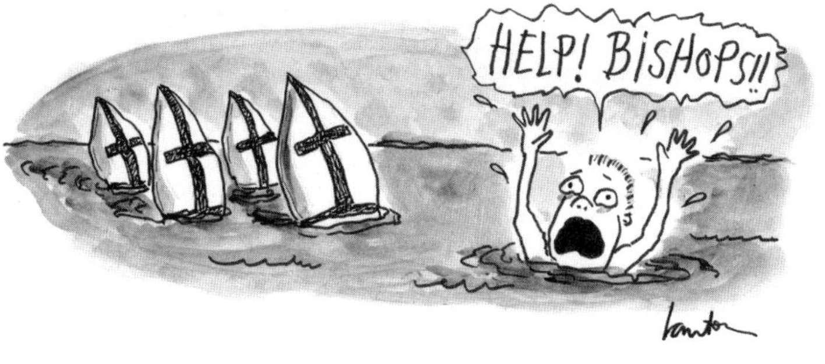
HELP! BISHOPS!!

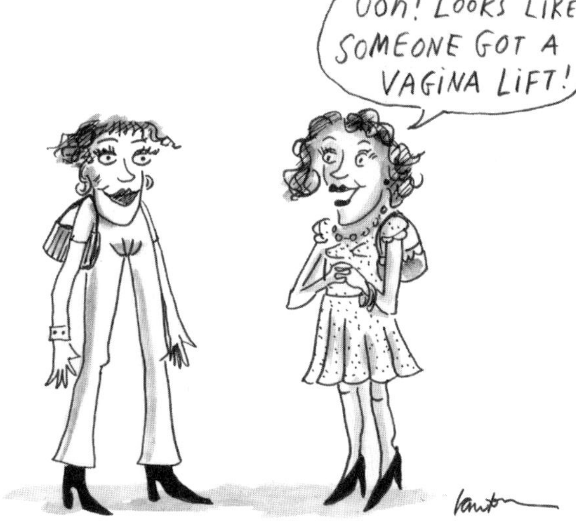
Ooh! LOOKS LIKE SOMEONE GOT A VAGINA LIFT!

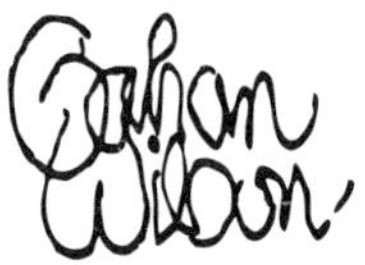

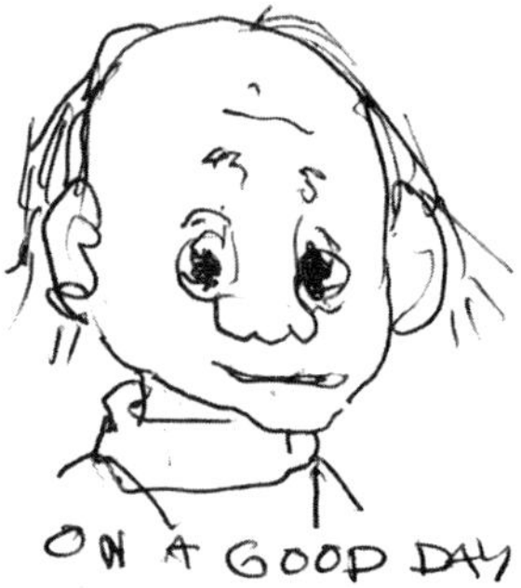
ON A GOOD DAY

Gahan Wilson

Frequently Asked Questions

- *Where do you get your ideas?*
  You tell me.

- *Which comes first, the picture or the caption?*
  They usually crowd in together.

- *How'd you get started?*
  I noticed I was drawing on walls and tried doing it on paper.

- *I admire . . .*
  Your nerve in asking these questions.

- *How do you deal with rejection?*
  I continue.

- *What are some things that make you laugh and why?*
  Depending on my mood, just about anything. I will admit the laughter is now and then bitter. But usually it's nice. Sometimes downright joyful.

- *I've got a great idea for a cartoon—wanna hear it?*
  Hey, would you look at the time—I've got to catch a train!

Infrequently Asked Questions

- *Have you mooned or been mooned more often in your life?*
  Neither.

- *What would make a terrible pizza topping?*
  Yet another pizza.

- *What might one expect to find at a really low-budget amusement park?*
  Myself killed by a faulty roller coaster.

- *What did the shepherd say to the three-legged sheepdog?*
  What say we go into another line of work?

Draw Something in This Space

. . . that will help us understand your childhood.

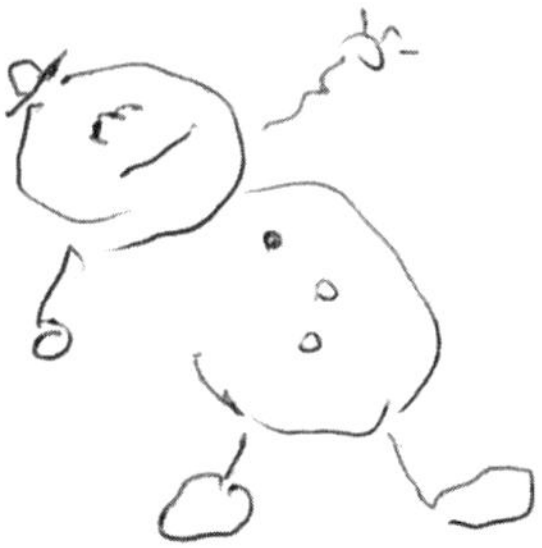

Draw Some Sort of Doodle

. . . using the random lines below as a starting point.

PARKWAY
29
378
BROOKLYN
17

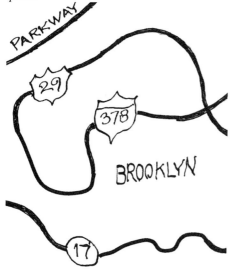

And Now for a Few More Questions . . .

- *What do you hate drawing?*
  I'm afraid you've mistaken me for somebody else.
- *Being as accurate as possible, how many desert island cartoons do you think you've come up with and submitted to* The New Yorker*?*
  Something like 250.
- *What's the funniest thing that you witnessed, overheard, or came up with that you couldn't figure out how to use in a cartoon?*
  So far I've been lucky enough not to run into it.

Naming Names

- *What name might you give to a mild-mannered, middle-aged, bespectacled dental assistant in one of your cartoons?*
  Lance.
- *Other than Lance, what name would you give to a twenty-eight-year-old entertainment lawyer with a blue-dyed fauxhawk who cycles on weekends?*
  Fred.
- *What would be a good name for a new, commercially unviable breakfast cereal?*
  Lance.
- *Come up with a name for an unpleasant medical procedure.*
  Lance.
- *If you used a pen name, what would it be?*
  Lance.

Complete the Pie Chart Below

. . . in a way that tells us something about your life or how you think.

THERE--
NOW IT'S DONE!

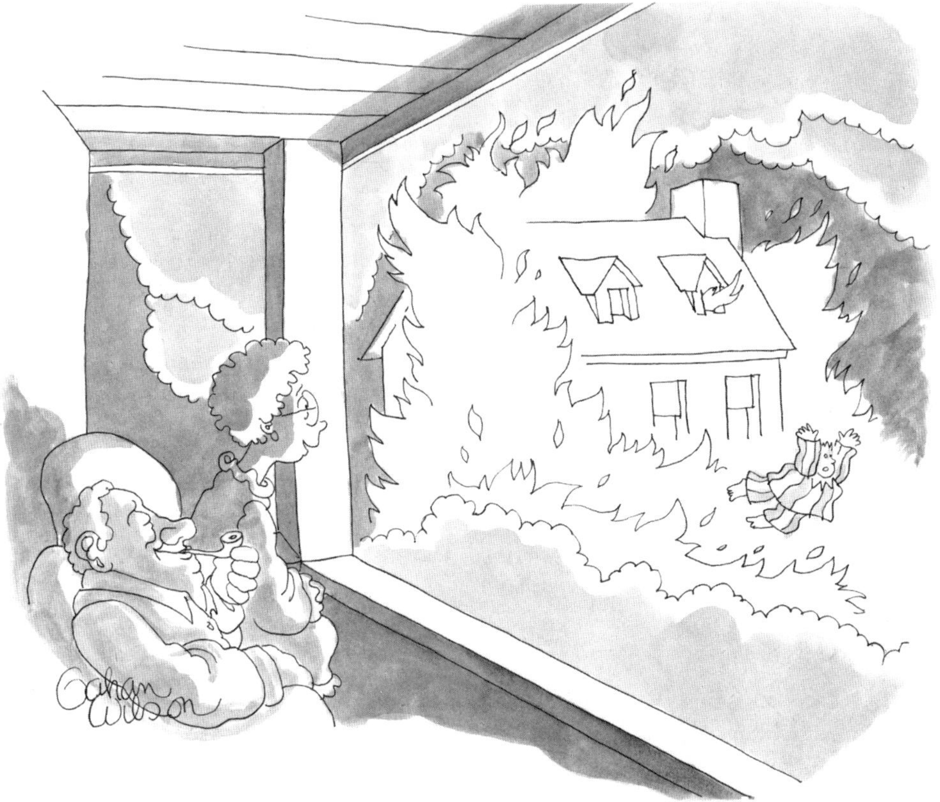
Gahan Wilson

"Well, you certainly were right about the power of prayer, dear!"

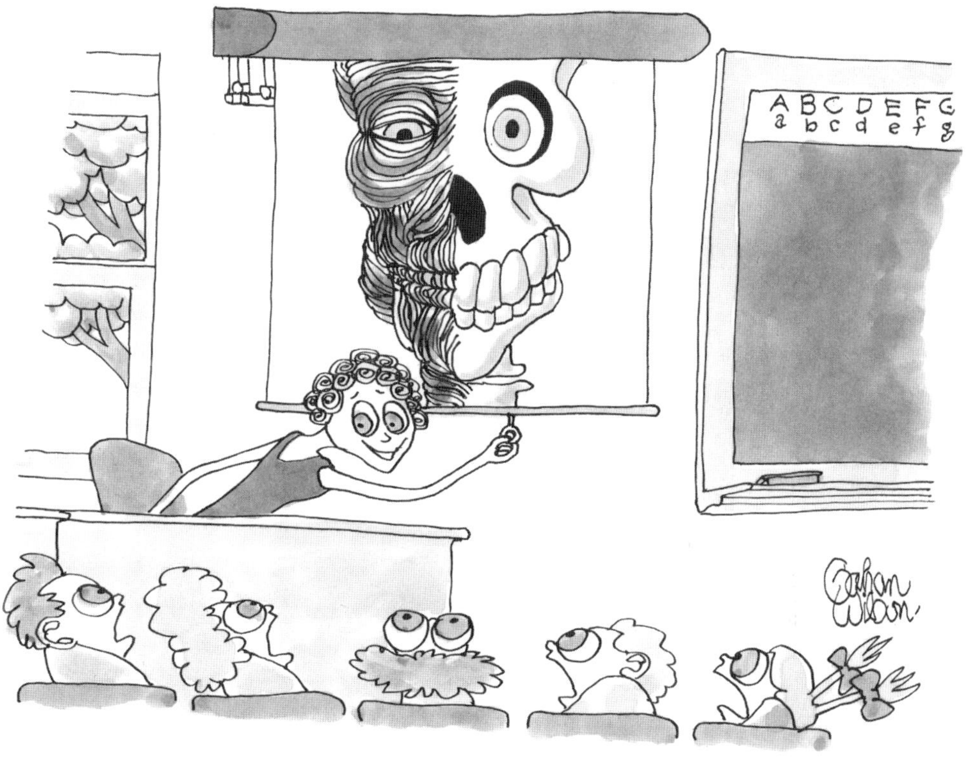
ABCDEFG
abcdefg
Gahan Wilson

"Sorry—this was supposed to be a map of Peru!"

"Some like to keep them as souvenirs, some don't."

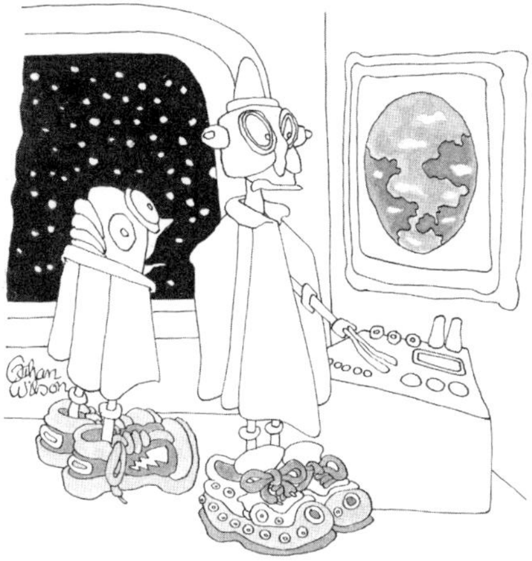
Gahan Wilson

"But if we destroy the planet Earth, they'll stop making these great cheap shoes!"

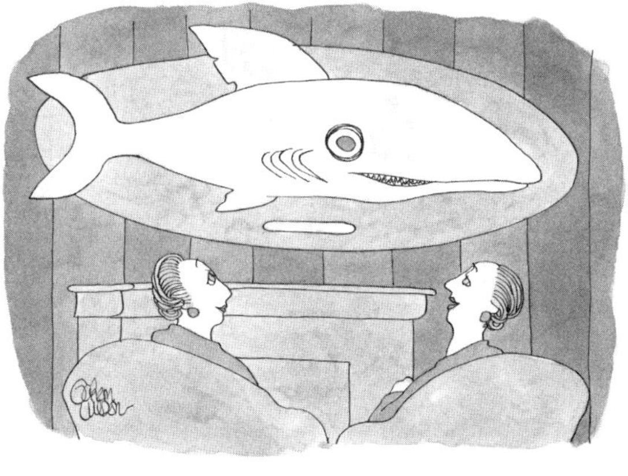
Gahan Wilson

"I had it stuffed and mounted as a sentimental gesture since it was the one that ate most of Roger."

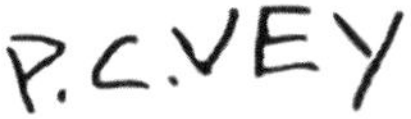
P.C.VEY

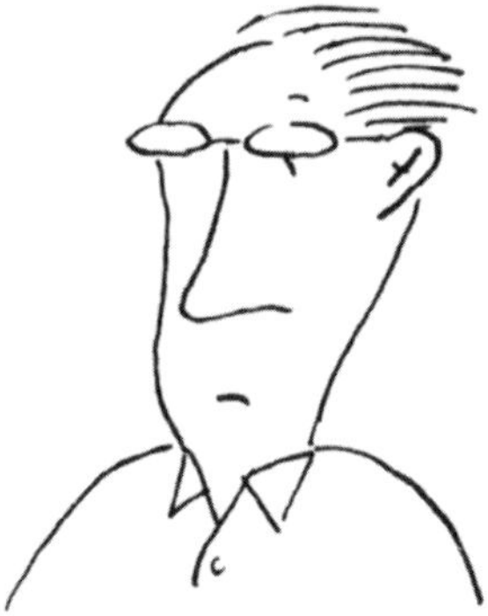

P. C. Vey

Frequently Asked Questions

- *Where do you get your ideas?*
  From a box on the shelf.

- *Which comes first, the picture or the caption?*
  One or the other.

- *How'd you get started?*
  At the beginning.

- *I admire . . .*
  The vibrancy of peas and carrots.

- *How do you deal with rejection?*
  In very colorful ways.

- *What are some things that make you laugh and why?*
  Long walks on the beach, fine wine, and sunsets. If I don't laugh at them, who will?

- *I've got a great idea for a cartoon—wanna hear it?*
  Sure.

Infrequently Asked Questions

- *Have you mooned or been mooned more often in your life?*
  I can't remember.

- *What would make a terrible pizza topping?*
  Cheese.

- *What might one expect to find at a really low-budget amusement park?*
  "Standing Still, the Ride . . ."

- *What did the shepherd say to the three-legged sheepdog?*
  Where's your other leg?

Draw Something in This Space

. . . that will help us understand your childhood.

DIRT
IN A
CAN

And Now for a Few More Questions . . .

- *What do you hate drawing?*
  Steam coming from a freshly slaughtered animal.

- *Being as accurate as possible, how many desert island cartoons do you think you've come up with and submitted to* The New Yorker*?*
  184.

- *What's the funniest thing that you witnessed, overheard, or came up with that you couldn't figure out how to use in a cartoon?*
  Naughty pine.

Naming Names

- *What name might you give to a mild-mannered, middle-aged, bespectacled dental assistant in one of your cartoons?*
  Lance.

- *Other than Lance, what name would you give to a twenty-eight-year-old entertainment lawyer with a blue-dyed fauxhawk who cycles on weekends?*
  Vance.

- *What would be a good name for a new, commercially unviable breakfast cereal?*
  Steam from a Freshly Slaughtered Animal.

- *Come up with a name for an unpleasant medical procedure.*
  A doctor extraction.

- *If you used a pen name, what would it be?*
  P. C. Vey.

Complete the Pie Chart Below

. . . in a way that tells us something about your life or how you think.

STUFF TO DO.
STUFF TO DO.
STUFF TO DO.
STUFF TO DO.

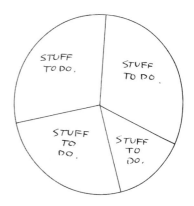

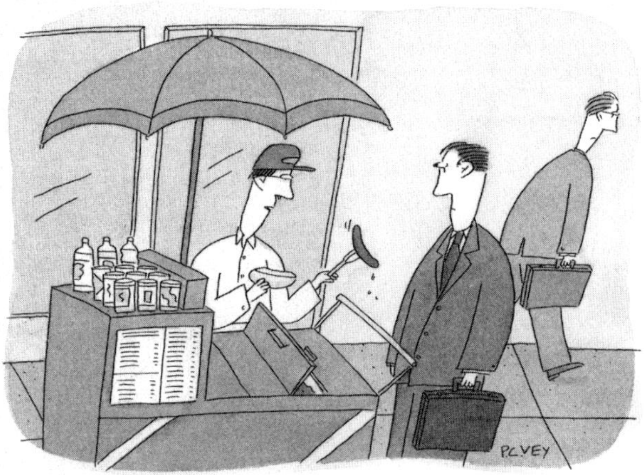
P.C.VEY

"Are you sure you don't want to lick it before I bun it?"

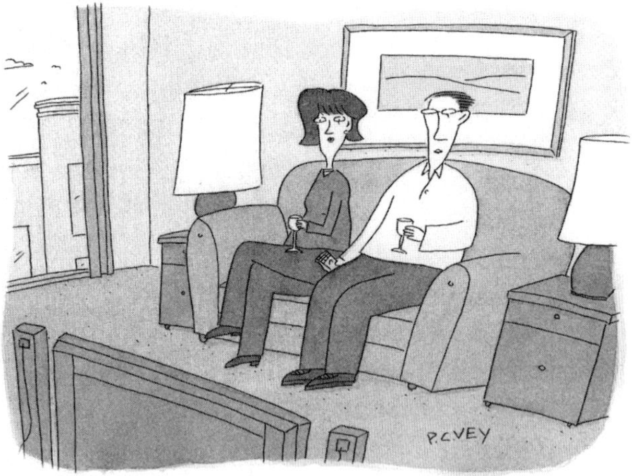
P.C.VEY

"You haven't seen disaster relief till you've seen it in high definition."

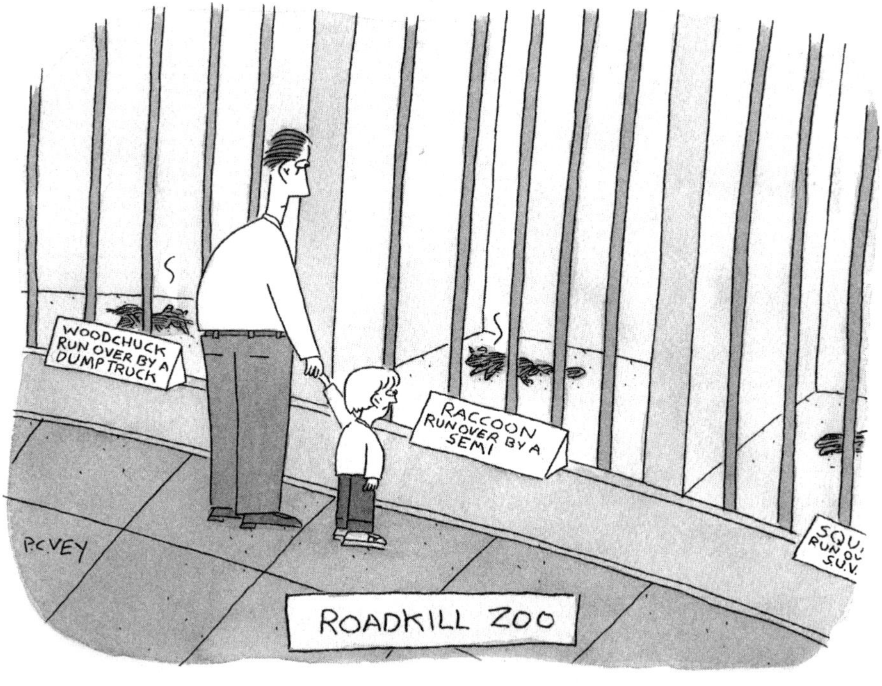
WOODCHUCK RUN OVER BY A DUMP TRUCK
RACCOON RUN OVER BY A SEMI
SQU
RUN OV
S.U.V.
P.C.VEY
ROADKILL ZOO

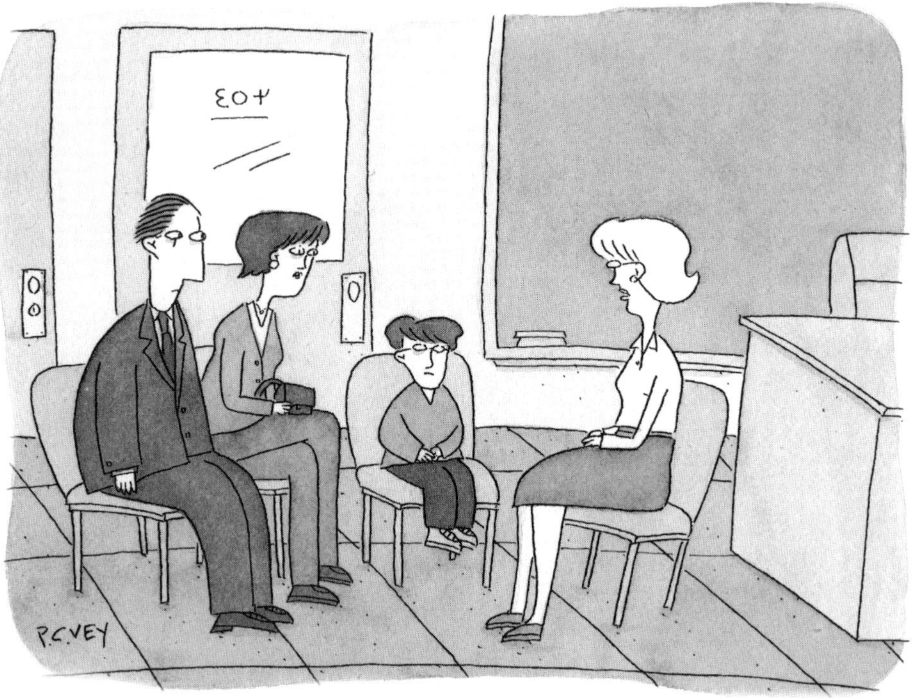
P.C.VEY

"He's at that awkward age when he tells his teachers valuable information about his parents."

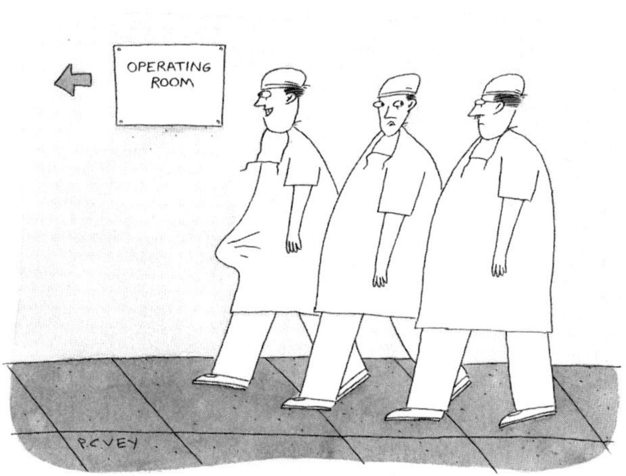
OPERATING ROOM
P.C.VEY

"If you ask me, Roger has the completely wrong attitude about gallbladder surgery."

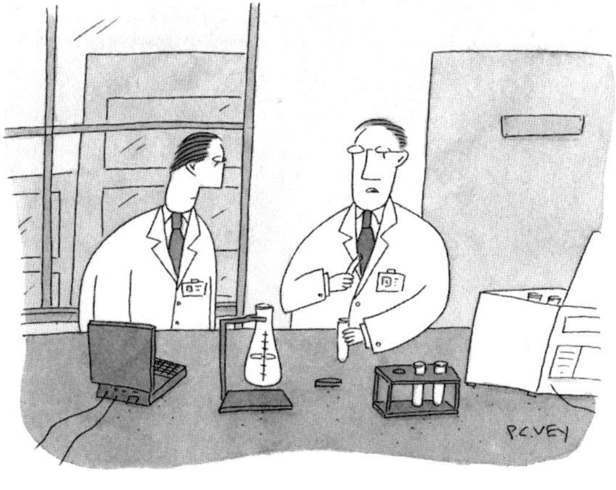
P.C.VEY

"These stem cells taste funny."

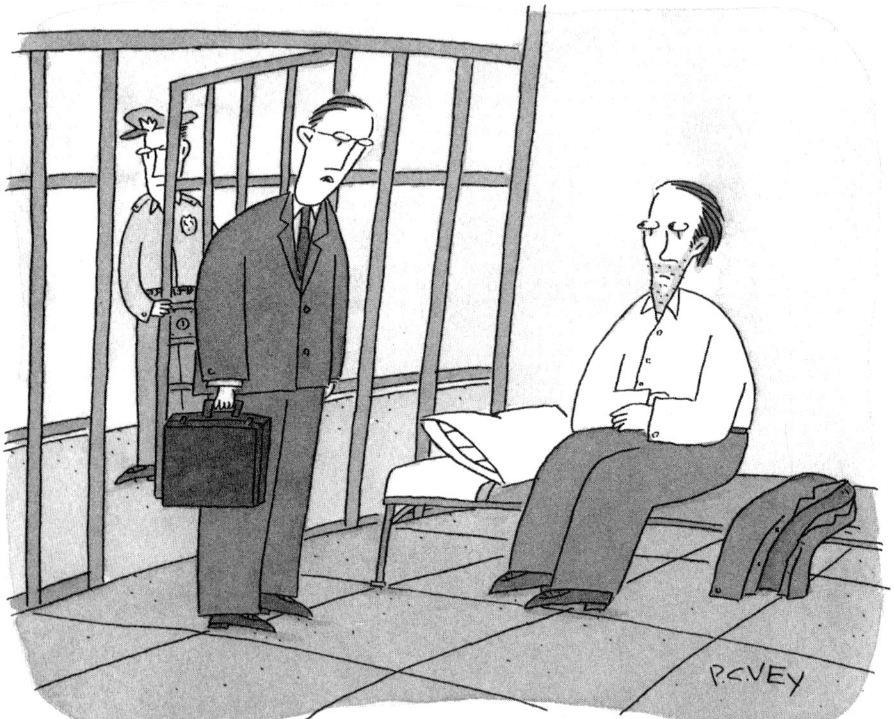
P.C.VEY

"They've agreed to drop the charges, but only if you agree never to stuff the turkey again."

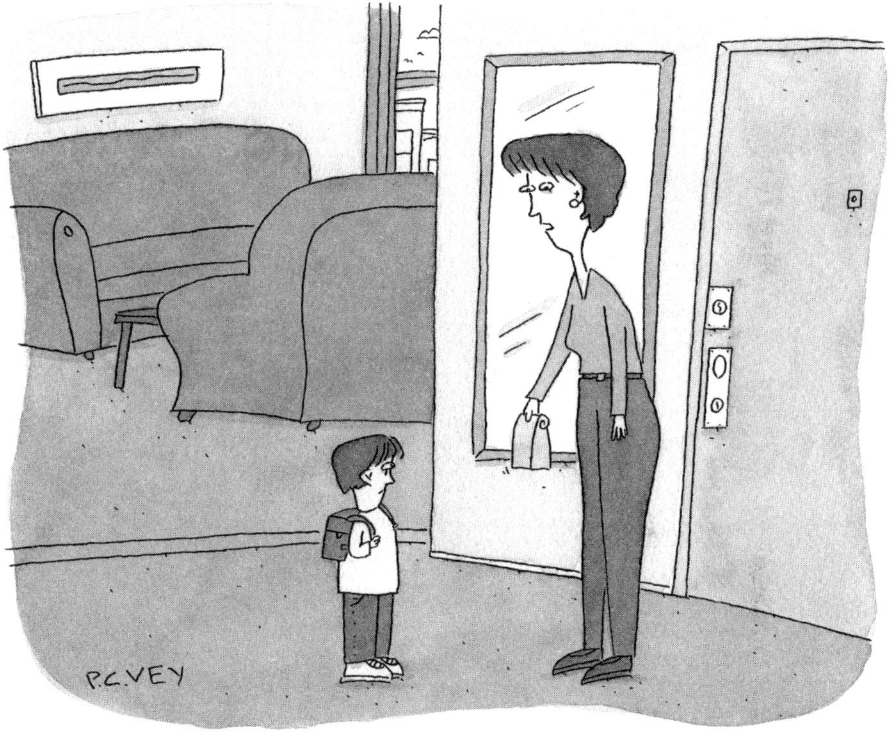
P.C.VEY

"It's something I brought back from the doctor."

PATTERSON

Jason Patterson

Frequently Asked Questions

- *Where do you get your ideas?*
  I think of my best ideas when I'm not trying to think of ideas.

- *Which comes first, the picture or the caption?*
  Picture.

- *How'd you get started?*
  I sold my first cartoon to a local paper for $20, in high school.

- *I admire . . .*
  People that like to draw serious grown-up things.

- *How do you deal with rejection?*
  I have this little trick where I just think about dinosaurs. I love dinosaurs. Then, I imagine the dinosaurs eating the cartoon editor.

- *What are some things that make you laugh and why?*
  People who like to draw serious grown-up things.

- *I've got a great idea for a cartoon—wanna hear it?*
  Ok, just keep in mind nine out of ten ideas are bad.

Infrequently Asked Questions

- *Have you mooned or been mooned more often in your life?*
  Been.

- *What would make a terrible pizza topping?*
  Corn.

- *What might one expect to find at a really low-budget amusement park?*
  Porn.

- *What did the shepherd say to the three-legged sheepdog?*
  How do you do?

And Now for a Few More Questions . . .

- *What do you hate drawing?*
  Cars. I can't seem to get them right.

- *Being as accurate as possible, how many desert island cartoons do you think you've come up with and submitted to* The New Yorker?
  Twenty.

■ *What's the funniest thing that you witnessed, overheard, or came up with that you couldn't figure out how to use in a cartoon?*
Someone farted on the subway really loud, but everyone was completely stone-faced about it. Killed me.

Draw Some Sort of Doodle

. . . using the random lines below as a starting point.

Naming Names

■ *What name might you give to a mild-mannered, middle-aged, bespectacled dental assistant in one of your cartoons?*
Steven.

■ *Other than Lance, what name would you give to a twenty-eight-year-old entertainment lawyer with a blue-dyed fauxhawk who cycles on weekends?*
Steve.

■ *What would be a good name for a new, commercially unviable breakfast cereal?*
Bacon Bits.

■ *Come up with a name for an unpleasant medical procedure.*
Brain transplant.

■ *If you used a pen name, what would it be?*
Linwood.

Complete the Pie Chart Below

. . . in a way that tells us something about your life or how you think.

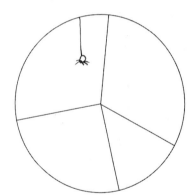

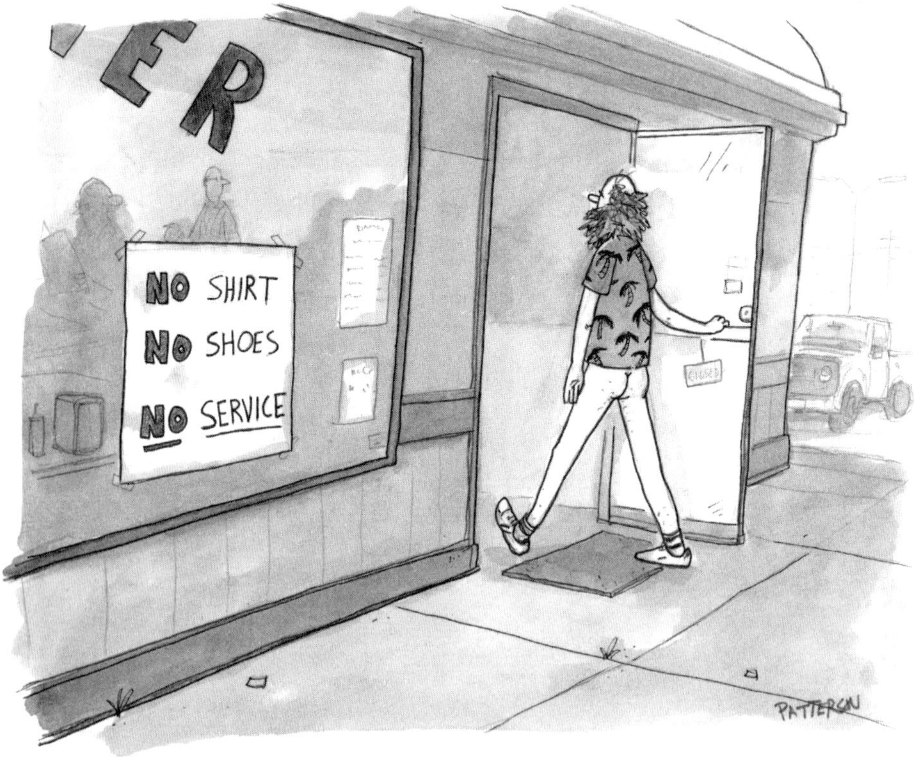
ER
NO SHIRT
NO SHOES
NO SERVICE
PATTERSON

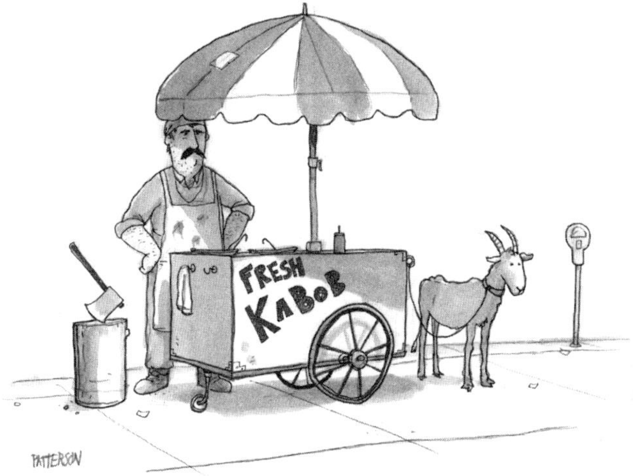
FRESH
KABOB
PATTERSON

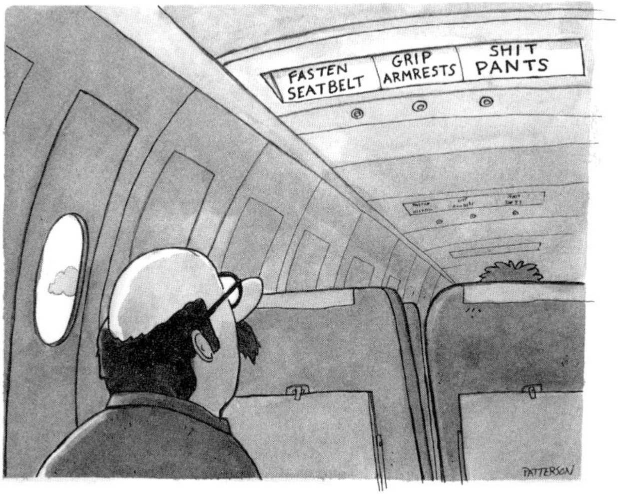
FASTEN
SEATBELT
GRIP
ARMRESTS
SHIT
PANTS
PATTERSON

Navied

Navied Mahdavian

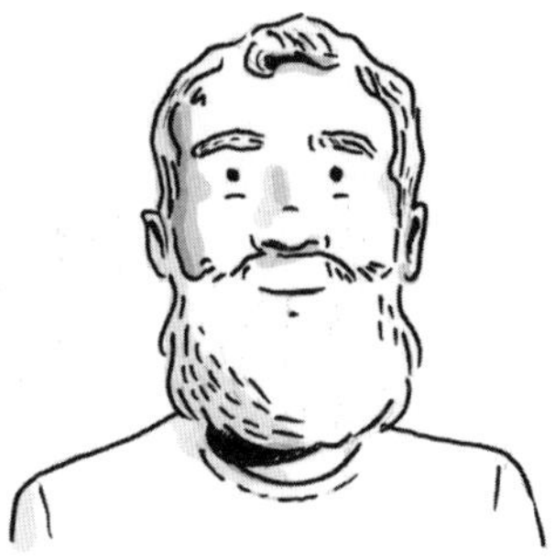

Frequently Asked Questions

- *Where do you get your ideas?*
  Typically, I sit very quietly with a notebook and pen, and when that doesn't work, I lay even more quietly on the couch. Once I've awoken hours later, I go back to sitting and remain sitting until I've thought of something funny. I am still sitting.

- *Which comes first, the picture or the caption?*
  Captions, if only because they take up less room than sketches in my notebook (speaking of which, will you buy me a new notebook?).

- *How'd you get started?*
  Before becoming a cartoonist, I taught the fifth grade where I learned most of my jokes. I started cartooning around this time, but none of my cartoons went over with my students as well as Uranus jokes.

- *I admire . . .*
  people who aren't taller than me.

- *How do you deal with rejection?*
  I post cartoons to social media where devoted followers like IG user ThisIsNotNaviedsMom post comments like "What a handsome boy!"

- *What are some things that make you laugh and why?*
  Uranus jokes.

- *I've got a great idea for a cartoon—wanna hear it?*
  Matt Diffee does! His number is 555-0781.

Infrequently Asked Questions

- *Have you mooned or been mooned more often in your life?*
  (‿ʏ‿) I am, in fact, mooning you right now.

- *What would make a terrible pizza topping?*
  There are no bad pizza toppings, only bad pizzas.

- *What might one expect to find at a really low-budget amusement park?*
  A sideshow featuring struggling cartoonists. "Gobble, gobble, we accept you. One of us!"

- *What did the shepherd say to the three-legged sheepdog?*
  "One leg down, three meals to go."

Draw Something in This Space

. . . that will help us understand your childhood.

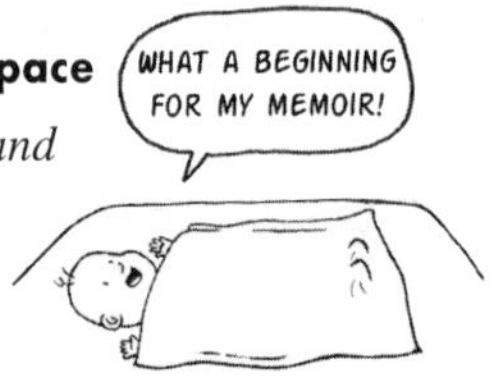
WHAT A BEGINNING FOR MY MEMOIR!

Draw Some Sort of Doodle

. . . using the random lines below as a starting point.

And Now for a Few More Questions . . .

- *What do you hate drawing?*
  The Roman playwright Terence once said, "I am human, I consider nothing human alien to me." Like Terence, I also am human. Unlike Terence, humans are alien to me, particularly when I have to draw them. This is probably why I draw so many animals in bed.

- *Being as accurate as possible, how many desert island cartoons do you think you've come up with and submitted to* The New Yorker*?*
  102. I know this because it specifies the number on this cease and desist letter I received from the desk of the cartoon editor.

- *What's the funniest thing that you witnessed, overheard, or came up with that you couldn't figure out how to use in a cartoon?*
  The abyss. I stared into it for too long, but then got sleepy.

Naming Names

- *What name might you give to a mild-mannered, middle-aged, bespectacled dental assistant in one of your cartoons?*
  Gary. Always Gary.

- *Other than Lance, what name would you give to a twenty-eight-year-old entertainment lawyer with a blue-dyed fauxhawk who cycles on weekends?*
  Garreth.

- *What would be a good name for a new, commercially unviable breakfast cereal?*
  Gary Flakes.

- *Come up with a name for an unpleasant medical procedure.*
  Gary-ectomy.

- *If you used a pen name, what would it be?*
  Gary.

Complete the Pie Chart Below

. . . in a way that tells us something about your life or how you think.

REPRESSION
FIXATION
PENIS ENVY
FANTASY

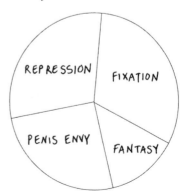

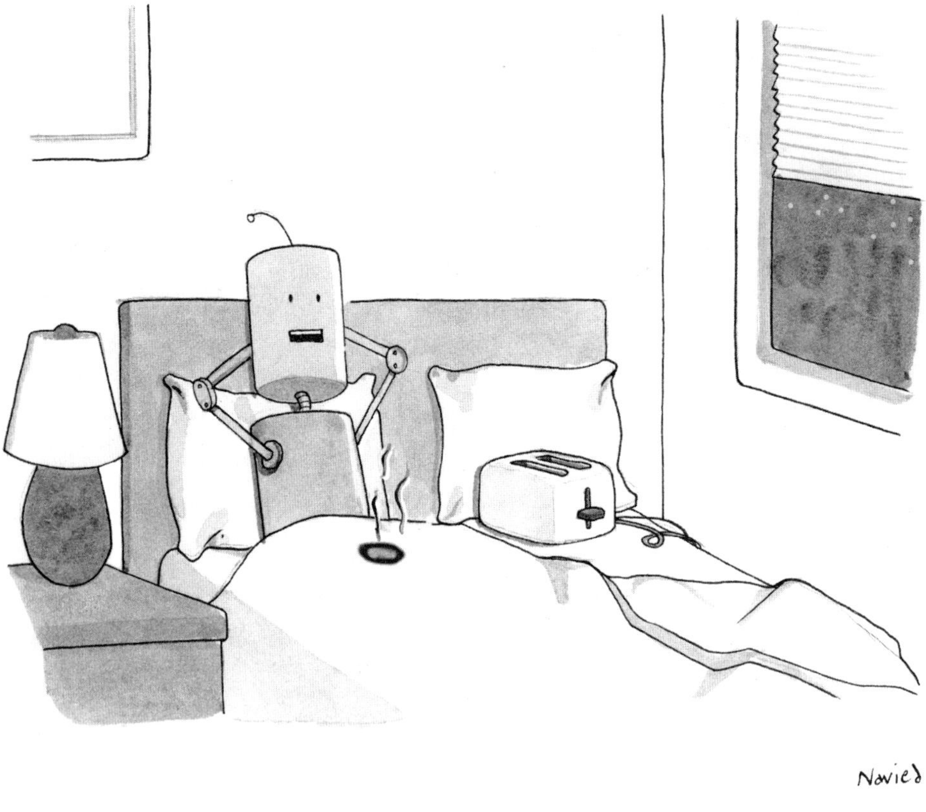
Navied

"Wow! So that was the bagel setting."

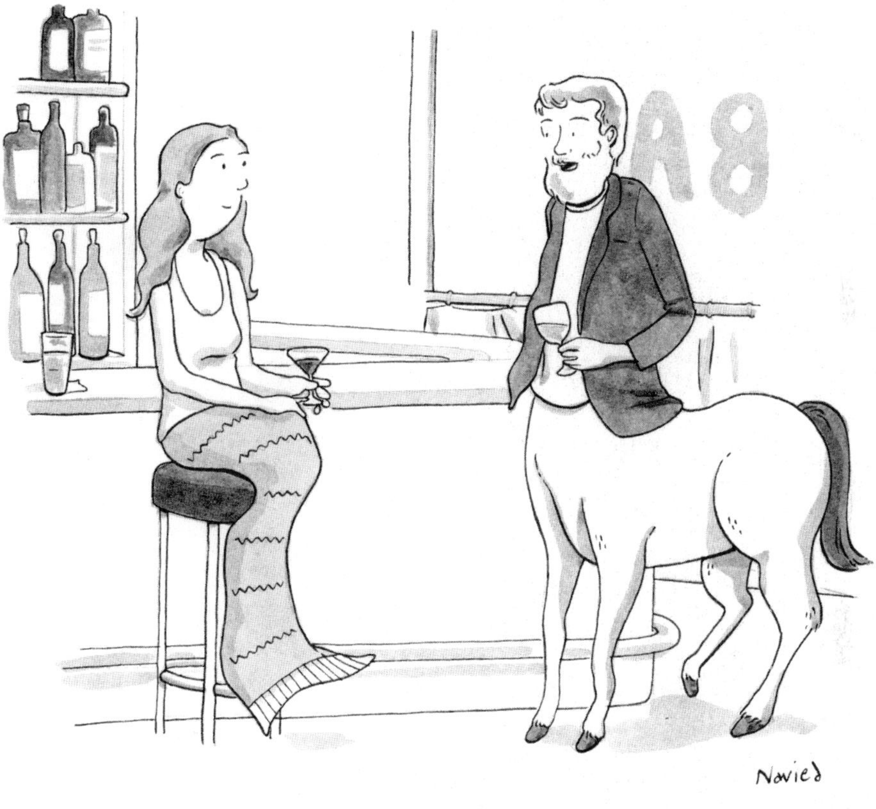
Navied

"For my dad, it was horses."

"You have one, two, three months to live."

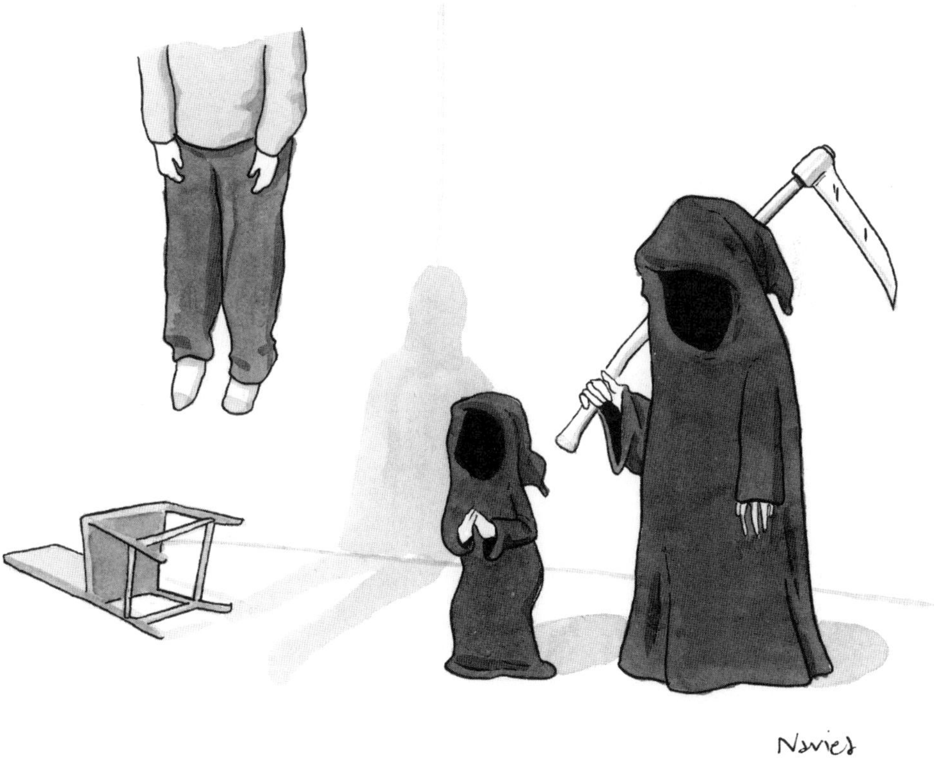
Navied

"Again, daddy, again!"

CAJ

Carolita Johnson

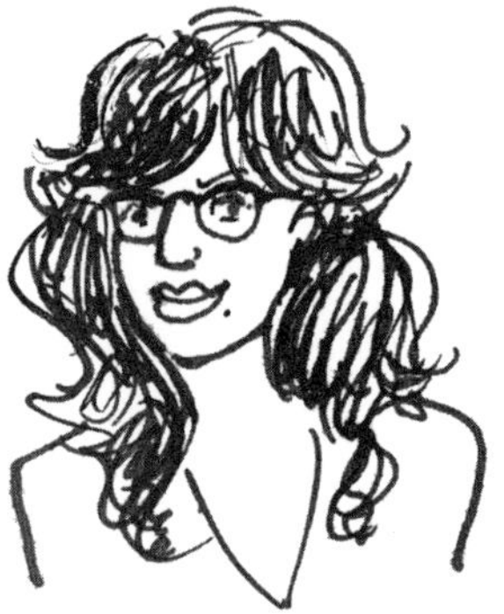

Frequently Asked Questions

- *Where do you get your ideas?*
  Not from the gag-writers who keep emailing me with proposals!

- *Which comes first, the picture or the caption?*
  70 percent the caption, 29 percent the picture, 1 percent both at the same time.

- *How'd you get started?*
  Don't get me started.

- *I admire . . .*
  People who get away with murder (metaphorically speaking, of course).

- *How do you deal with rejection?*
  Never giving up. Visiting the batting cage at Coney Island and naming all the softballs after the rejector(s). (They know who they are. . . .)

- *What are some things that make you laugh and why?*
  Men named Dick, birds called "tits," Edgar Allan Poe, very serious people, Saint Hildegard's remedy for leprosy,* my own jokes, and people who think that's wrong. Why? Because they can't help it.

- *I've got a great idea for a cartoon—wanna hear it?*
  NO!!!

Infrequently Asked Questions

- *Have you mooned or been mooned more often in your life?*
  I am mooning you right now.

- *What would make a terrible pizza topping?*
  What doesn't?

- *What might one expect to find at a really low-budget amusement park?*
  Me—I love low-budget amusement parks!

- *What did the shepherd say to the three-legged sheepdog?*
  Can you shoot a gun?

***Saint Hildegard's recipe for leprosy control includes a "modicum stercoris gallinarum."**

Draw Something in This Space

. . . that will help us understand your childhood.

And I now have four.
I only wanted four!
(9 yrs. old)
Someday I'll have as many flashlights as I want...

And Now for a Few More Questions . . .

- *What do you hate drawing?*
  Straight lines.
- *Being as accurate as possible, how many desert island cartoons do you think you've come up with and submitted to* The New Yorker*?*
  Fifteen, about a third sold.
- *What's the funniest thing that you witnessed, overheard, or came up with that you couldn't figure out how to use in a cartoon?*
  President Bush's administration.
  (So funny I forgot to laugh.)

Naming Names

- *What name might you give to a mild-mannered, middle-aged, bespectacled dental assistant in one of your cartoons?*
  Matthew.
- *Other than Lance, what name would you give to a twenty-eight-year-old entertainment lawyer with a blue-dyed fauxhawk who cycles on weekends?*
  Chad, Tad, Brad . . . any "ad" name.
- *What would be a good name for a new, commercially unviable breakfast cereal?*
  Gassies. Hairy Crunchballs.
- *Come up with a name for an unpleasant medical procedure.*
  Foreskinoplasty.

Complete the Pie Chart Below

. . . in a way that tells us something about your life or how you think.

1970 - 1983
NEARLY FATAL BOREDOM
1984 - 2000
ah - haaa!!
2000 - 2002
attempt at gainful employment
2002 → present.
"so long, suckers!" + ("the check is in the mail")

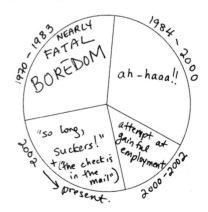

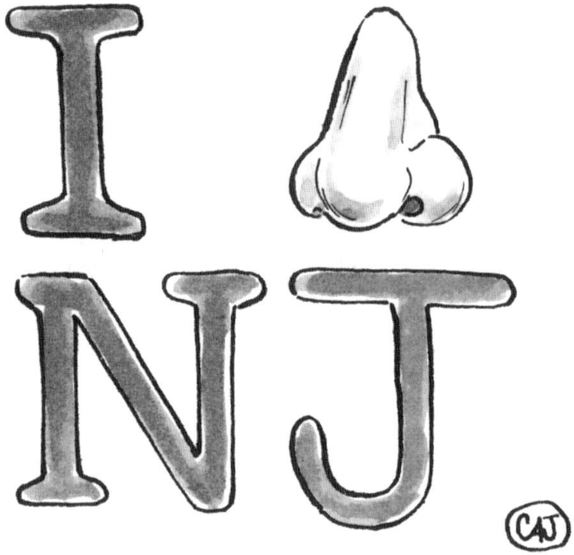
I
NJ

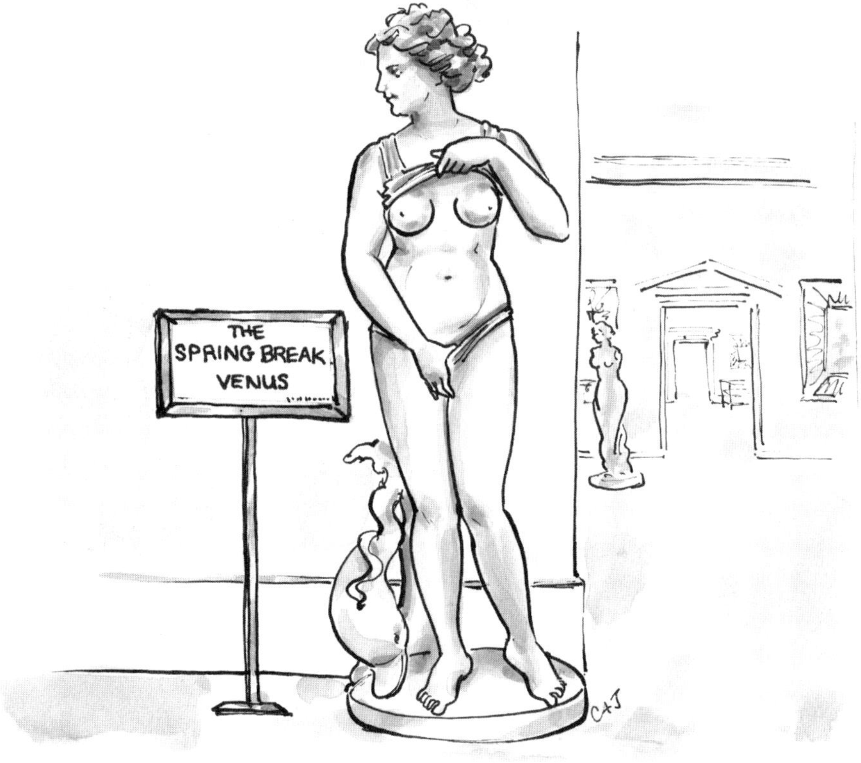
THE
SPRING BREAK
VENUS
C+J

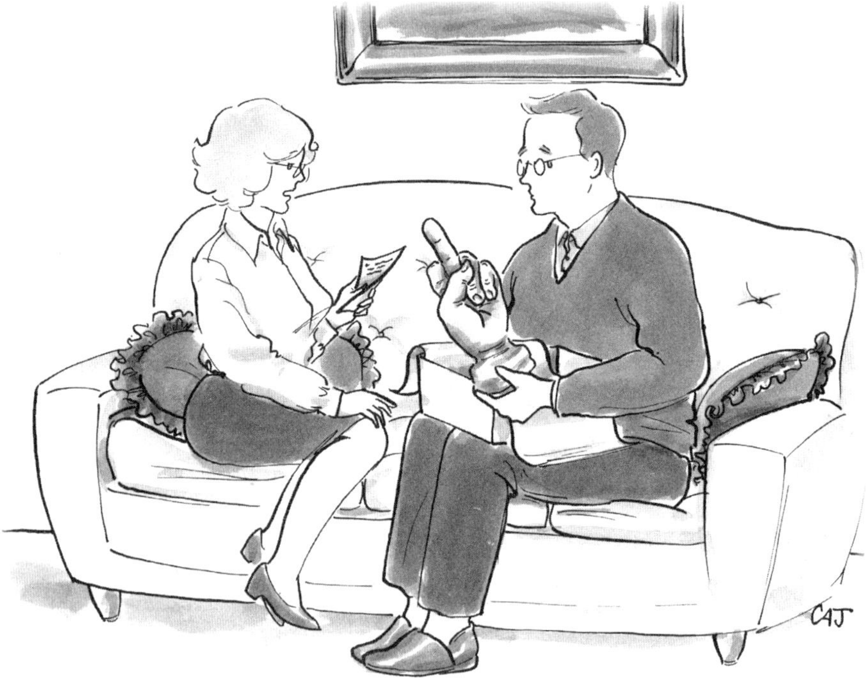
CAJ

"It's from Marcus at sculpture camp."

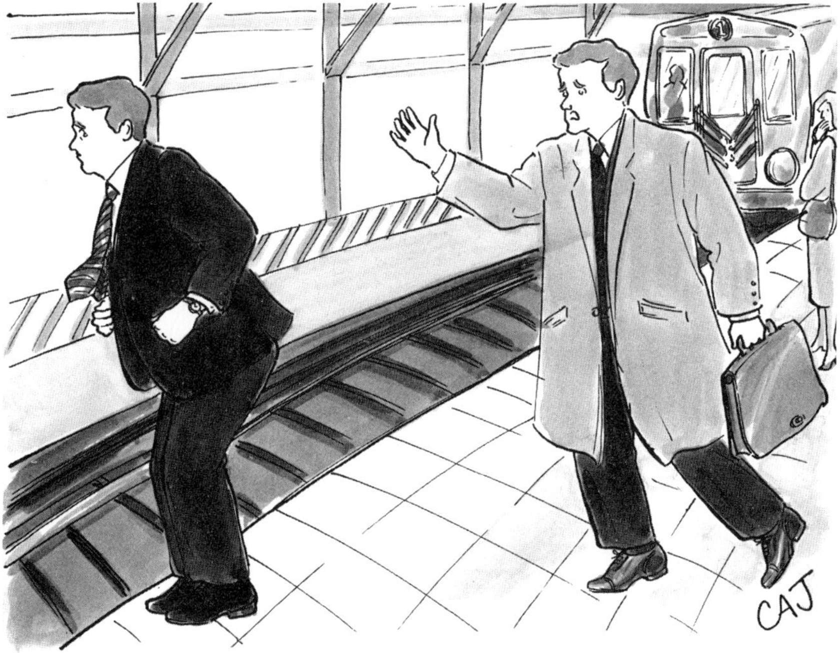
CAJ

"Wait. There's another train right behind this one."

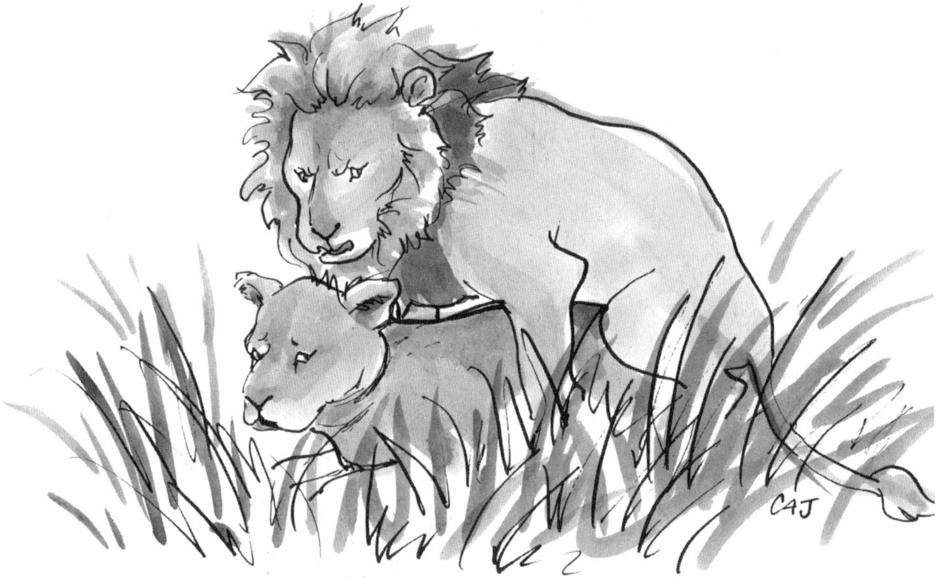
CAJ

"Those pervs from National Geographic are filming us again."

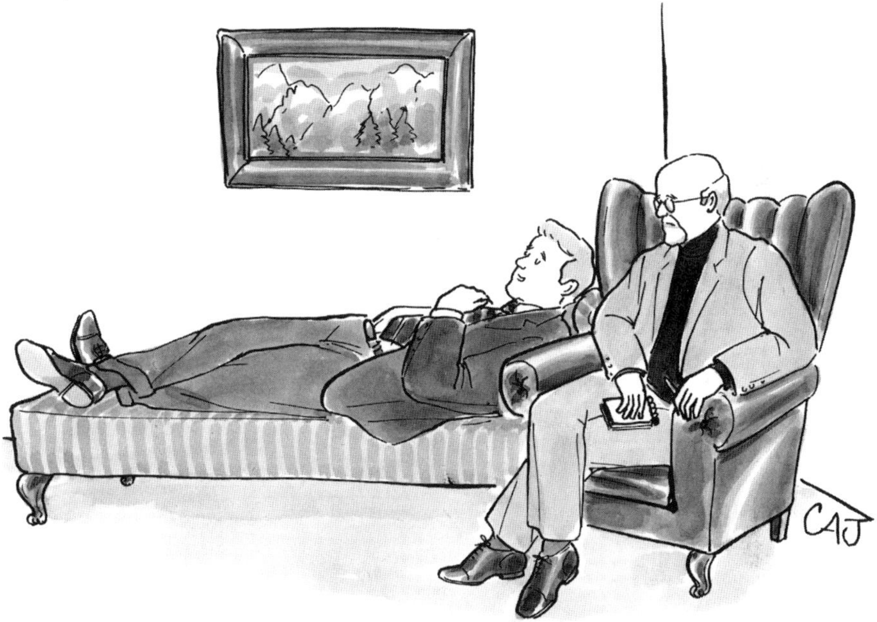
CAJ

"I was bound and beaten for what seemed like hours, and it only cost me a hundred bucks."

IF DOGS MADE PERFUME

Eau de Ass

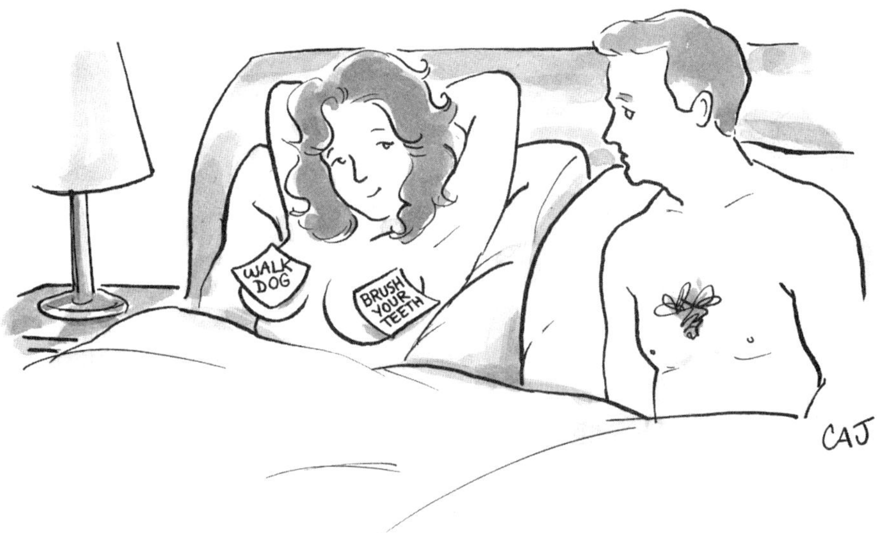
WALK DOG
BRUSH YOUR TEETH
CAJ

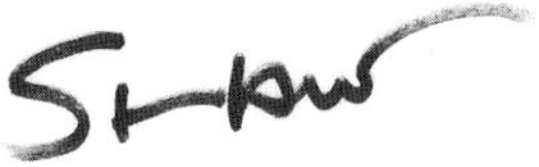
Shaw

Michael Shaw

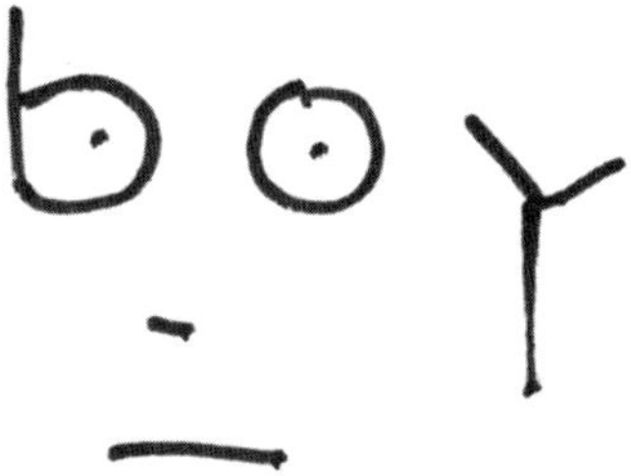
boy

Frequently Asked Questions

- *Where do you get your ideas?*
  I've never been asked that question.

- *Which comes first, the picture or the caption?*
  Actually, I have been asked that question—but not frequently.

- *How'd you get started?*

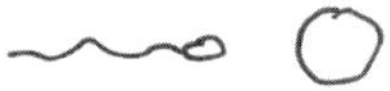

- *I admire . . .*
  Many, many people—but I would not let them suspect. I do admire my wife for putting up with me. And here's a shout-out to my fellow crusty Missourian, Mr. George Booth! James Thurber remains my favorite dead cartoonist.

- *How do you deal with rejection?*
  Think reproductively. My rejection rate would send even the most optimistic of souls into despair. But compared to the chances of the average sperm succeeding in its mission, my odds are quite good.

- *What are some things that make you laugh and why?*
  I laugh at things that aren't meant to be funny. Eternal World Television Network is hilarious.

  My motto—"Tragedy plus time equals comedy—but who has time anymore?"

  My favorite joke—"What did the sadist do to the masochist? Nothing."

- *I've got a great idea for a cartoon—wanna hear it?*
  I think you'd have to read it, instead. Two guys walk into a bar . . . the third guy ducked.

Infrequently Asked Questions

- *Have you moo[redacted]ed or been moo[redacted]ed more often in your life?*
  (Lived in Wisconsin.)

- *What would make a terrible pizza topping?*
  Foil.

- *What might one expect to find at a really low-budget amusement park?*
  God.

- *What did the shepherd say to the three-legged sheepdog?*
  Dog.

Draw Something in This Space

. . . that will help us understand your childhood.

NA NA
NA NA
NAA NAA!

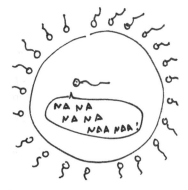

And Now for a Few More Questions . . .

Sorry, I'm using this space for a cartoon I've submited 127 times and have never sold.

V WL S
W NT D

- *What's the funniest thing that you witnessed, overheard, or came up with that you couldn't figure out how to use in a cartoon?*

"How's the fish?"

Complete the Pie Chart Below

. . . in a way that tells us something about your life or how you think.

PROCRASTINATE
PROCRASTINATE
PROCRASTINATE
PROCRASTINATE
PROCRASTINATE
PROCRASTINATE
PANIC!
PROCRASTINATE
PROCRASTINATE
PROCRASTINATE
PROCRASTINATE
PROCRASTINATE

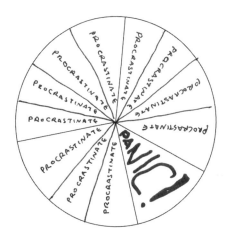

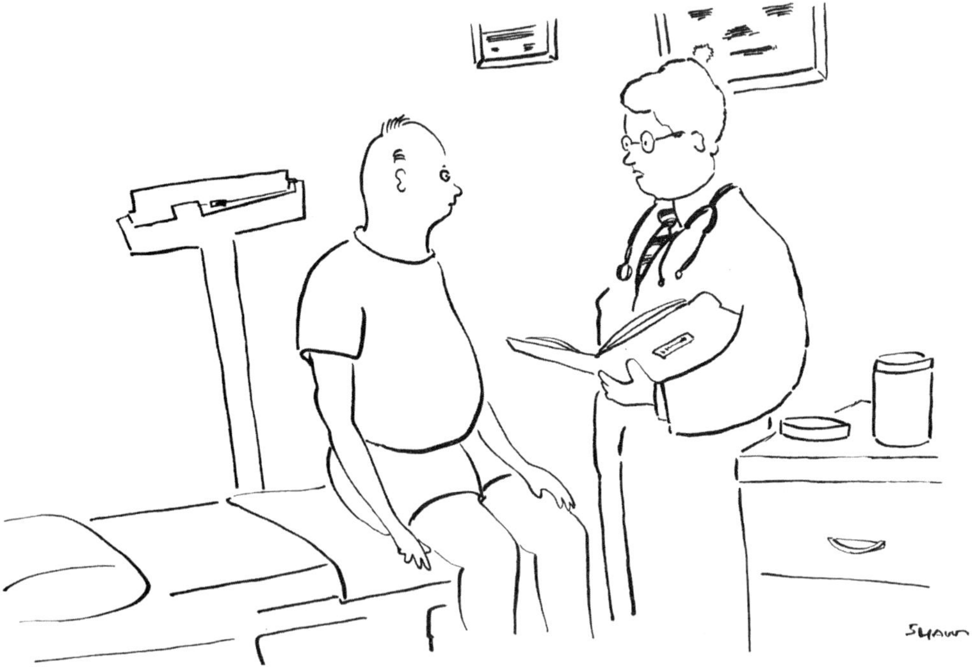
SHAW

"Now, this is going to feel like I'm sticking my finger up your ass."

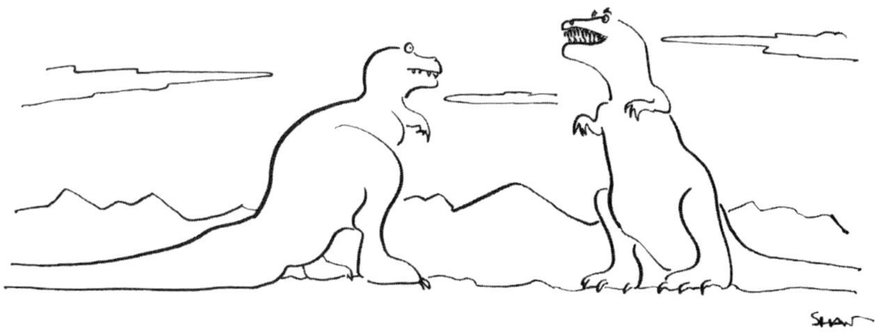
SHAW

"I'd give up being the most fearsome creature on the planet if I could just reach my weenie."

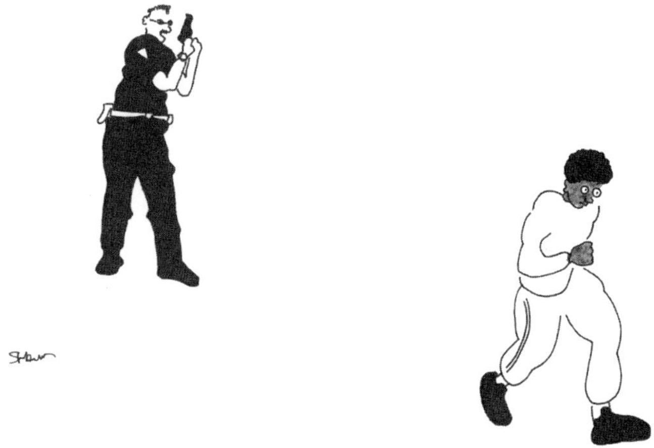
SHAW

"Stop and I'll shoot."

GIVING THE FINGER
GETTING THE FINGER
SHAW

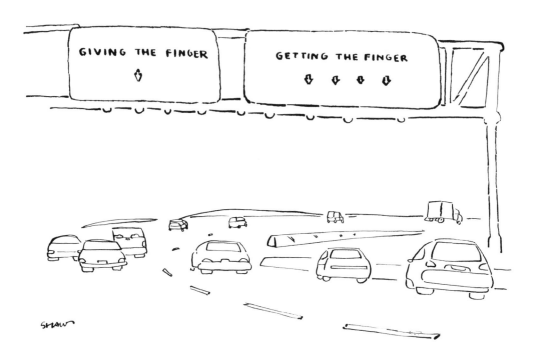

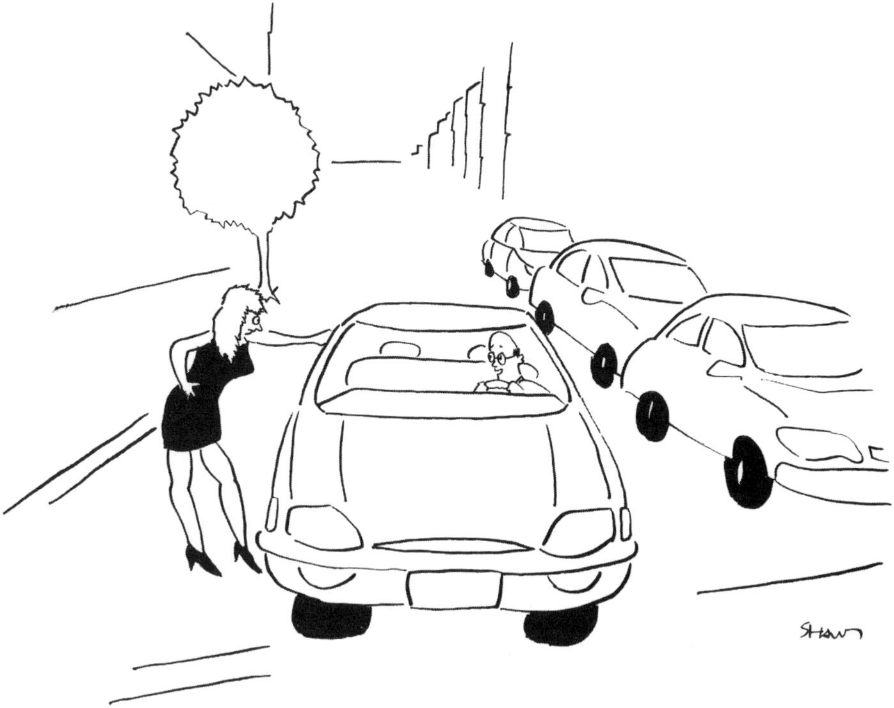
SHAW

"Throw in a prostate exam and you've got a deal!"

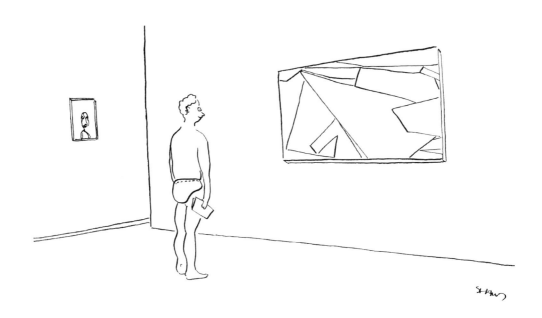

Half-price tighty-whitey day at the MoMA

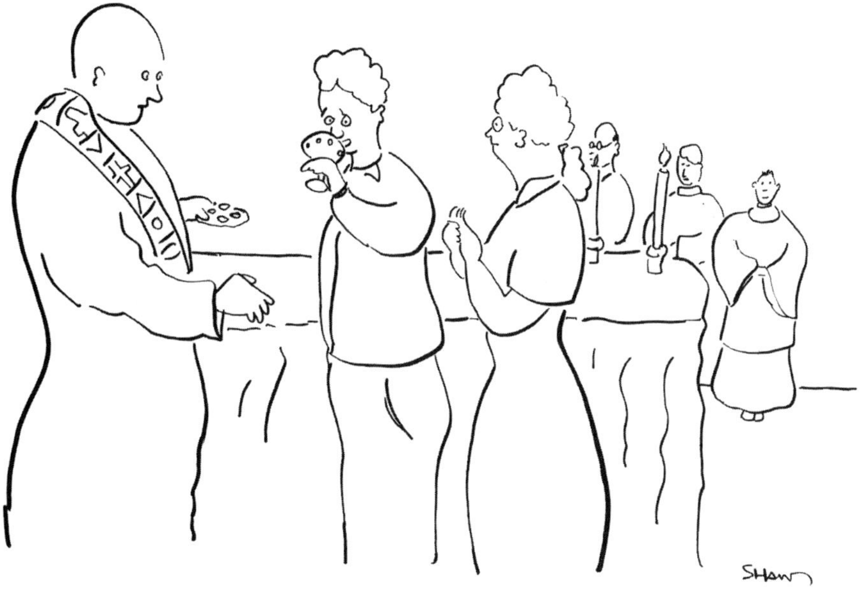
SHAW

"I'm getting earthy overtones of guilt, with just a hint of sexual frustration."

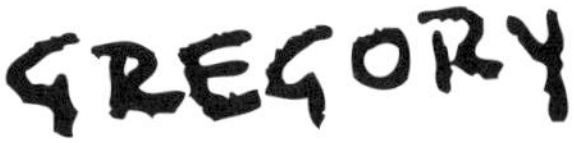
GREGORY

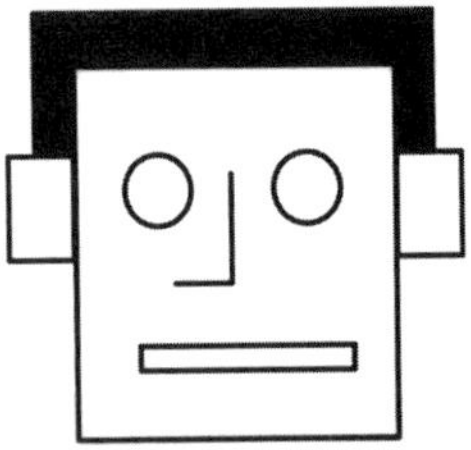

Alex Gregory

Frequently Asked Questions

- *Where do you get your ideas?*
  Target.

- *Which comes first, the picture or the caption?*
  They arrive together arm in arm.

- *How'd you get started?*
  Dad met Mom at some dance hall in New York.

- *I admire . . .*
  Nice buttocks, but I try not to be obvious about it. Sunglasses help.

- *How do you deal with rejection?*
  I remind myself that even though she's really attractive, if my new liver doesn't want to be a part of my life, I'm better off without her.

- *What are some things that make you laugh and why?*
  I am always amused by nunchucks. I can't recall ever hearing of a single incident where anyone has successfully used nunchucks to either defend himself or to attack someone else, yet they are illegal in three states. They can't be easily concealed, and they pose as much of a danger to the wielder as to the target. Presumably, if nunchucks were in any way effective, all soldiers and cops would carry them. And yet factories manufacture nunchucks every day. And every day some teenage boy covers his back and forearms in bruises in his futile quest to master the noble art of nunchuckery.

- *I've got a great idea for a cartoon—wanna hear it?*
  Just draw it and sign my name. I trust you.

Infrequently Asked Questions

- *Have you mooned or been mooned more often in your life?*
  There's been so much mooning in my life, it's impossible to calculate.

- *What would make a terrible pizza topping?*
  Gelatin beads filled with children's tears.

- *What might one expect to find at a really low-budget amusement park?*
  I wouldn't know. The amusement parks I attend are super classy.

■ *What did the shepherd say to the three-legged sheepdog?*
Come on, we're both lonely and sick of sheep.

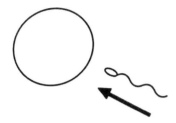

Draw Something in This Space

. . . that will help us understand your childhood.

And Now for a Few More Questions . . .

■ *What do you hate drawing?*
Cars, furniture, shoes, and windows—God, I hate drawing windows—no idea why.

■ *Being as accurate as possible, how many desert island cartoons do you think you've come up with and submitted to* The New Yorker?
No idea. Ten?

■ *What's the funniest thing that you witnessed, overheard, or came up with that you couldn't figure out how to use in a cartoon?*
The overabundance of fennel in restaurants.

Naming Names

■ *What name might you give to a mild-mannered, middle-aged, bespectacled dental assistant in one of your cartoons?*
Matt Diffee.

■ *Other than Lance, what name would you give to a twenty-eight-year-old entertainment lawyer with a blue-dyed fauxhawk who cycles on weekends?*
Matt Diffee.

■ *Come up with a name for an unpleasant medical procedure.*
I defy you to name a pleasant medical procedure.

■ *If you used a pen name, what would it be?*
For all of my criminal activity, I use the alias "Matt Diffee."

Complete the Pie Chart Below

. . . in a way that tells us something about your life or how you think.

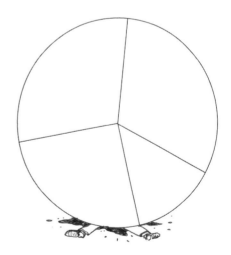

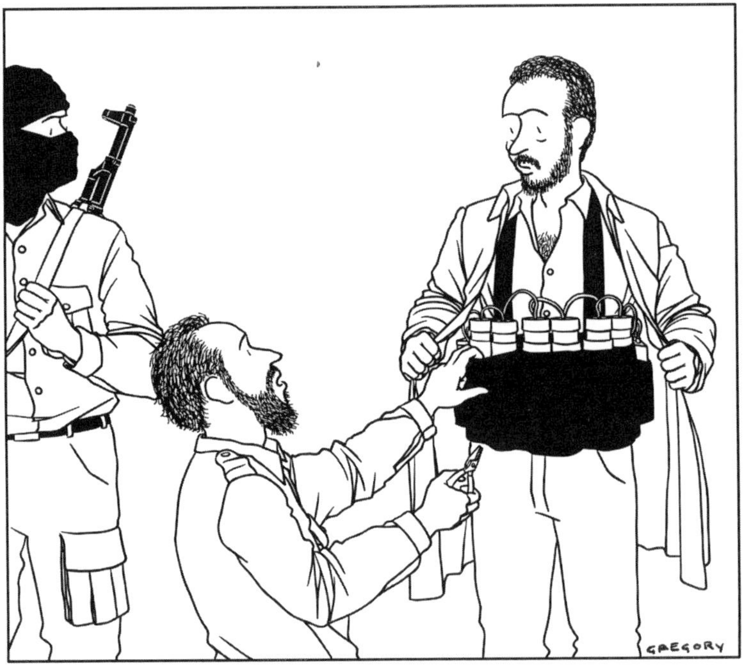
GREGORY

"Too snug?"

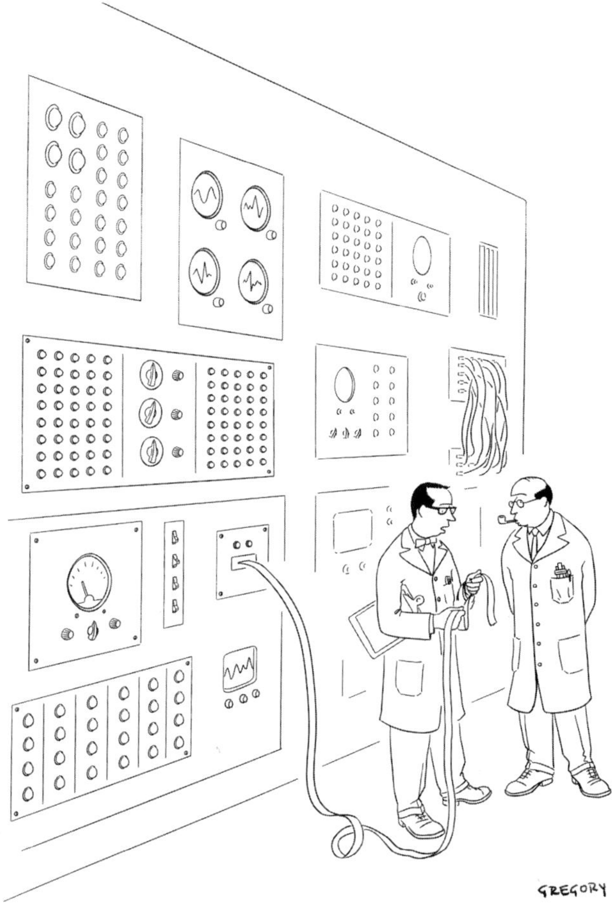
GREGORY

"The results are impressive, but it'll be decades before we can transmit and receive pornography."

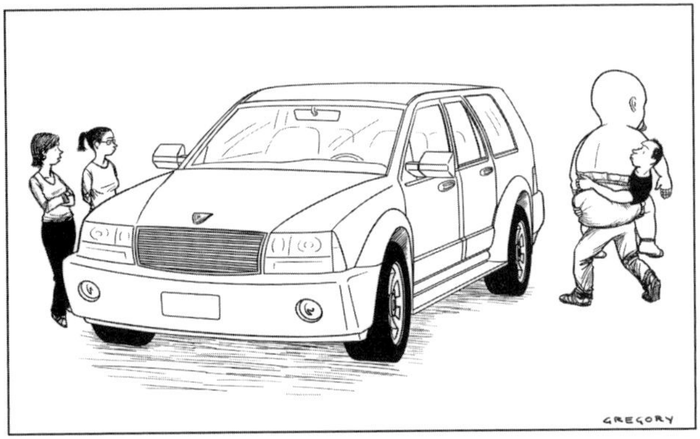
GREGORY

"We were dead set against getting an SUV until we had the baby."

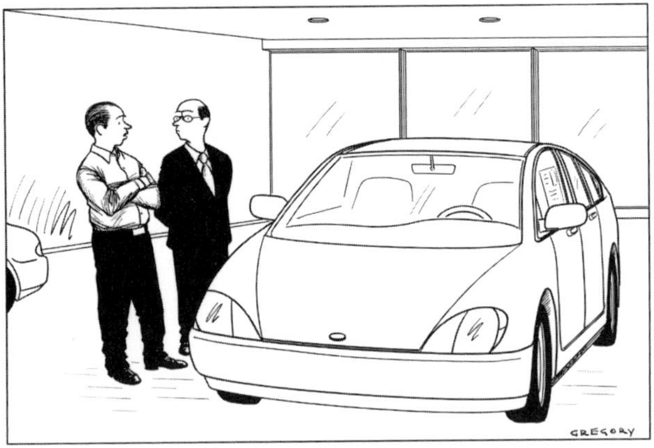
GREGORY

"Will the high mileage and low emissions make my penis seem bigger?"

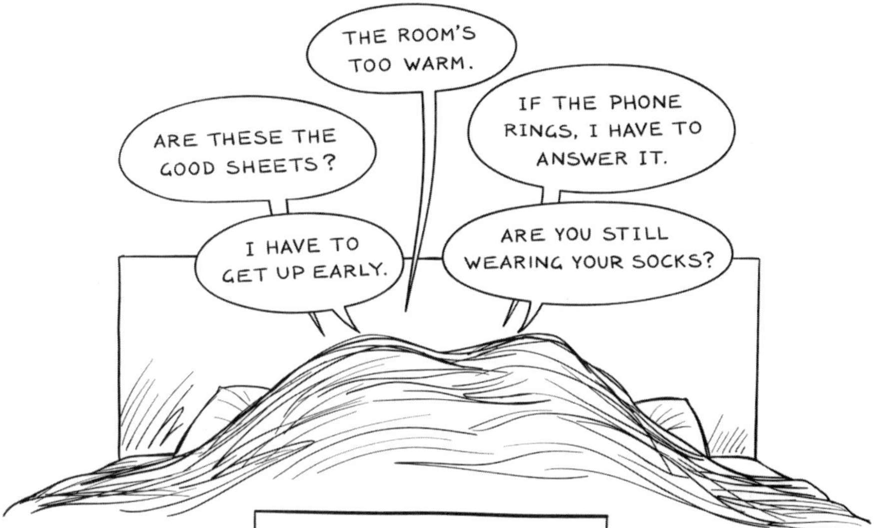
THE ROOM'S TOO WARM.
ARE THESE THE GOOD SHEETS?
IF THE PHONE RINGS, I HAVE TO ANSWER IT.
I HAVE TO GET UP EARLY.
ARE YOU STILL WEARING YOUR SOCKS?
GREGORY

ANAL SEX

OH, GOD–
PLEASE TELL
ME THIS ISN'T
TOFU CHEESE....
GREGORY

CARGO BRIEFS

GREGORY

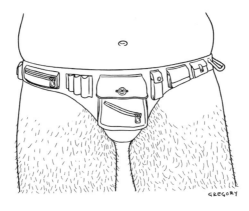

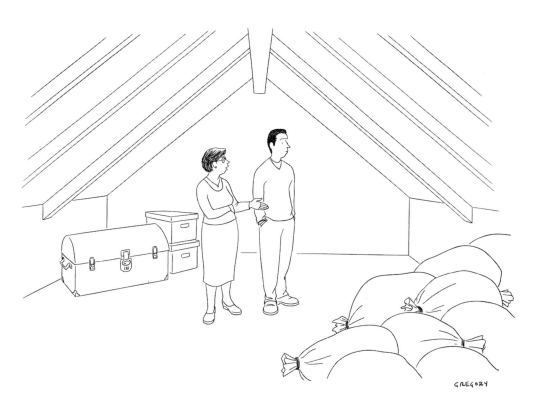

"We saved all your old diapers."

BURNS

Teresa Burns Parkhurst

Frequently Asked Questions

- *Where do you get your ideas?*
  From my Concept-O-Matic 1500.

- *Which comes first, the picture or the caption?*
  The egg.

- *How'd you get started?*
  My parents got wasted.

- *I admire . . .*
  People who adhere to the surgeon general's guidelines for wine consumption.

- *How do you deal with rejection?*
  Like a baby.

- *What are some things that make you laugh and why?*
  Marty Feldman's eyes, because they're funny. Duh.

- *I've got a great idea for a cartoon—wanna hear it?*
  Sure, because I'm too unassertive to say no.

Infrequently Asked Questions

- *Have you mooned or been mooned more often in your life?*
  Been mooned.

- *What would make a terrible pizza topping?*
  Sandals. Unless they were Jesus's.

- *What might one expect to find at a really low-budget amusement park?*
  Even skankier pedophiles.

- *What did the shepherd say to the three-legged sheepdog?*
  "I've got a great idea for a cartoon, want to hear it?"

Draw Something in This Space

. . . that will help us understand your childhood.

Draw Some Sort of Doodle

. . . using the random lines below as a starting point.

SHIT.

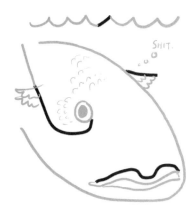

And Now for a Few More Questions . . .

- *What do you hate drawing?*

THE LETTER "G" (see?) AND CARS

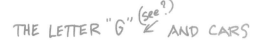

- *Being as accurate as possible, how many desert island cartoons do you think you've come up with and submitted to* The New Yorker*?*
  Three.

- *What's the funniest thing that you witnessed, overheard, or came up with that you couldn't figure out how to use in a cartoon?*
  Overweight beggars.

Naming Names

- *What name might you give to a mild-mannered, middle-aged, bespectacled dental assistant in one of your cartoons?*
  Dawn Koslowski.

- *Other than Lance, what name would you give to a twenty-eight-year-old entertainment lawyer with a blue-dyed fauxhawk who cycles on weekends?*
  Dale Philip Newton.

- *What would be a good name for a new, commercially unviable breakfast cereal?*
  Tuna-Os.

- *Come up with a name for an unpleasant medical procedure.*
  Rectumapalooza.

- *If you used a pen name, what would it be?*
  Bic.

Complete the Pie Chart Below

. . . in a way that tells us something about your life or how you think.

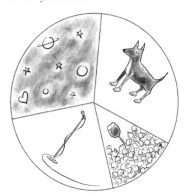

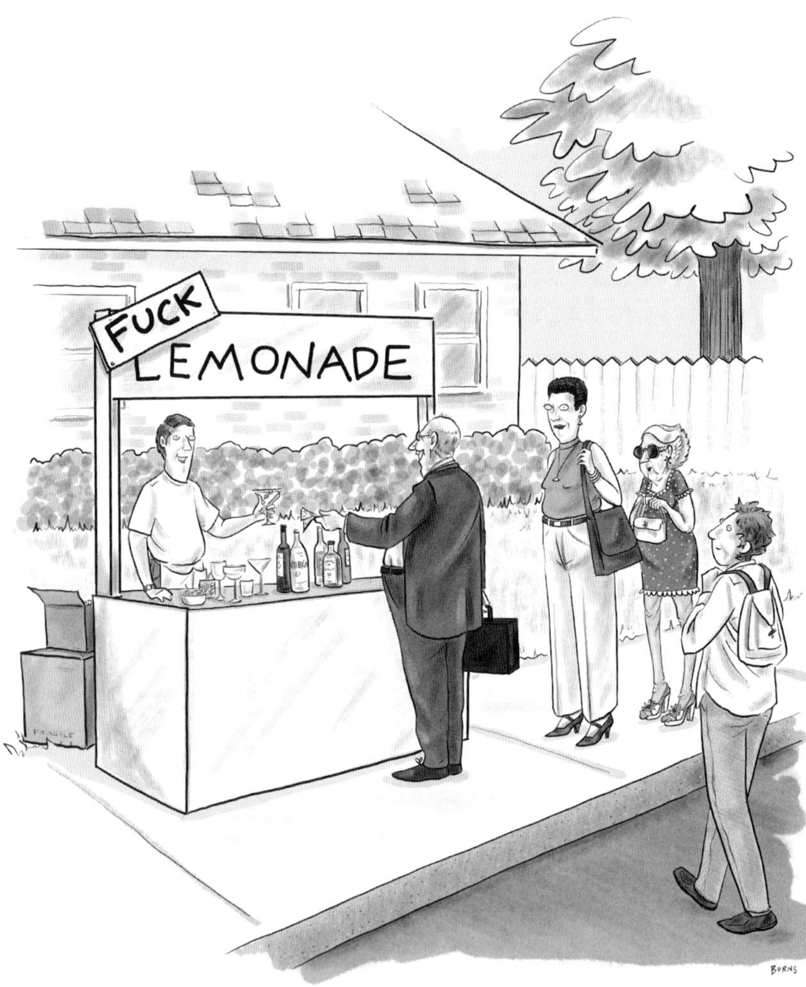
FUCK
LEMONADE
BURNS

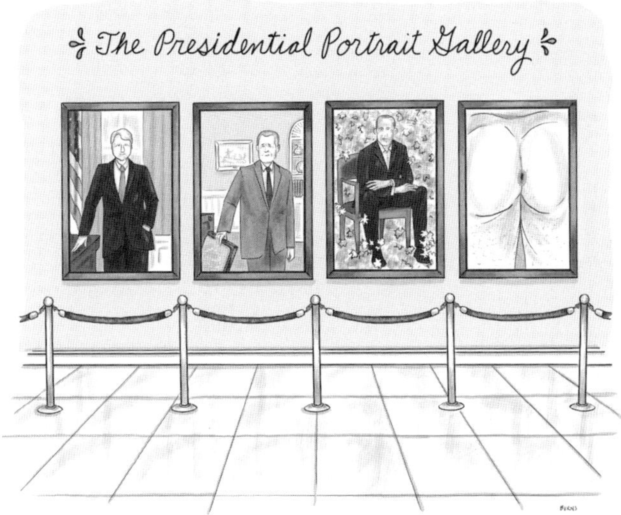
The Presidential Portrait Gallery
BURNS

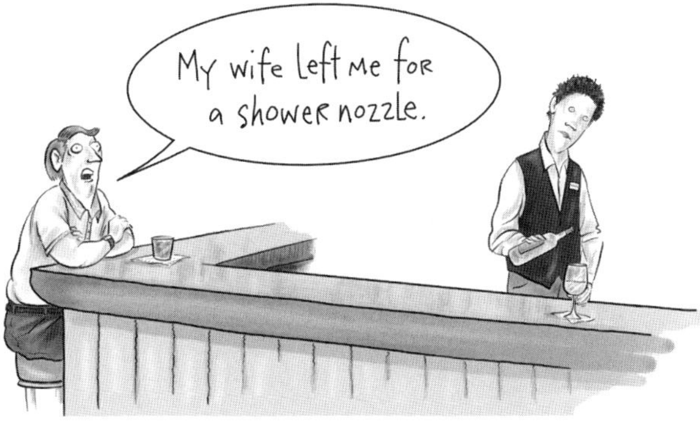
My wife left me for a shower nozzle.

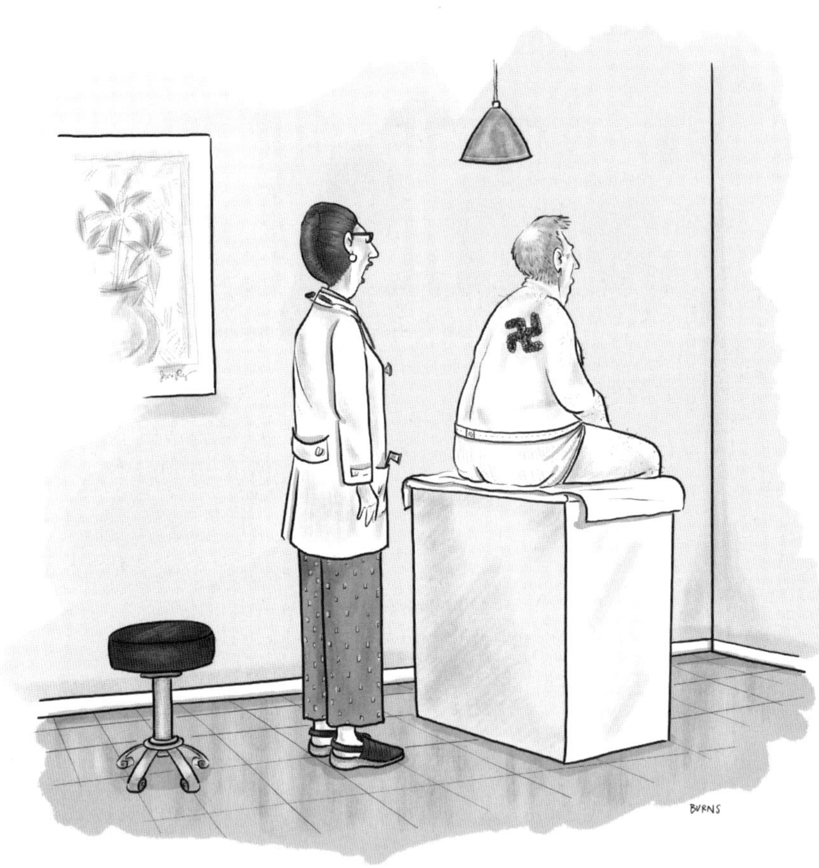
BURNS

"I don't like the look of that mole."

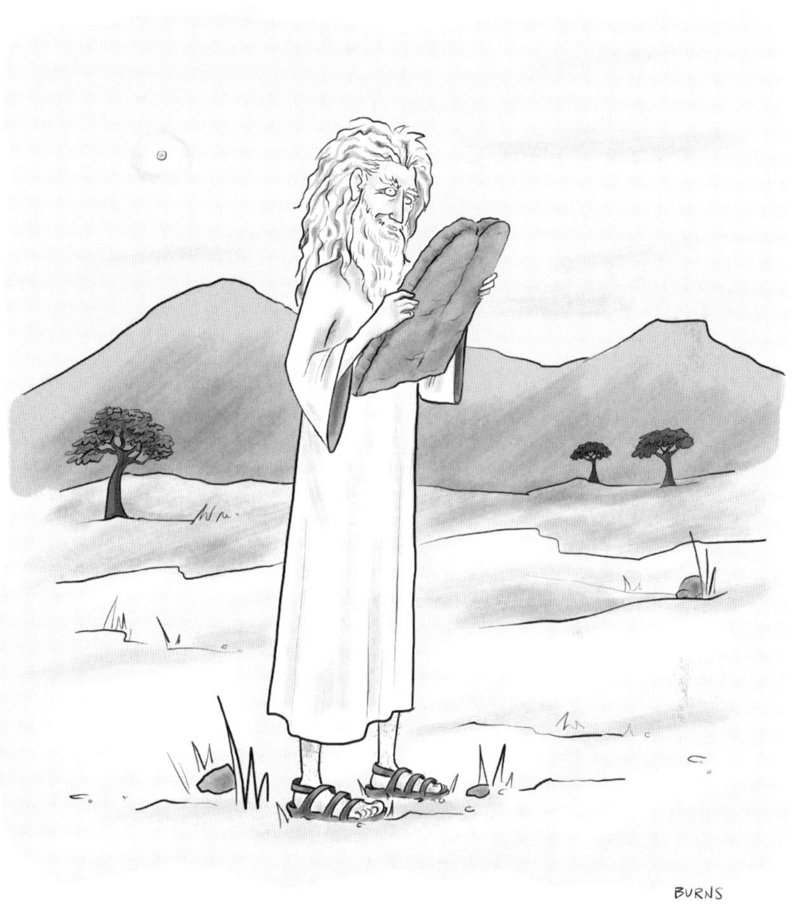
BURNS

*"Hmm, eleven commandments just doesn't sound right,
I'm taking out the one about white guys dancing."*

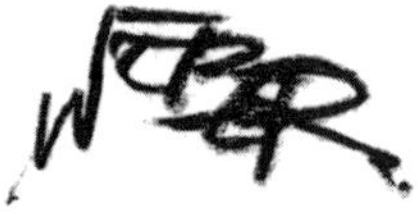
WEBER

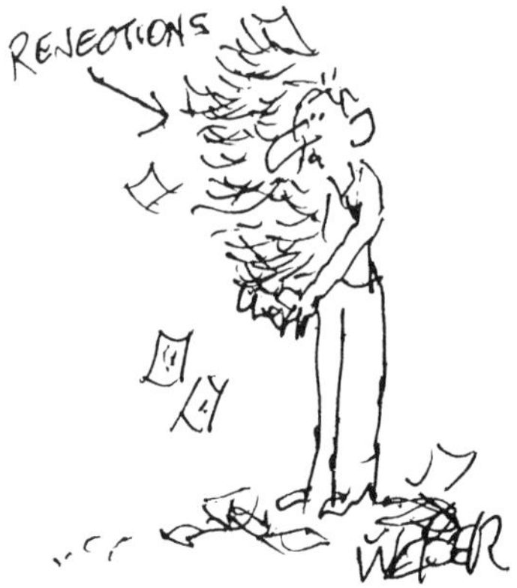
REJECTIONS
WEBER

Robert Weber

Frequently Asked Questions

- *Where do you get your ideas?*
  You think I'd tell you?
- *Which comes first, the picture or the caption?*
  Both.
- *How'd you get started?*
  Doing spots for magazines.
- *I admire . . .*
  All accountants.
- *How do you deal with rejection?*
  Sink into a deep depression.
- *What are some things that make you laugh and why?*
  Can't think of anything, actually.
- *I've got a great idea for a cartoon—wanna hear it?*
  You think I'd tell you?

Infrequently Asked Questions

- *Have you mooned or been mooned more often in your life?*
  Let's not go there.
- *What would make a terrible pizza topping?*
  That's for you to answer.
- *What might one expect to find at a really low-budget amusement park?*
  A lot of dashed expectations.
- *What did the shepherd say to the three-legged sheepdog?*
  Please pass the brandy.

And Now for a Few More Questions . . .

- *What do you hate drawing?*
  Money from savings account.

- *Being as accurate as possible, how many desert island cartoons do you think you've come up with and submitted to* The New Yorker*?*
  64,000.

- *What's the funniest thing that you witnessed, overheard, or came up with that you couldn't figure out how to use in a cartoon?*
  Recovering from bilateral knee surgery.

Draw Some Sort of Doodle

. . . using the random lines below as a starting point.

YOU SAID IT!

Naming Names

- *What name might you give to a mild-mannered, middle-aged, bespectacled dental assistant in one of your cartoons?*
  Zandra-Lois.

- *Other than Lance, what name would you give to a twenty-eight-year-old entertainment lawyer with a blue-dyed fauxhawk who cycles on weekends?*
  Horace Boris.

- *What would be a good name for a new, commercially unviable breakfast cereal?*
  Organ-Iky.

- *Come up with a name for an unpleasant medical procedure.*
  Opsy.

- *If you used a pen name, what would it be?*
  Waterman.

Complete the Pie Chart Below

. . . in a way that tells us something about your life or how you think.

APPLE
LEMON MERENGUE
STRAW-BERRY RUBARB
PIZZA

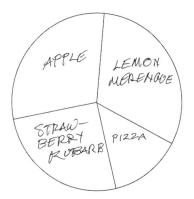

"How many times have I told you to keep your elbows off the table?"

"*Wanna see me fake an orgasm?*"

"*Do you mind if I use your thong as a bookmark?*"

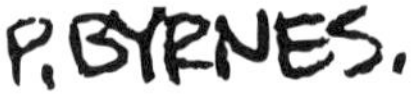
P. BYRNES.

Pat Byrnes

Frequently Asked Questions

- *Where do you get your ideas?*
  Is that what you mean by frequently asked questions?

- *Which comes first, the picture or the caption?*
  Yes.

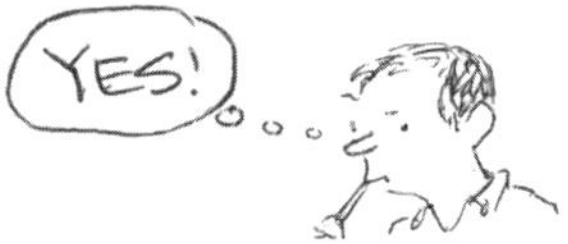
YES!

- *How'd you get started?*
  The same as everyone else. All kids start out drawing cartoons. Some of us simply don't stop.

- *I admire . . .*
  My cutie's mommy.

- *How do you deal with rejection?*
  I've been an ad writer, a comedian, an actor, and I couldn't find a woman to marry me until I was forty-three. I deal with rejection like you deal with an old friend.

- *What are some things that make you laugh and why?*
  Corporate jargon because it doesn't fool me. The Three Stooges' "O Elaine" sketch because it is a magical blend of the high and the low. The way my daughter instantly imitates people's embarrassing noises because she is only sixteen months old and can get away with it—and she knows it!

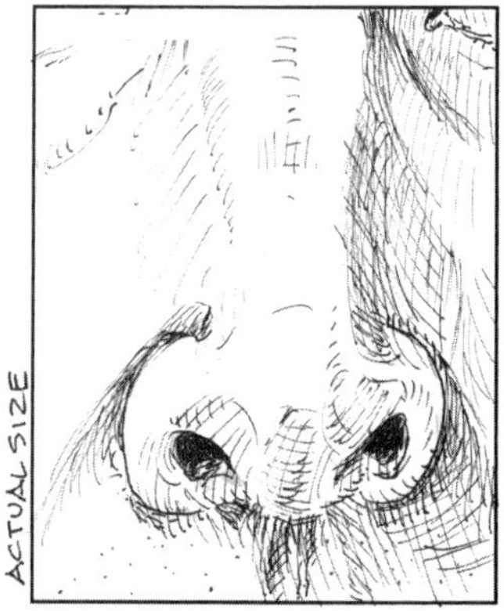
ACTUAL SIZE

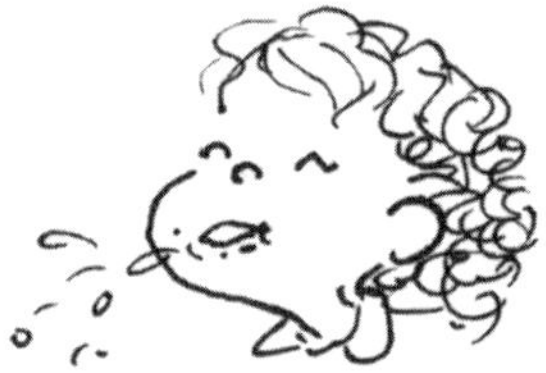

- *I've got a great idea for a cartoon—wanna hear it?*
  No, I want to see it.

Infrequently Asked Questions

- *Have you mooned or been mooned more often in your life?*
  I've successfully repressed those memories, thank you very much.

- *What would make a terrible pizza topping?*
  Snickers bars, based on how awful they taste deep-fried on a stick.

- *What might one expect to find at a really low-budget amusement park?*
  The Tunnel of Cousins.

- *What did the shepherd say to the three-legged sheepdog?*
  Shake.

And Now for a Few More Questions . . .

- *What do you hate drawing?*
  A blank.

- *Being as accurate as possible, how many desert island cartoons do you think you've come up with and submitted to* The New Yorker*?*
  Azores < x < Indonesia.

- *What's the funniest thing that you witnessed, overheard, or came up with that you couldn't figure out how to use in a cartoon?*

+
+
+
BUT YOU REALLY HAD TO BE THERE.

Naming Names

- *What name might you give to a mild-mannered, middle-aged, bespectacled dental assistant in one of your cartoons?*
  Llewelyn.

- *Other than Lance, what name would you give to a twenty-eight-year-old entertainment lawyer with a blue-dyed fauxhawk who cycles on weekends?*
  Chaz.

- *What would be a good name for a new, commercially unviable breakfast cereal?*
  Tac-Os: "It's a fiesta in your mouth!"

- *Come up with a name for an unpleasant medical procedure.*
  Bone Flushing.

- *If you used a pen name, what would it be?*
  Uni-ball Jetstream.

Complete the Pie Chart Below

. . . in a way that tells us something about your life or how you think.

KEY LIME
APPLE
LEMON MERINGUE
DUTCH APPLE

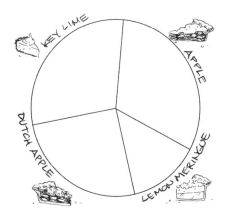

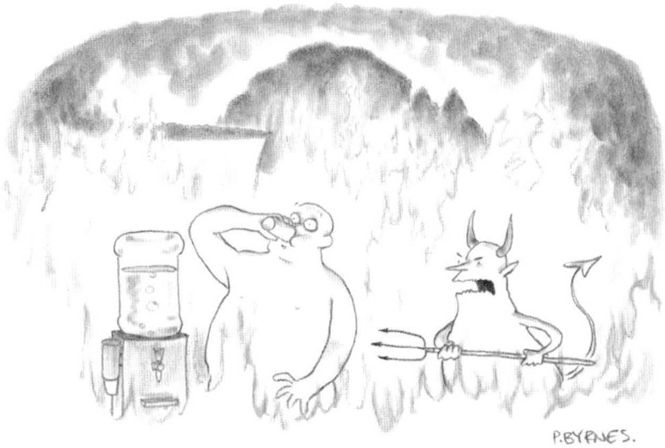
P.BYRNES.

"Hey, get away from the urinal."

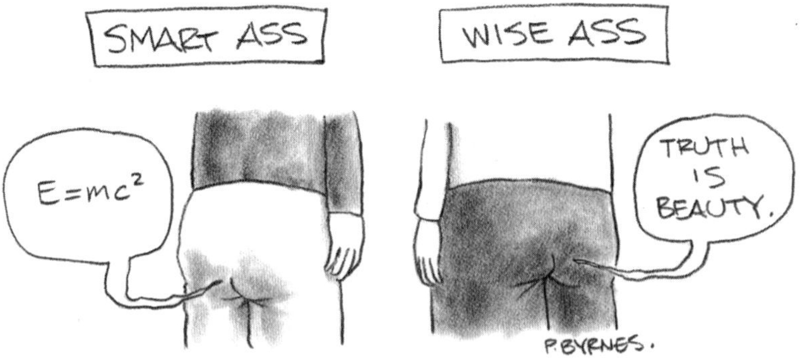
SMART ASS
WISE ASS
E=mc²
TRUTH IS BEAUTY.
P.BYRNES.

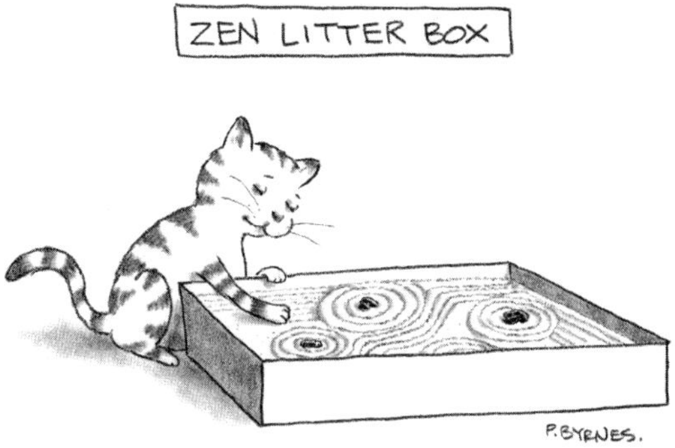
ZEN LITTER BOX
P.BYRNES.

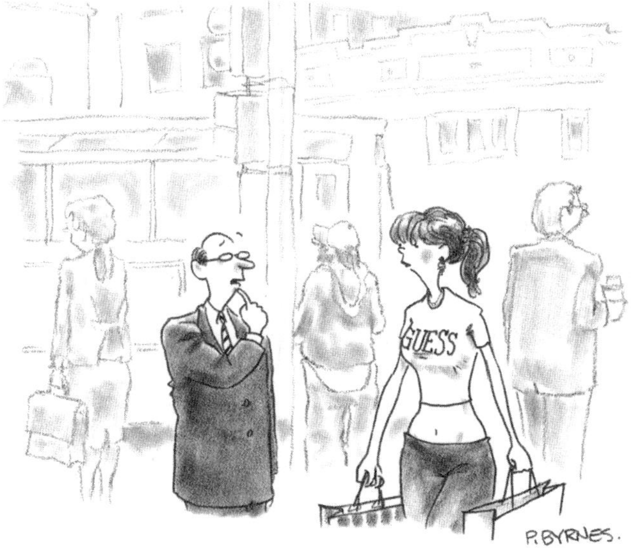
GUESS
P.BYRNES.

"34-C?"

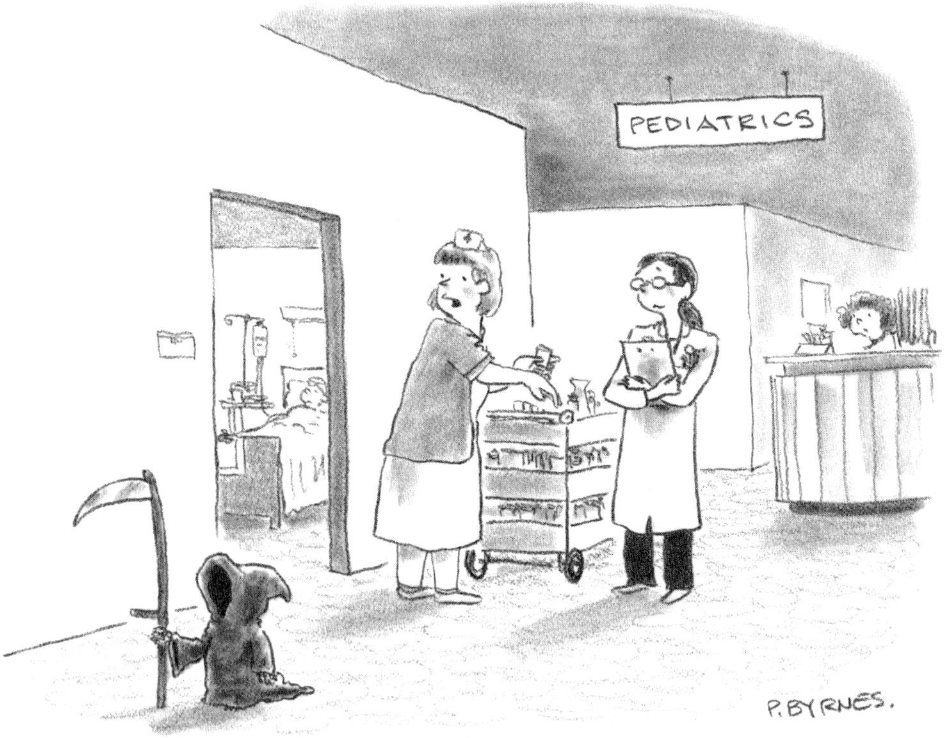
PEDIATRICS
P. BYRNES.

"It would be sad if he wasn't so damned cute."

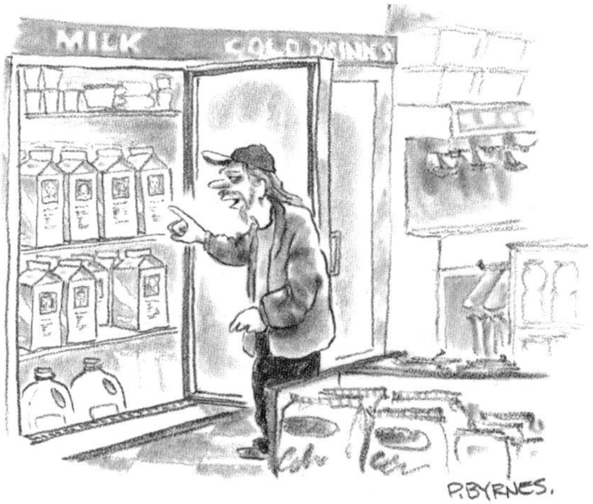
MILK
COLD DRINKS
P. BYRNES.

"Got 'im, got 'im, need 'im, need 'im . . ."

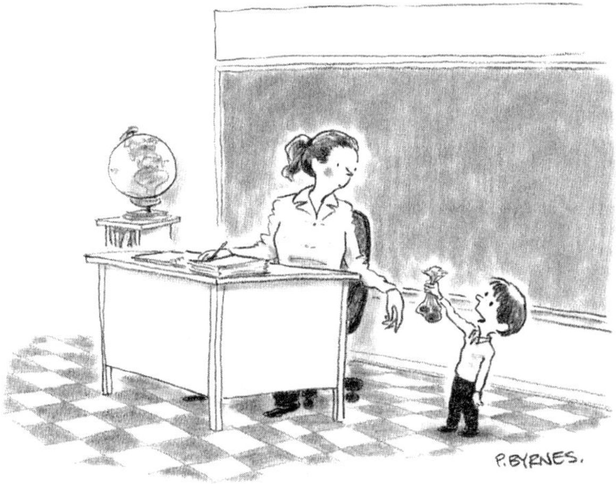
P. BYRNES.

"Remember how I said my dog ate it and you said that was no excuse?"

B. Smaller

Barbara Smaller

Frequently Asked Questions

■ *Where do you get your ideas?*
I'm guessing, China.

■ *Which comes first, the picture or the caption?*
The chicken.

■ *How'd you get started?*
I was at a bookstore and I came across a book called, *How to Draw Cartoons.* I didn't actually buy the book, but I did give it a thorough looking over.

■ *I admire . . .*
Bob Mankoff, of course . . . oh, and Gandhi.

■ *How do you deal with rejection?*
Hey, it just means more cartoons for me.

■ *What are some things that make you laugh and why?*
Sex and death, sometimes I think sex is the funniest, and sometimes I think it's the other way around.

■ *I've got a great idea for a cartoon—wanna hear it?*
One great idea is of no use, I need at least ten great ideas.

Infrequently Asked Questions

■ *Have you mooned or been mooned more often in your life?*
I am not now, and have never been, a member of the Rev. Sun Myung Moon's church.

■ *What would make a terrible pizza topping?*
14.5-gauge baling wire.

■ *What might one expect to find at a really low-budget amusement park?*
Sit & Spin.

Draw Something in This Space

. . . that will help us understand your childhood.

And Now for a Few More Questions . . .

- *What do you hate drawing?*
  Since I am not now, and never was, a twelve-year-old boy: cars.

- *Being as accurate as possible, how many desert island cartoons do you think you've come up with and submitted to* The New Yorker*?*
  4.7.

- *What's the funniest thing that you witnessed, overheard, or came up with that you couldn't figure out how to use in a cartoon?*
  Things that involve cars.

Naming Names

- *What name might you give to a mild-mannered, middle-aged, bespectacled dental assistant in one of your cartoons?*
  Matt.

- *Other than Lance, what name would you give to a twenty-eight-year-old entertainment lawyer with a blue-dyed fauxhawk who cycles on weekends?*
  Bob.

- *What would be a good name for a new, commercially unviable breakfast cereal?*
  Sexual Intercourse Flakes.

- *Come up with a name for an unpleasant medical procedure.*
  What would be the name of a *pleasant* medical procedure?

- *If you used a pen name, what would it be?*
  B. Larger.

Complete the Pie Chart Below

. . . in a way that tells us something about your life or how you think.

product placement
sleeping
napping
Rhubarb

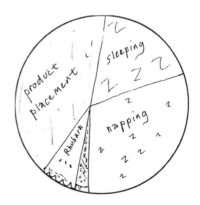

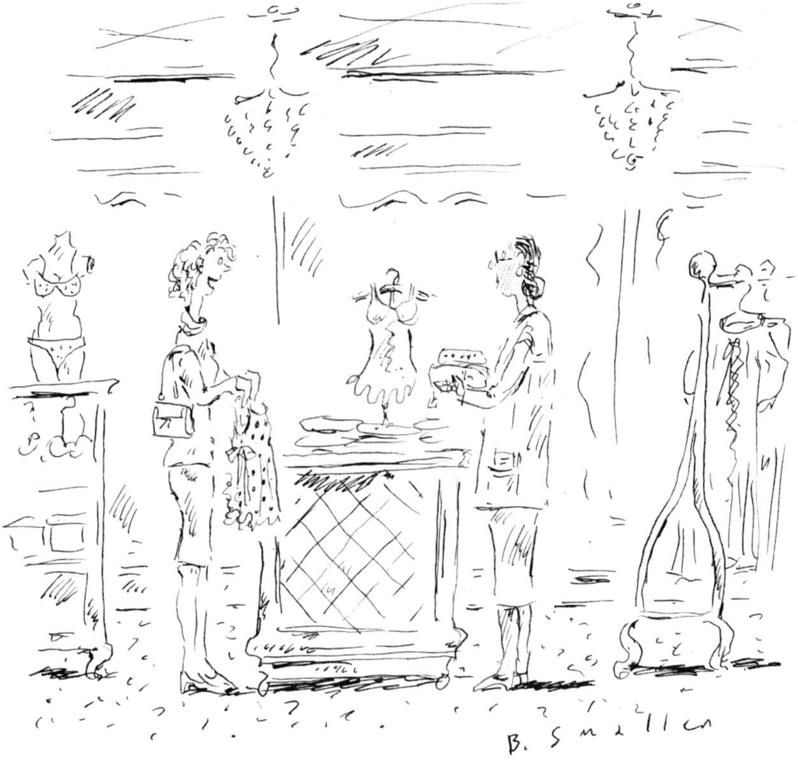
B. Smaller

"Does it say 'I'm ovulating'?"

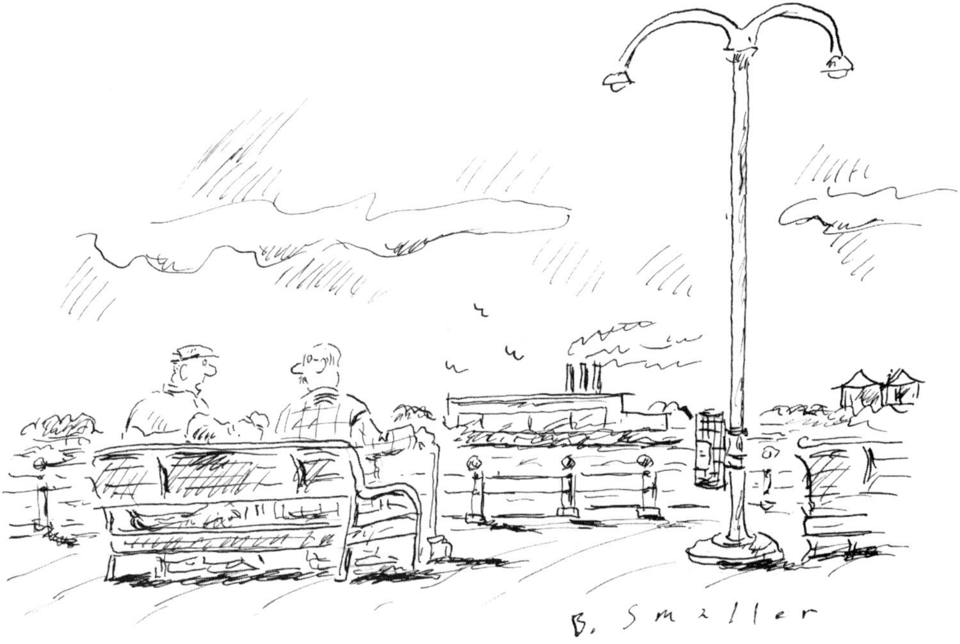
B. Smaller

"I can afford to die or I can afford to be sick, but I can't afford to be sick and then die."

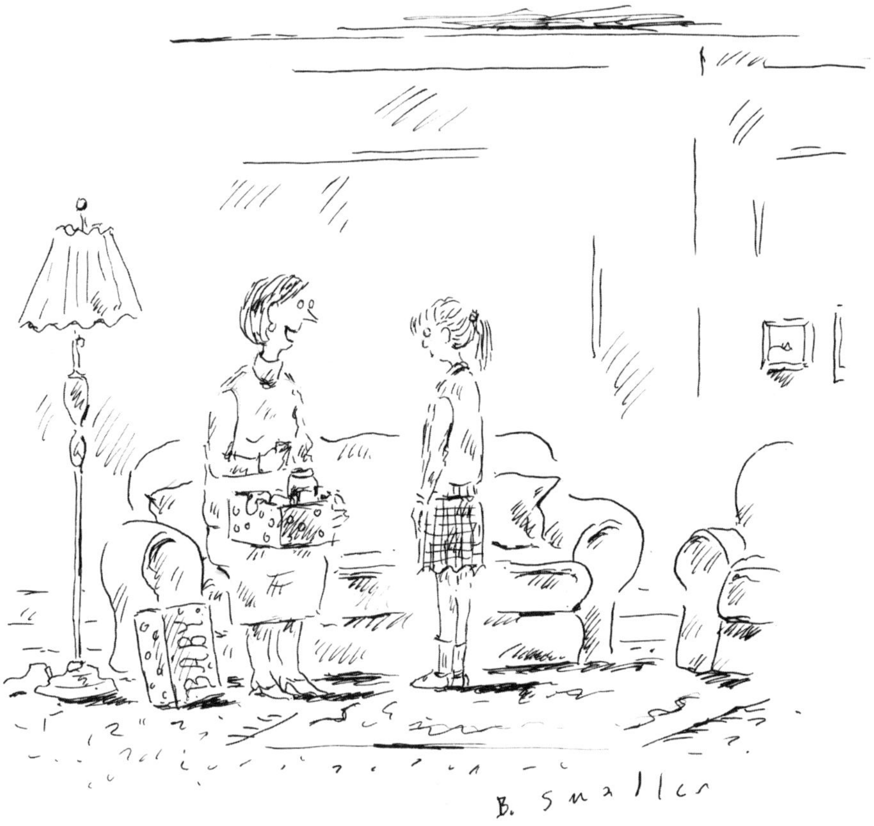
BABY

"Here's a lock of your hair, your first tooth, and your placenta."

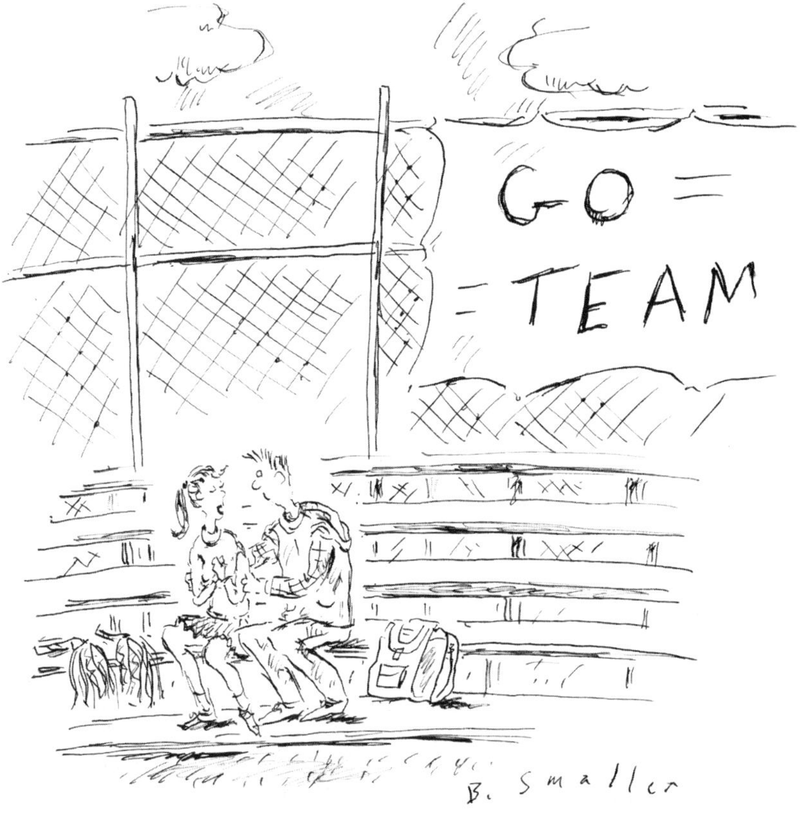
GO
TEAM
B. Smaller

"No, Justin. I'm saving myself for college."

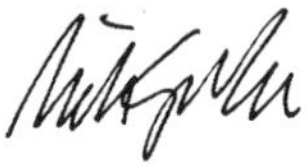

Rich Sparks

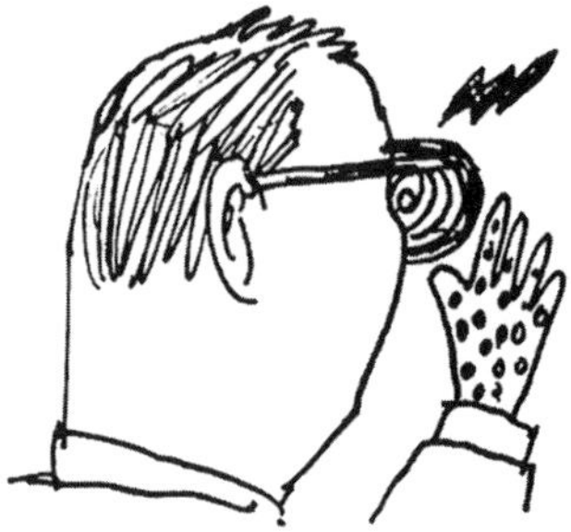

Frequently Asked Questions

- *Where do you get your ideas?*
  In the shower or watching TV. Sometimes simultaneously.

- *Which comes first, the picture or the caption?*
  The picture, then the caption, then I change the picture, then I change the caption.

- *How'd you get started?*
  Drawing for trade journals. I think most people are familiar with my work in *HVAC Monthly*.

- *I admire . . .*
  people who fish.

- *How do you deal with rejection?*
  Fishing. I mean, if I knew how.

- *What are some things that make you laugh and why?*
  I'm still waiting for it, but someone slipping on a banana peel would slay me. Because that would mean the actual Singularity is here, when cartoons and reality merge.

- *I've got a great idea for a cartoon—wanna hear it?*
  A mule couple walk into a fertility clinic . . .

Infrequently Asked Questions

- *Have you mooned or been mooned more often in your life?*
  Tried doing it once, but my flat ass doesn't describe a moon shape, so all it did was sow confusion and panic. So my answer is I don't know.

- *What would make a terrible pizza topping?*
  Vegetables.

- *What might one expect to find at a really low-budget amusement park?*
  Tilt-A-Squirrel.

- *What did the shepherd say to the three-legged sheepdog?*
  "I don't pay you to stand around all day."

Draw Something in This Space

. . . that will help us understand your childhood.

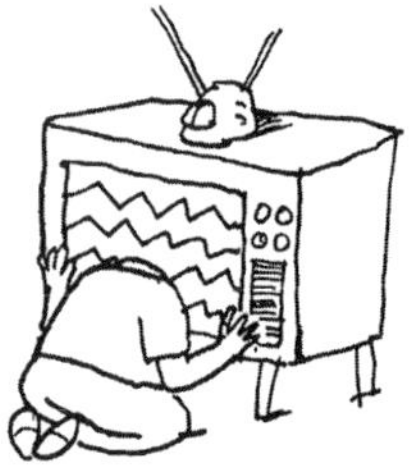

And Now for a Few More Questions . . .

- *What do you hate drawing?*
  Straight lines.

- *Being as accurate as possible, how many desert island cartoons do you think you've come up with and submitted to* The New Yorker?
  There's no name for that number.

- *What's the funniest thing that you witnessed, overheard, or came up with that you couldn't figure out how to use in a cartoon?*
  My parents divorcing.

Draw Some Sort of Doodle

. . . using the random lines below as a starting point.

Naming Names

- *What name might you give to a mild-mannered, middle-aged, bespectacled dental assistant in one of your cartoons?*
  Gary. Wait. Larry? No, Gary.

- *Other than Lance, what name would you give to a twenty-eight-year-old entertainment lawyer with a blue-dyed fauxhawk who cycles on weekends?*
  Larry?

- *What would be a good name for a new, commercially unviable breakfast cereal?*
  Poli-O's.

- *Come up with a name for an unpleasant medical procedure.*
  Urethral Rescissoring.

- *If you used a pen name, what would it be?*
  Dick Sparks.

Complete the Pie Chart Below

. . . in a way that tells us something about your life or how you think.

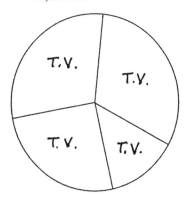

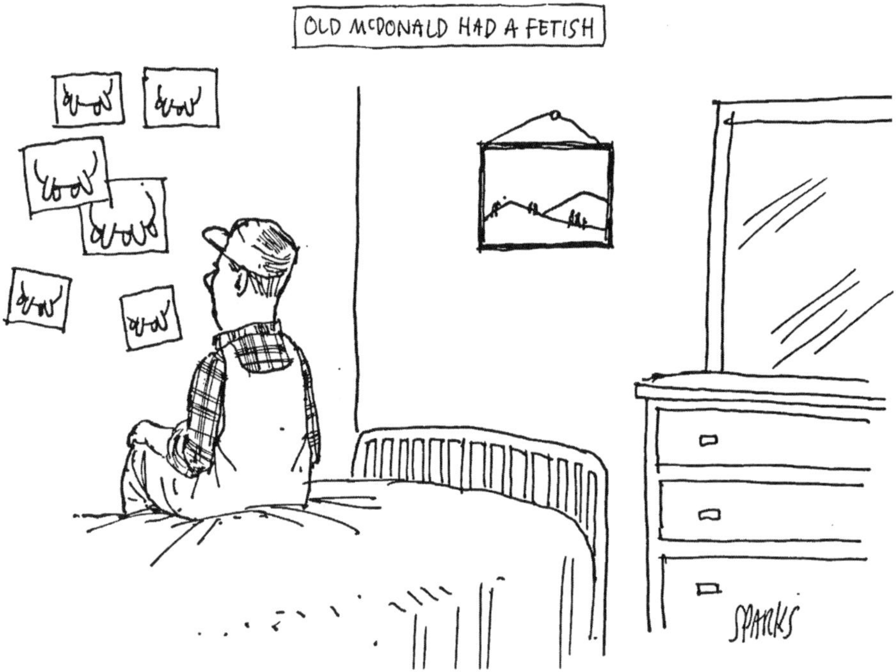
OLD McDONALD HAD A FETISH
SPARKS

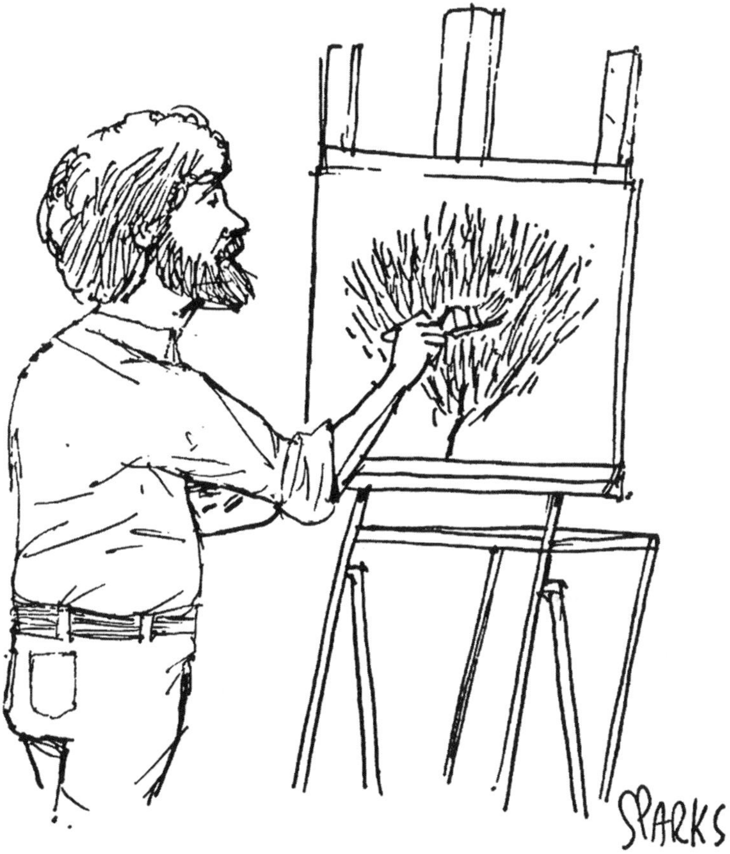
SPARKS

"And here's a happy little bush."

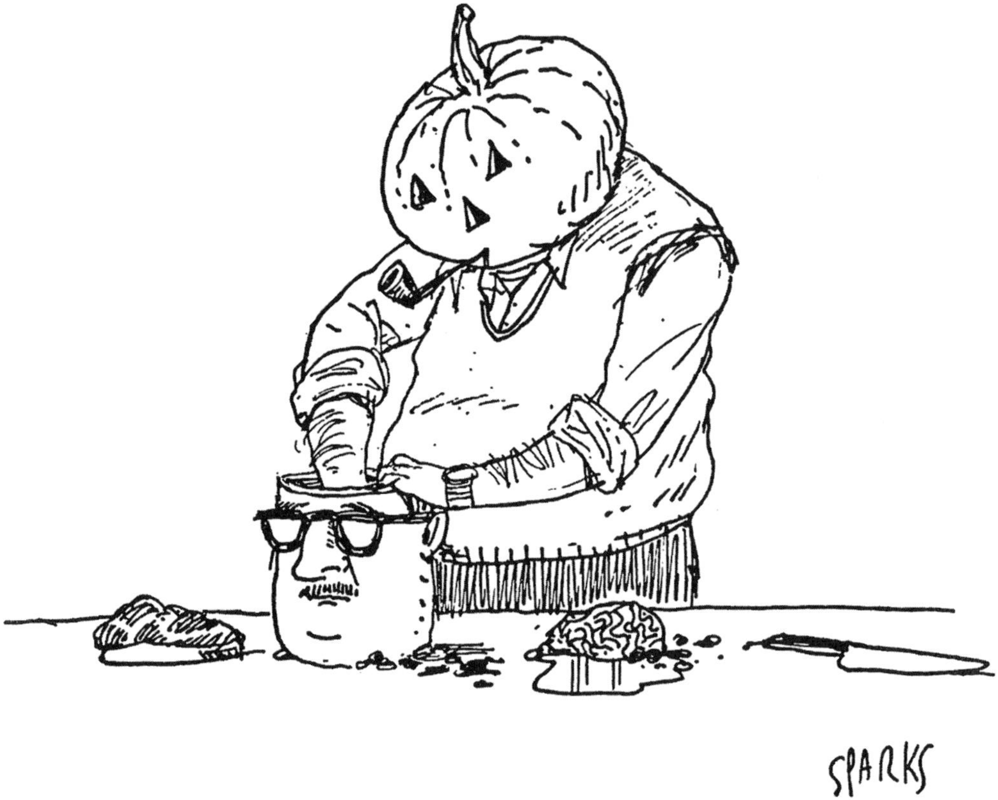
SPARKS

SPARKS

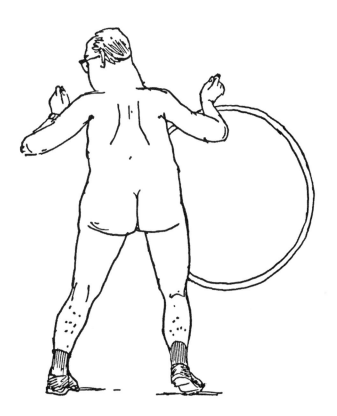

Drew Dernavich

Frequently Asked Questions

- *Where do you get your ideas?*
  Behind that tall, shiny-looking thingy with the knob on it, right across from you. No, not that one. The other one.

- *Which comes first, the picture or the caption?*
  The idea.

- *How'd you get started?*
  With my first idea.

- *I admire . . .*
  Anyone whose job it is to make decisions other than whether the word *Wednesday* is funnier than the word *Thursday*.

- *How do you deal with rejection?*
  Denial. I bottle up my anger. Someday I will unleash it on society. I will give you a few days' notice, though.

- *What are some things that make you laugh and why?*
  I pretty much laugh at everything. When I was nine, my teacher told me I'd probably laugh at a grapefruit. Since then, I have

found grapefruits to be hysterically funny. Humor can, and should, be found in everything in life. If you can't find it, you're an unhealthy person. But being unhealthy is funny, so . . . can you see the vicious (and humorous) cycle?

- *I've got a great idea for a cartoon—wanna hear it?*
  How about a beer instead?

Infrequently Asked Questions

- *Have you mooned or been mooned more often in your life?*
  After a long day of work, I love to go out and get mooned.

- *What would make a terrible pizza topping?*
  Nostalgia.

- *What might one expect to find at a really low-budget amusement park?*
  Matt Diffee, eating circus peanuts.

- *What did the shepherd say to the three-legged sheepdog?*
I've got a great idea for a cartoon—wanna hear it?

And Now for a Few More Questions . . .

- *What do you hate drawing?*
Shrubbery. Feet. Tiny little details.

- *Being as accurate as possible, how many desert island cartoons do you think you've come up with and submitted to* The New Yorker?
Fourteen.

- *What's the funniest thing that you witnessed, overheard, or came up with that you couldn't figure out how to use in a cartoon?*
There used to be a blind man at my subway stop who would feel for his seat by plunging his stick into everybody's crotch. His aim was painfully accurate. People were terrified. It was great theatre. I could never make it any funnier than it was.

Naming Names

- *What name might you give to a mild-mannered, middle-aged, bespectacled dental assistant in one of your cartoons?*
Nacho Panza.

- *Other than Lance, what name would you give to a twenty-eight-year-old entertainment lawyer with a blue-dyed fauxhawk who cycles on weekends?*
Chad.

- *What would be a good name for a new, commercially unviable breakfast cereal?*
Individually Wrapped Rice Krispies.

- *Come up with a name for an unpleasant medical procedure.*
Lemon meringue. (The procedure is so painful I couldn't name it for what it really is.)

- *If you used a pen name, what would it be?*
Marcus Chicken-Stock.*

Complete the Pie Chart Below

. . . in a way that tells us something about your life or how you think.

---

*with apologies to John Hodgman

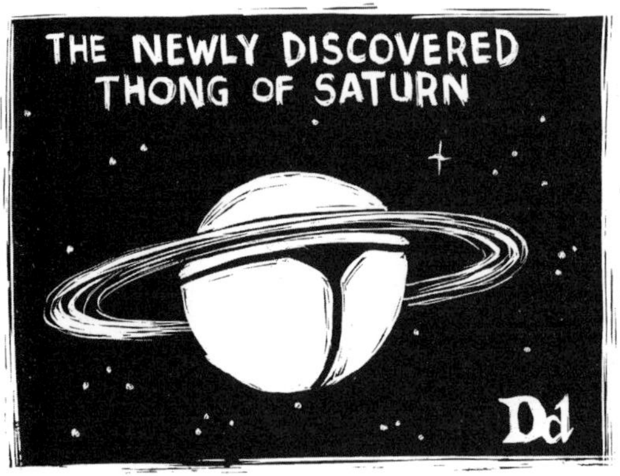
THE NEWLY DISCOVERED
THONG OF SATURN
Dd

THE PROSTATE MONOLOGUES

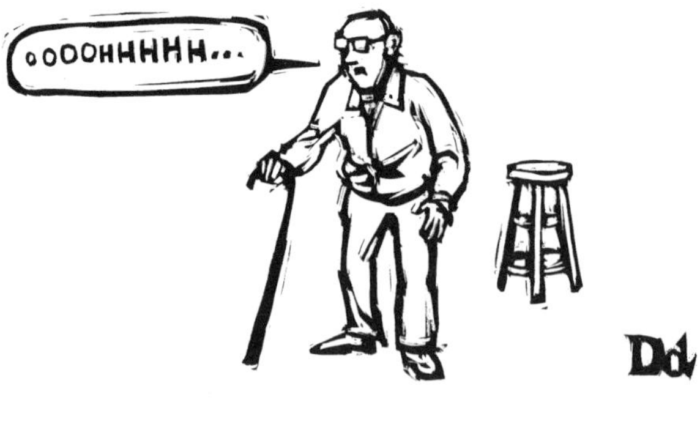
oOOOHHHHH...
Dd

"Okay, up there, let's give 'er another try."

"Will it be just a cleaning or the full hour of sensual dentistry?"

"I faked your New Year's resolution."

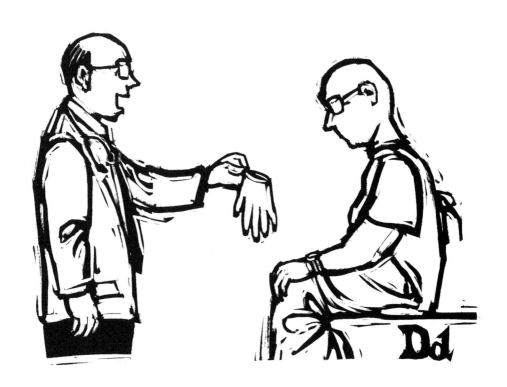

"Give a man an exam and he'll be healthy for a day;
teach a man to examine himself and he'll be healthy for a lifetime."

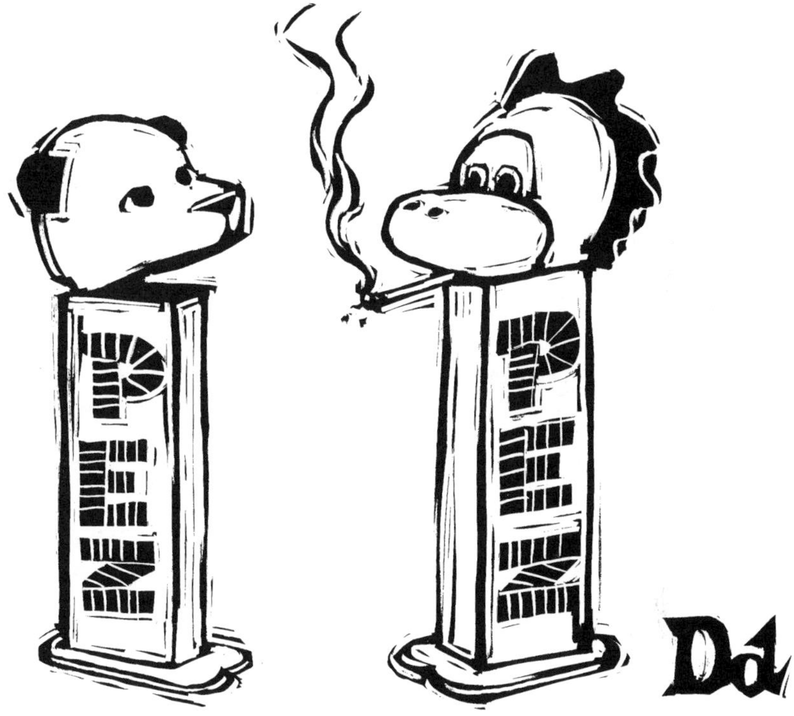
PEZ
PEZ

"Are you going to dispense candy with that mouth?"

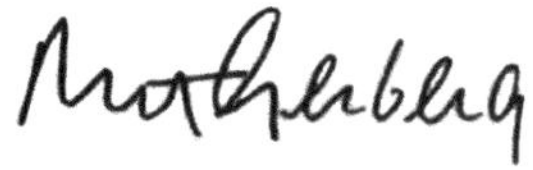

Mort Gerberg

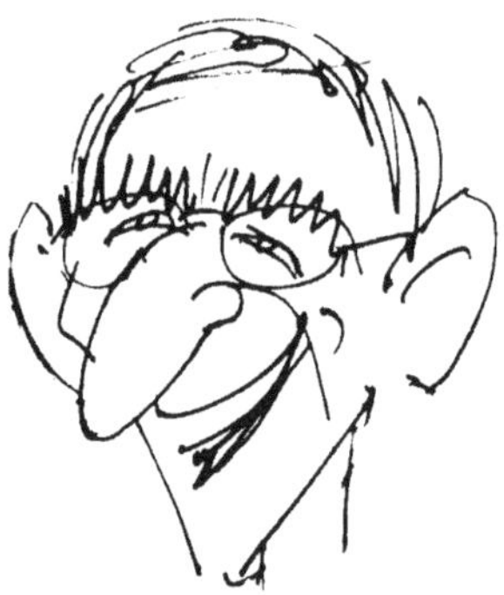

Frequently Asked Questions

- *Where do you get your ideas?*
  I put a tooth under my pillow when I go to sleep. The next morning, when I wake up, there they are!

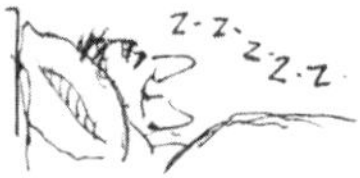
z-z-z-z-z

- *Which comes first, the picture or the caption?*
  The one that's more turned on from the foreplay.

- *How'd you get started?*
  Well, the way I understand it, first my father and mother had sex with each other . . .

- *I admire . . .*
  People who get to be 80 so they can ski for free at Alta—and I'm very partial to great bread.

- *How do you deal with rejection?*
  I try to remember that my wife, the career counselor, keeps telling me that I am not my work—but I keep forgetting that.

- *What are some things that make you laugh and why?*
  I can't name them because I never know in advance what they might be—they're "things" I see or hear in any random moment, and because, like most cartoonists, my head is wired weirdly, I simply experience them as "funny."

- *I've got a great idea for a cartoon—wanna hear it?*
  What? *What? What* did you say? Sorry, but my hearing aid is on the fritz and I can't . . . *What? WHAT?* You ate a *DEER*?!

Infrequently Asked Questions

- *Have you mooned or been mooned more often in your life?*

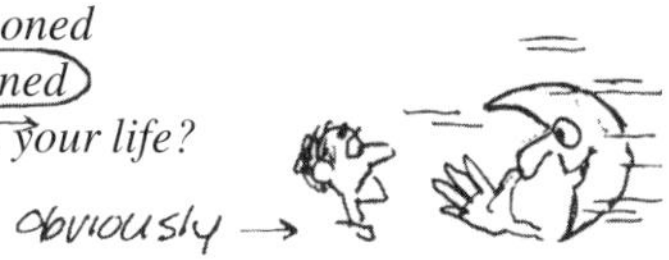
obviously

- *What would make a terrible pizza topping?*
  A big, fat meditating Buddhist monk.

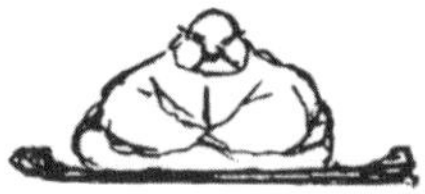

- *What might one expect to find at a really low-budget amusement park?*
  A flashlight-lit copy of the Gettysburg Address, with a scratchy soundtrack of "The Battle Hymn of the Republic" sung by John Ashcroft.

- *What did the shepherd say to the three-legged sheepdog?*

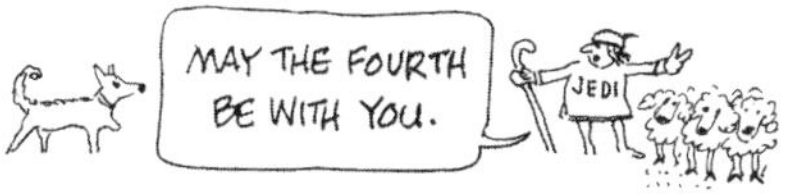
MAY THE FOURTH BE WITH YOU.
JEDI

Draw Something in This Space

. . . that will help us understand your childhood.

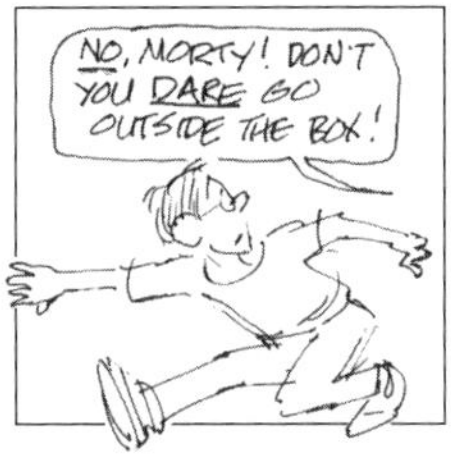
NO, MORTY! DON'T YOU DARE GO OUTSIDE THE BOX!

And Now for a Few More Questions . . .

- *What do you hate drawing?*
  I hate drawing attention to myself. (*Hah*! Now *there's* a laugh!)

- *Being as accurate as possible, how many desert island cartoons do you think you've come up with and submitted to* The New Yorker*?*
  Only four—because I ran out of little bottles to stuff the drawings in.

- *What's the funniest thing that you witnessed, overheard, or came up with that you couldn't figure out how to use in a cartoon?*
  George Bush's shipboard "Mission Accomplished" scene. Because it was already 100 percent pure self-satire, it was satire-proof—and I cried because I hadn't thought of the idea myself.

Naming Names

- *What name might you give to a mild-mannered, middle-aged, bespectacled dental assistant in one of your cartoons?*
  Flossie.

- *Other than Lance, what name would you give to a twenty-eight-year-old entertainment lawyer with a blue-dyed fauxhawk who cycles on weekends?*
  Geary Wheeler.

- *Come up with a name for an unpleasant medical procedure.*
  Upyouroscopy.

- *If you used a pen name, what would it be?*
  Monsieur Mont Blanc.

Complete the Pie Chart Below

. . . in a way that tells us something about your life or how you think.

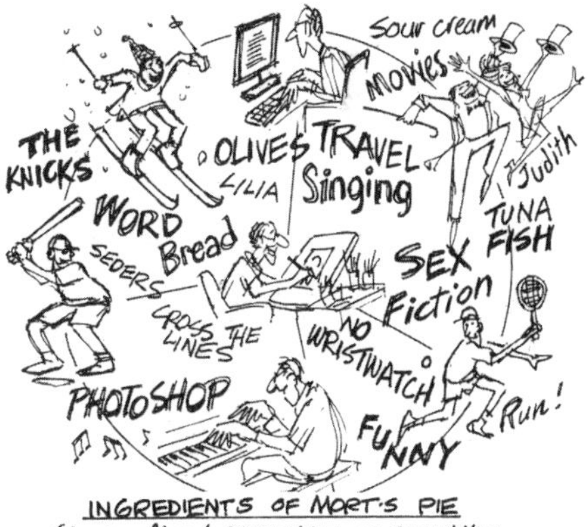
Sour cream
Movies
THE KNICKS
OLIVES
LILIA
TRAVEL
Singing
Judith
TUNA FISH
WORD
Bread
SEDERS
SEX
Fiction
CROSS THE LINES
NO WRISTWATCH
PHOTOSHOP
FUNNY
Run!

INGREDIENTS OF MORT'S PIE
(in no fixed proportion or quantity, which change every day.)

"Take a shower first. You smell like a chimney."

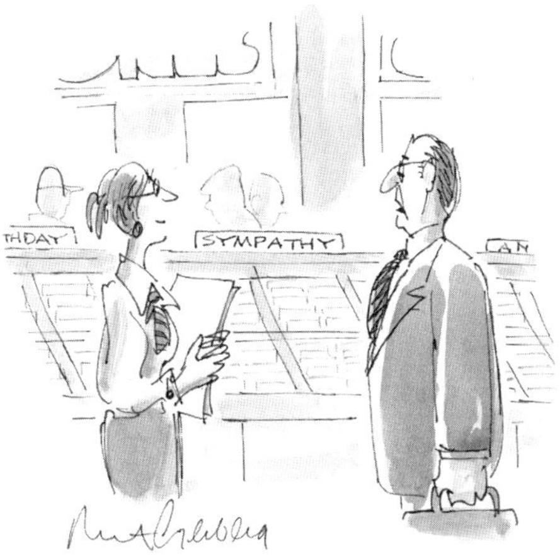
SYMPATHY

"I'm looking for a card that says 'Sorry about the herpes.'"

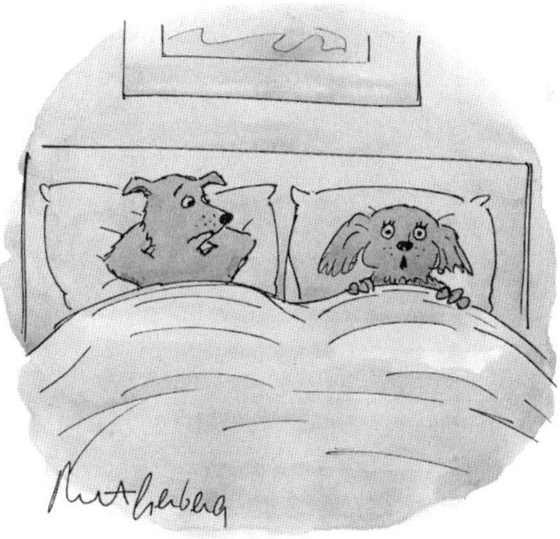

"No, no—it was great. It's just that sometime I'd like to try it missionary style."

"I knew it! You've been sleeping with that Rapunzel bitch!"

"Lately I've had uncontrollable cravings for venison."

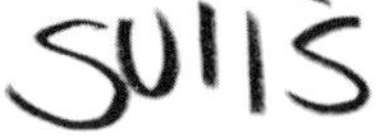
SUITS

Julia Suits

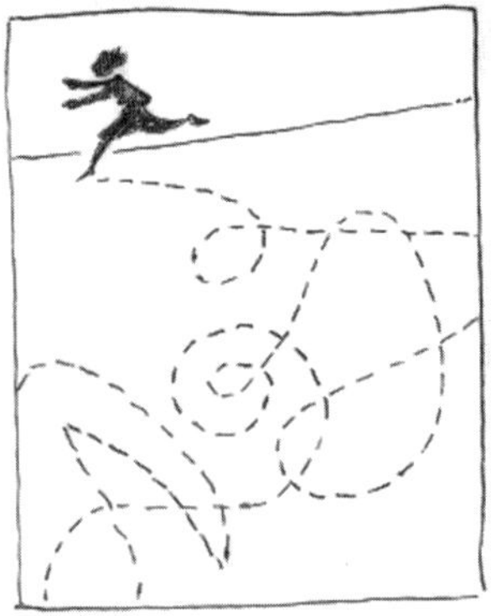

Frequently Asked Questions

- *Where do you get your ideas?*
  Personal experiences and observations, reading, radio, TV—in that order. Everything is stored in my head; it accumulates mercilessly. Best ideas come out of NOWHERE! Fun.

- *Which comes first, the picture or the caption?*
  The caption, 90 percent.

- *How'd you get started?*
  One day I decided I wanted to draw cartoons for *The New Yorker*. So, as in tennis—where I had to hit a million balls to achieve a desired skill level—I began the task of drawing a million (actually, several hundred) cartoons.

- *I admire . . .*
  Mountain goats. They are not afraid of heights, and they can cling to just about any surface.

- *How do you deal with rejection?*
  Ointment.

- *What are some things that make you laugh and why?*
  What: Genius comedians, guffawing babies. Why: The science or psychology behind it escapes me.

- *I've got a great idea for a cartoon—wanna hear it?*
  Sure! I need to practice my fake laugh.

Infrequently Asked Questions

- *Have you mooned or been mooned more often in your life?*
  Once. It was not a waxing gibbon . . . more like a gibbon in need of a waxing.

- *What would make a terrible pizza topping?*
  A manhole cover.

- *What might one expect to find at a really low-budget amusement park?*
  A higher percentage of safety violations.

- *What did the shepherd say to the three-legged sheepdog?*
  Nothing. The three-legged dog and the shepherd lived in different parts of the world: the dog in Canton, Ohio, the shepherd in Béziers, France.

Draw Some Sort of Doodle

. . . using the random lines below as a starting point.

Someone holding a toy car while smoking a pipe.

And Now for a Few More Questions . . .

- *What do you hate drawing?*
  Auditoriums or places with a lot of seating and/or crowds of people.

- *Being as accurate as possible, how many desert island cartoons do you think you've come up with and submitted to* The New Yorker*?*
  Twenty-five.

- *What's the ~~funniest~~* weird, pathetic, horrific *thing that you witnessed, overheard, or came up with that you couldn't figure out how to use in a cartoon?*
  I once "borrowed" $20 from a corpse.

Naming Names

- *What name might you give to a mild-mannered, middle-aged, bespectacled dental assistant in one of your cartoons?*
  Colleen, Yvonne, Lynette, Latrineesha, Pegotty.

- *Other than Lance, what name would you give to a twenty-eight-year-old entertainment lawyer with a blue-dyed fauxhawk who cycles on weekends?*
  Travis, Damian, Ethan, Owen.

- *What would be a good name for a new, commercially unviable breakfast cereal?*
  DingleberriO's or Now Wheatier Wheaties.

- *Come up with a name for an unpleasant medical procedure.*
  Nipplectomy.

- *If you used a pen name, what would it be?*
  Beva Lebourveau.

Complete the Pie Chart Below

. . . in a way that tells us something about your life or how you think.

THINGS I CAN SEE RIGHT NOW WHILE SITTING AT MY DESK.
WILD TURKEYS in yard
MY SONS READING THE PAPER
CAST IRON TAPE DISPENSER
circa 1937
COFFEE CUP
NEVER JUDGE

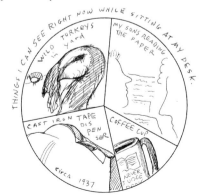

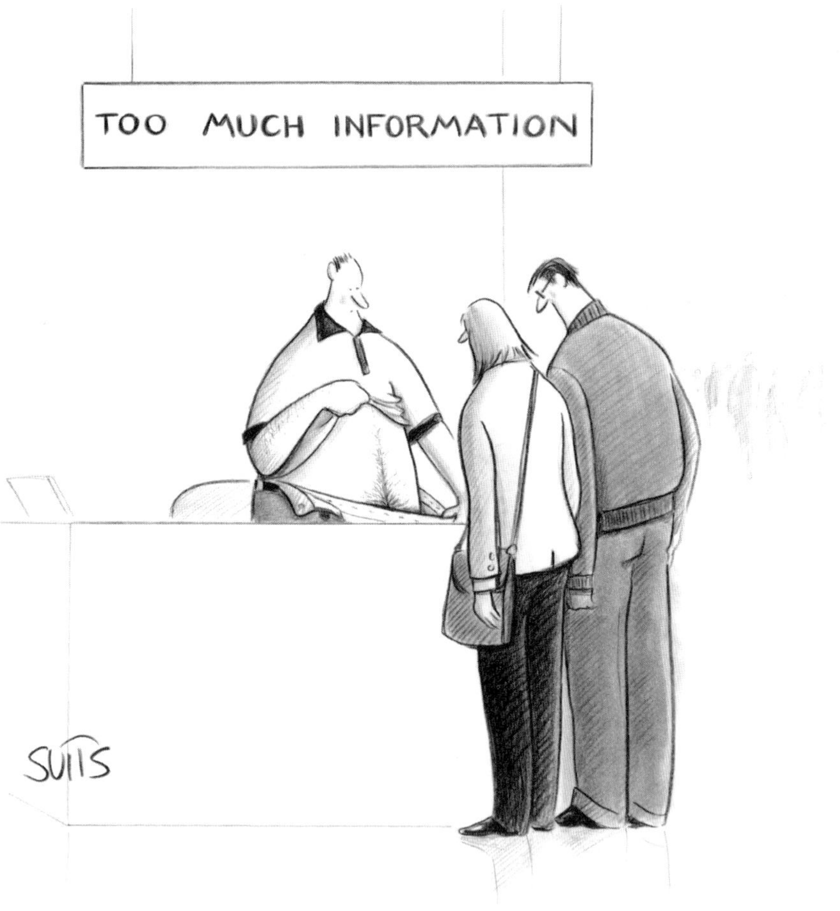
TOO MUCH INFORMATION
SUITS

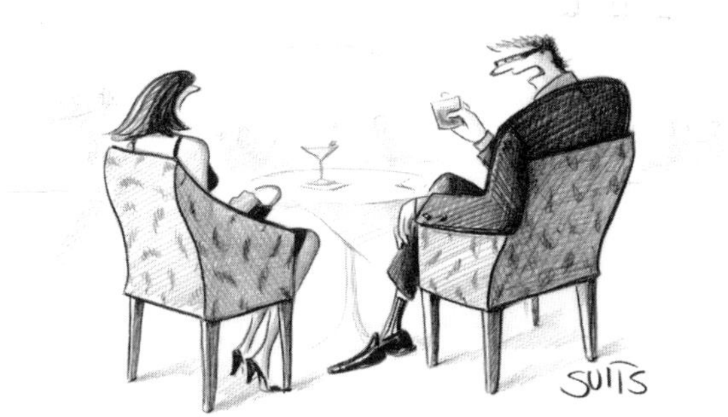
SUITS

"Enough about my penis. What's new with the ol' vagina?"

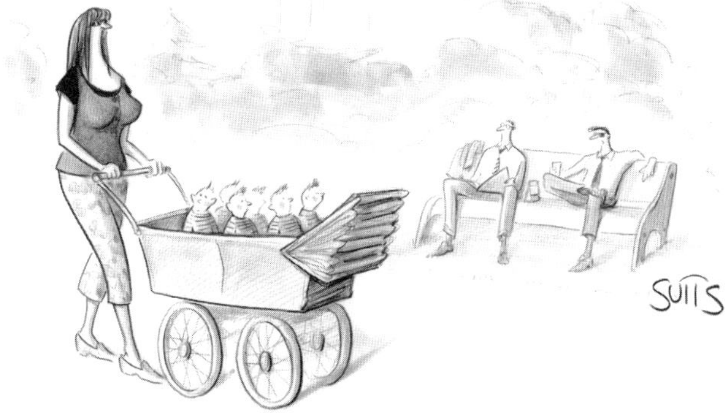
SUITS

"Check those babies out."

JON ADAMS

Jon Adams

Frequently Asked Questions

- *Where do you get your ideas?*
  It would be wrong to call them "my" ideas since they all come from God.

- *Which comes first, the picture or the caption?*
  They tend to come simultaneously, though sometimes when a cartoon doesn't sell I may recaption it to something entirely new in the hopes that sells. Which it doesn't.

- *How'd you get started?*
  I started working professionally in comics when I was in high school, but didn't have an interest in single panel cartoons until many years later when Matt Petty, the Art Director of the *San Francisco Chronicle*, invited me to create a weekly single-panel strip. It was called Friendship Town. Before sending those cartoons to the *Chronicle*, I figured I may as well submit them to *The New Yorker* where they would be rejected. Eventually the *Chronicle* canceled it's independent comics section, but a few years later I decided to start submitting to *The New Yorker* again, this time opting to impose upon long-time *New Yorker* cartoonist Emily Flake, who was also a good friend from high school. She vouched for me, which I think helped.

- *I admire . . .*
  Extroverts.

- *What are some things that make you laugh and why?*
  The one thing that consistently makes me laugh is watching people try to pull open locked doors. Because it's fucking hilarious.

- *I've got a great idea for a cartoon—wanna hear it?*
  Please, no.

Infrequently Asked Questions

- *Have you mooned or been mooned more often in your life?*
  What does staring at my butt in the mirror count as?

- *What would make a terrible pizza topping?*
  Olives.

- *What might one expect to find at a really low-budget amusement park?*
  Low-budget people?

- *What did the shepherd say to the three-legged sheepdog?*
  "Quit rubbing in how many legs you have." Or: "Mess up again and I'll take another leg."

Draw Something in This Space

. . . that will help us understand your childhood.

WHY

And Now for a Few More Questions . . .

- *What do you hate drawing?*
  Everything but people.

- *Being as accurate as possible, how many desert island cartoons do you think you've come up with and submitted to* The New Yorker*?*
  The very first cartoon I sold to *The New Yorker* was a desert island cartoon. I've probably submitted 50 or so, several of which can be seen in the new desert island cartoon collection *Send Help! A Collection of Marooned Cartoons* (ISBN: 9780316262798) edited by myself and *New Yorker* cartoonist Ellis Rosen, and featuring over 100 other cartoonists including Matthew Diffee who says, "*Send Help!* is the greatest book I've ever been in."

- *What's the funniest thing that you witnessed, overheard, or came up with that you couldn't figure out how to use in a cartoon?*
  In a Boston food court there's a set of glass doors that look like they would open but don't and I spent about an hour watching multiple people try to open them. It was one of the happiest moments of my life.

Naming Names

- *What name might you give to a mild-mannered, middle-aged, bespectacled dental assistant in one of your cartoons?*
  Darcy.

- *Other than Lance, what name would you give to a twenty-eight-year-old entertainment lawyer with a blue-dyed fauxhawk who cycles on weekends?*
  Now that you've suggested Lance, it's the only name I can think of. Maybe Lance Jr.? Blanche?

- *What would be a good name for a new, commercially unviable breakfast cereal?*
  Frosted Truffle-Os.

- *Come up with a name for an unpleasant medical procedure.*
  Alimentary Canal Removal.

- *If you used a pen name, what would it be?*
  I do use a pen name. It's Ted Wilson.

Complete the Pie Chart Below

. . . in a way that tells us something about your life or how you think.

Movies.
Movies.
Movies.
Movies.

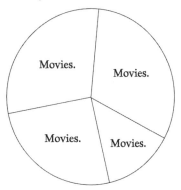

JON ADAMS

"Don't worry, when I get home I'm going to make sure someone dedicates a bench to everything that happened here."

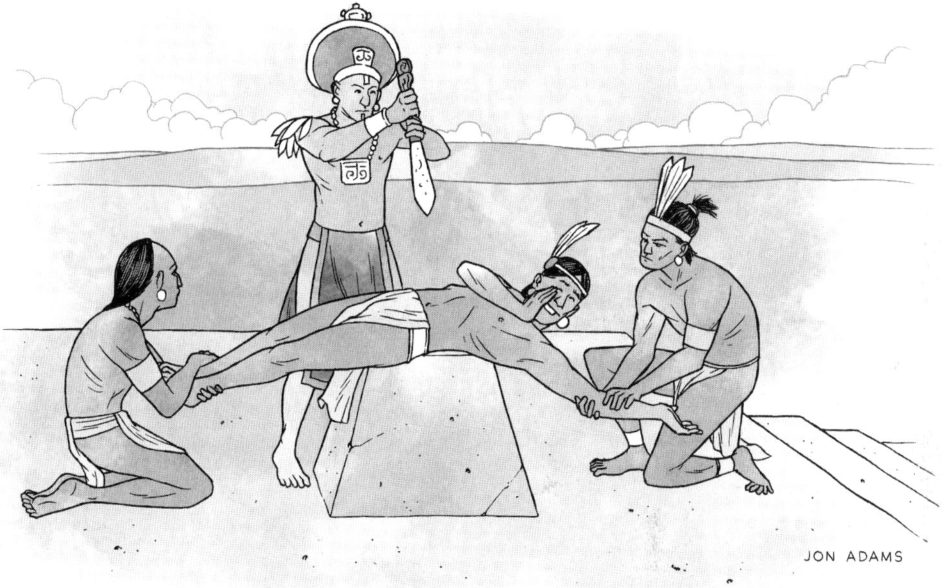
JON ADAMS

"Looks like I'm not a good-for-nothing after all, am I, Mom?"

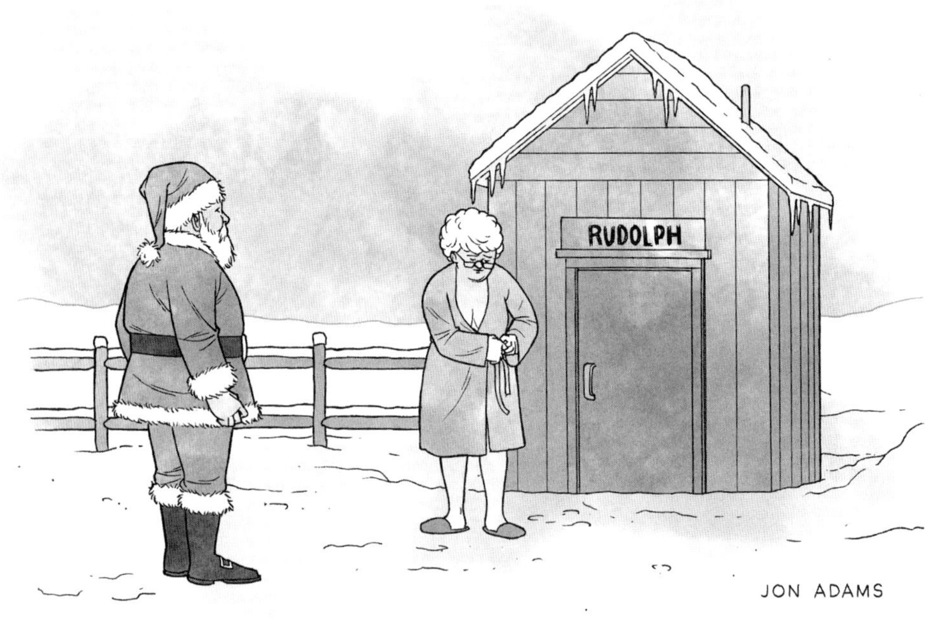
RUDOLPH
JON ADAMS

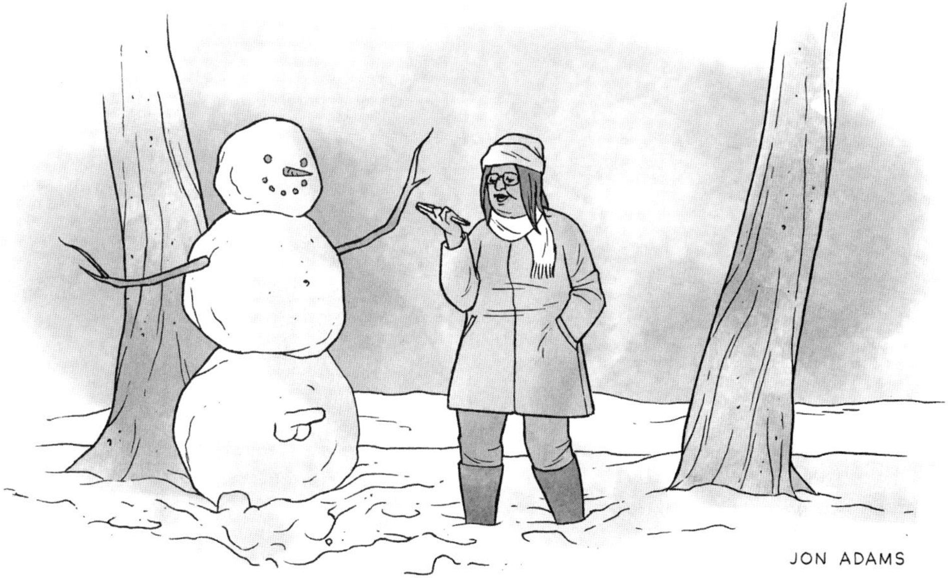
JON ADAMS

"Hey Siri, where can I buy a magic hat?"

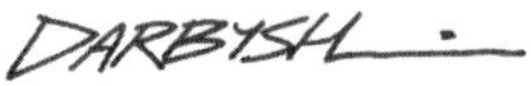

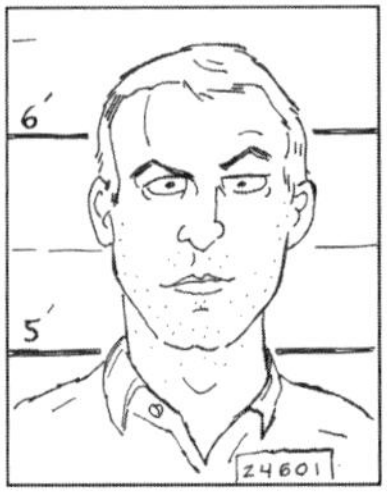
6'
5'
24601

C. Covert Darbyshire

Frequently Asked Questions

- *Where do you get your ideas?*
  I rework Drew Dernavich and Matt Diffee's rejects.

- *Which comes first, the picture or the caption?*
  1) Egg
  2) Caption
  3) Google images
  4) Rubber glove
  5) Chicken
  6) Picture

- *How'd you get started?*
  Photos of Mankoff.

- *I admire . . .*
  The work of Charles Schulz (*Peanuts*), Gary Larson (*The Far Side*), Matt Groening (*Life in Hell*), and the cartoonists at *The New Yorker* who continually crank out great work—like Jack Ziegler.

- *How do you deal with rejection?*
  First, shock, then denial, followed by anger, confusion, depression, and eventually, through self-medication, acceptance.

- *What are some things that make you laugh and why?*
  Will Ferrell—funniest man alive, *Seinfeld* reruns, the movie *Rushmore,* any movie by Pixar, *America's Funniest Home Videos,* Conan O'Brien, my kids, other cartoonists.

- *I've got a great idea for a cartoon—wanna hear it?*
  Hold that thought. . . .

Infrequently Asked Questions

- *Have you mooned or been mooned more often in your life?*
  Been. I used to train baboons in Nairobi.

- *What would make a terrible pizza topping?*
  Gravy.

- *What might one expect to find at a really low-budget amusement park?*
  People being mauled by lions.

- *What did the shepherd say to the three-legged sheepdog?*
  How was the amusement park?

Draw Something in This Space

. . . that will help us understand your childhood.

GAS

And Now for a Few More Questions . . .

- *What do you hate drawing?*
  Fudge (with nuts).

- *Being as accurate as possible, how many desert island cartoons do you think you've come up with and submitted to* The New Yorker*?*
  36.37, if you count this one.

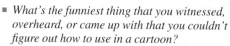

- *What's the funniest thing that you witnessed, overheard, or came up with that you couldn't figure out how to use in a cartoon?*
  A car dealership where each car, in addition to a spare tire, comes with a German midget mechanic in a case—in the back, next to the tire.

Naming Names

- *What name might you give to a mild-mannered, middle-aged, bespectacled dental assistant in one of your cartoons?*
  Wendall.

- *Other than Lance, what name would you give to a twenty-eight-year-old entertainment lawyer with a blue-dyed fauxhawk who cycles on weekends?*
  Dexter.

- *What would be a good name for a new, commercially unviable breakfast cereal?*
  Bowel Movers.

- *Come up with a name for an unpleasant medical procedure.*
  Johnsonectomy.

- *If you used a pen name, what would it be?*
  Dexter Wendallston.

Complete the Pie Chart Below

. . . in a way that tells us something about your life or how you think.

REASONS WHY I SHOULD HAVE AN IPOD BUT DON'T.
NUMBER OF PEOPLE STARVING IN AFRICA WITH NO IPOD.
NUMBER OF SONGS I'D TOTALLY PUT ON MY IPOD IF I WERE GOING TO AFRICA.
BONO.

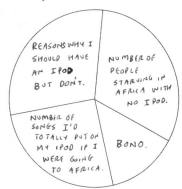

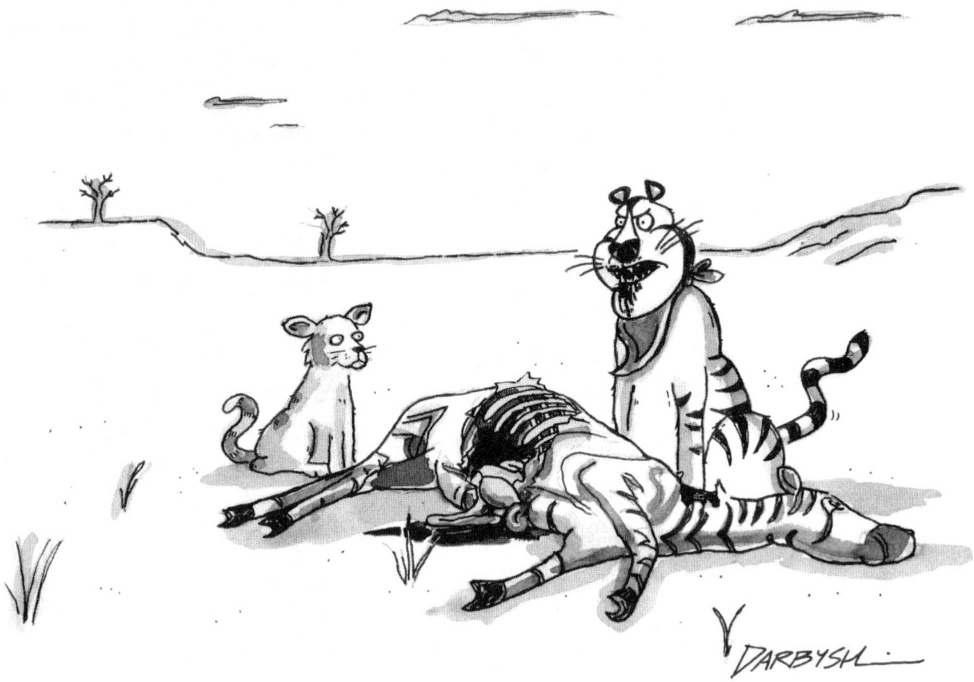
DARBYSH

"Sure, it was a sweet gig, but I'm a carnivore for Pete's sake."

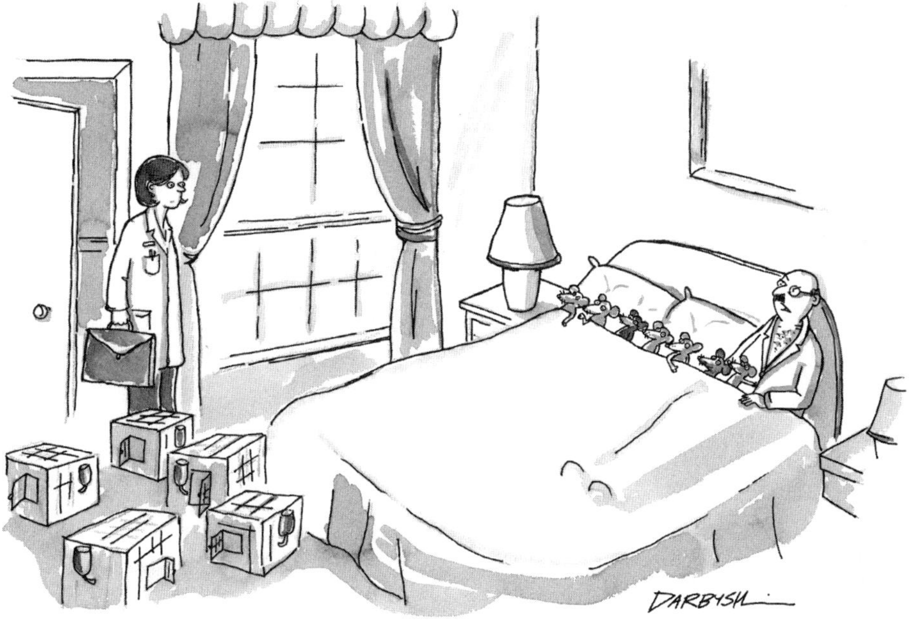
DARBYSH

"Yes, it's exactly what it looks like, and no, I don't know where this leaves us and our research."

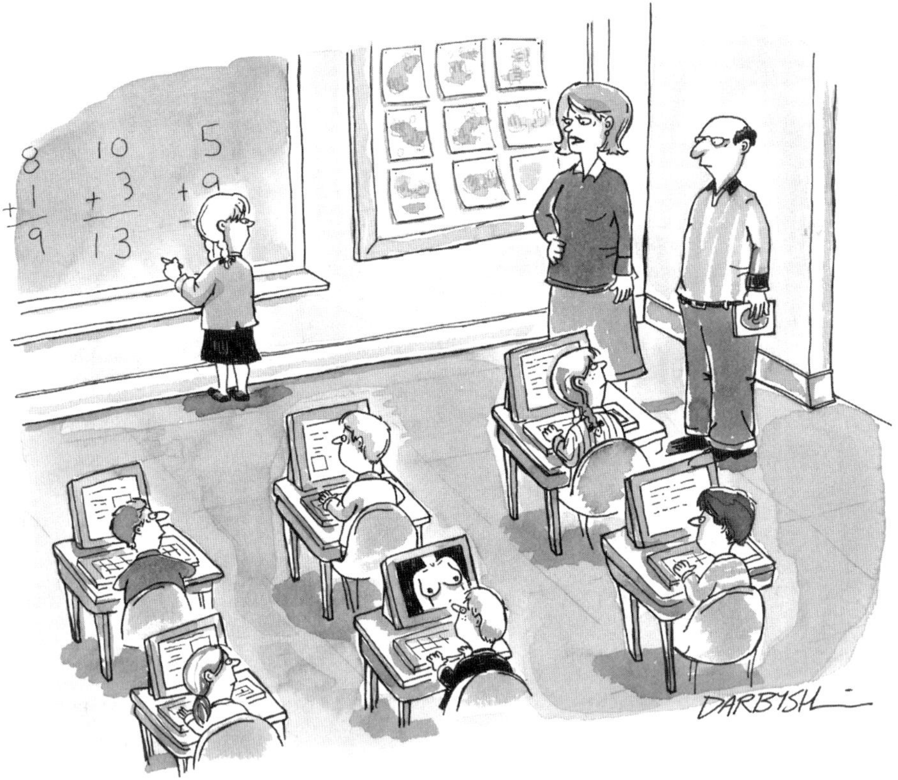
8
+1
9
10
+3
13
5
+9
DARBYSHIRE

"Who else needs Mr. Cornelson to reinstall the porn filter?"

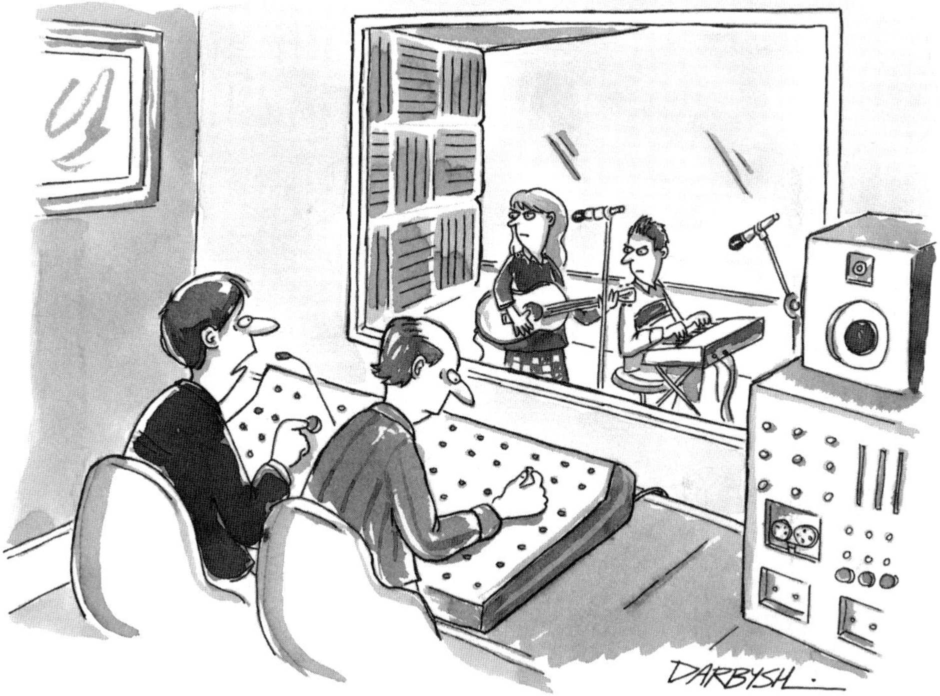
DARBYSH.

"That was nice—but this time with a little more of that Canadian angst."

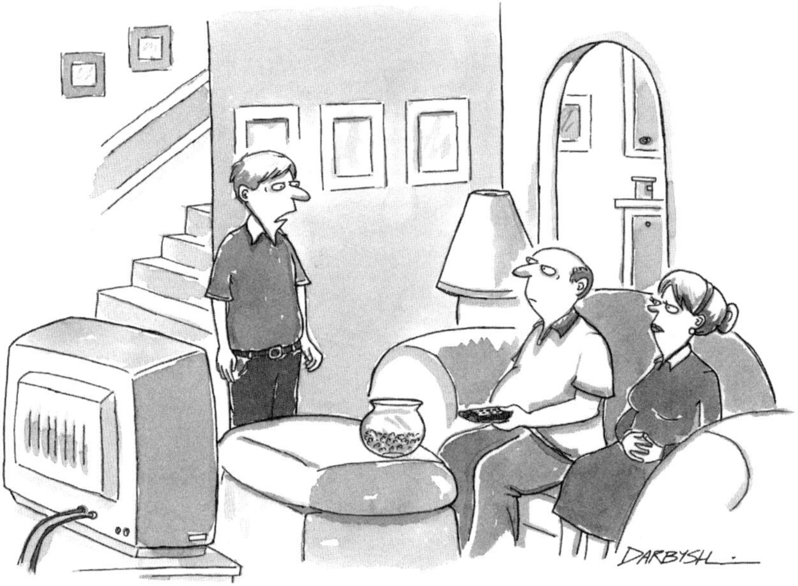
DARBYSH

"Mom, Dad, as you both know, I collect vintage dolls and listen to Cher regularly and without irony. I work as a perfume consultant at Bloomingdale's and am currently working on getting a degree in massage therapy. I own four glitter wigs, I use the word 'fabulous' way too much, and I, of course, love a cabaret. I also have a tattoo on the inside of my left ankle that says 'Ronald Forever,' who happens to be my quote unquote roommate going on five and a half years. . . . Oh, and I'm currently wearing stilettos. Stop me if you know where I'm going with this. . . ."

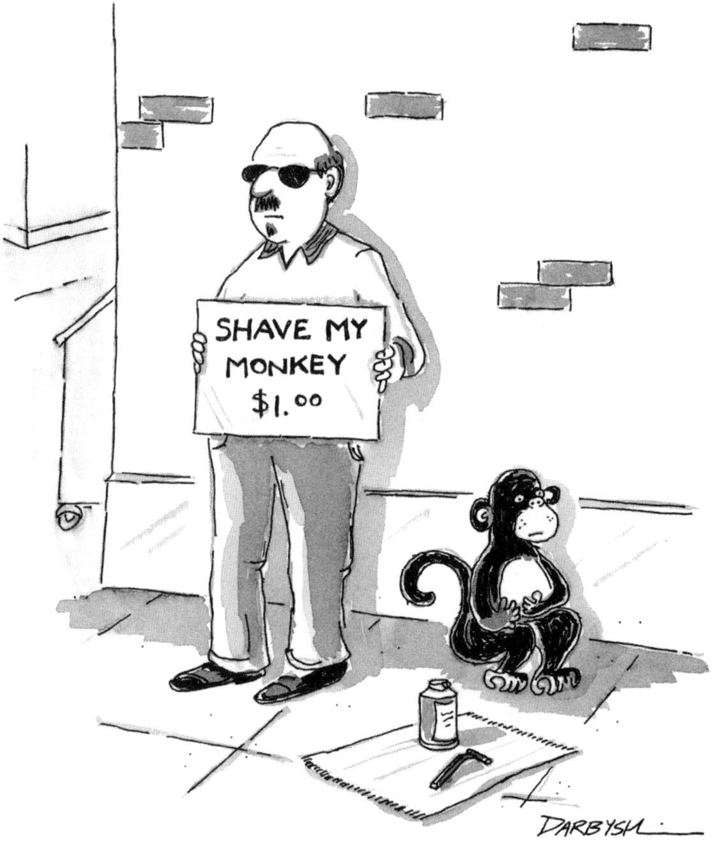
SHAVE MY
MONKEY
$1.00
DARBYSH

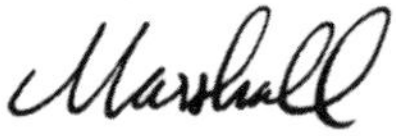

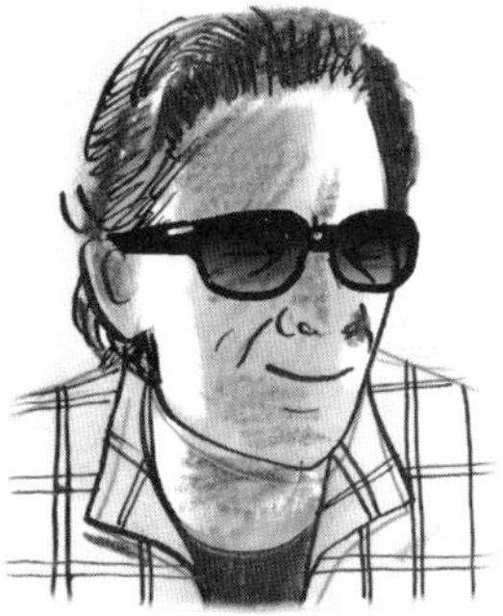

Marshall Hopkins

Frequently Asked Questions

- *Where do you get your ideas?*
  50 percent dead cartoonists.
  50 percent thin air.

- *Which comes first, the picture or the caption?*
  The picture usually comes first, and then I attach the caption with glue and a large mallet.

- *How'd you get started?*
  Coffee.

- *I admire . . .*
  Stanley Tucci.

- *How do you deal with rejection?*
  I buy another self-help audiobook.

- *What are some things that make you laugh and why?*
  A good fake accent because they're like magic. That person shouldn't sound like that, but somehow they do.

- *I've got a great idea for a cartoon—wanna hear it?*
  Absolutely, just sign right here.

Infrequently Asked Questions

- *Have you mooned or been mooned more often in your life?*
  Been mooned, I guess.

- *What would make a terrible pizza topping?*
  Liquid helium.

- *What might one expect to find at a really low-budget amusement park?*
  Tetanus.

- *What did the shepherd say to the three-legged sheepdog?*
  Let us know what happens on *General Hospital*.

And Now for a Few More Questions . . .

- *What do you hate drawing?*
  That Calvin peeing from *Calvin & Hobbes*.

- *Being as accurate as possible, how many desert island cartoons do you think you've come up with and submitted to* The New Yorker*?*
  Around twenty to twenty-five.

- *What's the funniest thing that you witnessed, overheard, or came up with that you couldn't figure out how to use in a cartoon?*

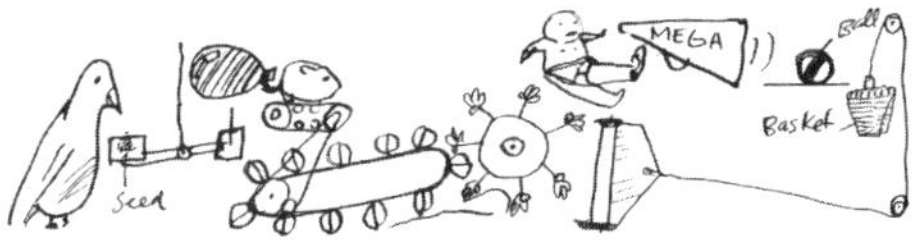
MEGA
Ball
Basket
Seed

Draw Some Sort of Doodle

. . . using the random lines below as a starting point.

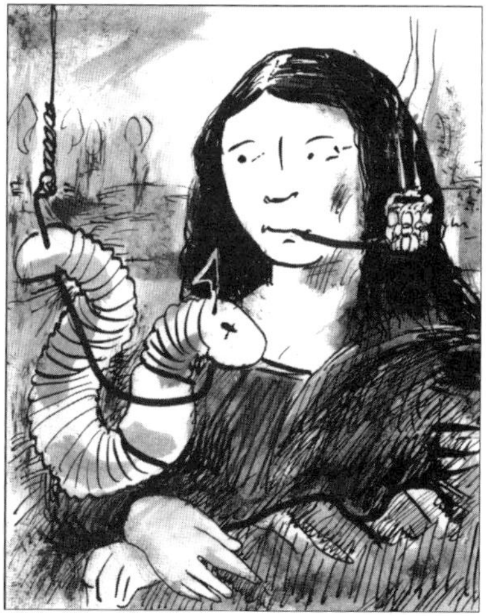

Naming Names

- *What name might you give to a mild-mannered, middle-aged, bespectacled dental assistant in one of your cartoons?*
  Hopkins.
- *Other than Lance, what name would you give to a twenty-eight-year-old entertainment lawyer with a blue-dyed fauxhawk who cycles on weekends?*
  Hillary Clinton.
- *What would be a good name for a new, commercially unviable breakfast cereal?*
  Coco Meth.
- *Come up with a name for an unpleasant medical procedure.*
  Buttectomy.
- *If you used a pen name, what would it be?*
  George Booth.

Complete the Pie Chart Below

. . . in a way that tells us something about your life or how you think.

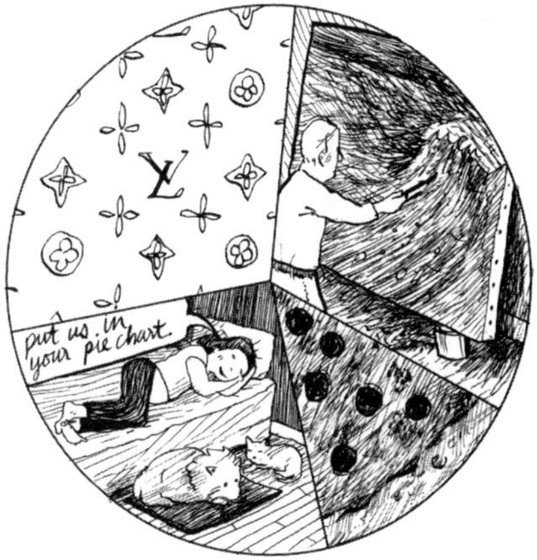
put us in your pie chart.

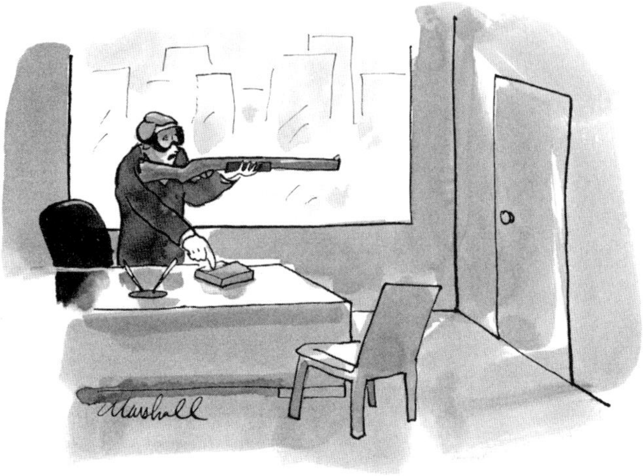
Marshall

"Pull."

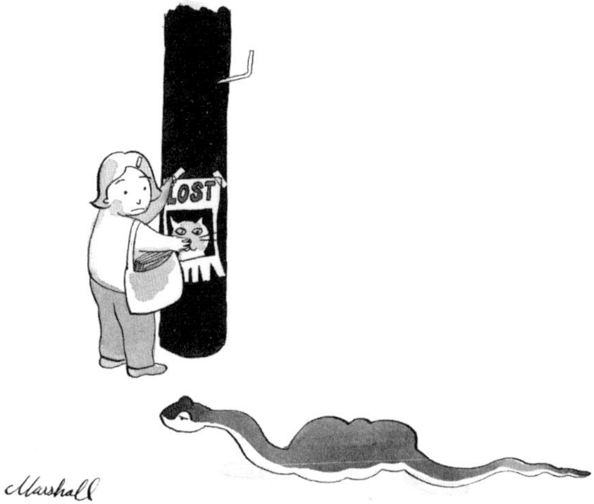
LOST
Marshall

"Look, Ma."

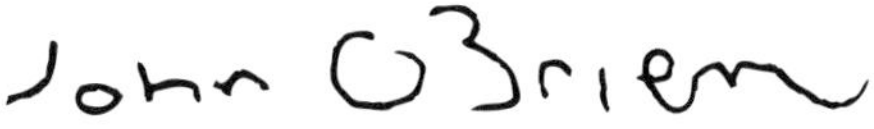

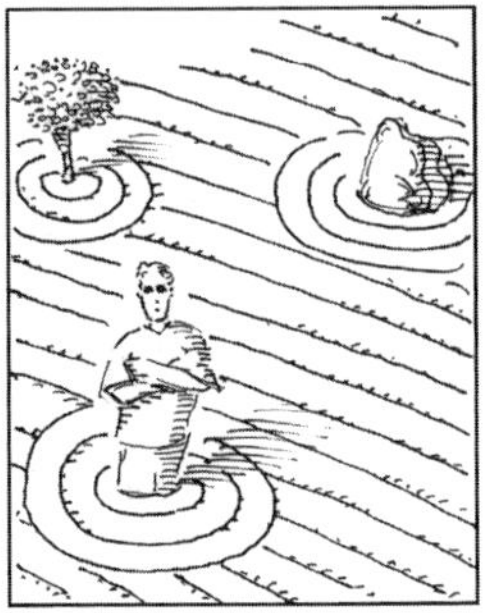

John O'Brien

Frequently Asked Questions

- *Where do you get your ideas?*

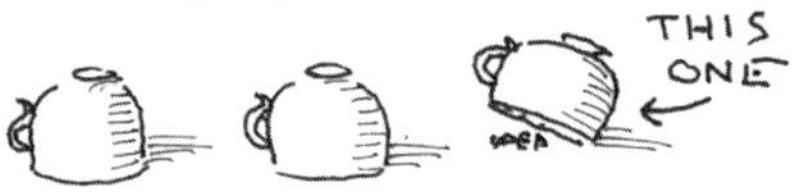
THIS ONE

- *Which comes first, the picture or the caption?*

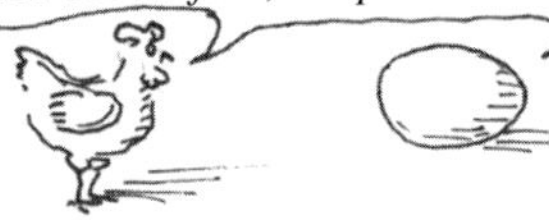

- *How'd you get started?*

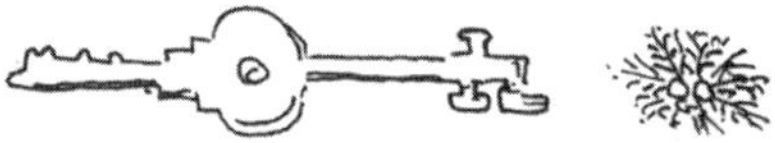

- *I admire . . .*
  Pranksters, wiseguys, and cheapshot artists.

- *How do you deal with rejection?*
  I put my ATM card back in the slot with the black stripe facing down and to the right . . . then I repeat the process.

- *What are some things that make you laugh and why?*
  The absurd, vaudeville skits, the sophomoric, other peoples' misfortunes.
  Why? Come on!

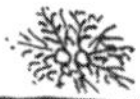

- *I've got a great idea for a cartoon—wanna hear it?*

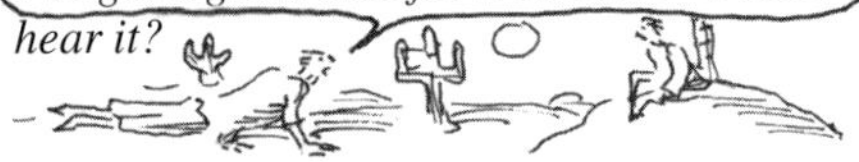

Infrequently Asked Questions

- *Have you mooned or been mooned more often in your life?*

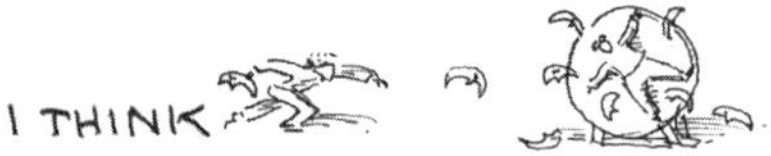
I THINK

- *What would make a terrible pizza topping?*
  The unwashed hands of a restaurant employee returning from the restroom?

- *What might one expect to find at a really low-budget amusement park?*
  Dangling keys.

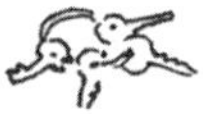

- *What did the shepherd say to the three-legged sheepdog?*

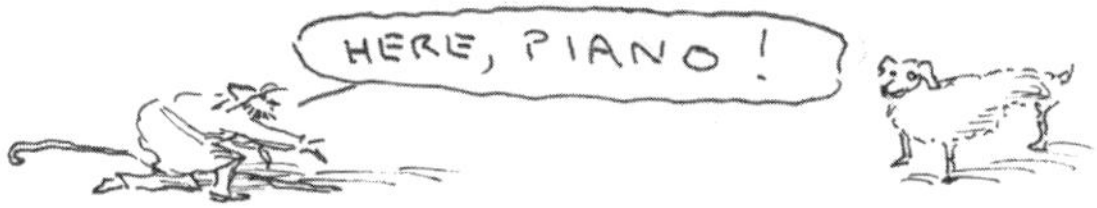
HERE, PIANO!

And Now for a Few More Questions . . .

- *What do you hate drawing?*
  If I knew, I'd have to shoot myself.

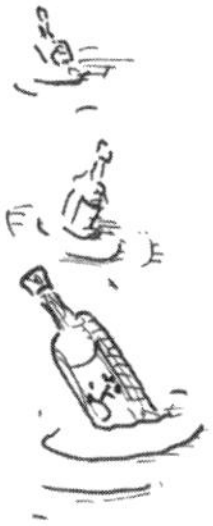

- *Being as accurate as possible, how many desert island cartoons do you think you've come up with and submitted to* The New Yorker*?*
  Many, but I'm not sure if the bottles washed up in Manhattan yet.

- *What's the funniest thing that you witnessed, overheard, or came up with that you couldn't figure out how to use in a cartoon?*

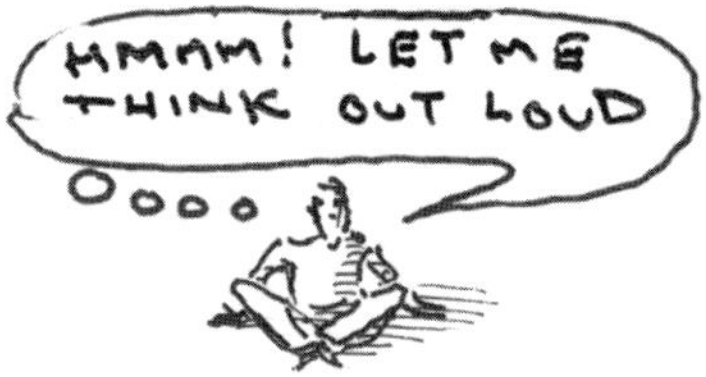
HMMM! LET ME THINK OUT LOUD
Oooo

Naming Names

- *What name might you give to a mild-mannered, middle-aged, bespectacled dental assistant in one of your cartoons?*
  Hugh Brushmore, Perry Donis, Ginger Vitus, Kay Nines, E. Namel, X. Traction, N. Cisors, D. Kaye . . . ok, ok, I'll stop.

- *Other than Lance, what name would you give to a twenty-eight-year-old entertainment lawyer with a blue-dyed fauxhawk who cycles on weekends?*
  Any name I feel like calling him, and he'll thank me for it while I'm dating his girlfriend.

- *What would be a good name for a new, commercially unviable breakfast cereal?*

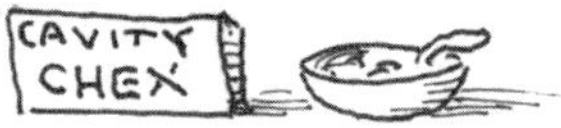
CAVITY CHEX

- *Come up with a name for an unpleasant medical procedure.*
  The-doctor-has-to-catch-a-flight-to-Miami-so-we're-rescheduling-you-for-next-Monday-sorry-about-the-seven-hour-wait-ectomy.

- *If you used a pen name, what would it be?*
  I'm still waiting for the test results. If it's a boy, I'll call it Bic; and if it's a girl, Koh-i-noor.

Complete the Pie Chart Below

. . . in a way that tells us something about your life or how you think.

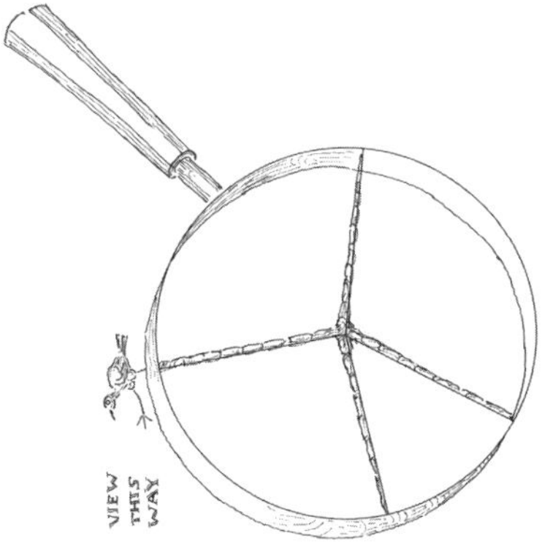
VIEW THIS WAY

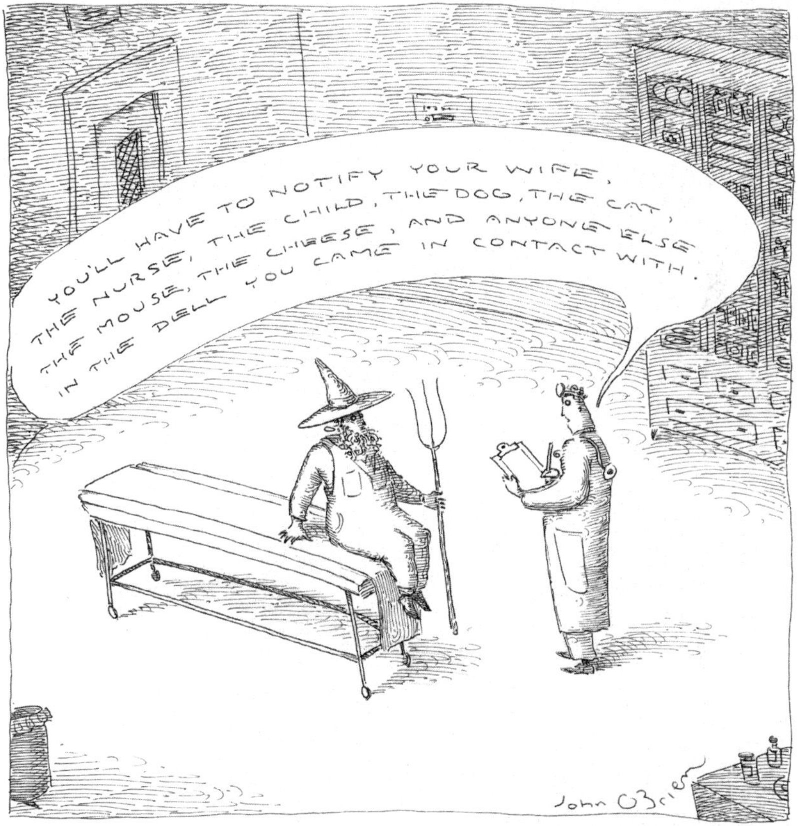
YOU'LL HAVE TO NOTIFY YOUR WIFE,
THE NURSE, THE CHILD, THE DOG, THE CAT,
THE MOUSE, THE CHEESE, AND ANYONE ELSE
IN THE DELL YOU CAME IN CONTACT WITH.
John O'Brien

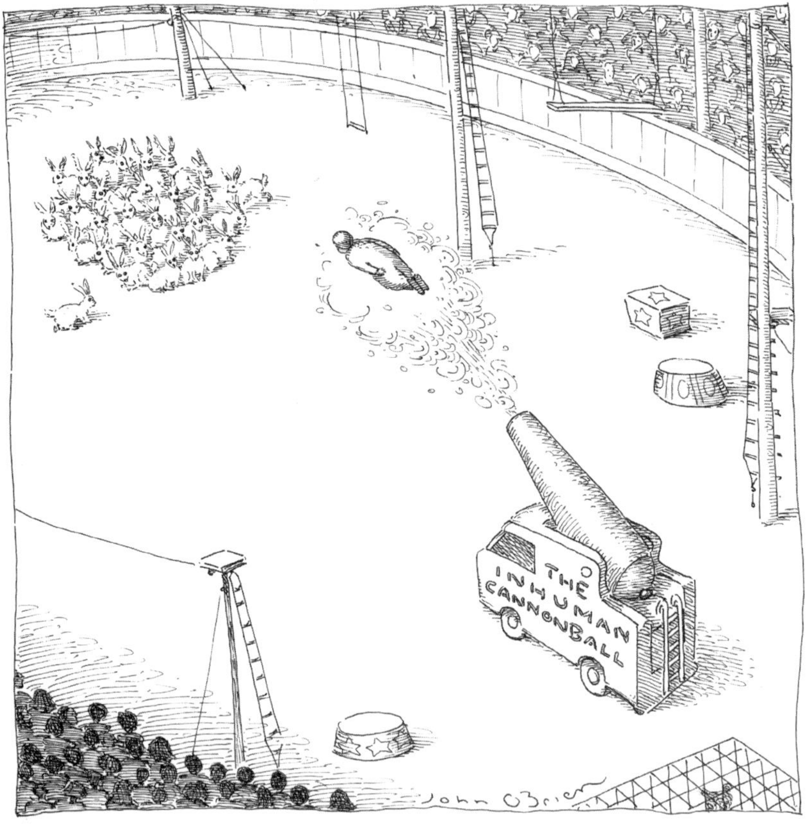
THE
INHUMAN
CANNONBALL
John O'Brien

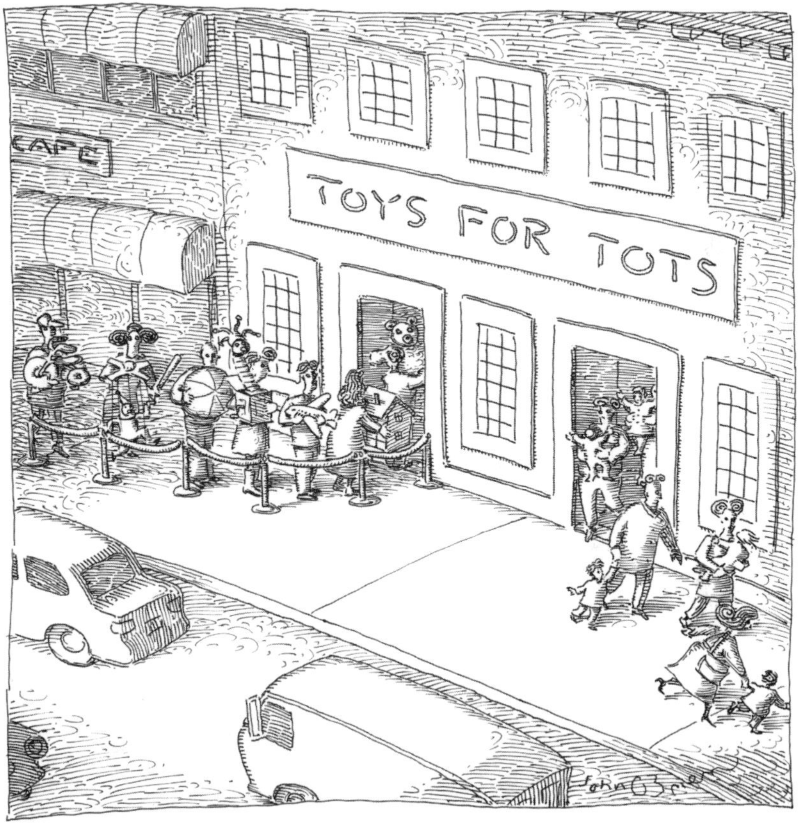
CAFE
TOYS FOR TOTS

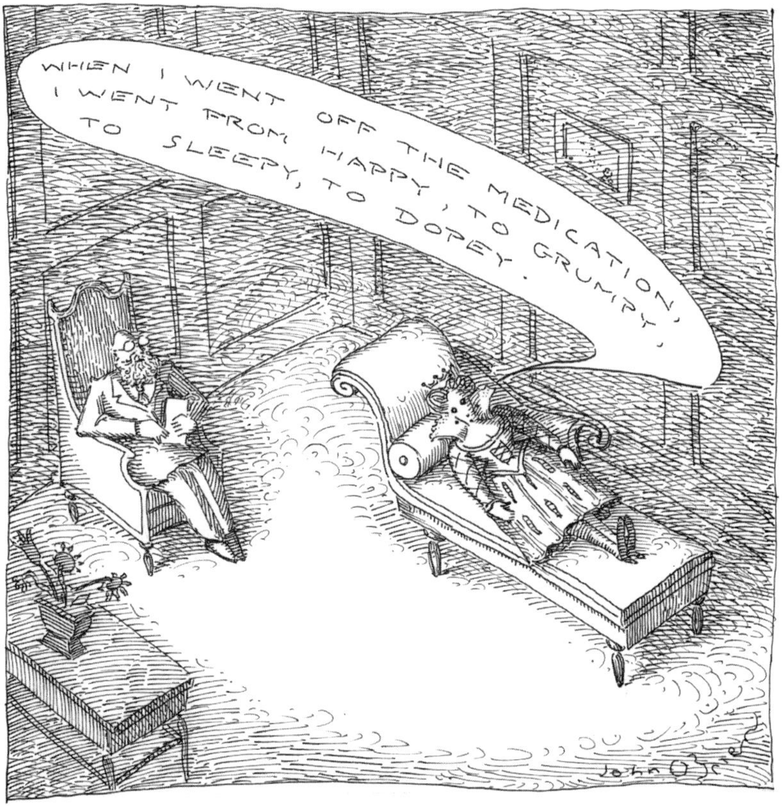
WHEN I WENT OFF THE MEDICATION, I WENT FROM HAPPY, TO GRUMPY, TO SLEEPY, TO DOPEY.
John O'Brien

Kanin

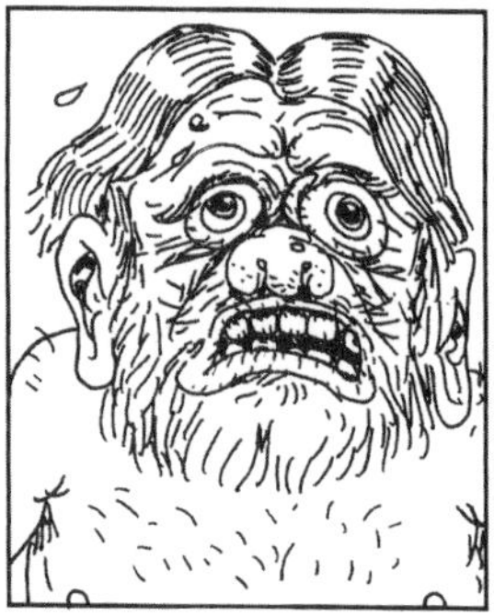

Zachary Kanin

Frequently Asked Questions

- *Where do you get your ideas?*
  A friend of a friend.

- *Which comes first, the picture or the caption?*
  He gives them to me in code, sometimes with no pictures.

- *How'd you get started?*
  Technical high school for cartooning.

- *I admire . . .*
  Charles Burns, Little Walter, Alice Neel, Chris Onstad, Max Beckmann, Aretha Franklin, my parents, Batman.

- *How do you deal with rejection?*
  The same as anyone else—I dust off my pants, pat down my hair, get back up on that horse, and tell it we're gonna be married whether he likes it or not, and there's not a damned army in the world that can keep us apart.

- *What are some things that make you laugh and why?*
  Worms. They have no shame!

- *I've got a great idea for a cartoon—wanna hear it?*
  Is it in code?

Infrequently Asked Questions

- *Have you mooned or been mooned more often in your life?*
  Is it mooning if you never wear pants?

- *What would make a terrible pizza topping?*
  Anything except cheese or tomato.

- *What might one expect to find at a really low-budget amusement park?*
  A ride where a guy pushes old people out of wheelchairs into mud.

- *What did the shepherd say to the three-legged sheepdog?*
  Follow your dreams.

And Now for a Few More Questions . . .

- ~~*What*~~ why *do you hate drawing?*
  I don't. Look.

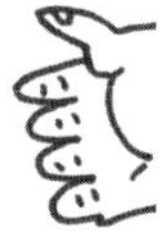

■ *Being as accurate as possible, how many desert island cartoons do you think you've come up with and submitted to* The New Yorker?
5,000.

Nobel Prize Committee?

■ *What's the funniest thing that you witnessed, overheard, or came up with that you couldn't figure out how to use in a cartoon?*
There is a YouTube clip of Frasier falling off a stage that I'm really in love with.

Draw Some Sort of Doodle

. . . using the random lines below as a starting point.

Naming Names

■ *What name might you give to a mild-mannered, middle-aged, bespectacled dental assistant in one of your cartoons?*
Robert Throngman.

■ *Other than Lance, what name would you give to a twenty-eight-year-old entertainment lawyer with a blue-dyed fauxhawk who cycles on weekends?*
Elliot Crogan-Josh.

■ *What would be a good name for a new, commercially unviable breakfast cereal?*
Assholes.

■ *Come up with a name for an unpleasant medical procedure.*
"Feeling-up"-expulsion.

■ *If you used a pen name, what would it be?*
Wart Manhog.

Complete The Pie Chart Below

. . . in a way that tells us something about your life or how you think.

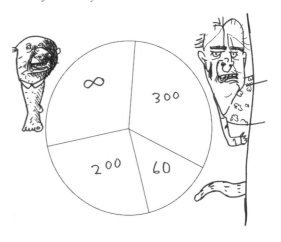

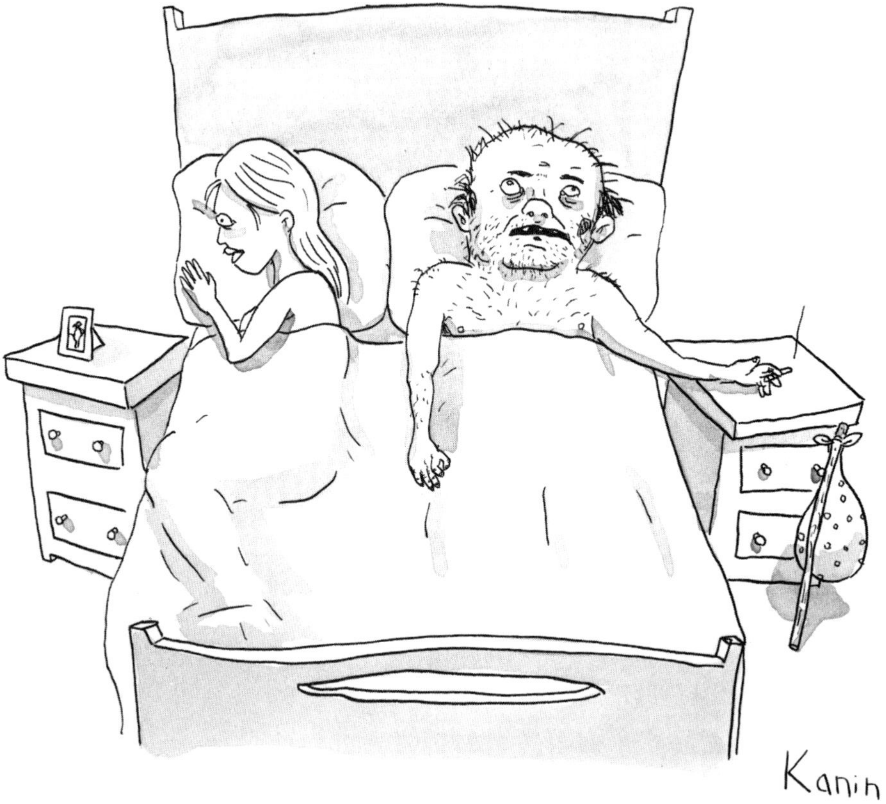
Kanin

"I really would've just settled for some spare change."

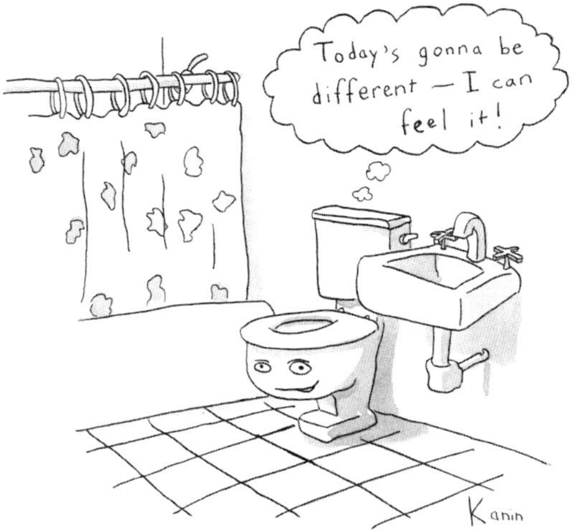
Today's gonna be different — I can feel it!
Kanin

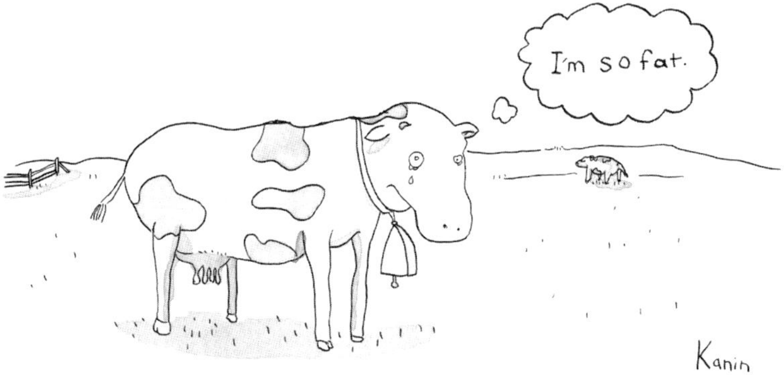
I'm so fat.
Kanin

SAD COW DISEASE

e. flake

Emily Flake

Frequently Asked Questions

- *Where do you get your ideas?*
  What? Wait, why are you asking? Stay the hell away from my secret idea-finding spot!

- *Which comes first, the picture or the caption?*
  Oh, God, the caption. And then, with much anguish and foot-dragging, the picture. Actually, there's anguish and foot-dragging with both, but still, caption first.

- *How'd you get started?*
  I lured Bob Mankoff to a dank basement and put him in front of the hot lights 'til he agreed to buy a cartoon. Kidding, kidding, first I did a strip in some alt-weeklies. Then the basement thing.

- *I admire . . .*
  Are we talking other cartoonists, or personal qualities? If the former, Will McPhail, Ed Steed, and Joe Dator fill me with the blackest most bilious envy. Roz Chast and Lynda Barry are my queens. If I could draw like anyone, it would be Eleanor Davis or Edel Rodriguez or Graham Roumieu. Personal qualities: honesty, hard work, decency, and the ability to admire others' work without falling into a pit of self-lacerating despair.

- *How do you deal with rejection?*
  Eat that shit for *breakfast.*

- *What are some things that make you laugh and why?*
  My favorite are the laughs that live in between sorrow, shame, and absurdity, because I am a terrible person.

- *I've got a great idea for a cartoon—wanna hear it?*
  I TOLD you get AWAY from my secret idea hoard!

Infrequently Asked Questions

- *Have you mooned or been mooned more often in your life?*
  Sir, there is a *lady* present.

- *What would make a terrible pizza topping?*
  Old flip-phones, don't ask me how I know.

- *What might one expect to find at a really low-budget amusement park?*
  My fuckin' REAL dad, last I heard.

- *What did the shepherd say to the three-legged sheepdog?*
  What workers' comp???

Draw Some Sort of Doodle

. . . using the random lines below as a starting point.

HEY BABY
YOU WANNA
NO NO
PLEASE I DO NOT

And Now for a Few More Questions . . .

- *What do you hate drawing?*
  Cars and buildings, just the worst. (I read this as "why do you hate drawing" at first and wondered if my therapist wrote this.)

- *Being as accurate as possible, how many desert island cartoons do you think you've come up with and submitted to* The New Yorker*?*
  Honestly, like twenty?? And one of them I actually love and they KEEP NOT BUYING IT.

- *What's the funniest thing that you witnessed, overheard, or came up with that you couldn't figure out how to use in a cartoon?*
  A little girl on the subway who snarled "I'm not fuckin' five, I'm fuckin' *seven*."

Naming Names

- *What name might you give to a mild-mannered, middle-aged, bespectacled dental assistant in one of your cartoons?*
  Gary, and that's the only right answer.

- *Other than Lance, what name would you give to a twenty-eight-year-old entertainment lawyer with a blue-dyed fauxhawk who cycles on weekends?*
  Colton, ugh, I hate that guy.

- *What would be a good name for a new, commercially unviable breakfast cereal?*
  Flerbs (also available in strawberry!).

- *Come up with a name for an unpleasant medical procedure.*
  Also Gary. (Failing that, "clitoral debridement") (Oh, God, I'm very sorry.)

- *If you used a pen name, what would it be?*
  Winsor Ann Newton (I'll be here all night, folks!).

Complete the Pie Chart Below

. . . in a way that tells us something about your life or how you think.

HELP

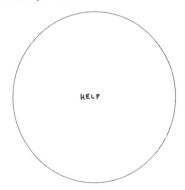

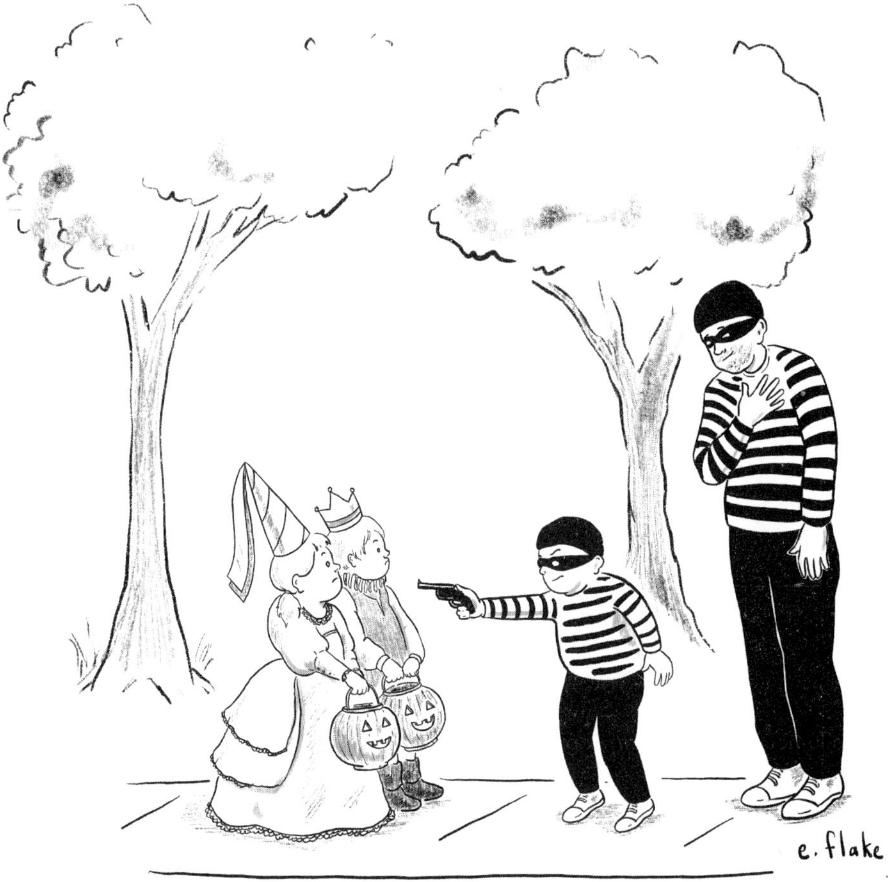
e. flake

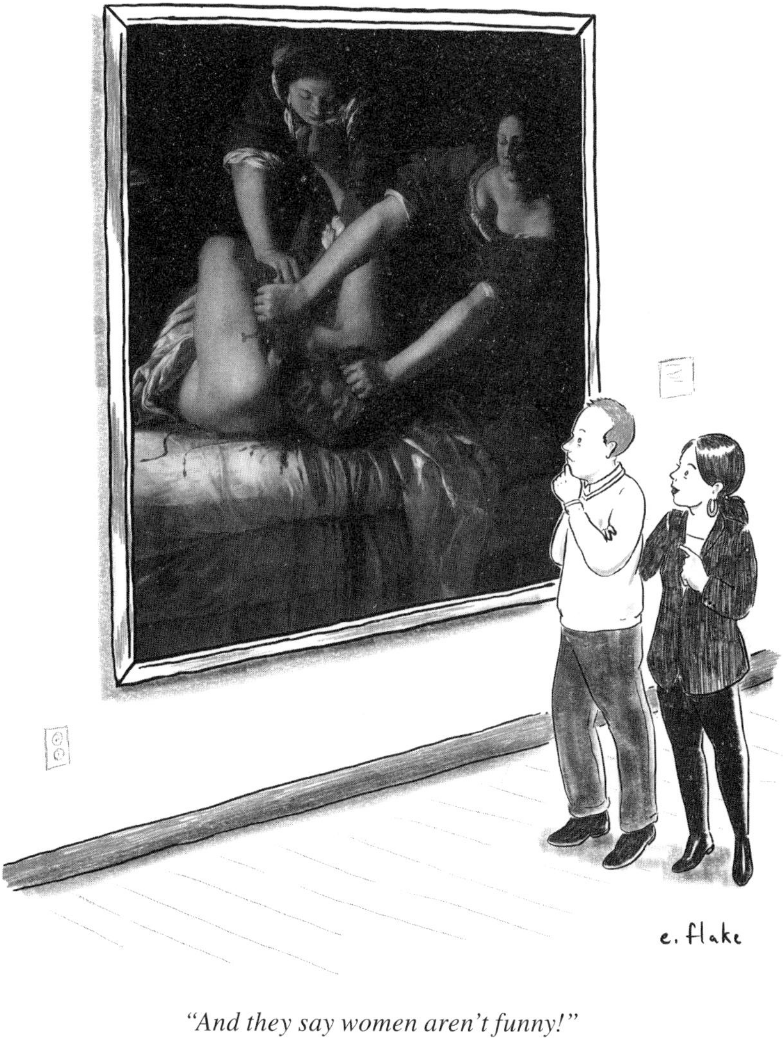
e. flake

"And they say women aren't funny!"

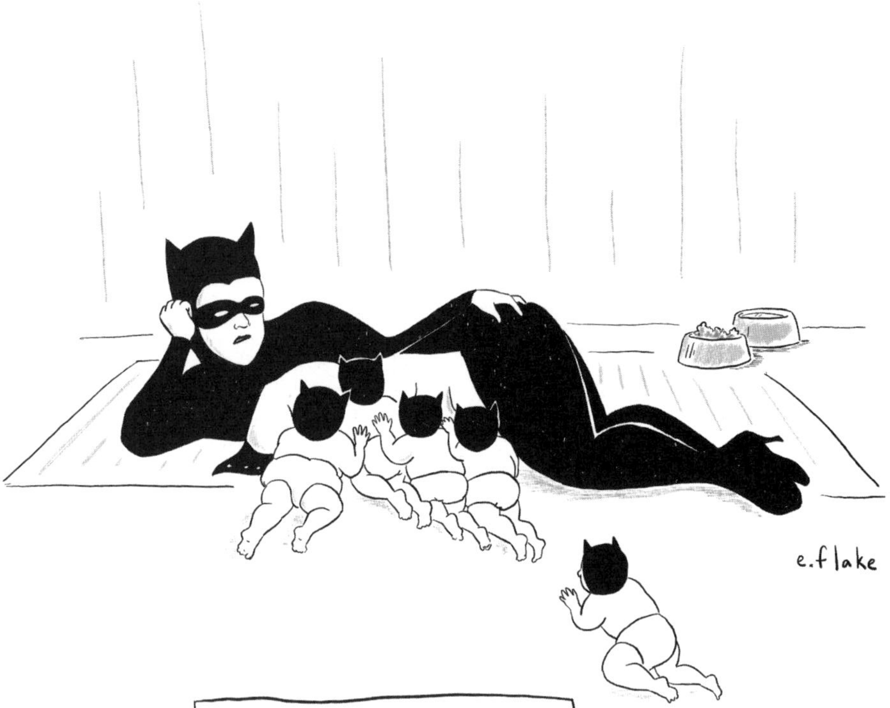
e.flake

CATWOMAN AT HOME

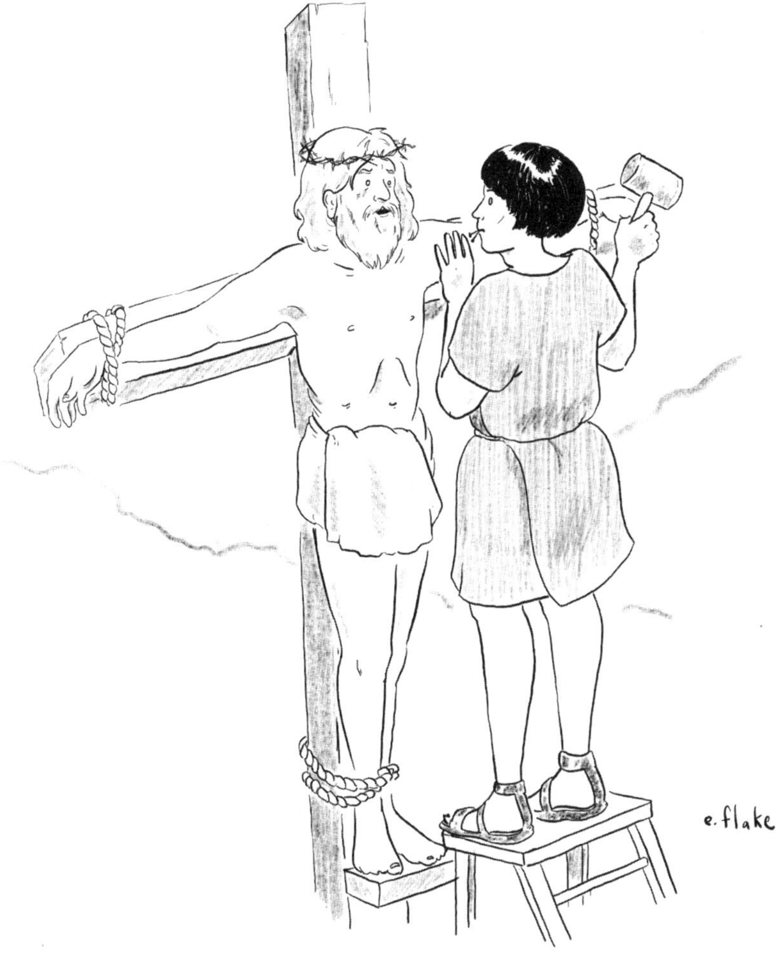
e. flake

"As a carpenter, I think you're gonna want galvanized."

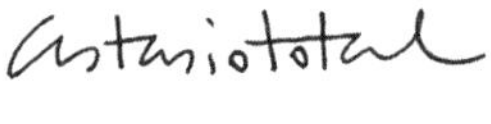

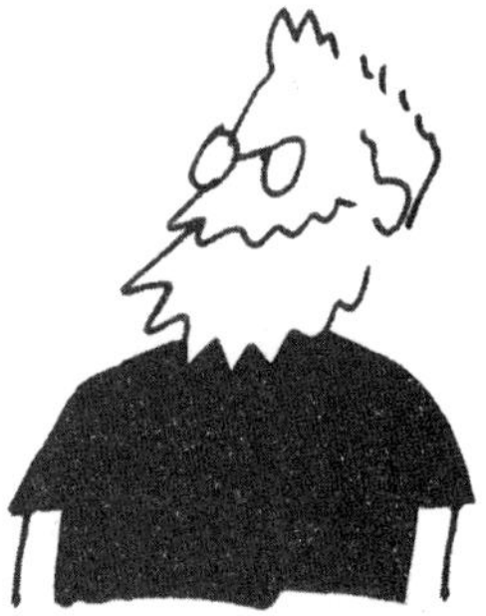

Juan Astasio Soriano

Frequently Asked Questions

- *Where do you get your ideas?*
  A ouija board.

- *Which comes first, the picture or the caption?*
  You get the thing letter by letter. It gets a bit tedious sometimes, but I would advise against complaining.

- *How'd you get started?*
  I'll place my fingers on the planchette and say "If there is someone with us today, please say something funny."

- *I admire . . .*
  My cats.

- *How do you deal with rejection?*
  I pet my cats.

- *What are some things that make you laugh and why?*
  Anything serious. If you can't laugh at something it's probably because you are not taking it seriously enough.

- *I've got a great idea for a cartoon—wanna hear it?*
  Yes! Tell it to my cats.

Infrequently Asked Questions

- *Have you mooned or been mooned more often in your life?*
  I think the latter.

- *What would make a terrible pizza topping?*
  Fingernails.

- *What might one expect to find at a really low-budget amusement park?*
  A significant number of severed limbs.

- *What did the shepherd say to the three-legged sheepdog?*
  That wouldn't have happened if you were a cat.

Draw Something in This Space

. . . that will help us understand your childhood.

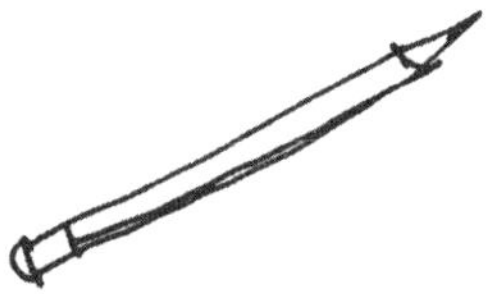

Draw Some Sort of Doodle

. . . using the random lines below as a starting point.

And Now for a Few More Questions . . .

- *What do you hate drawing?*
  I have a hard time with noses, front view.

- *Being as accurate as possible, how many desert island cartoons do you think you've come up with and submitted to* The New Yorker?
  Just four.

- *What's the funniest thing that you witnessed, overheard, or came up with that you couldn't figure out how to use in a cartoon?*
  In my opinion, funny things don't make good cartoons. The best ones come from turning something unfunny into hilarious.

Naming Names

- *What name might you give to a mild-mannered, middle-aged, bespectacled dental assistant in one of your cartoons?*
  Gwendolyn.

- *Other than Lance, what name would you give to a twenty-eight-year-old entertainment lawyer with a blue-dyed fauxhawk who cycles on weekends?*
  Chad.

- *What would be a good name for a new, commercially unviable breakfast cereal?*
  Turdios.

- *Come up with a name for an unpleasant medical procedure.*
  Triple Anal Giulianisectomy.

- *If you used a pen name, what would it be?*
  Castell, Faber Castell.

Complete the Pie Chart Below

. . . in a way that tells us something about your life or how you think.

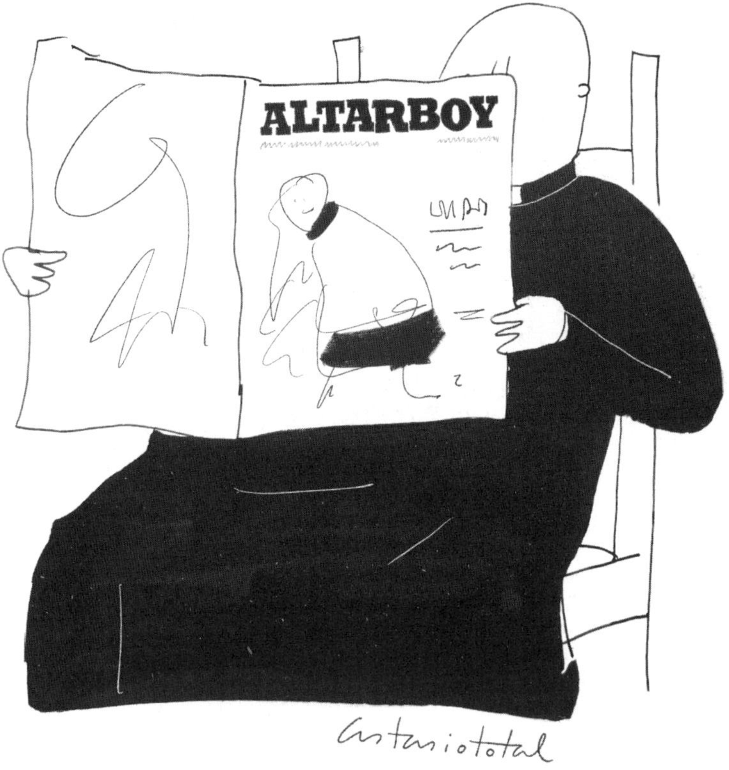
ALTARBOY
Castaniototal

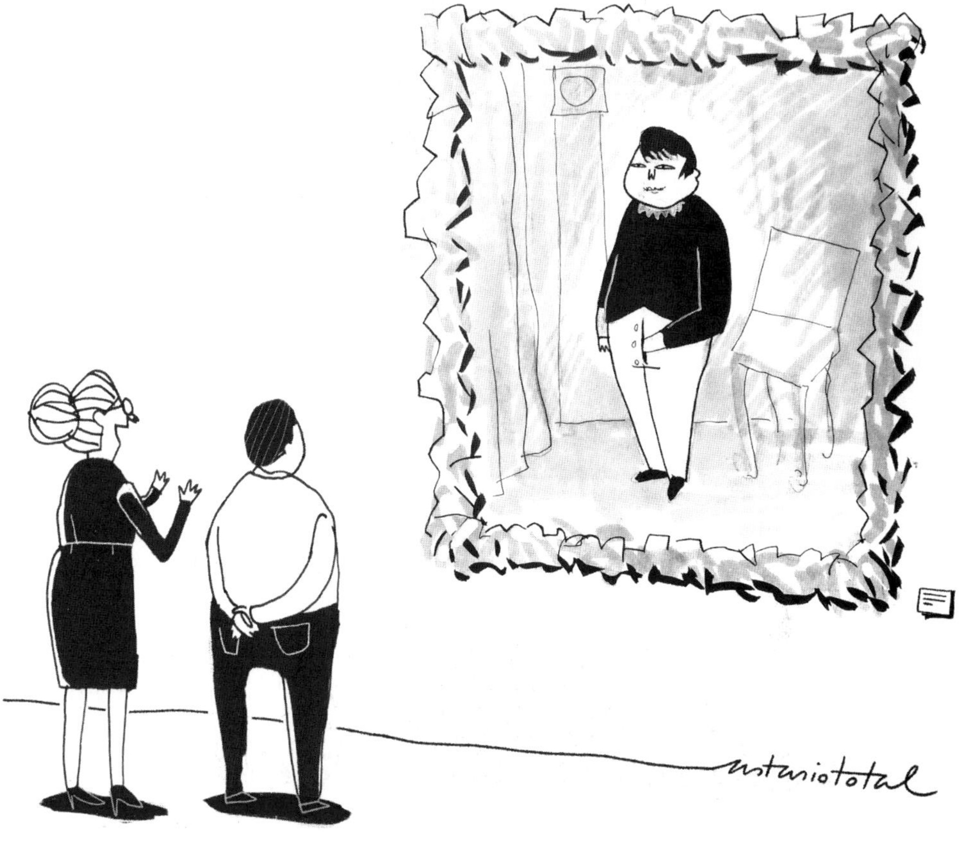
astasiototal

"My personal favorite, 'Teenaged Napoleon.'"

THE NEW GOLDEN AGE OF SPACE EXPLORATION
BEZOS'S BLUE ORIGIN
BRANSON'S SILVER MAGNUM
MUSK'S WHITE MEGADONG
Antoniototal

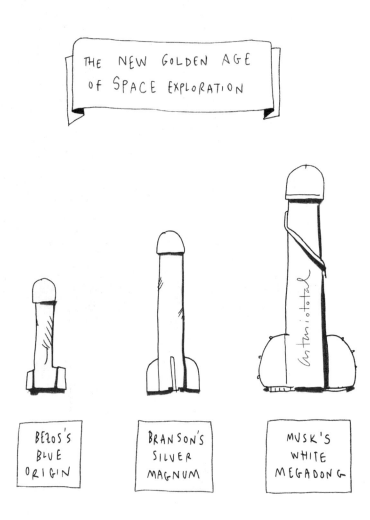

"God bless YouTube."

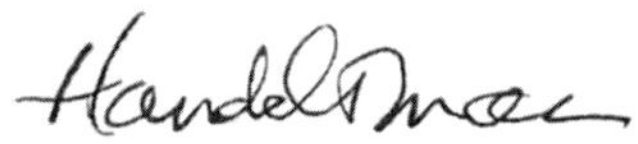

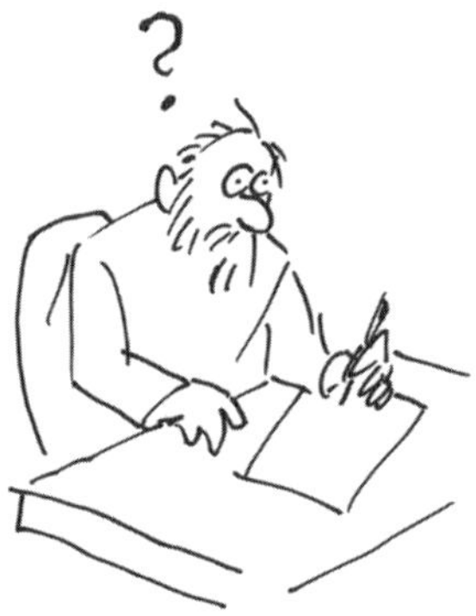

J. B. Handelsman

Frequently Asked Questions

- *Where do you get your ideas?*
  I steal them, accidentally, of course.

- *Which comes first, the picture or the caption?*
  The idea comes all at once.

- *How'd you get started?*
  Like Abou Ben Adhem, I awoke from a deep dream of peace.

- *On a scale of 1 to 10 (1 being not very much at all and 10 being quite a bit), how much do you enjoy bowling?*
  4.

- *How often do you curse?*
  10.

- *How close have you ever come to getting a tattoo?*
  1.

- *I've got a great idea for a cartoon—wanna hear it?*
  Please spare me.

Infrequently Asked Questions

- *Have you mooned or been mooned more often in your life?*
  Question not understood.

- *What would make a terrible pizza topping?*
  Editors' brains, if any.

- *What might one expect to find at a really low-budget amusement park?*
  Nothing.

- *What did the shepherd say to the three-legged sheepdog?*
  You have my profoundest sympathy.

And Now for a Few More Questions . . .

- *What do you hate drawing?*
  I don't hate drawing anything.

- *Being as accurate as possible, how many desert island cartoons do you think you've come up with and submitted to* The New Yorker*?*
  Four.

- *What's the funniest thing that you witnessed, overheard, or came up with that you couldn't figure out how to use in a cartoon?*
  Can't remember.

Draw Some Sort of Doodle

. . . using the random lines below as a starting point.

THESE ARE SPERM CELLS AND I WOULDN'T DARE INTERFERE WITH THEM.

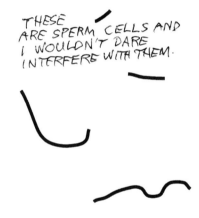

Naming Names

- *What name might you give to a mild-mannered, middle-aged, bespectacled dental assistant in one of your cartoons?*
  Handelsman.

- *Other than Lance, what name would you give to a twenty-eight-year-old entertainment lawyer with a blue-dyed fauxhawk who cycles on weekends?*
  James.

- *What would be a good name for a commercially unviable cereal?*
  Stupid flakes.

- *Come up with a name for an unpleasant medical procedure.*
  Brain removal, followed by appointment as editor.

- *If you used a pen name, what would it be?*
  Jughead.

Complete the Pie Chart Below

. . . in a way that tells us something about your life or how you think.

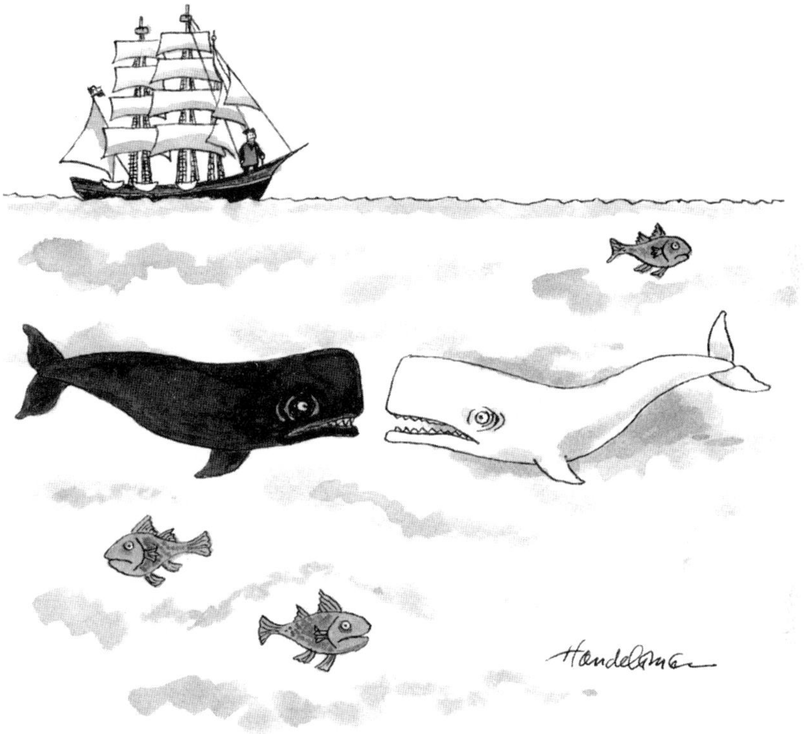
Handelsman

"The name's Moby Richard. Who's he callin' Dick?"

Michael Crawford

Frequently Asked Questions

- *Where do you get your ideas?*
  My best friend's girl.

- *Which comes first, the picture or the caption?*
  You Americans!

- *How'd you get started?*
  In the spring, the larvae hatch and the cycle begins again.

- *I admire . . .*
  People who mind their own beeswax.

- *How do you deal with rejection?*
  I just keep pinching myself!

- *What are some things that make you laugh and why?*
  Taken a walk down 8th Avenue lately?

- *I've got a great idea for a cartoon—wanna hear it?*
  Maybe we can touch base in hell.

Infrequently Asked Questions

- *Have you mooned or been mooned more often in your life?*
  You late-rising professionals!

- *My first cartoon . . .*
  Sold for fitty bucks.

- *What might one expect to find at a really low-budget amusement park?*
  Rabid Beaver Petting Zoo.

- *What did the shepherd say to the three-legged sheepdog?*
  You want my number?

And Now for a Few More Questions . . .

- *What do you hate drawing?*
  My best friend's girl.

- *Being as accurate as possible, how many desert island cartoons do you think you've come up with and submitted to* The New Yorker?
  Three. Zero.

- *What's the funniest thing that you witnessed, overheard, or came up with that you couldn't figure out how to use in a cartoon?*
Jesus in the "Twelve Apostles or Less" line at Fairway.

Draw Something in This Space

. . . that will help us understand your childhood.

Naming Names

- *What name might you give to a mild-mannered, middle-aged, bespectacled dental assistant in one of your cartoons?*
Nursey Nurse.

- *Other than Lance, what name would you give to a twenty-eight-year-old entertainment lawyer with a blue-dyed fauxhawk who cycles on weekends?*
Whoa! You've got a lot of anger.

- *What would be a good name for a new, commercially unviable breakfast cereal?*
Barf Loops.

- *Come up with a name for an unpleasant medical procedure.*
A peckerectomy.

- *If you used a pen name, what would it be?*
Uniball Gel Impact.

Complete the Pie Chart Below

. . . in a way that tells us something about your life or how you think.

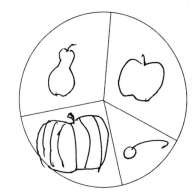

"Going to be long over there, Mr. Happy? I need to get my casserole in."

"Give me a hint. I'm sleeping with a lot of lobbyists."

"Wanna swap?"

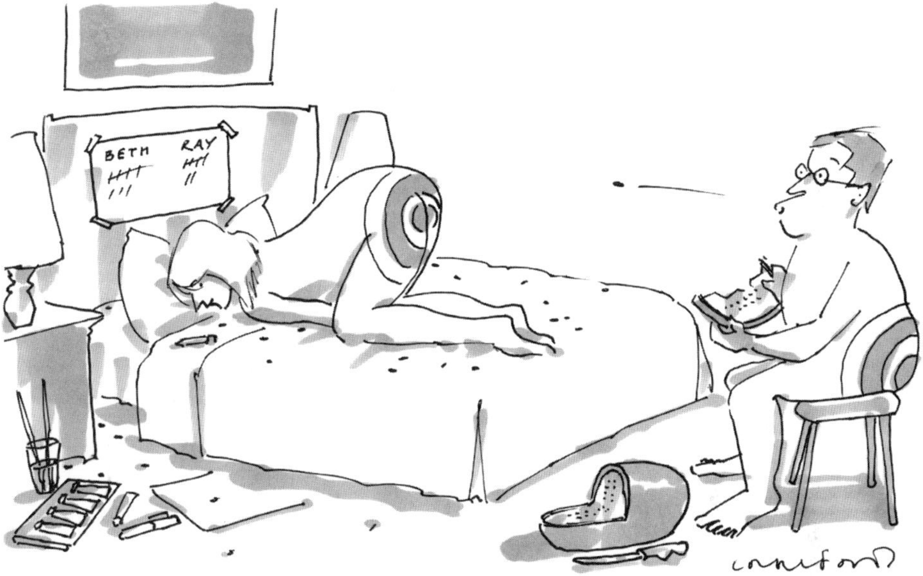
BETH
RAY

LET THE SUMMER GAMES BEGIN!

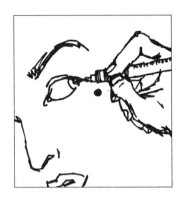

MARISA
ACOCELLA
MARCHETTO

Marisa Acocella Marchetto

Frequently Asked Questions

- *Where do you get your ideas?*
  If I knew, I'd have more. Just kidding. From life.

- *Which comes first, the picture or the caption?*
  The egg.

- *How'd you get started?*
  See above.

- *I admire . . .*
  Anyone who makes me laugh.

- *How do you deal with rejection?*
  Rejection is crack.

- *What are some things that make you laugh and why?*
  Trauma and embarassment make me laugh—because after you get over the initial feeling of mortification, it's always the best material.

- *I've got a great idea for a cartoon—wanna hear it?*
  Please, then you'll ask me to draw it. Nope. No way.

Infrequently Asked Questions

- *Have you mooned or been mooned more often in your life?*
  I prefer the sun.

- *What would make a terrible pizza topping?*
  A top hat.

- *What might one expect to find at a really low-budget amusement park?*
  No one having any fun.

- *What did the shepherd say to the three-legged sheepdog?*
  "Herd any good jokes?"
  I can't believe I wrote that.

Draw Something in This Space

. . . that will help us understand your childhood.

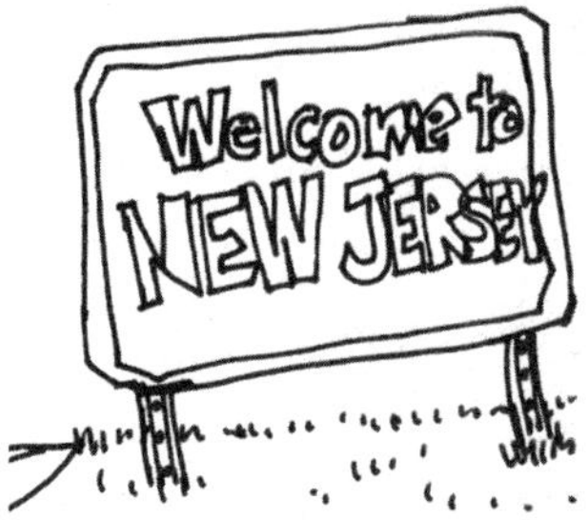
Welcome to
NEW JERSEY

And Now for a Few More Questions . . .

- *What do you hate drawing?*
  Babies.

- *Being as accurate as possible, how many desert island cartoons do you think you've come up with and submitted to* The New Yorker*?*
  Actually, none.

- *What's the funniest thing that you witnessed, overheard, or came up with that you couldn't figure out how to use in a cartoon?*
  If I told you, then I'd be giving you material.

Naming Names

- *What name might you give to a mild-mannered, middle-aged, bespectacled dental assistant in one of your cartoons?*
  Esther.

- *Other than Lance, what name would you give to a twenty-eight-year-old entertainment lawyer with a blue-dyed fauxhawk who cycles on weekends?*
  Jonathan.

- *What would be a good name for a new, commercially unviable breakfast cereal?*
  Cereal Killer.

- *Come up with a name for an unpleasant medical procedure.*
  What medical procedure is pleasant?

- *If you used a pen name, what would it be?*
  Rapidograph.

Complete the Pie Chart Below

. . . in a way that tells us something about your life or how you think.

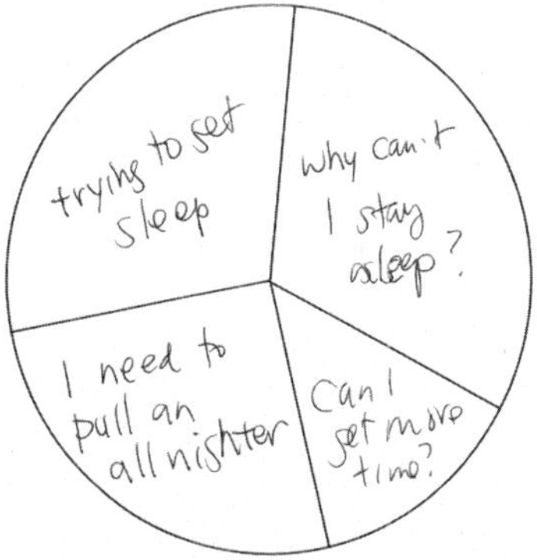
trying to get sleep
why can't I stay asleep?
I need to pull an all nighter
Can I get more time?

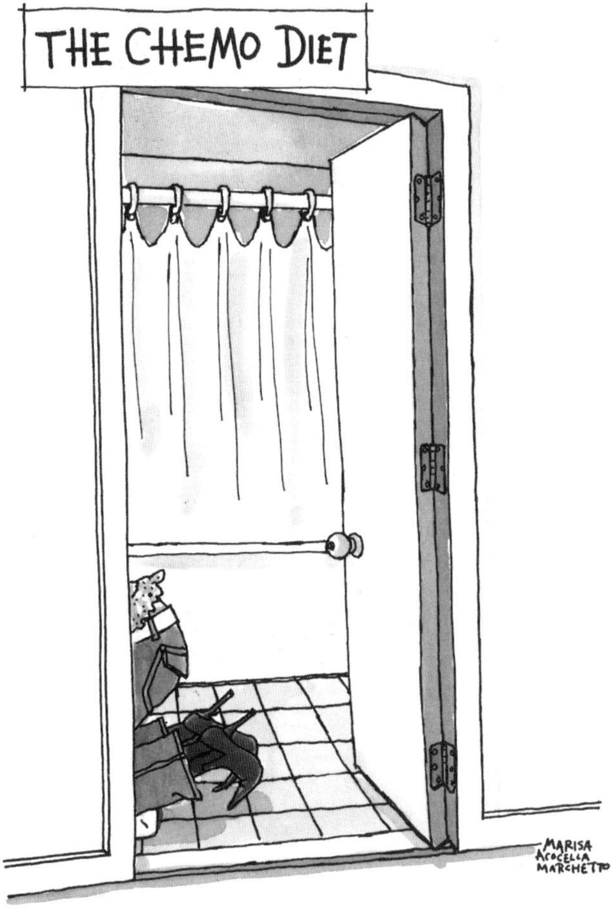
THE CHEMO DIET
MARISA ACOCELLA MARCHETTO

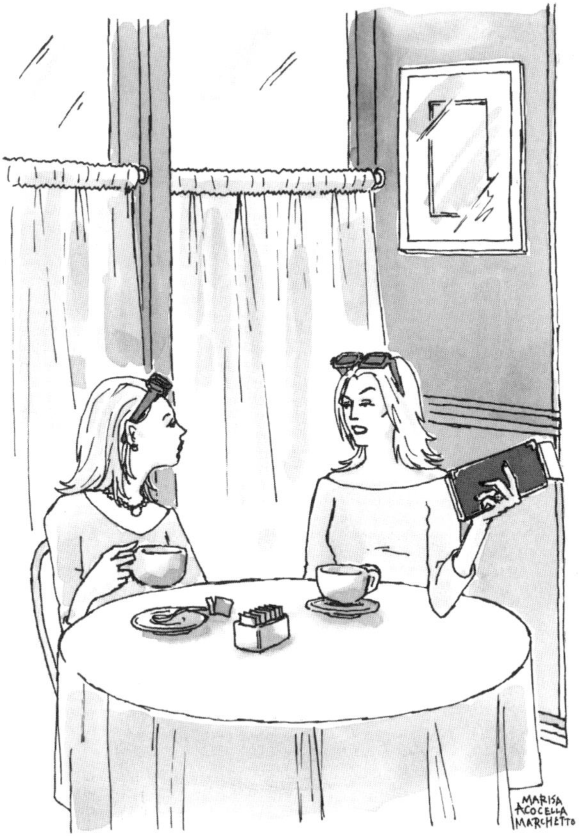
MARISA
ACOCELLA
MARCHETTO

"Your husband got the last one. This one's on mine."

JESUS CHRISTO
INRI
MARISA ACOCELLA MARCHETTO

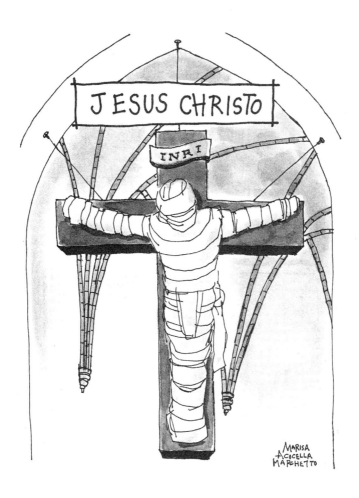

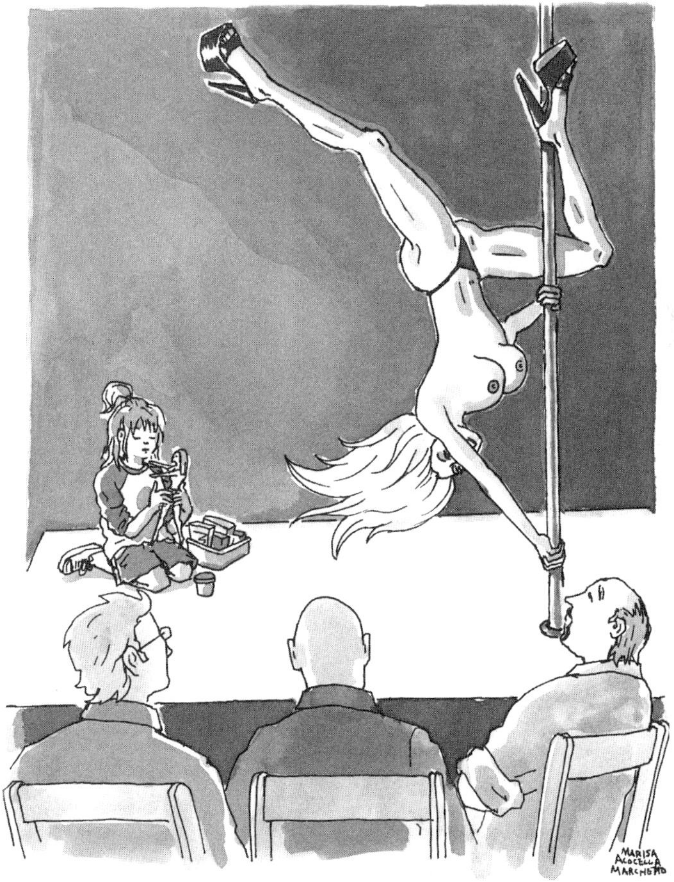
MARISA ACOCELLA MARCHETTO

"It's 'Take Your Daughter to Work Day.'"

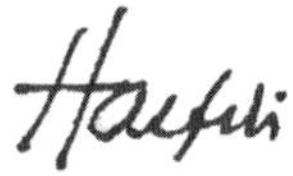

William Haefeli

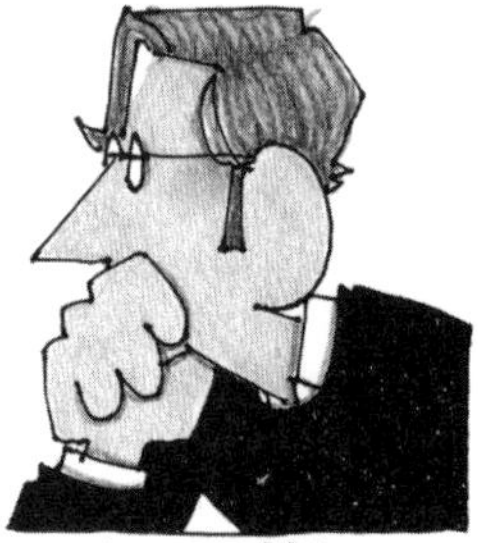

circa 1990
(Based on self-portrait that ran in Punch)

Frequently Asked Questions

- *Where do you get your ideas?*
  Rummaging around in my brain.

- *Which comes first, the picture or the caption?*
  Caption.

- *How'd you get started?*
  With great enthusiasm!

- *I admire . . .*
  The cartoonists Charles Saxon, for the lushness of his drawings and the keenness of his observations, and Gluyas Williams, for how well he captured his times and the precision of his drawing (I can't catch him cheating). For diplomacy, I'm not mentioning living cartoonists.

- *How do you deal with rejection?*
  No cartoon is ever definitively rejected. There's always a chance to resubmit it at a later date or sell it elsewhere. However, some cartoons and their topics have a certain shelf life, and it is always sad when they don't get sold by their "sell-by" date.

- *What are some things that make you laugh and why?*
  TV SHOWS: *NewsRadio*: The funny comes from so many directions: character comedy, verbal humor, slapstick, obscure cultural references. It can be subtle, broad, off-the-wall. The *Mary Tyler Moore Show*: Mary is so nice. *Fawlty Towers*: Basil is so awful.
  MOVIES: Harold Lloyd and his wonderful 1920s American energy. I love when attractive and sophisticated people are nonchalantly goofy. e.g., Cary Grant in most of his comedies; Capucine in the original *Pink Panther* when she hits her head on the bar or falls into the closet.
  BOOKS: I can't say because my taste in humorous writing keeps changing. What I found funny twenty years ago seems tedious now.

- *I've got a great idea for a cartoon—wanna hear it?*
  No.

Infrequently Asked Questions

- *Have you mooned or been mooned more often in your life?*
  Equal.

- *What would make a terrible pizza topping?*
  Shoelaces.

- *What might one expect to find at a really low-budget amusement park?*
  Pizza with shoelaces.

- *What did the shepherd say to the three-legged sheepdog?*
  Here, eat my pizza with shoelaces.

Draw Something in This Space

. . . that will help us understand your childhood.

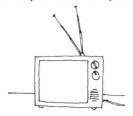

And Now for A Few More Questions . . .

- *What do you hate drawing?*
  Concentric circles.

- *Being as accurate as possible, how many desert island cartoons do you think you've come up with and submitted to* The New Yorker*?*
  Twelve.

- *What's the funniest thing that you witnessed, overheard, or came up with that you couldn't figure out how to use in a cartoon?*
  Don't you mean one that I couldn't figure out how to use in a cartoon *yet*?

Naming Names

- *What name might you give to a mild-mannered, middle-aged, bespectacled dental assistant in one of your cartoons?*
  Flossie. (Wouldn't everyone?)

- *Other than Lance, what name would you give to a twenty-eight-year-old entertainment lawyer with a blue-dyed fauxhawk who cycles on weekends?*
  H.B. (For "handlebar" cuz he cycles, and/or "handle bar" cuz he's a lawyer.)

- *What would be a good name for a new, commercially unviable breakfast cereal?*
  Ugh-ums!

- *Come up with a name for an unpleasant medical procedure.*
  Hatchet job.

Complete the Pie Chart Below

. . . in a way that tells us something about your life or how you think.

60 percent work
20 percent thinking about work
19 percent thinking about work while sleeping
1 percent pretending not to be thinking about work (for the benefit of others)

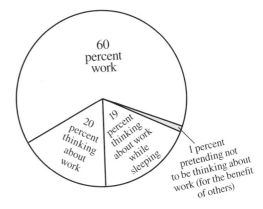

*"Mommy wants you to have everything she had when
she was growing up—starting with divorced parents."*

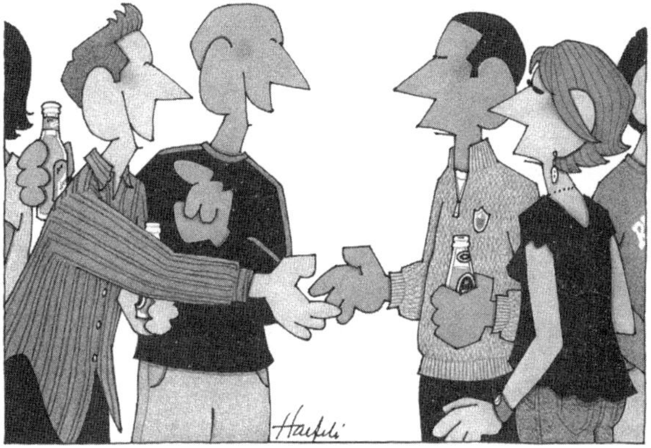
Haefeli

"This is Jerry. His family used to own my family."

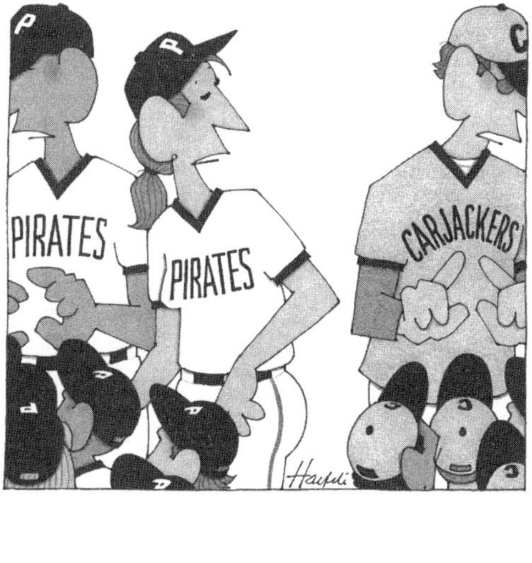
PIRATES
PIRATES
CARJACKERS
Haefeli

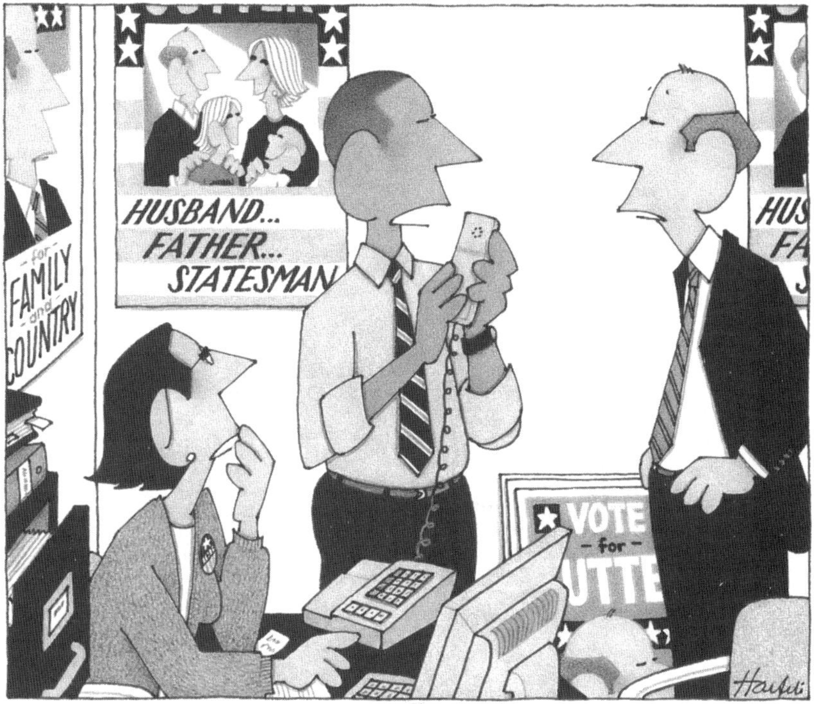
HUSBAND...
FATHER...
STATESMAN
for
FAMILY
and
COUNTRY
VOTE
for

"He claims he has you on video—how can I put this?—'courting the gay vote.'"

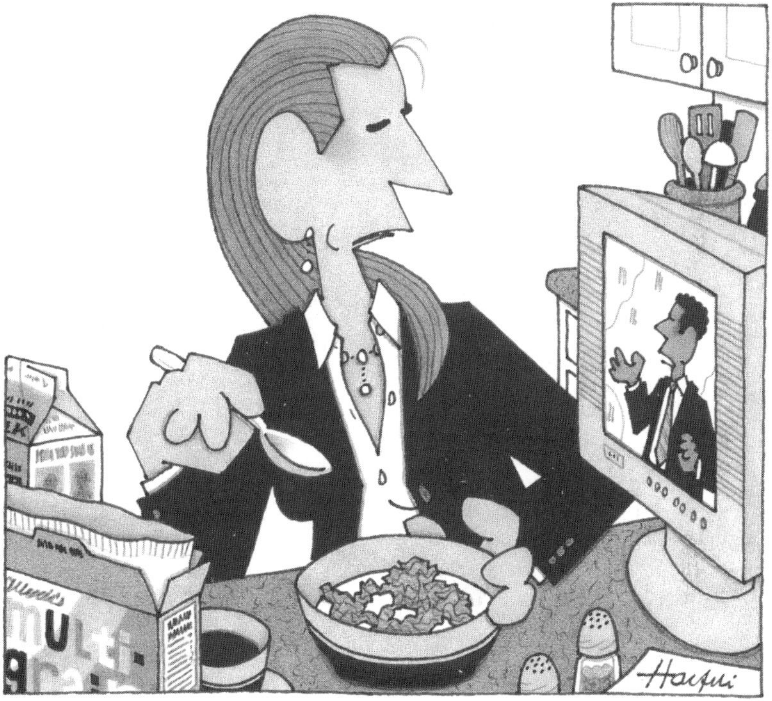
Haefeli

"For those of you headed to the office, today will be 68 degrees and fluorescent."

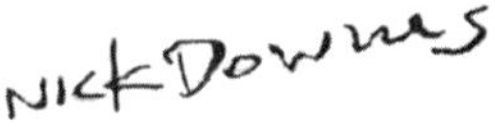
NICK DOWNES

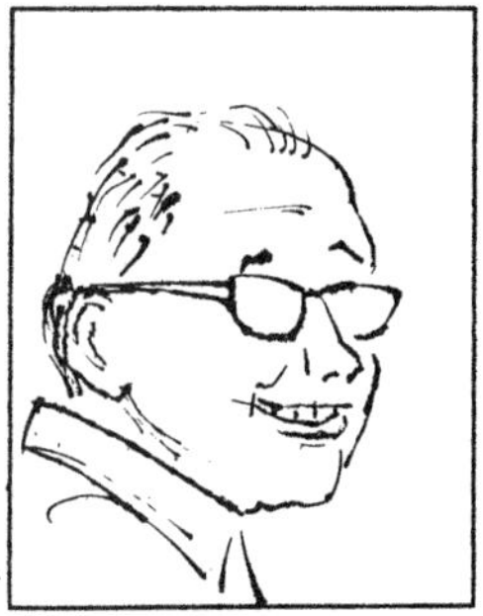

Nick Downes

Frequently Asked Questions

- *Where do you get your ideas?*
  Out of extremely thin (anorexic, really) air.
- *Which comes first, the picture or the caption?*
  The caption—absolutely no staying power.
- *How'd you get started?*
  As a twinkle in my dad's rather myopic eye, I guess.
- *I admire . . .*
  From afar.
- *How do you deal with rejection?*
  Stunned disbelief.
- *What are some things that make you laugh and why?*
  Things that are funny precisely because they aren't supposed to be at all.
- *I've got a great idea for a cartoon—wanna hear it?*
  Save it for when I'm a desperate, dried-up hack. Okay, let's hear it.

Infrequently Asked Questions

- *Have you mooned or been mooned more often in your life?*
  I was slightly mooned, once. Sort of a crescent mooning.
- *What would make a terrible pizza topping?*
  Blood, sweat, and tears.
- *What might one expect to find at a really low-budget amusement park?*
  A Pitch 'n' Putt 'n' Pass Out.
- *What did the shepherd say to the three-legged sheepdog?*
  We'll always have Paris What'sername.

Draw Some Sort of Doodle

. . . using the random lines below as a starting point.

And Now for a Few More Questions . . .

- *What do you hate drawing?*
  Sometimes, yes.

- *Being as accurate as possible, how many desert island cartoons do you think you've come up with and submitted to* The New Yorker?
  104.

- *What's the funniest thing that you witnessed, overheard, or came up with that you couldn't figure out how to use in a cartoon?*
  Tail end of a conversation among a group of men I walked by in Brooklyn, ". . . it was a closed casket—what does that tell me?"

Naming Names

- *What name might you give to a mild-mannered, middle-aged, bespectacled dental assistant in one of your cartoons?*
  Rence 'n' Spitt.

- *Other than Lance, what name would you give to a twenty-eight-year-old entertainment lawyer with a blue-dyed fauxhawk who cycles on weekends?*
  Sue.

- *What would be a good name for a new, commercially unviable breakfast cereal?*
  Luckless Charms.

- *Come up with a name for an unpleasant medical procedure.*
  Tag Team Neurosurgery.

- *If you used a pen name, what would it be?*
  Phineas T. Farquar.

Complete the Pie Chart Below

. . . in a way that tells us something about your life or how you think.

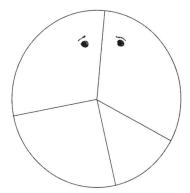

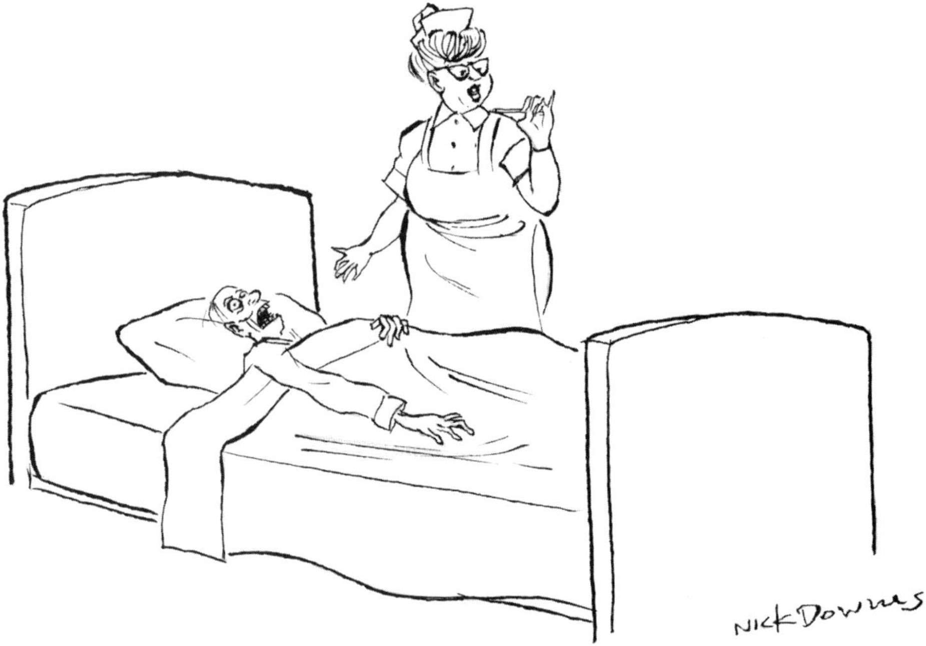
NICK DOWNES

"Oh my, your fever's way down."

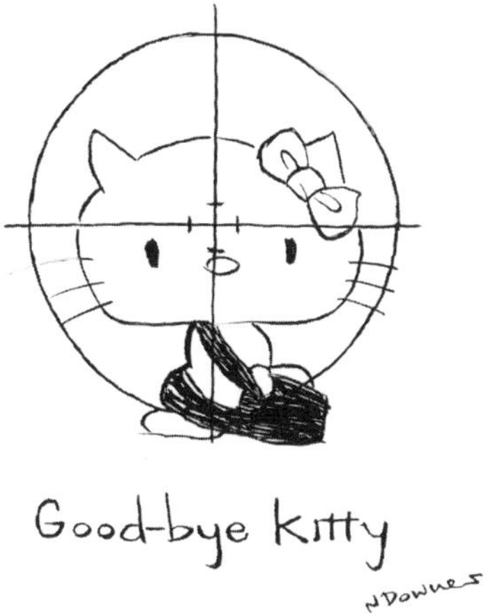
NDOWNES

Good-bye Kitty

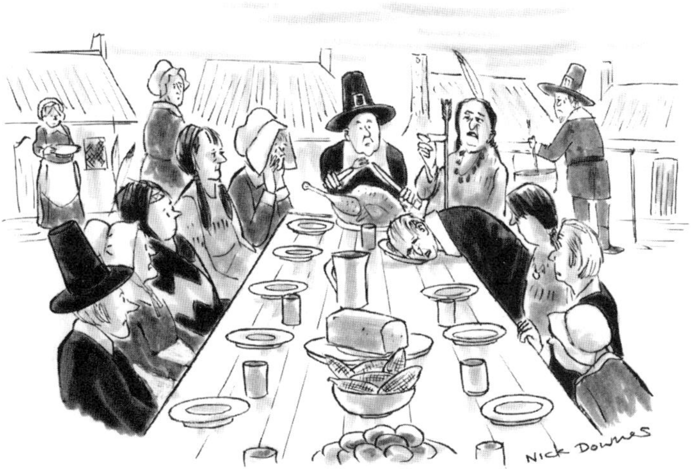
NICK DOWNES

"Running Deer sends his regrets."

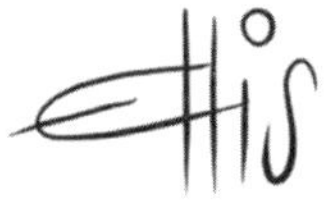

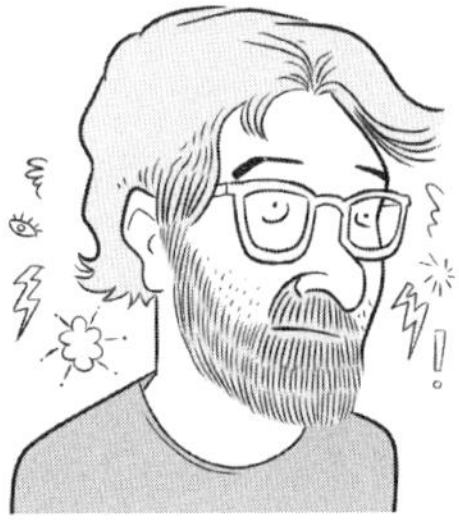

Ellis Rosen

Frequently Asked Questions

- *Where do you get your ideas?*
  I go into the future and steal my own ideas, then go back and draw them. It's technically a paradox, but whatever works, right?

- *Which comes first, the picture or the caption?*
  Depends on the cartoon. For instance, for a cartoon in which I came up with the caption first, I would have started off with the caption first.

- *How'd you get started?*
  The same way as all cartoonists: three years at Stanford studying law, an assigned clerkship with an ethically dubious judge, a brief stint as a defense attorney followed by four years as an oil lobbyist. After that I was Governor for three years, followed by a money laundering scandal, a forced resignation, disbarment, a very public trial, a very public divorce and a ghost-written auto-biography that was critically panned for having "purposefully misleading information." Around that time I started submitting cartoons to *The New Yorker* and the rest is history.

- *How do you deal with rejection?*
  I go into the future and yell at myself for having such bad ideas.

- *What are some things that make you laugh and why?*
  In 2012, a woman named Cecilia Giménez set out to restore a painting of Jesus and botched it up so bad that the painting is now referred to as "Monkey Christ." This is the greatest story in the history of both art and comedy. No one will ever create a better work of art and no one will ever do anything funnier.

- *I've got a great idea for a cartoon—wanna hear it?*
  Not right now! I have to keep this bus going above 50 miles per hour or it will explode!

Infrequently Asked Questions

- *Have you mooned or been mooned more often in your life?*
  We are all being mooned, all the time, by the invisible butt of the marketplace.

- *What would make a terrible pizza topping?*
  The invisible butt of the marketplace.

- *What might one expect to find at a really low-budget amusement park?*
  The cyclone! Like, an actual cyclone! Run!

Draw Something in This Space

. . . that will help us understand your childhood.

BENJAMIN BUTTON STOLE MY LIFE'S STORY!

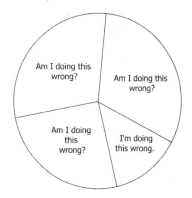

And Now for a Few More Questions . . .

- *What do you hate drawing?*

  Yes.

- *Being as accurate as possible, how many desert island cartoons do you think you've come up with and submitted to* The New Yorker*?*

  Twelve or so . . . hey! This just occurred to me . . . you know what would be a great idea? A whole book of desert island cartoons called *Send Help! A Collection of Marooned Cartoons* that you can buy online or at any bookstore.

- *What's the funniest thing that you witnessed, overheard, or came up with that you couldn't figure out how to use in a cartoon?*

  I've been trying to come up with a joke about how the permanence of death and the concept of eternity scare me so much that I can't go one day without thinking "I am going to die some day and *it will last forever,*" and then I get a mild stomachache and I desperately need to distract myself with some frivolous form of entertainment and then, wait, what were we talking about?

Naming Names

- *What name might you give to a mild-mannered, middle-aged, bespectacled dental assistant in one of your cartoons?*

  Ned, Herb, Lisa, or Claire. Meek characters are Ned, Herb, Lisa, or Claire. Grumpy old characters are Linda, Sharon, Murray, Mitch, or Frank. All other characters are Jim or Sarah.

- *Other than Lance, what name would you give to a twenty-eight-year-old entertainment lawyer with a blue-dyed fauxhawk who cycles on weekends?*

  Jim or Sarah.

- *What would be a good name for a new, commercially unviable breakfast cereal?*

  Cap'n Crunch's Oops! All Gallbladder.

- *Come up with a name for an unpleasant medical procedure.*

  Doctor Crunch's Oops! Gallbladder Removal.

- *If you used a pen name, what would it be?*

  Ellis Rosen but not *that* Ellis Rosen.

Complete the Pie Chart Below

. . . in a way that tells us something about your life or how you think.

Am I doing this wrong?
Am I doing this wrong?
Am I doing this wrong?
I'm doing this wrong.

"Can we talk about the moaning?"

"This changes everything."

"That one looks like a mushroom."

"But my biggest fetish is working too hard."

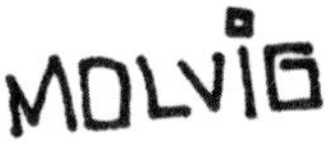

MOLVIG

Ariel Molvig

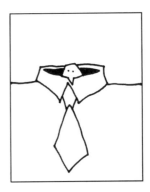

Frequently Asked Questions

- *Where do you get your ideas?*
  It's unsightly, but the doctors think stem cells may help.

- *Which comes first, the picture or the caption?*

THE CAPTION GOES DOWN WITH THE

- *How'd you get started?*

$$\frac{CLEVER\ LITTLE\ HANDS + SOCIAL\ PARIAH}{CARTOONIST}$$

- *I admire . . .*
  Clear vision in dark times.

- *How do you deal with rejection?*
  A pillow is a great way to hide a rejection.

- *What are some things that make you laugh and why?*
  A kick to someone else's gonads. Laughter is an instinctual reflex of relief that one's own

gonads are unscathed. Anything funny is a metaphorical gonad assault.

- *I've got a great idea for a cartoon—wanna hear it?*
  No. Stop showing off.

Infrequently Asked Questions

- *Have you mooned or been mooned more often in your life?*
  I've practiced A LOT in the mirror, but I figure that's a wash.

- *What would make a terrible pizza topping?*
  Another Bush presidency.

- *What might one expect to find at a really low-budget amusement park?*
  "F Train: The Ride."

- *What did the shepherd say to the three-legged sheepdog?*
  Thanks for dinner. That was delish.

Draw Some Sort of Doodle

... *using the random lines below as a starting point.*

And Now for a Few More Questions . . .

- *What do you hate drawing?*
  Speaking as a cartoonist—horses. Speaking as a horse—carriages.

- *Being as accurate as possible, how many desert island cartoons do you think you've come up with and submitted to* The New Yorker?
  2 lbs. 7.5 oz.

- *What's the funniest thing that you witnessed, overheard, or came up with that you couldn't figure out how to use in a cartoon?*
  That's a hard one, humor is so subtle and subjective . . . probably King Kong coating Manhattan with huge monkey feces.

- *Most cartoonists I know are . . .*
  Rarely invited to play Pictionary.

Naming Names

- *Other than Lance, what name would you give to a twenty-eight-year-old entertainment lawyer with a blue-dyed fauxhawk who cycles on weekends?*
  Houston, Austin, but not Corpus Christi.

- *Come up with a name for an unpleasant medical procedure.*
  Eugenbertholdfriedrichbrechtomy.

- *If you used a pen name, what would it be?*
  Bic.

Complete the Pie Chart Below

... *in a way that tells us something about your life or how you think.*

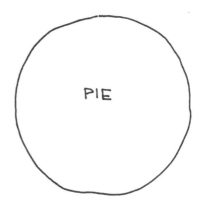

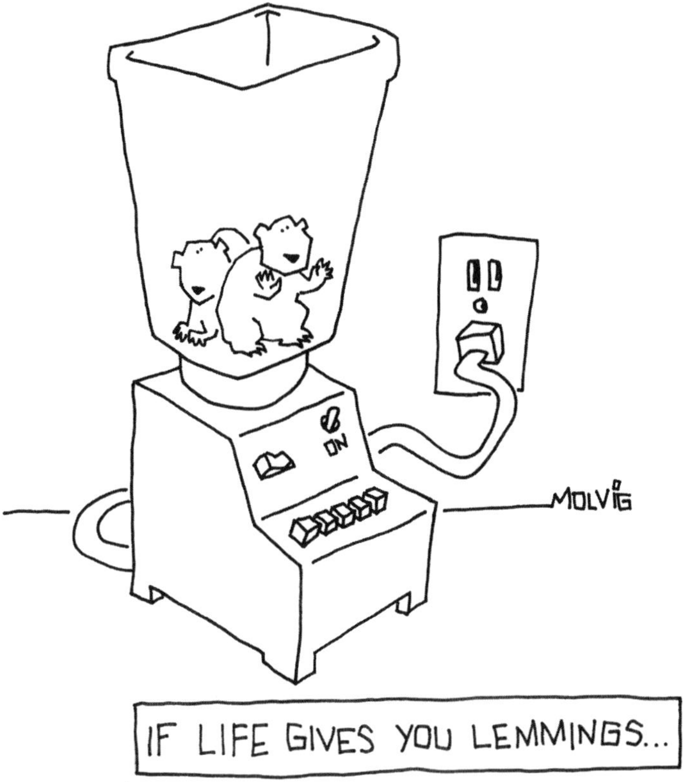
ON
MOLVIG
IF LIFE GIVES YOU LEMMINGS...

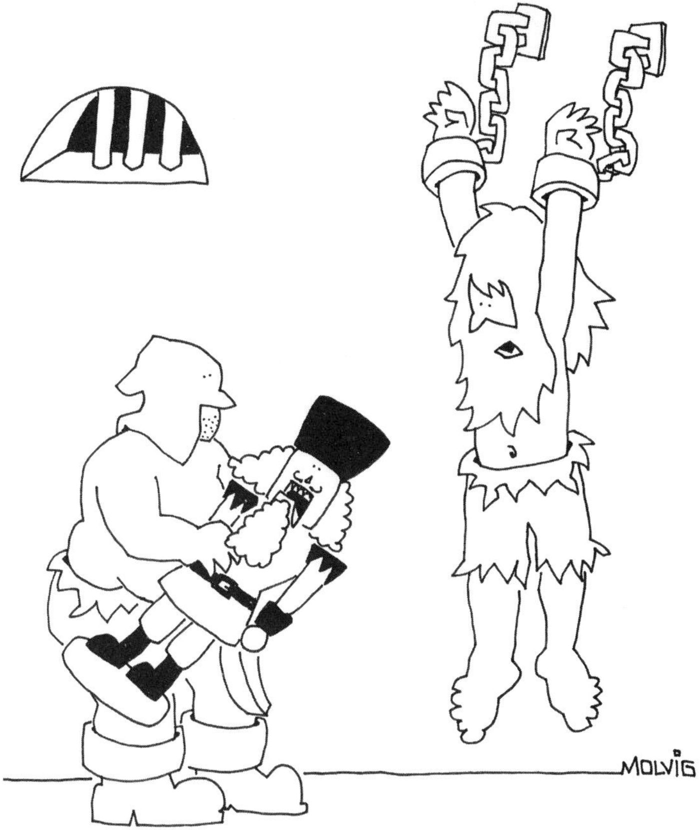
MOLVIG

"I'll talk."

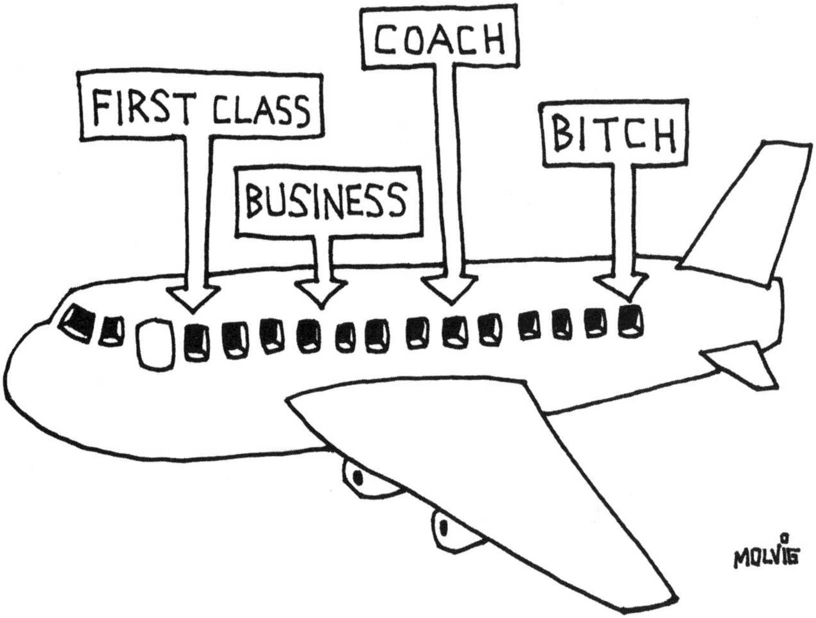
COACH
FIRST CLASS
BITCH
BUSINESS
MOLVIG

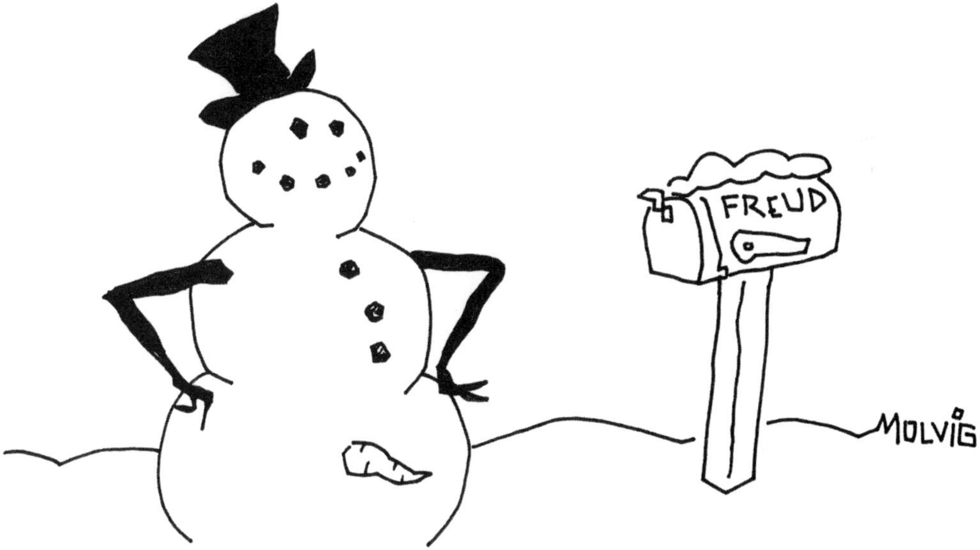
FREUD
MOLVIG

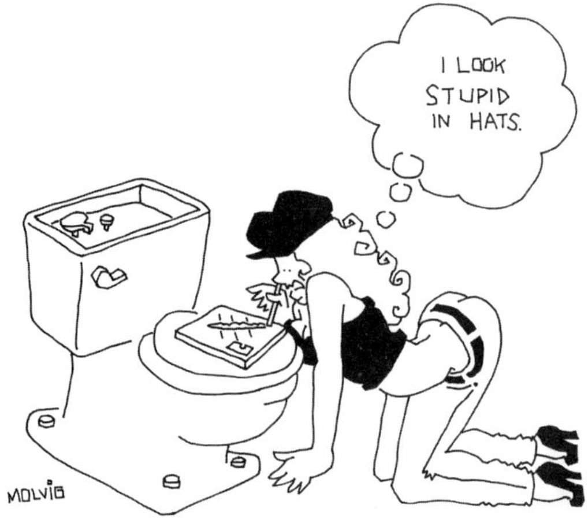
I LOOK STUPID IN HATS.
MOLVIG

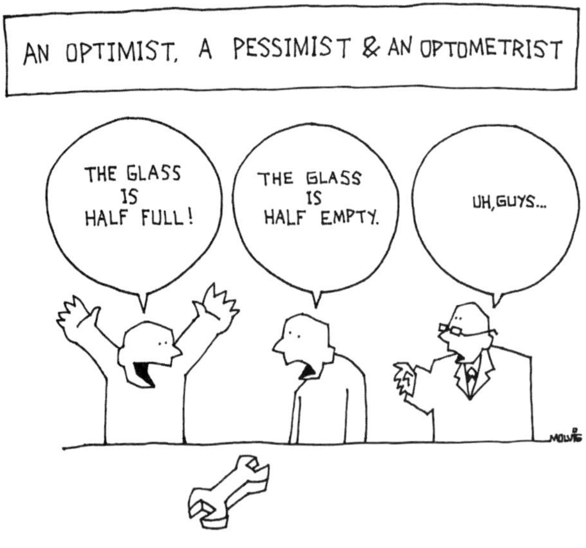
AN OPTIMIST, A PESSIMIST & AN OPTOMETRIST
THE GLASS IS HALF FULL!
THE GLASS IS HALF EMPTY.
UH, GUYS...
MOLVIG

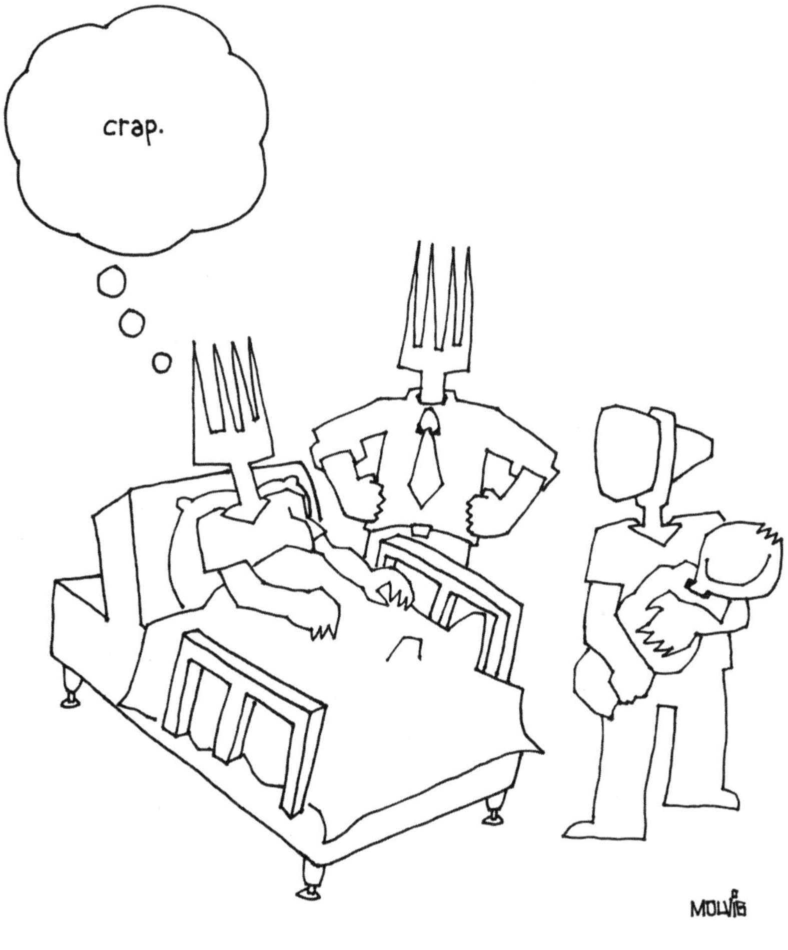
crap.
MOLVIG

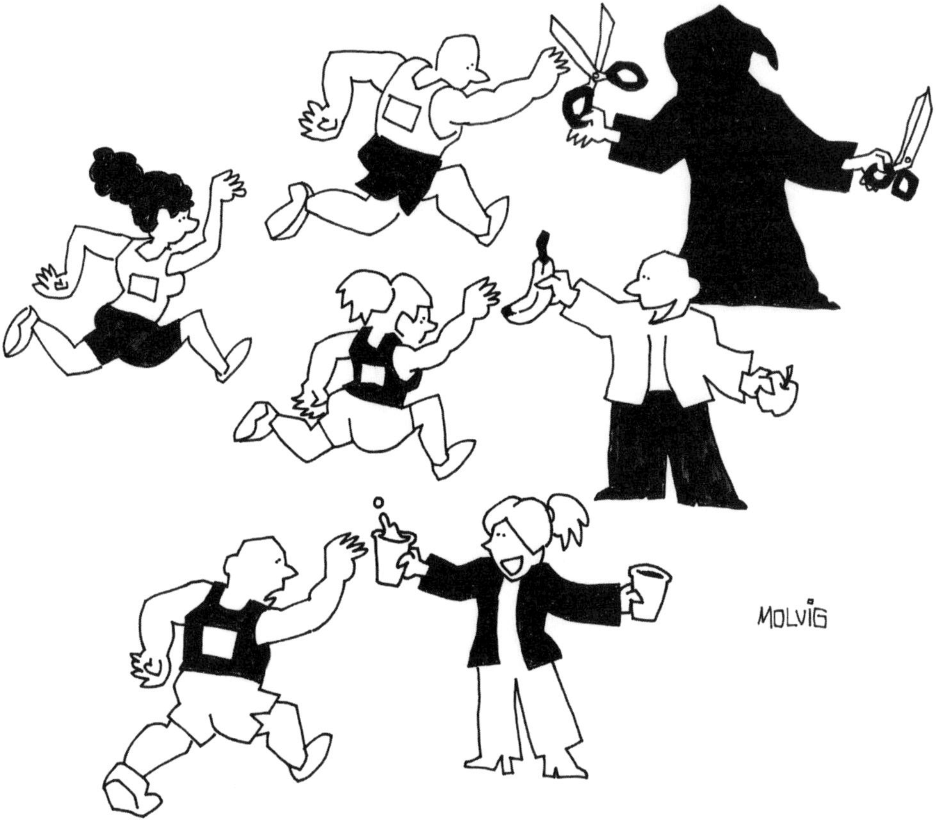
MOLVIG

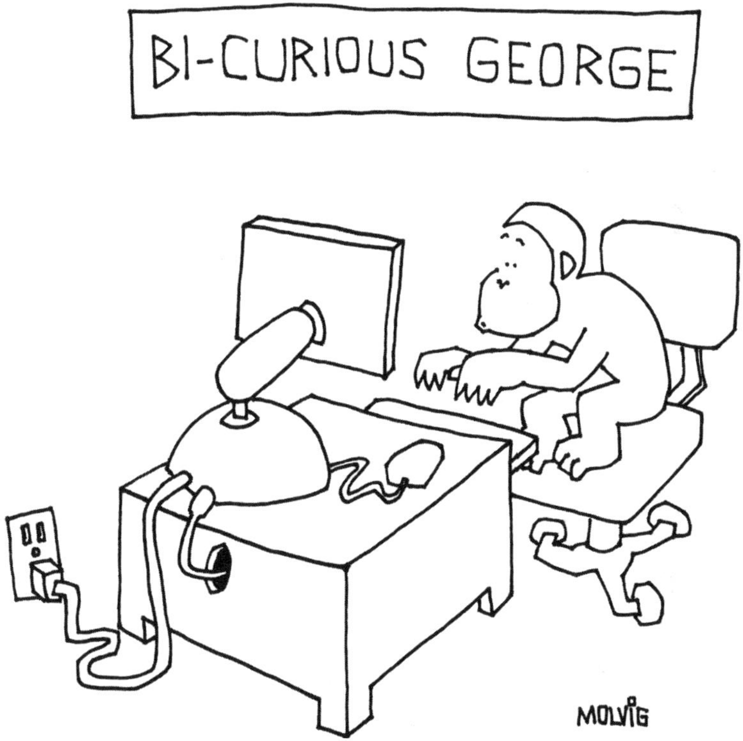
BI-CURIOUS GEORGE
MOLVIG

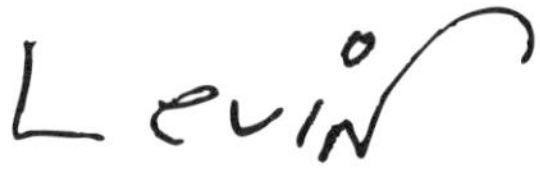
Levin

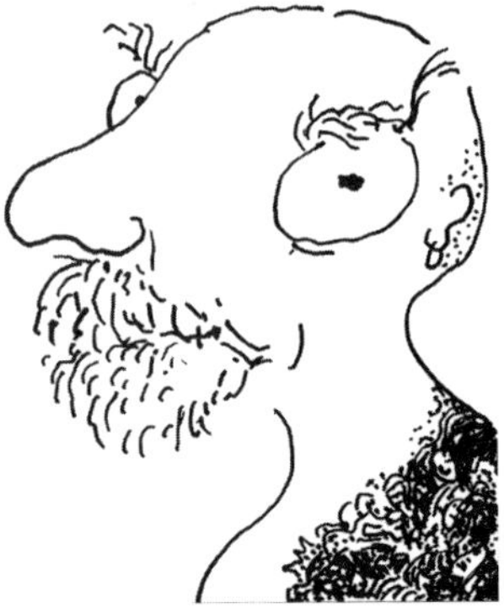

Arnie Levin

Frequently Asked Questions

- *Where do you get your ideas?*
  I don't *get* ideas, *they* come to me.

- *Which comes first, the picture or the caption?*
  The one who phoned ahead.

- *How'd you get started?*
  When I was in my mid-twenties, I had an auto accident in which I broke my hip and dislocated both of my shoulders. My mom had a copy of *Writer's Digest* in which there was a "how-to" for sending batches of cartoons to magazines.

- *I admire . . .*
  Lee Lorenz and Victoria Roberts who are back . . . on their own terms . . .

- *How do you deal with rejection?*
  Denial—wonder—rebuttal—composure . . .

- *What are some things that make you laugh and why?*
  Someone carving a pumpkin (a sadistic laugh). An email from a lawyer in Hong Kong, asking me to join in on a scheme for millions of dollars . . . (just makes me happy). *Curb Your Enthusiasm* (out loud). A White House press conference . . . (anticipated joy). Overhearing dialogue of a policeman giving directions to someone. Putting my underwear on backward, unintentional guffaw.

- *I've got a great idea for a cartoon—wanna hear it?*
  EH?

Infrequently Asked Questions

- *Have you mooned or been mooned more often in your life?*
  I was once half mooned.

- *What would make a terrible pizza topping?*
  Terrible ingredients.

- *What might one expect to find at a really low-budget amusement park?*
  Ambulances.

- *What did the shepherd say to the three-legged sheepdog?*
  Let's see the pirouette again.

Draw Something in This Space

. . . that will help us understand your childhood.

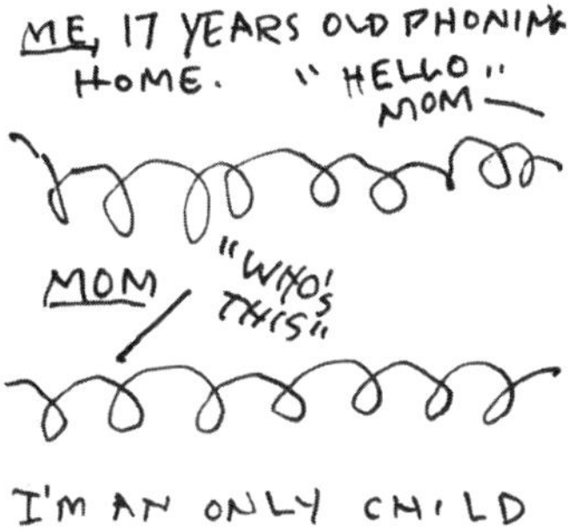
ME, 17 YEARS OLD PHONING HOME. "HELLO MOM—"
MOM "WHO'S THIS!"
I'M AN ONLY CHILD

And Now for a Few More Questions . . .

- *What do you hate drawing?*

  Bowling pins. I have never been able to freehand one I liked. Even the ones I tried to do mechanically. . . . Also horses' legs . . .

- *Being as accurate as possible, how many desert island cartoons do you think you've come up with and submitted to* The New Yorker*?*

  Two . . . sold them both.

- *What's the funniest thing that you witnessed, overheard, or came up with that you couldn't figure out how to use in a cartoon?*

  More perplexing than funny . . . The electric warning signs on the highways that read:
  It's the Law!
  Move Over for Stopped Emergency Vehicles.

Naming Names

- *What name might you give to a mild-mannered, middle-aged, bespectacled dental assistant in one of your cartoons?*

  Dwane.

- *Other than Lance, what name would you give to a twenty-eight-year-old entertainment lawyer with a blue-dyed fauxhawk who cycles on weekends?*

  Cash.

- *What would be a good name for a new, commercially unviable breakfast cereal?*

  Algae.

- *Come up with a name for an unpleasant medical procedure.*

  Co-payment.

- *If you used a pen name, what would it be?*

  Speedball.

Complete the Pie Chart Below

. . . in a way that tells us something about your life or how you think.

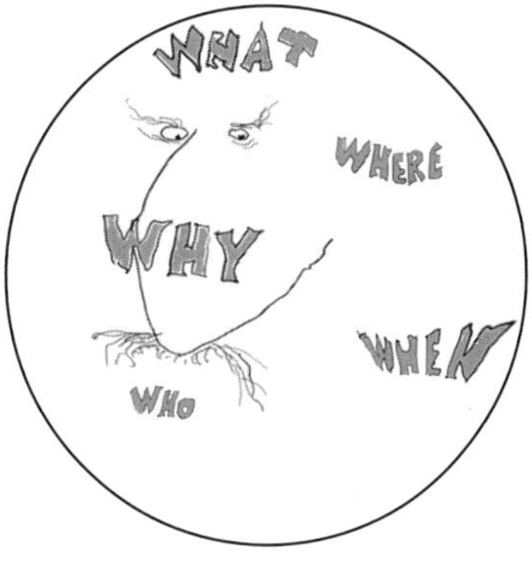
WHAT
WHERE
WHY
WHEN
WHO

"Perhaps I'm not hearing you right, stranger. Did you just call me 'cupcake'?"

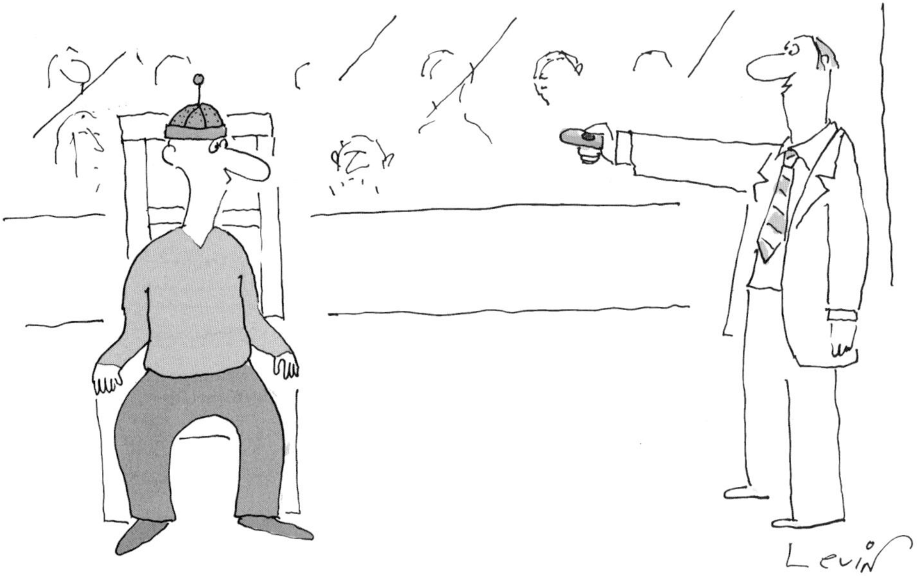
Levin

"My wife! My best tie!"

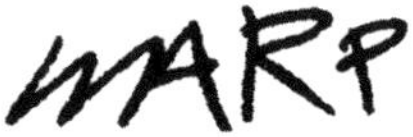
WARP

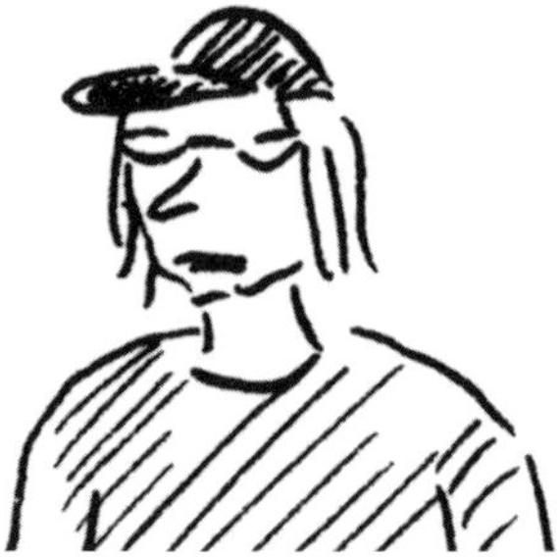

Kim Warp

Frequently Asked Questions

- *Where do you get your ideas?*
  Brooding, obsessing, daydreaming.
- *Which comes first, the picture or the caption?*
  The embryonic idea comes at once—then evolves.
- *How'd you get started?*
  We had drawing time every day.
- *I admire . . .*
  Other cartoonists' pens.
- *How do you deal with rejection?*
  I don't think about it. I just draw more.
- *What are some things that make you laugh and why?*
  I laugh at everything—it's a problem.
- *I've got a great idea for a cartoon—wanna hear it?*
  No, but Diffee does!

Infrequently Asked Questions

- *Have you mooned or been mooned more often in your life?*
  The pets moon me every day.
- *What would make a terrible pizza topping?*
  Cat food—right, Mom?
- *What might one expect to find at a really low-budget amusement park?*
  Teeny tiny roller coasters.
- *What did the shepherd say to the three-legged sheepdog?*
  I just hope it was empathetic and not some dumb joke.

And Now for a Few More Questions . . .

- *What do you hate drawing?*
  Nothing.
- *Being as accurate as possible, how many desert island cartoons do you think you've come up with and submitted to* The New Yorker*?*
  Twelve and a half.

- *What's the funniest thing that you witnessed, overheard, or came up with that you couldn't figure out how to use in a cartoon?*
  Nice try, Diffee!

Draw Something in This Space

. . . that will help us understand your childhood.

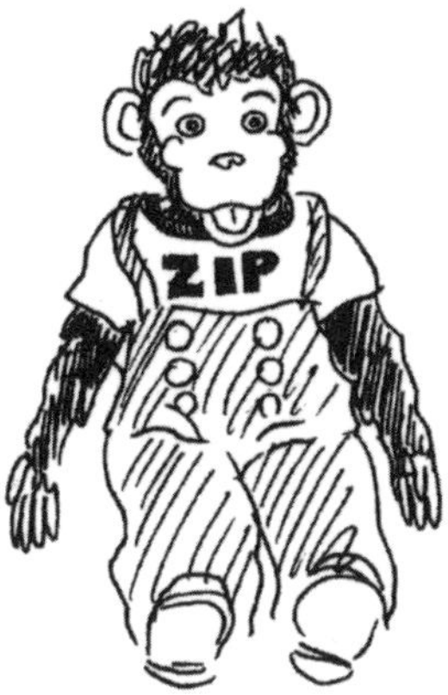
ZIP

Naming Names

- *What name might you give to a mild-mannered, middle-aged, bespectacled dental assistant in one of your cartoons?*
  Amy.

- *Other than Lance, what name would you give to a twenty-eight-year-old entertainment lawyer with a blue-dyed fauxhawk who cycles on weekends?*
  Josh.

- *What would be a good name for a new, commercially unviable breakfast cereal?*
  Chunks.

- *Come up with a name for an unpleasant medical procedure.*
  Nosectomy.

- *If you used a pen name, what would it be?*
  Warp—but it's not.

Complete the Pie Chart Below

. . . in a way that tells us something about your life or how you think.

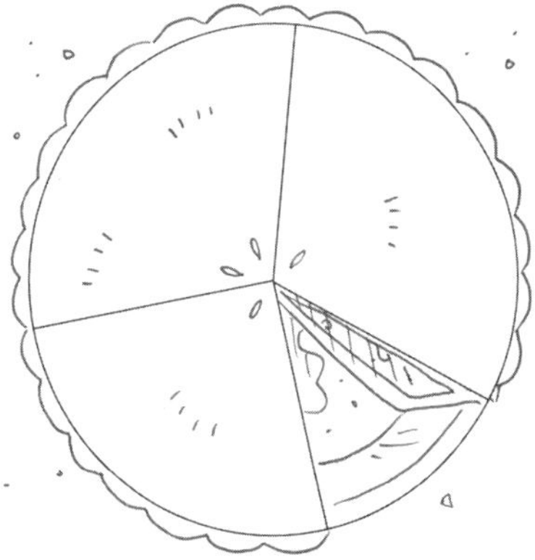

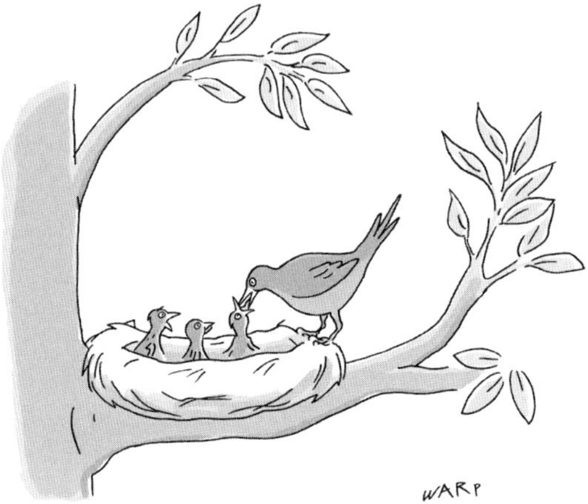
WARP

"Smoothies again?"

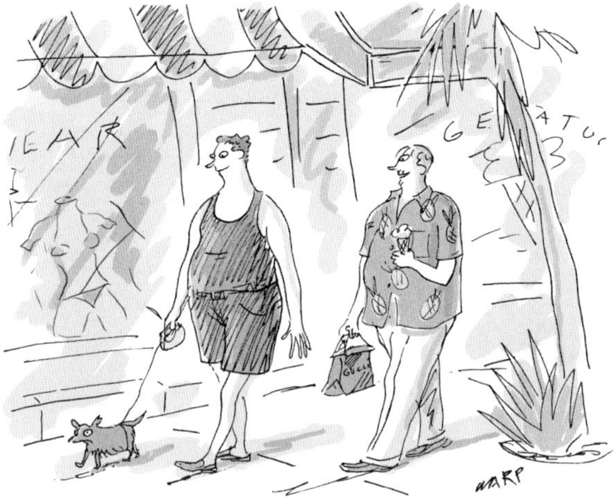
WARP

"Who even knew they made dog thongs?"

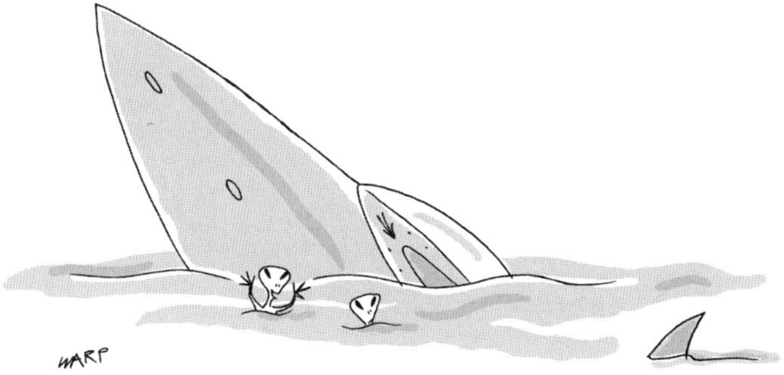
WARP

"We're saved! We're saved!"

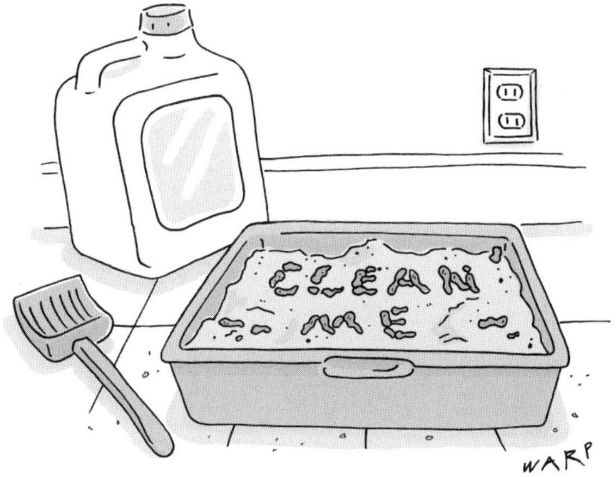
CLEAN
ME
WARP

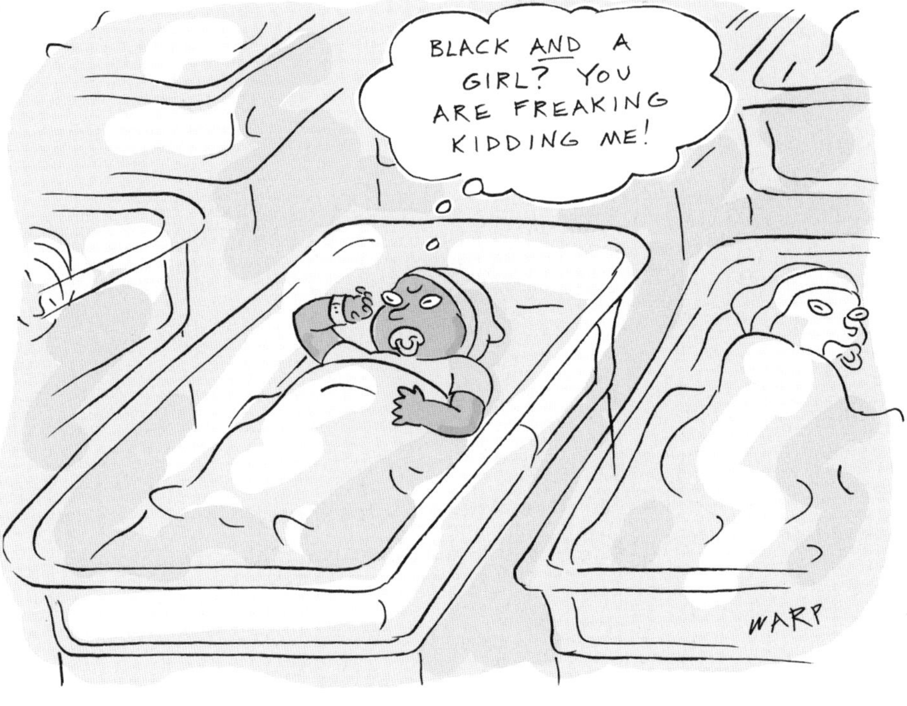
BLACK AND A GIRL? YOU ARE FREAKING KIDDING ME!
WARP

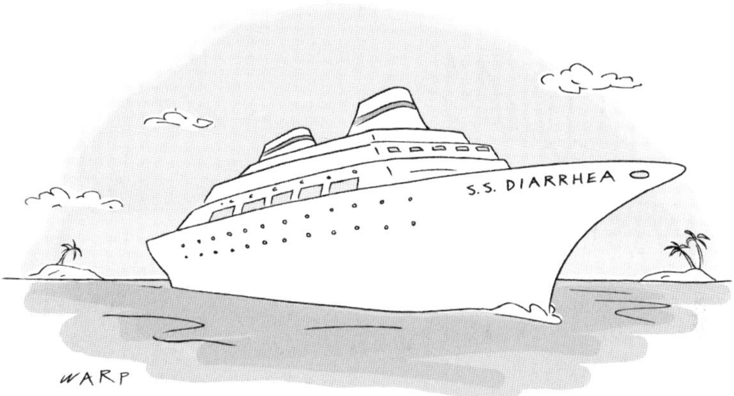
S.S. DIARRHEA
WARP

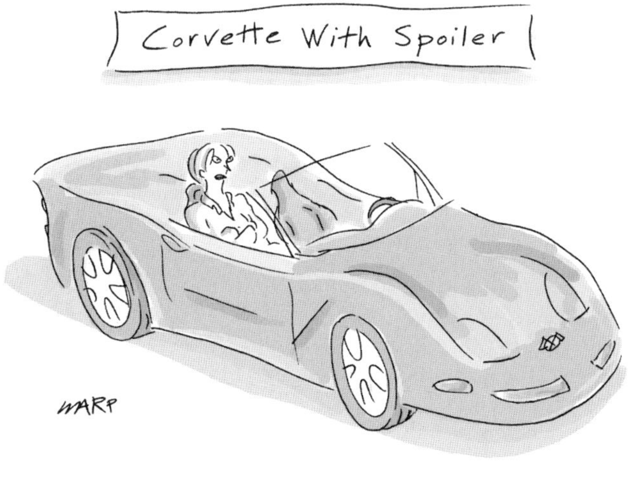
Corvette With Spoiler
WARP

Eric Lewis

ME
OLLIE
DAISY

Frequently Asked Questions

- *Where do you get your ideas?*
  At a place off Route 6 called Idea Barn.

- *Which comes first, the picture or the caption?*
  It's best when they come at the same time. What?!

- *How'd you get started?*
  I blew Bob at a party.

OLLIE AGAIN

- *I admire . . .*
  Jerry Garcia and George Herriman (creator of *Krazy Kat*).

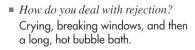

- *How do you deal with rejection?*
  Crying, breaking windows, and then a long, hot bubble bath.

- *What are some things that make you laugh and why?*
  My cats—Oliver and Daisy. Because they're never phony or contrived, and yet they do goofy things. For example, Daisy nurses on my earlobes.

- *I've got a great idea for a cartoon—wanna hear it?*
  NO!!! Okay, yes, Mom, tell me. . . .

Infrequently Asked Questions

- *Have you mooned or been mooned more often in your life?*
  I wish I could say, but I've completely repressed those memories.

- *What would make a terrible pizza topping?*
  Fried dark matter.

- *What might one expect to find at a really low-budget amusement park?*
  A View-Master reel library.

- *What did the shepherd say to the three-legged sheepdog?*
  I got nothin'.

Draw Something in This Space

. . . that will help us understand your childhood.

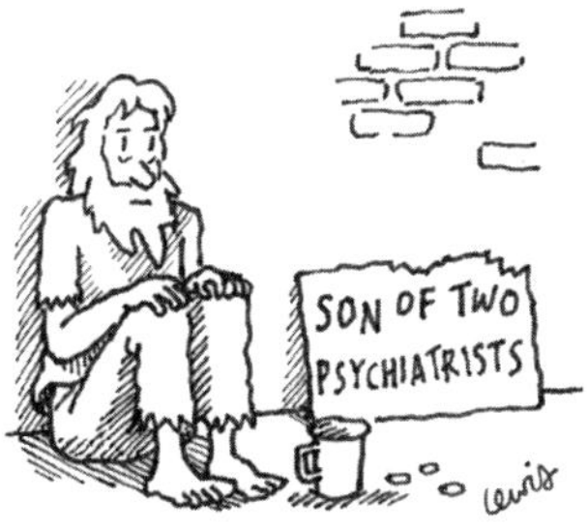
SON OF TWO PSYCHIATRISTS
lewis

And Now for a Few More Questions . . .

- *What do you hate drawing?*
  Perspective. I don't even believe in perspective, actually. It's just a theory!

- *Being as accurate as possible, how many desert island cartoons do you think you've come up with and submitted to* The New Yorker*?*
  Maybe fifty. Sold two!

- *What's the funniest thing that you witnessed, overheard, or came up with that you couldn't figure out how to use in a cartoon?*
  I'm convinced that Dick Cheney has some kind of emergency escape pod that could bring him safely to the moon in a time of crisis.

Naming Names

- *What name might you give to a mild-mannered, middle-aged, bespectacled dental assistant in one of your cartoons?*
  Matt Diffee.

- *Other than Lance, what name would you give to a twenty-eight-year-old entertainment lawyer with a blue-dyed fauxhawk who cycles on weekends?*
  Matthew Diffee.

- *Come up with a name for an unpleasant medical procedure.*
  Laser Urethrabrasion.

- *If you used a pen name, what would it be?*
  Dr. Sanford Sharpie.

Complete the Pie Chart Below

. . . in a way that tells us something about your life or how you think.

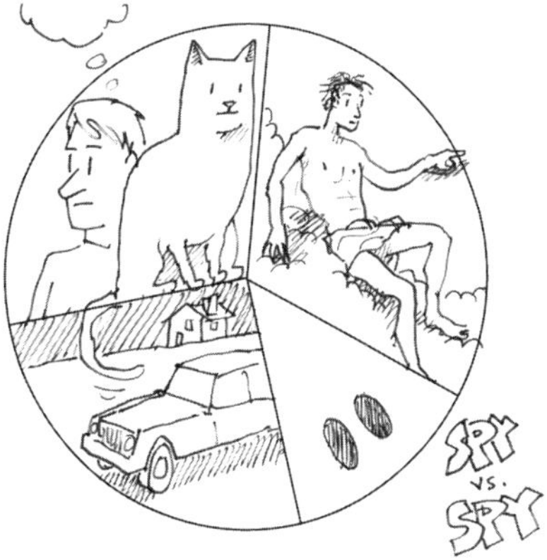
SPY VS. SPY

"If I ever start showing signs of Stockholm syndrome, kill me."

MOMS GONE WILD

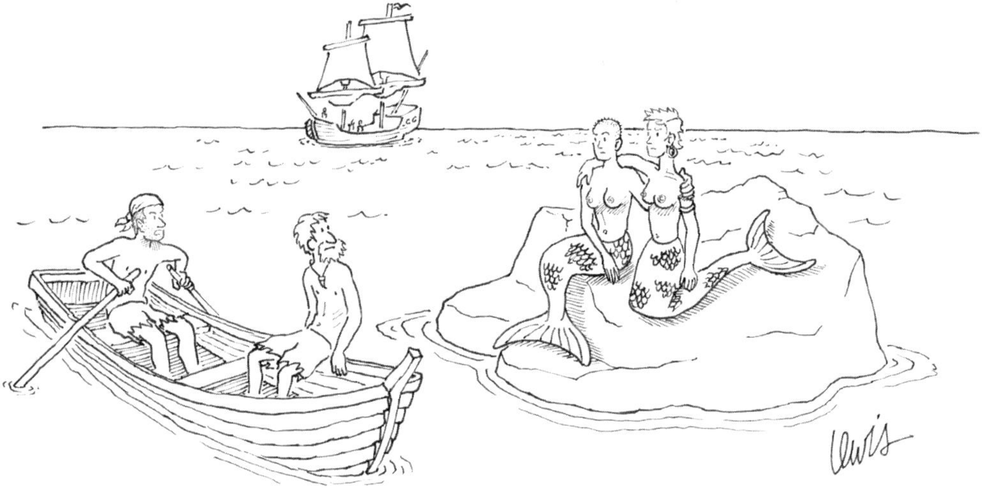
lewis

"Arrg. Just our luck!"

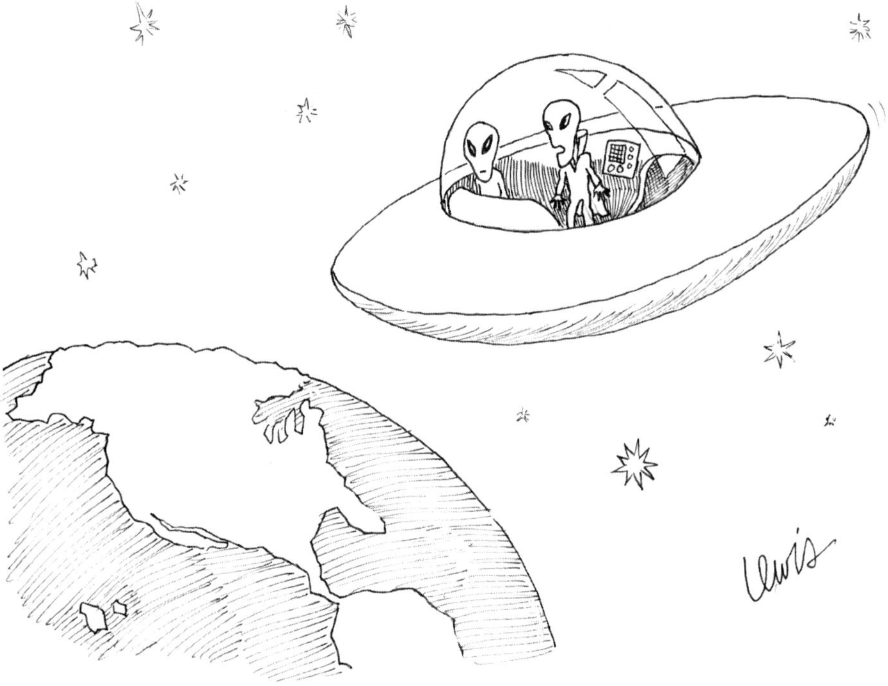
Lewis

"Hold that thought. I have to go take a number five."

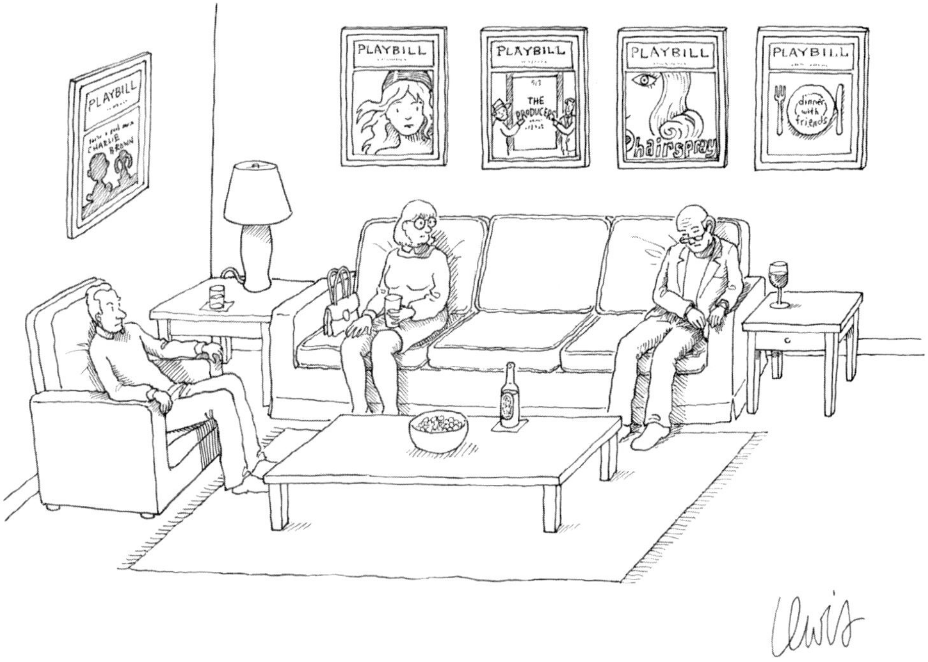
PLAYBILL
CHARLIE BROWN
PLAYBILL
PLAYBILL
THE PRODUCERS
PLAYBILL
hairspray
PLAYBILL
dinner with friends

ANOTHER DISAPPOINTING PARTY AT THE PLAYBILL MANSION

WOMEN'S SYNCHRONIZED PEEING

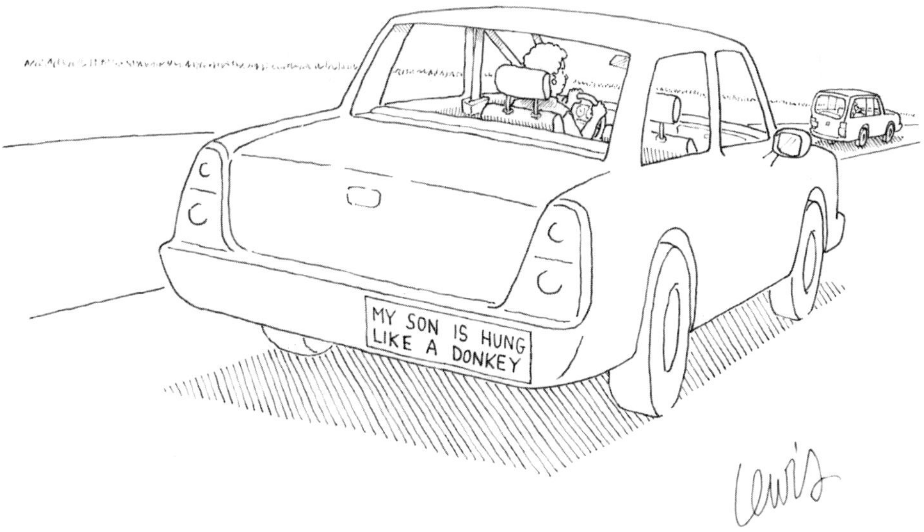
MY SON IS HUNG
LIKE A DONKEY
Lewis

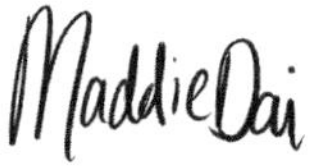
MaddieDai

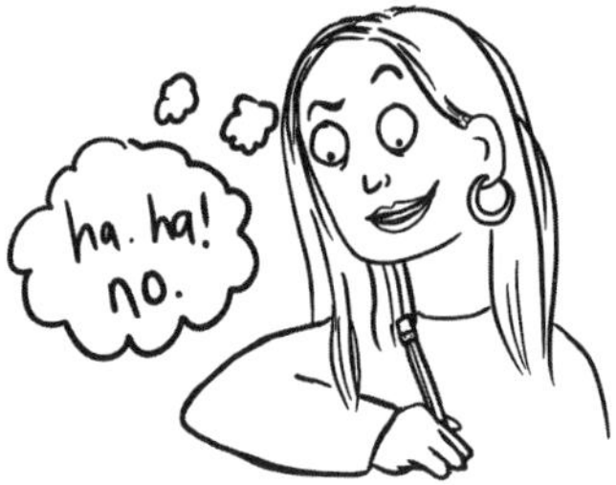
ha. ha!
no.

Maddie Dai

Frequently Asked Questions

- *Where do you get your ideas?*
  Bought them in bulk when I was starting out.

- *Which comes first, the picture or the caption?*
  The general idea, then the drawing. The caption is written on my notes app, then rewritten in the dying seconds before the weekly deadline.

- *How'd you get started?*
  Needed to get rich fast.

- *I admire . . .*
  People who use cartooning to get rich fast.

- *How do you deal with rejection?*
  Like a good deed that's paid forward, I pass it on. Refuse the love of a wealthy admirer. Frown at a smiling baby. Turn down a stable, societally productive job.

- *What are some things that make you laugh and why?*
  So many things, I'm a generous laugher. I move through the world at a low-grade chuckle.

- *I've got a great idea for a cartoon—wanna hear it?*
  God yes, I'll trade you my firstborn child for it.

Infrequently Asked Questions

- *Have you mooned or been mooned more often in your life?*
  I haven't wholeheartedly mooned, has always been a nervous half crescent, but I have absolutely been mooned. I'm a modern, cosmopolitan woman, aren't I? Circa 2002 I couldn't take two steps without being mooned by the young gentlemen of the neighborhood.

- *What would make a terrible pizza topping?*
  A low-budget amusement park.

- *What might one expect to find at a really low-budget amusement park?*
  The pizza with the terrible topping.

- *What did the shepherd say to the three-legged sheepdog?*
  Wait, is that a third leg, or are you a two legged dog that's happy to see me?

Draw Something in This Space

. . . *that will help us understand your childhood.*

LET'S RIDE!

And Now for a Few More Questions . . .

■ *What do you hate drawing?*
Never learned the correct way to hold a pencil.

■ *Being as accurate as possible, how many desert island cartoons do you think you've come up with and submitted to* The New Yorker?
Sent five, sold one. Sorry, I'm sure those are rookie numbers. Most things that have happened to me on desert islands were very serious and unsuited to the cartoon form.

■ *What's the funniest thing that you witnessed, overheard, or came up with that you couldn't figure out how to use in a cartoon?*
Other people's better cartoons.

Naming Names

■ *What name might you give to a mild-mannered, middle-aged, bespectacled dental assistant in one of your cartoons?*
Colin.

■ *Other than Lance, what name would you give to a twenty-eight-year-old entertainment lawyer with a blue-dyed fauxhawk who cycles on weekends?*
Colin.

■ *What would be a good name for a new, commercially unviable breakfast cereal?*
Colin Crunch.

■ *Come up with a name for an unpleasant medical procedure.*
Colinoscopy.

■ *If you used a pen name, what would it be?*
Colin.

Complete the Pie Chart Below

. . . *in a way that tells us something about your life or how you think.*

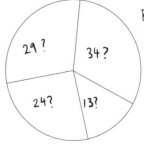

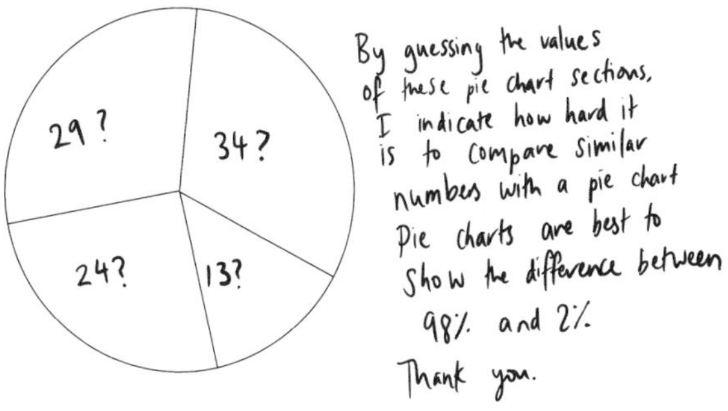

29 ?   34 ?
24 ?   13 ?

By guessing the values of these pie chart sections, I indicate how hard it is to compare similar numbers with a pie chart. Pie charts are best to show the difference between 98% and 2%. Thank you.

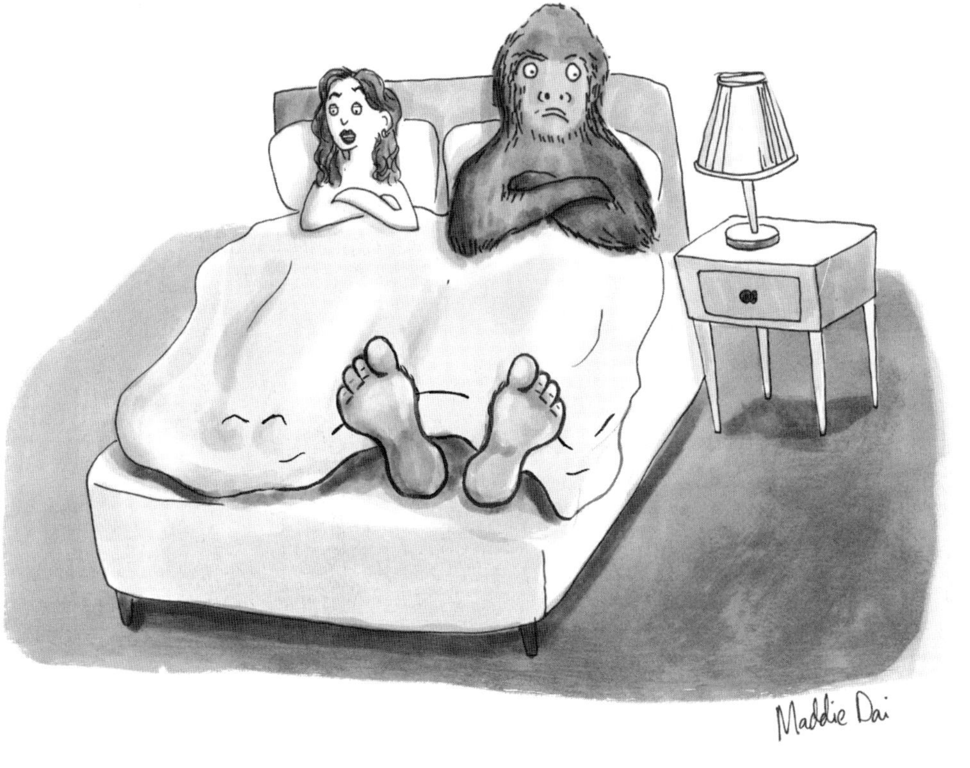
Maddie Dai

"I don't think it was that crazy of an assumption."

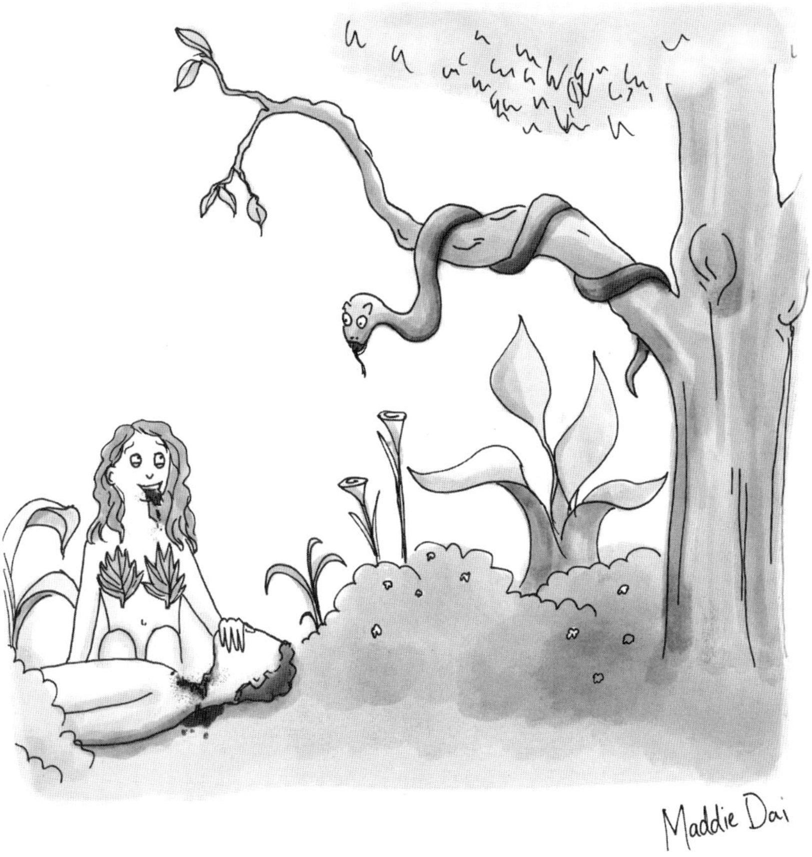
Maddie Dai

"No Eve! Not that apple!"

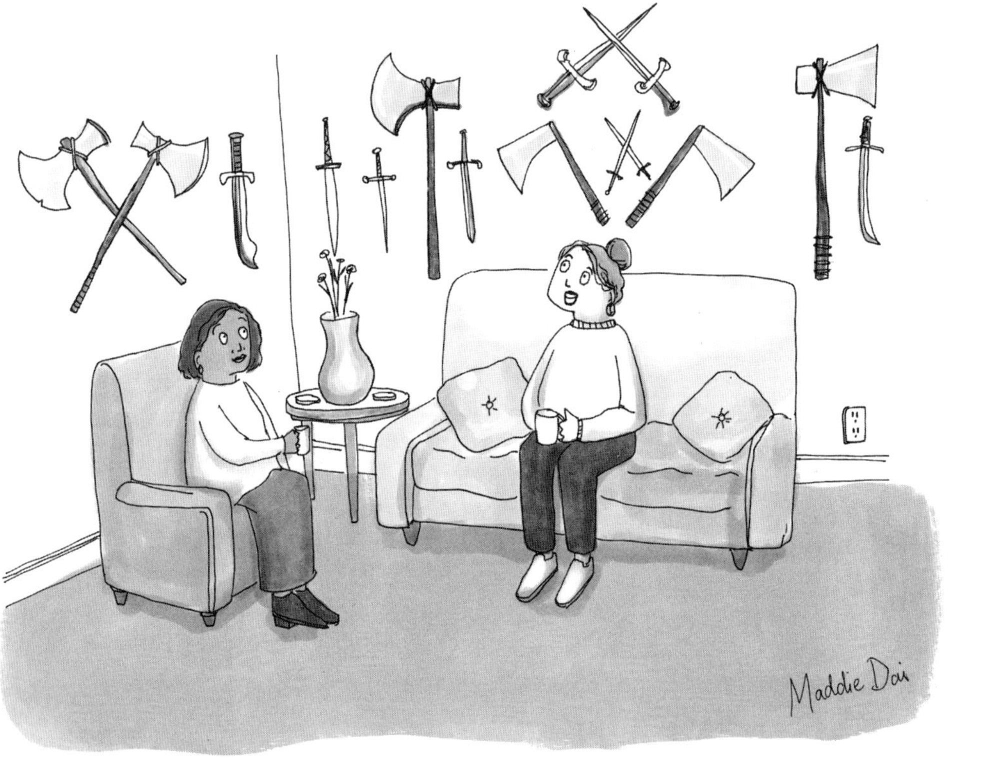
Maddie Dai

"He has to buy one every time he gets me tampons."

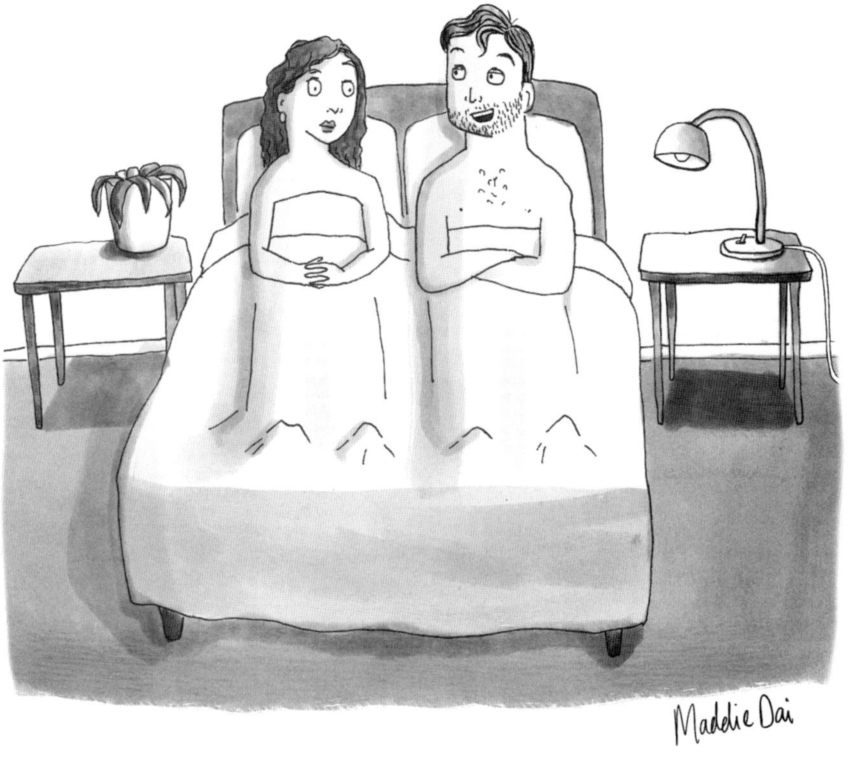
Maddie Dai

"In many industries failing fast is a widely celebrated iteratative process."

S.Harris

Sidney Harris

Frequently Asked Questions

- *Where do you get your ideas?*
  Mostly, while sitting—rarely standing.

- *Which comes first, the ~~picture or the caption~~?*
  VAGUE IDEA, THEN THE
  CAPTION.

- *How'd you get started?*
  I had nothing else to do.

- *I admire . . .*
  Zero Mostel, Mae West, Gene Tierney, George Gershwin, Jimmy Durante, Woody Allen, Lena Horne, Mel Brooks, Michael Jordan, Clara Bow, Rita Hayworth (Margarita Cansino), Carl Sagan, Arlo Guthrie, Mike Tyson, Lauren Bacall, Sandy Koufax, and those two dynamite ladies, Marisa Tomei and Rosie Perez. I could probably think of some people who weren't born in Brooklyn who could also be mentioned here, but these will do.

- *How do you deal with rejection?*
  A freelance cartoonist obviously has a short attention span, or he'd be writing something longer than single sentences, so, fortunately, I forget the rejections very soon.

- *What are some things that make you laugh and why?*
  Sid Caesar always makes me laugh—although it's often more than just laughter; others do only occasionally.

- *I've got a great idea for a cartoon—wanna hear it?*
  NO!

Infrequently Asked Questions

- *Have you mooned or been mooned more often in your life?*
  No.

- *What would make a terrible pizza topping?*
  Cheese and tomato sauce.

- *What might one expect to find at a really low-budget amusement park?*
  One bumper car.

- *What did the shepherd say to the three-legged sheepdog?*
  Here, tripod!

Draw Some Sort of Doodle

. . . using the random lines below as a starting point.

And Now for a Few More Questions . . .

- *What do you hate drawing?*
  Shoes. Socks are easier.

- *Being as accurate as possible, how many desert island cartoons do you think you've come up with and submitted to* The New Yorker*?*
  Two.

- *What's the funniest thing that you witnessed, overheard, or came up with that you couldn't figure out how to use in a cartoon?*
  Never saw anything funny.

Naming Names

- *What name might you give to a mild-mannered, middle-aged, bespectacled dental assistant in one of your cartoons?*
  Fritzi.

- *Other than Lance, what name would you give to a twenty-eight-year-old entertainment lawyer with a blue-dyed fauxhawk who cycles on weekends?*
  Fritz.

- *What would be a good name for a new, commercially unviable breakfast cereal?*
  Ritz.

- *Come up with a name for an unpleasant medical procedure.*
  Itz.

- *If you used a pen name, what would it be?*
  If it was the state pen: 376148902.

Complete the Pie Chart Below

. . . in a way that tells us something about your life or how you think.

Thomas Pynchon
Rembrandt
Art Tatum
Lemon Meringue

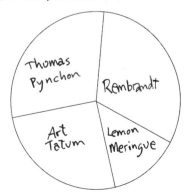

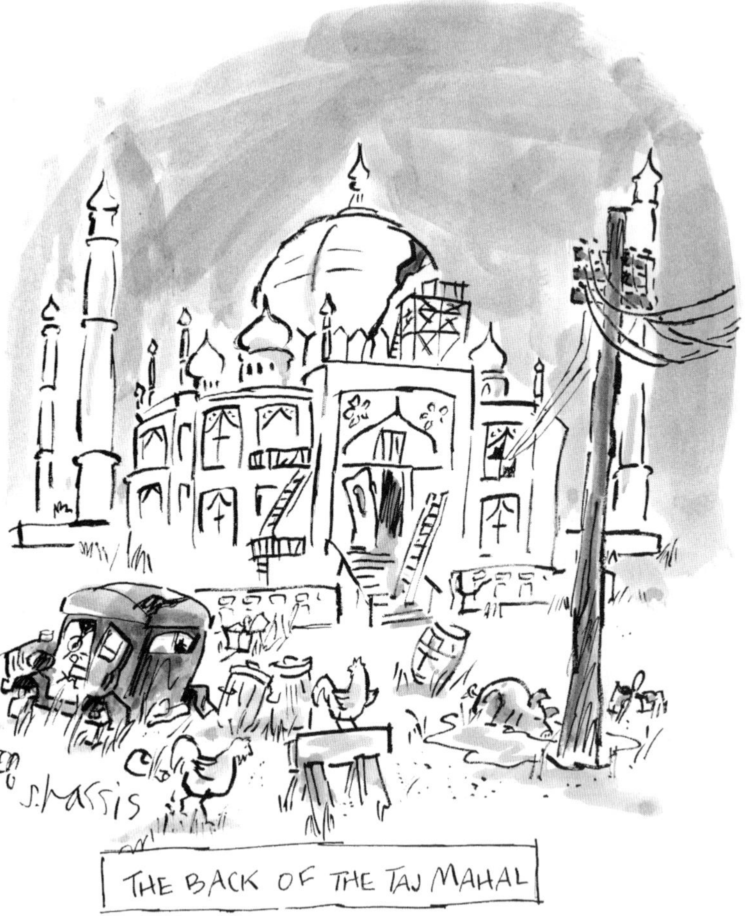
S. Gross

THE BACK OF THE TAJ MAHAL

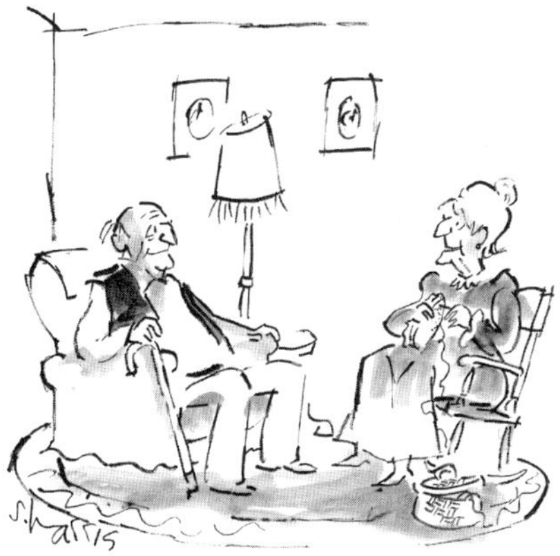
s.harris

"Now that the kids and grandkids are grown I can get back to doing more erotic embroidery."

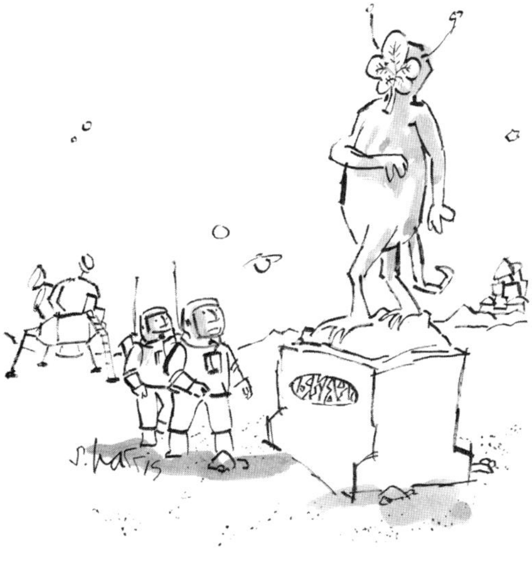
s.harris

J. C. Duffy

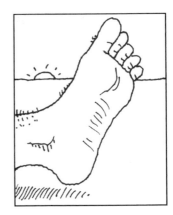

Frequently Asked Questions

- *Where do you get your ideas?*
  The Idea Place.

- *Which comes first, the picture or the caption?*
  Usually, the caption, sometimes the picture.

- *How'd you get started?*
  Hey, when it comes to how I got started, don't get me started!

- *I admire . . .*
  The dimples behind a woman's knees, and Gandhi.

- *How do you deal with rejection?*
  Alcohol and meaningless sex.

- *What are some things that make you laugh and why?*
  A man slipping on a banana peel, a person throwing a clock out the window in order to see time fly, a chicken (funny already!) crossing the road, but only when it's "to get to the other side," obviously, I'm easily amused.

- *I've got a great idea for a cartoon—wanna hear it?*
  I used to say no; now I say yes, but the ideas usually suck.

Infrequently Asked Questions

- *Have you mooned or been mooned more often in your life?*
  It's a tie: mooner, never. Moonee, never.

- *What would make a terrible pizza topping?*
  A human head.

- *What might one expect to find at a really low-budget amusement park?*
  Fifty percent polyester cotton candy.

- *What did the shepherd say to the three-legged sheepdog?*
  Come here often?

Draw Something in This Space

. . . that will help us understand your childhood.

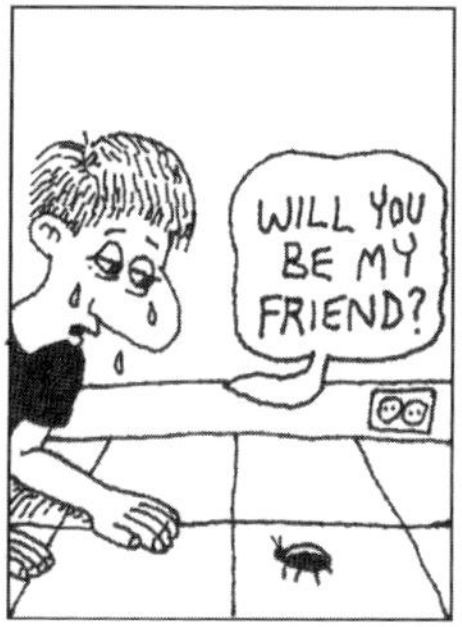
WILL YOU BE MY FRIEND?

And Now for a Few More Questions . . .

- *What do you hate drawing?*
  Crowds, bicycles, iron lung machines.

- *Being as accurate as possible, how many desert island cartoons do you think you've come up with and submitted to* The New Yorker*?*
  Maybe thirty or so.

- *What's the funniest thing that you witnessed, overheard, or came up with that you couldn't figure out how to use in a cartoon?*
  Whatever it is, I'm saving it for use in a noncartoon.

Naming Names

- *What name might you give to a mild-mannered, middle-aged, bespectacled dental assistant in one of your cartoons?*
  Prunella.

- *Other than Lance, what name would you give to a twenty-eight-year-old entertainment lawyer with a blue-dyed fauxhawk who cycles on weekends?*
  Vance.

- *What would be a good name for a new, commercially unviable breakfast cereal?*
  Mouse Clusters.

- *Come up with a name for an unpleasant medical procedure.*
  Surgery.

- *If you used a pen name, what would it be?*
  Chad Manwaring.

Complete the Pie Chart Below

. . . in a way that tells us something about your life or how you think.

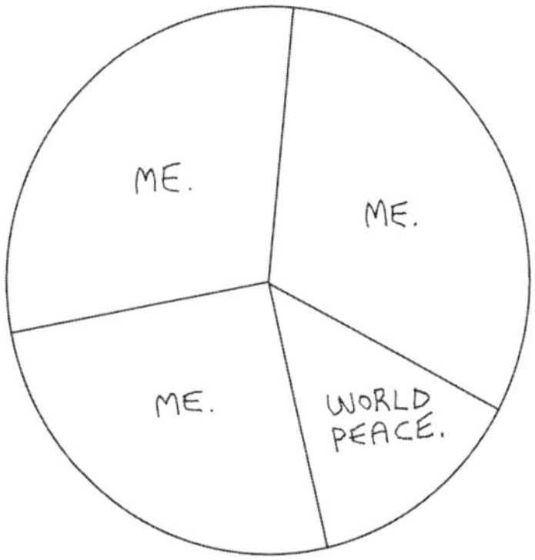
ME.
ME.
ME.
WORLD PEACE.

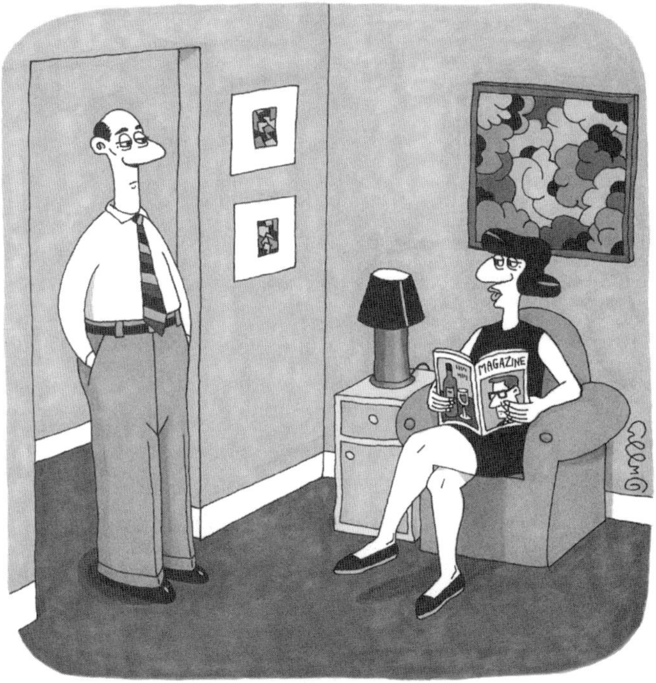
MAGAZINE

"I think your tailor has seriously miscalculated your rise, Herbert."

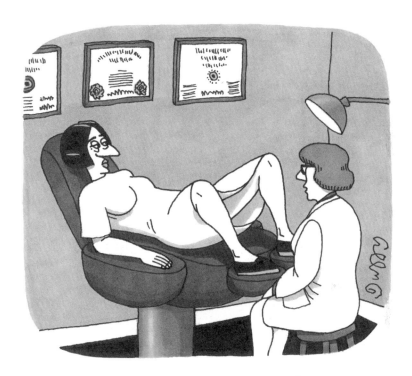

"I spy London, I spy France . . . neither of which rhymes with 'yeast infection.'"

"Could I do this with an imaginary friend?"

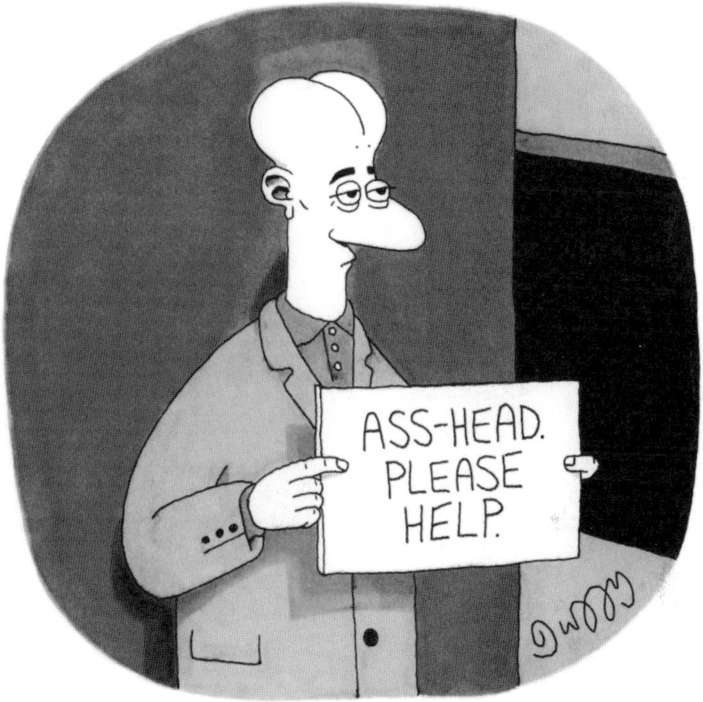
ASS-HEAD.
PLEASE
HELP.
DUFFY

"Waiter, there's a fly in my soup, and ironically, there's also a crouton in my shit."

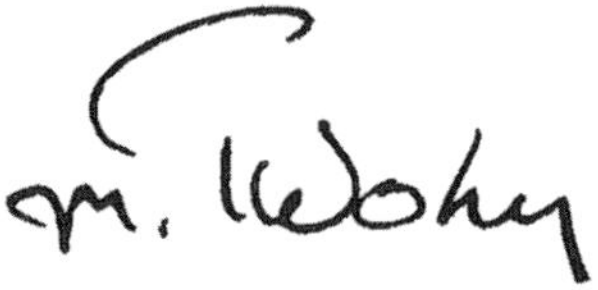

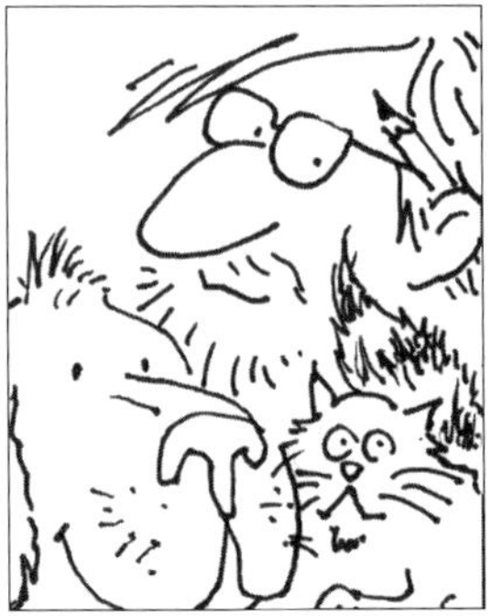

Mike Twohy

Frequently Asked Questions

- *Where do you get your ideas?*
  I think of them.

- *Which comes first, the picture or the caption?*
  A few random words and then doodling.

- *How'd you get started?*
  A guy asked me to draw up some gags he'd been carrying in his wallet for thirty years.

- *I admire . . .*
  Paul Klee, Dr. Seuss, Abraham Lincoln.

- *What are some things that make you laugh and why?*
  Political satire.
  Cauliflower ears.
  Bushisms.
  Pit toilets.

- *How do you deal with rejection?*

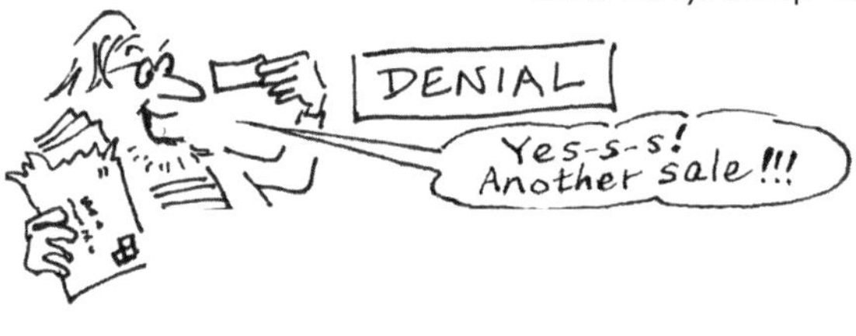
DENIAL
Yes-s-s! Another sale!!!

- *I've got a great idea for a cartoon—wanna hear it?*
  Sure—abuse me.

Infrequently Asked Questions

- *Have you mooned or been mooned more often in your life?*
  Hopefully, the Lord understands my mooning was always preemptive.

- *What would make a terrible pizza topping?*
  Scrabble tiles.

- *What might one expect to find at a really low-budget amusement park?*
  Sticky railings.

- *What did the shepherd say to the three-legged sheepdog?*
  Don't worry. Sheep can't count.

Draw Something in This Space

. . . that will help us understand your childhood.

And Now for a Few More Questions . . .

■ *What do you hate drawing?*
Casts of thousands and detailed architecture.

■ *Being as accurate as possible, how many desert island cartoons do you think you've come up with and submitted to* The New Yorker*?*
Seven (five my first year).

■ *What's the funniest thing that you witnessed, overheard, or came up with that you couldn't figure out how to use in a cartoon?*
Numerous cartoons that other people did.

Naming Names

■ *What name might you give to a mild-mannered, middle-aged, bespectacled dental assistant in one of your cartoons?*
Susan.

■ *Other than Lance, what name would you give to a twenty-eight-year-old entertainment lawyer with a blue-dyed fauxhawk who cycles on weekends?*
Reg.

■ *What would be a good name for a new, commercially unviable breakfast cereal?*
Transfatty-Os.

■ *Come up with a name for an unpleasant medical procedure.*
They've all been invented.

■ *If you used a pen name, what would it be?*
2E.

Complete the Pie Chart Below

. . . in a way that tells us something about your life or how you think.

"Underwear is aisle nine."

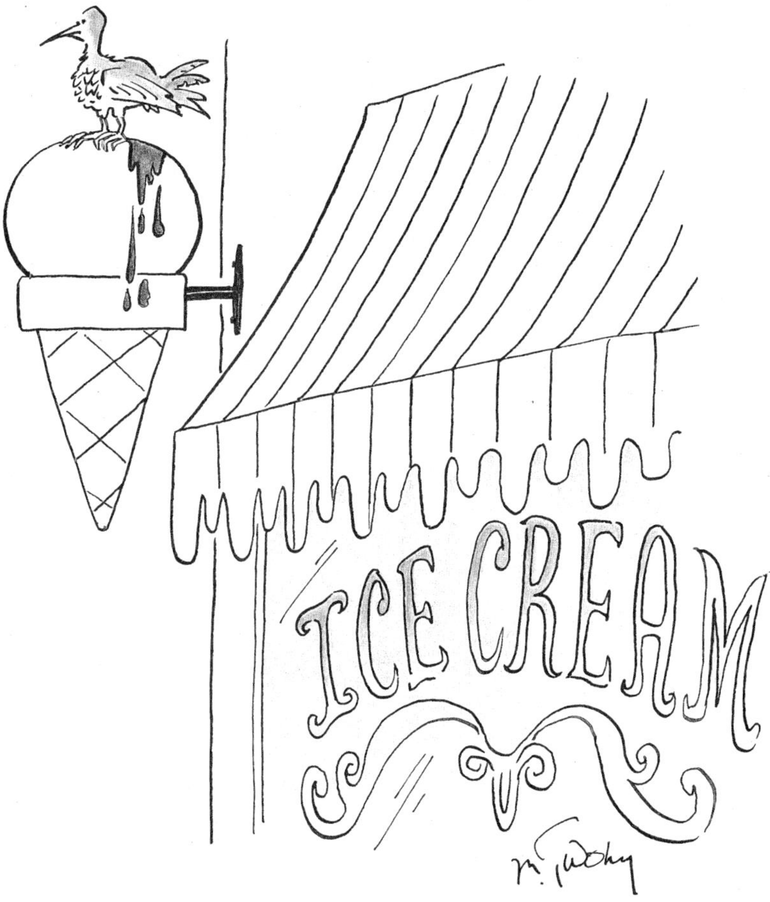
ICE CREAM
M. Twohy

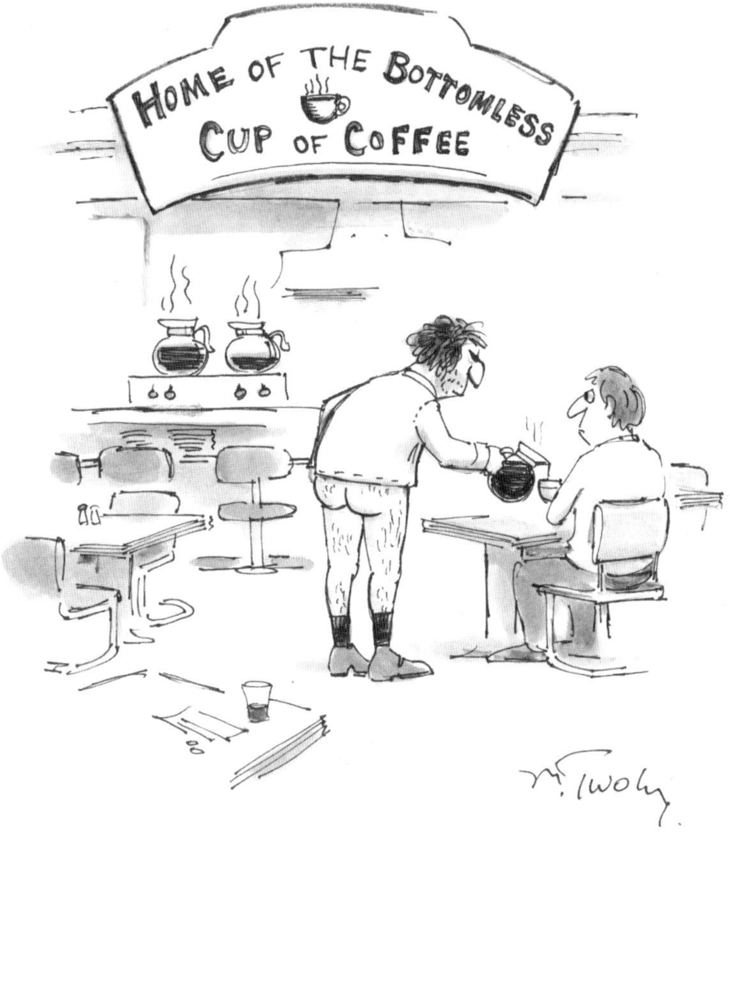
HOME OF THE BOTTOMLESS
CUP OF COFFEE

"Anchored on the far side, we have the oldest ship in the fleet."

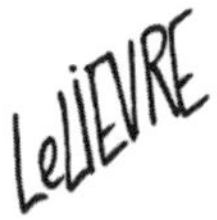
LeLIEVRE

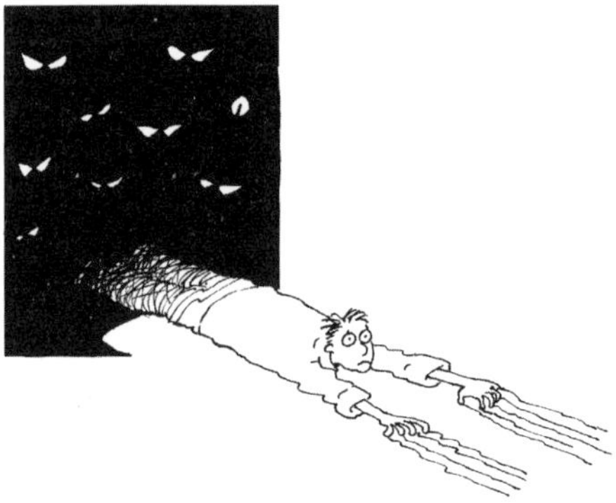

Glen Le Lievre

Frequently Asked Questions

- *Where do you get your ideas?*
  Southwest corner of East 62nd Street—facing north.

- *Which comes first, the picture or the caption?*
  The piction.

- *How'd you get started?*
  My dad had sex with my mom.

- *I admire . . .*
  Van Gogh. Anyone who'd cut off their ear and send it to a prostitute is a-okay in my book.

- *How do you deal with rejection?*
  Sacrifice a chicken over the magazine.

- *I've got a great idea for a cartoon—wanna hear it?*
  No.

- *I've got a great idea for a cartoon—wanna hear it?*
  No!

- *I've got a great idea for a cartoon—wanna hear it?*
  Noooo!

Infrequently Asked Questions

- *Have you mooned or been mooned more often in your life?*
  Avoiding both—lycanthropy.

- *What would make a terrible pizza topping?*
  New Jersey.

- *What might one expect to find at a really low-budget amusement park?*
  Escalator: The Ride!

- *What did the shepherd say to the three-legged sheepdog?*
  I've got a great idea for a cartoon—wanna hear it?

Draw Some Sort of Doodle

. . . using the random lines below as a starting point.

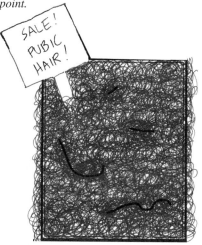

And Now for a Few More Questions . . .

- *What do you hate drawing?*
Boxes filled with hair.

- *Being as accurate as possible, how many desert island cartoons do you think you've come up with and submitted to* The New Yorker?
Five.

- *What's the funniest thing that you witnessed, overheard, or came up with that you couldn't figure out how to use in a cartoon?*
A desert island.

Naming Names

- *What name might you give to a mild-mannered, middle-aged, bespectacled dental assistant in one of your cartoons?*
Hey, you over there, in the corner.

- *Other than Lance, what name would you give to a twenty-eight-year-old entertainment lawyer with a blue-dyed fauxhawk who cycles on weekends?*
Ian Denial.

- *What would be a good name for a new, commercially unviable breakfast cereal?*
Hair Ballios!

- *Come up with a name for an unpleasant medical procedure.*
Astralianization.

- *If you used a pen name, what would it be?*
Paper Mate.

Complete the Pie Chart Below

. . . in a way that tells us something about your life or how you think.

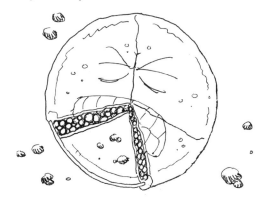

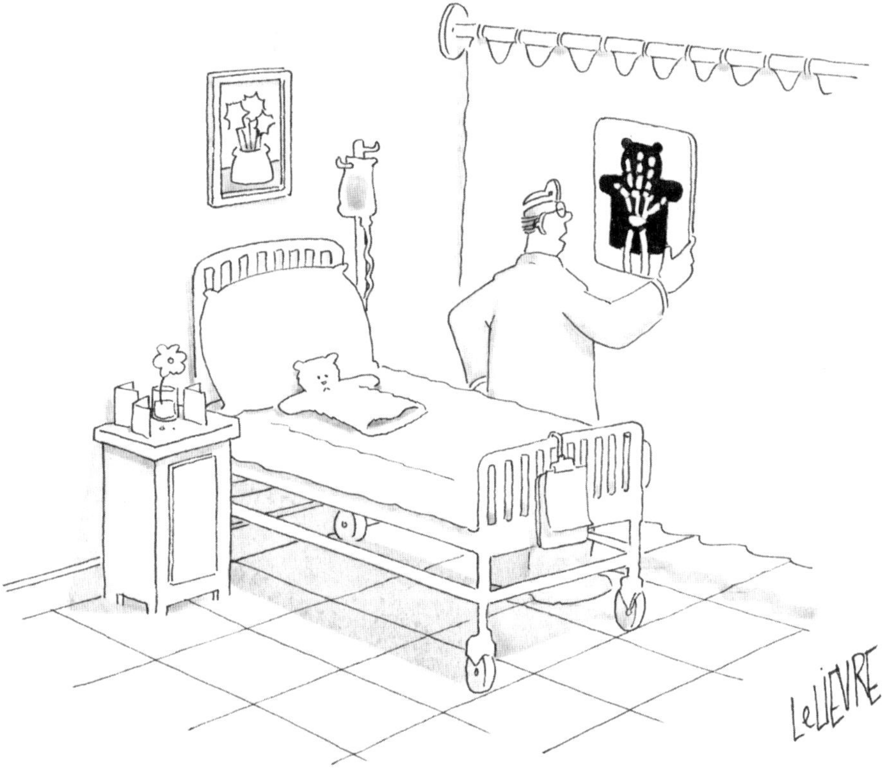
LeLIEVRE

"Well, we removed the growth, but the operation has left you paralyzed from the neck down."

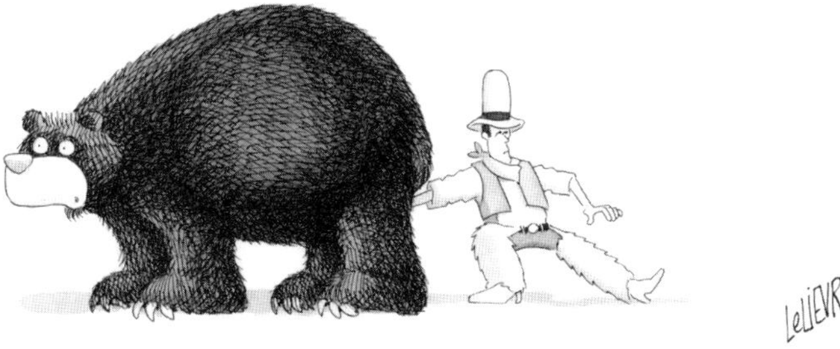
LeLIEVRE

HIGH STAKES TEXAS HOLD 'EM.

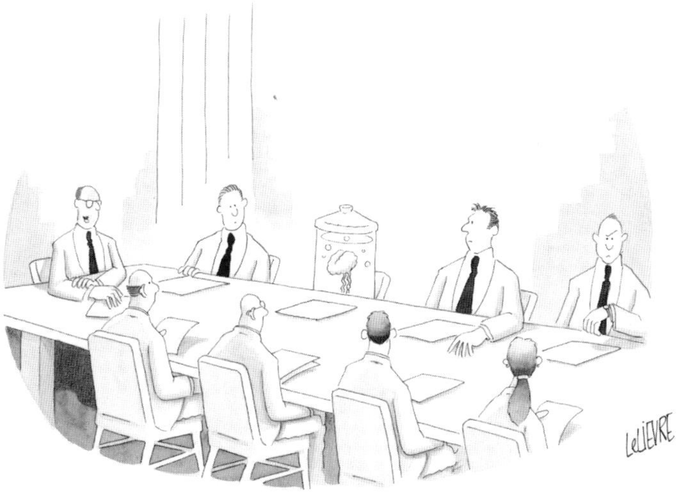
LeLIEVRE

"But first let's all congratulate Ted on his return to work."

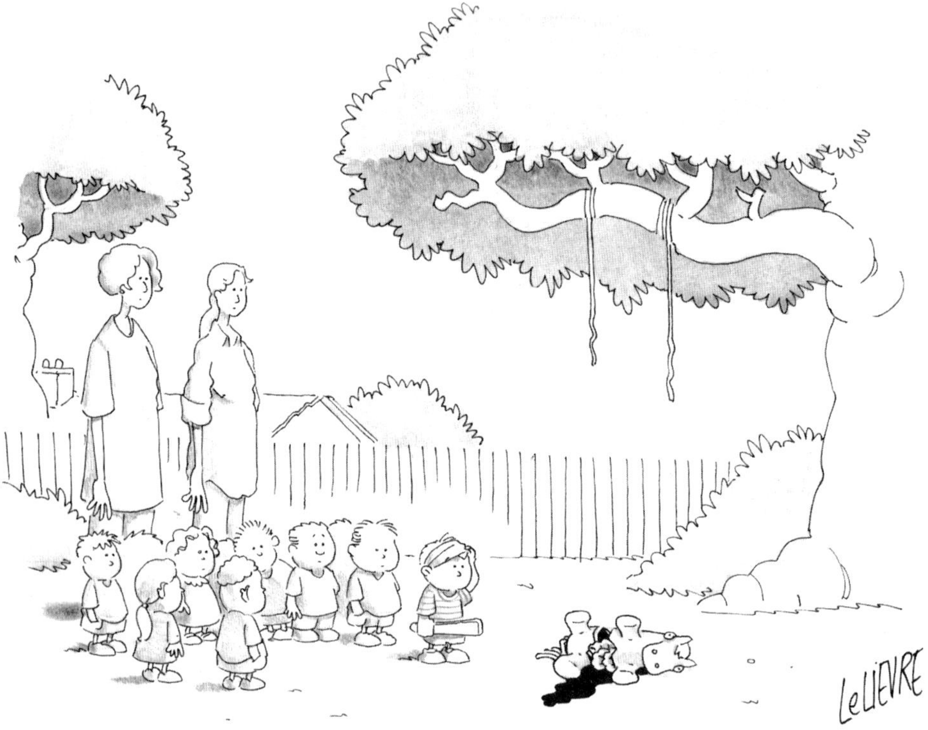
LeLIEVRE

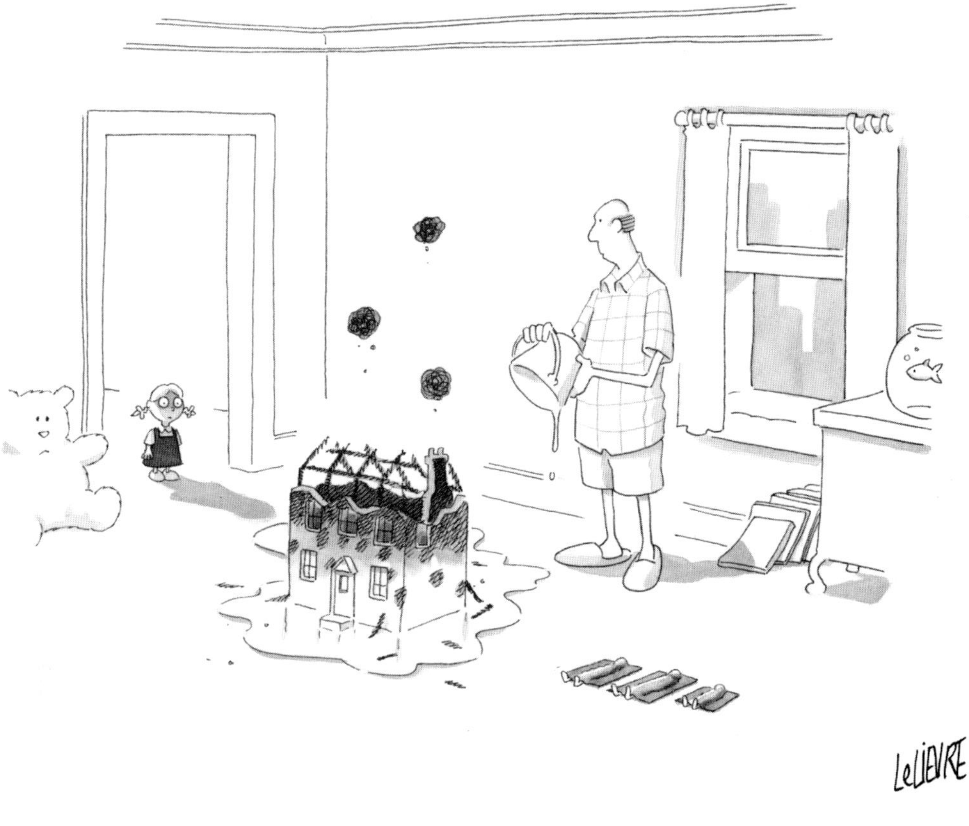

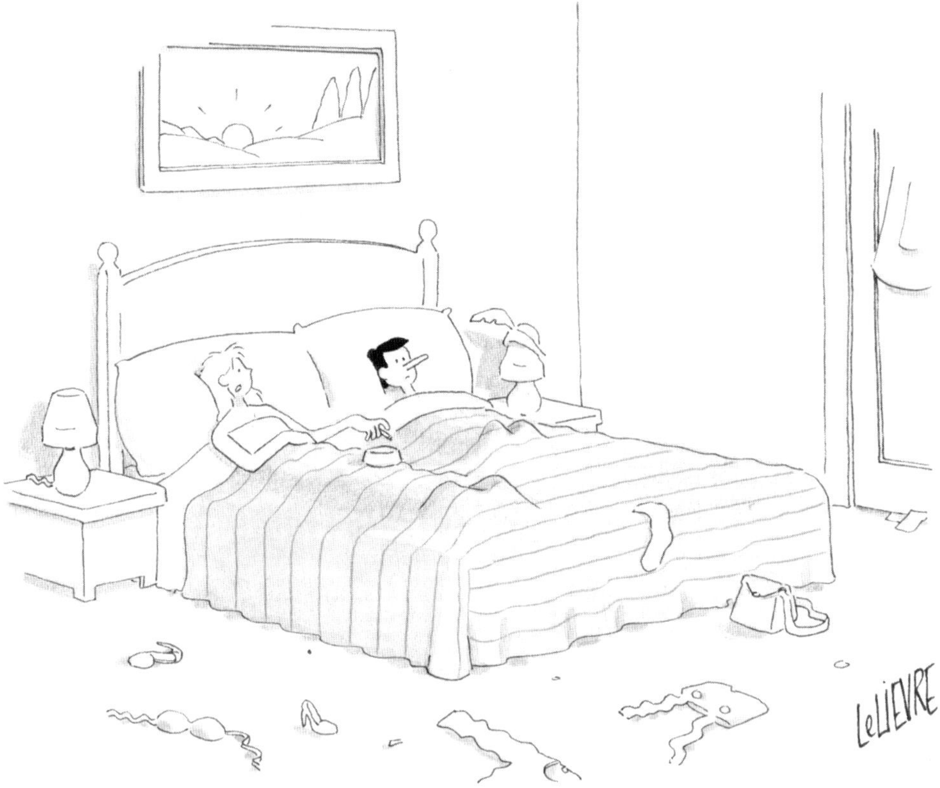
LeLIEVRE

"Lie to me again."

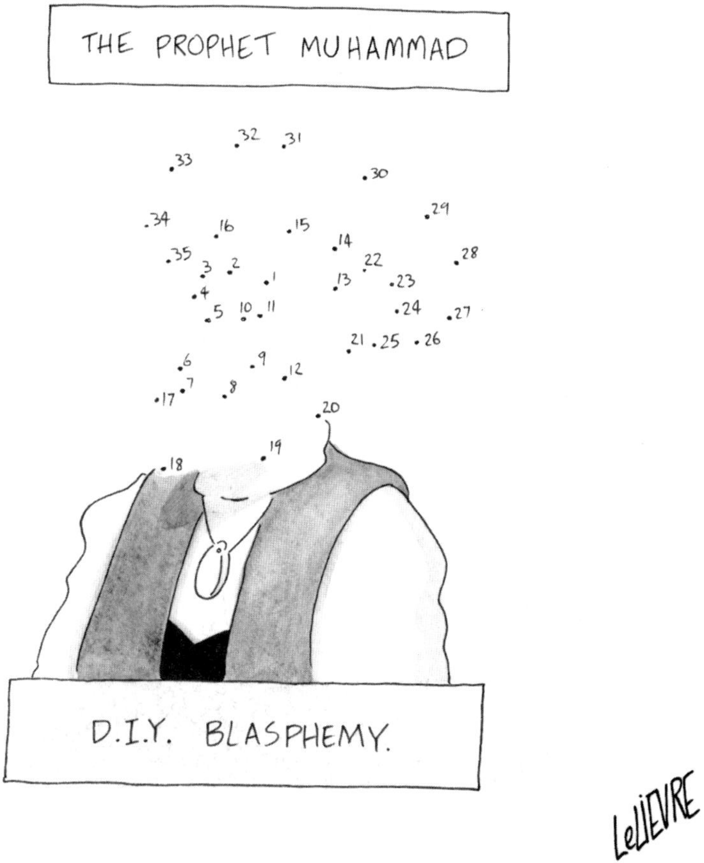
THE PROPHET MUHAMMAD
D.I.Y. BLASPHEMY.
LeLIEVRE

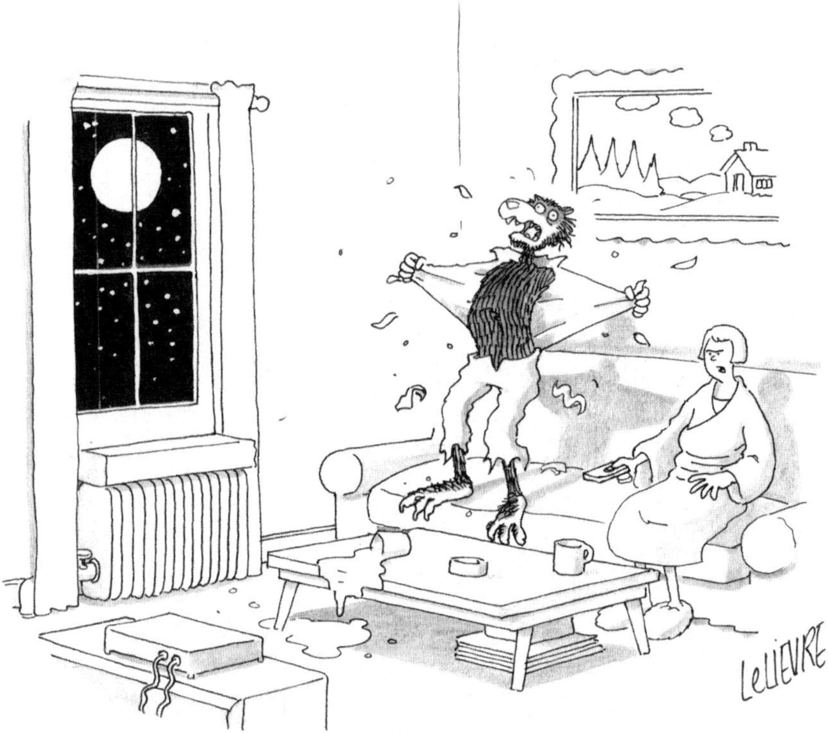
LeLIEVRE

"You're lucky. I'm turning into my mother."

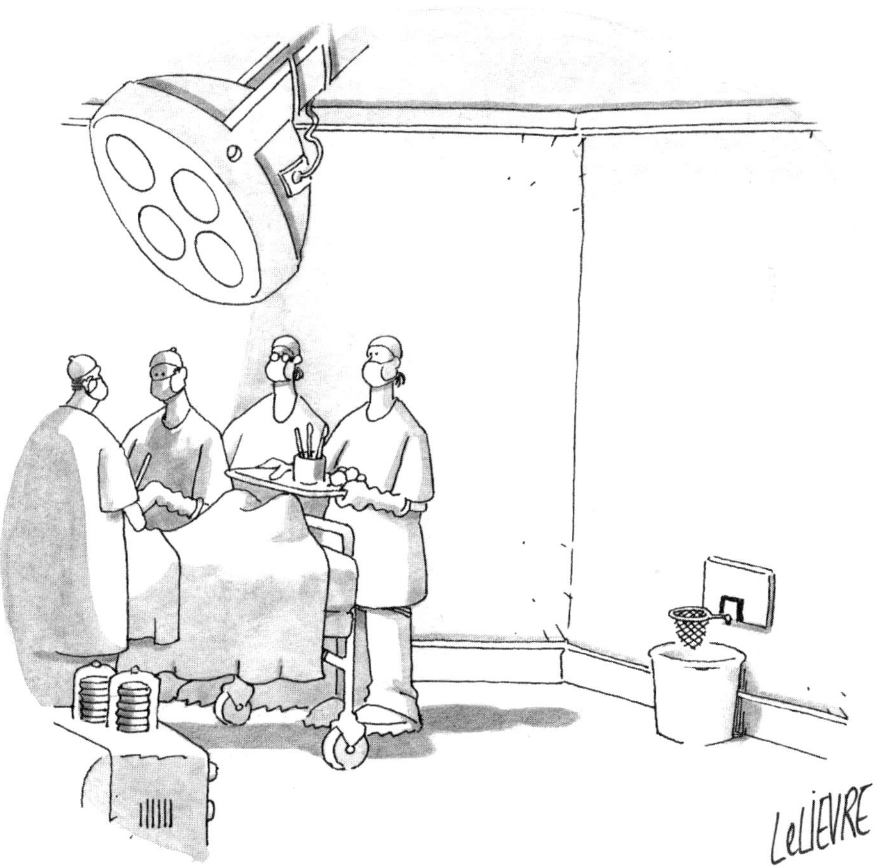
LeLIEVRE

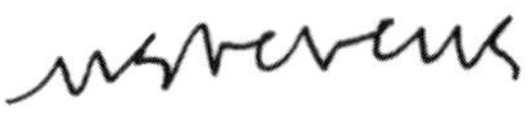

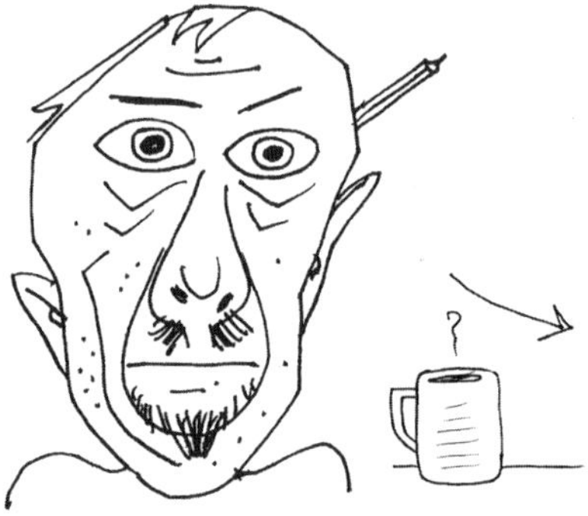

Mick Stevens

Frequently Asked Questions

- *Where do you get your ideas?*
  reallyfunnycartoonideas2makeurich.com.

- *Which comes first, the picture or the caption?*
  The picture. No, the caption. No, the picture. No . . . (I think I smell my circuits overheating.)

- *How'd you get started?*
  Jumper cables were involved.

- *I admire . . .*
  John Coltrane, Jimmy Carter, Jennifer Lopez, and Daffy Duck.

- *How do you deal with rejection?*
  Rant. Rave. Shake my fist at God. Throw the phone across the room.

- *What are some things that make you laugh and why?*
  The human condition, the State of the Union, presidential politics . . . because it's not manly to cry.

- *I've got a great idea for a cartoon—wanna hear it?*
  Define *great*.

Infrequently Asked Questions

- *Have you mooned or been mooned more often in your life?*
  Define *mooned*.

- *What would make a terrible pizza topping?*
  Spanish moss.

- *What might one expect to find at a really low-budget amusement park?*
  A child-powered carousel.

- *What did the shepherd say to the three-legged sheepdog?*
  Where's the other fourth of the flock?

Draw Something in This Space

. . . that will help us understand your childhood.

And Now for a Few More Questions . . .

- *What do you hate drawing?*
  Big religious murals. No commissions, please.

- *Being as accurate as possible, how many desert island cartoons do you think you've come up with and submitted to* The New Yorker*?*
  4,268 as of this week. Hold on, I just got another idea. . . .

- *What's the funniest thing that you witnessed, overheard, or came up with that you couldn't figure out how to use in a cartoon?*
  A conversation between two trees I overheard during an LSD experience in my youth. (You had to be there.)

Naming Names

- *What name might you give to a mild-mannered, middle-aged, bespectacled dental assistant in one of your cartoons?*
  Tubby Molarbuster.

- *Other than Lance, what name would you give to a twenty-eight-year-old entertainment lawyer with a blue-dyed fauxhawk who cycles on weekends?*
  Spinner Greasely.

- *What would be a good name for a new, commercially unviable breakfast cereal?*
  Nuts 'n' Bolts.

- *Come up with a name for an unpleasant medical procedure.*
  Coronary Overpass.

- *If you used a pen name, what would it be?*
  Max Doubt.

Complete the Pie Chart Below

. . . in a way that tells us something about your life or how you think.

TUESDAY
WEDNESDAY
MONDAY
THURSDAY
FRIDAY
SATURDAY
SUNDAY

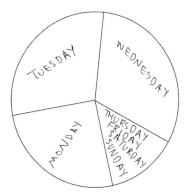

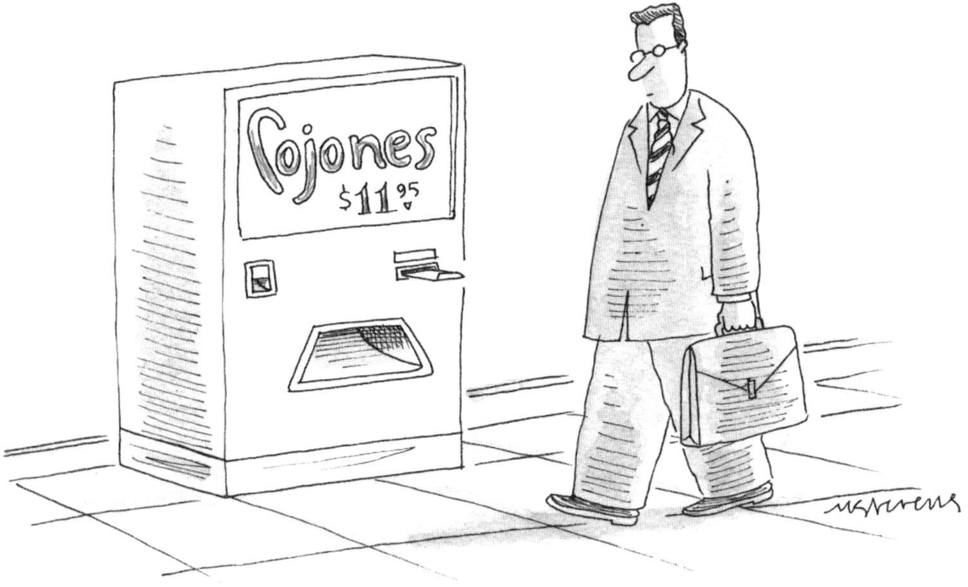
Cojones
$11.95
MSTEVENS

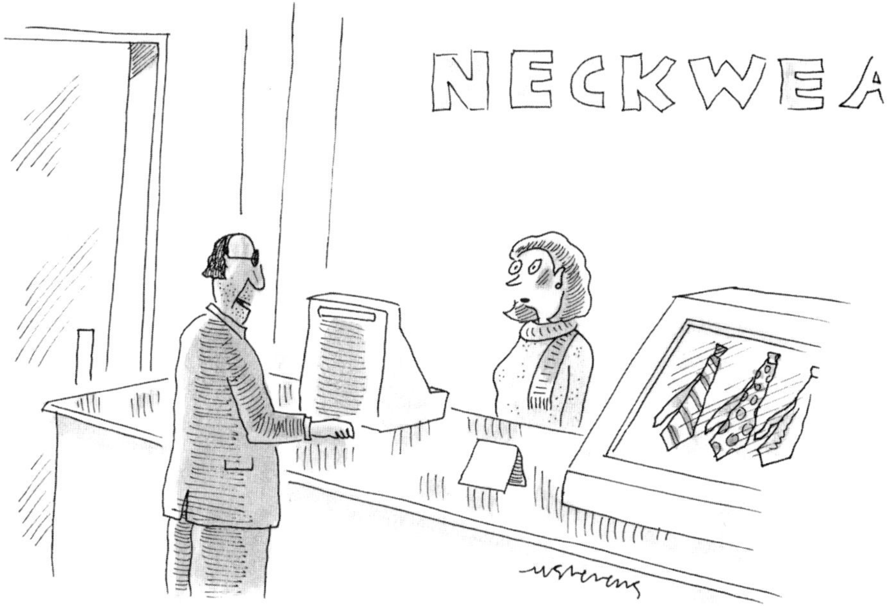
NECKWEA
mstevens

"I'm looking for a tie that says 'I'm not wearing any underwear.'"

"*I don't know how to say this, but I've found someone else.*"

"I'm in for killing a guy for snoring."

"Sorry about the reception, Lou. I grabbed my enchilada by mistake."

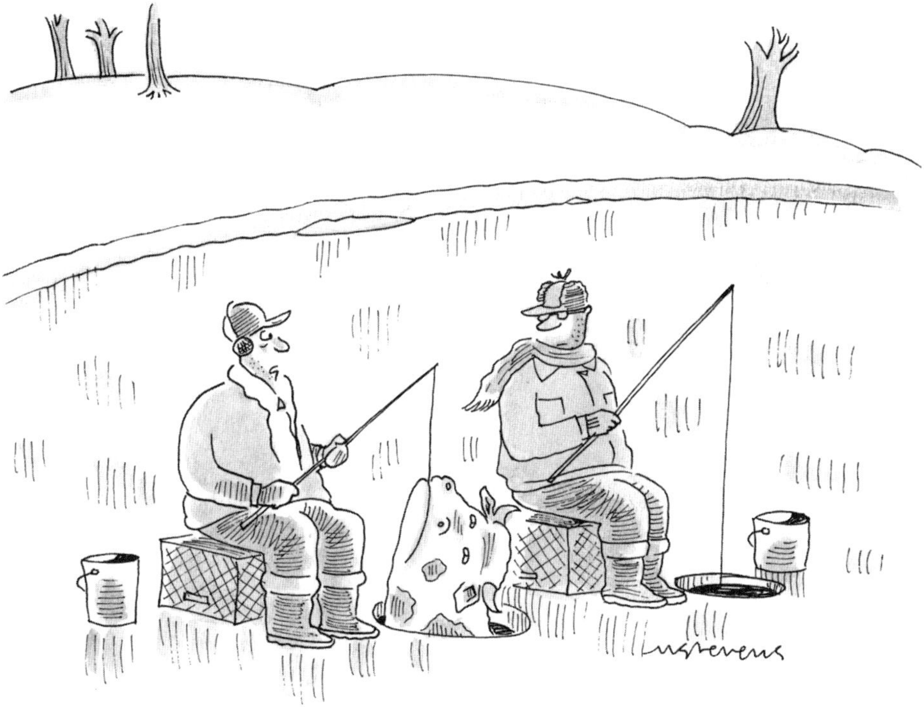
mstevens

"I just can't seem to get the hang of it."

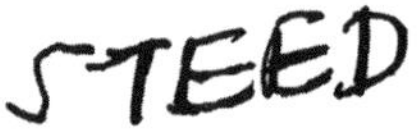
STEED

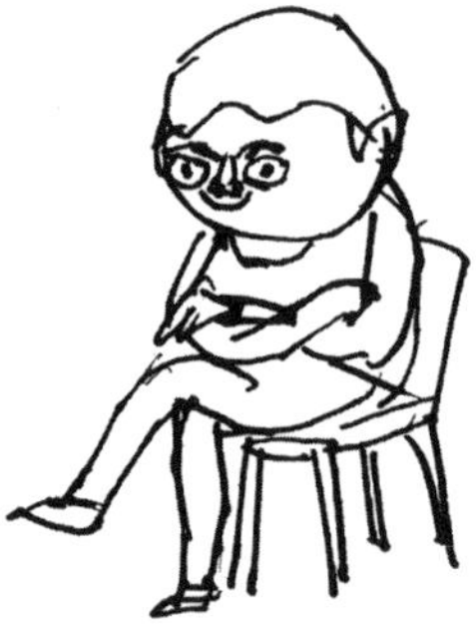

Ed Steed

Frequently Asked Questions

- *Where do you get your ideas?*
  From my drawings.
- *Which comes first, the picture or the caption?*
  The picture.
- *How'd you get started?*
  Drew a picture. Then thought of a caption.
- *I admire . . .*
  . . . d you more before I got to know you.
- *How do you deal with rejection?*
  Rejection is just an anagram of Eric Jeton.
- *What are some things that make you laugh and why?*
  Ears, ties, flags, crucifixes, weapons, fruit, robots, cups, curtains, gloves, dreams, cowboys, string, teeth, horses, jewellery, astronauts, tennis, musical instruments, priests, furniture, boats, hats, crocodiles, etc.
- *I've got a great idea for a cartoon—wanna hear it?*
  Definitely not.

Infrequently Asked Questions

- *Have you mooned or been mooned more often in your life?*
  Same number for both as of this morning.
- *What would make a terrible pizza topping?*
  Extra cheese.
- *What might one expect to find at a really low-budget amusement park?*
  People having a nice time away from amusement park snobs like you.
- *What did the shepherd say to the three-legged sheepdog?*
  "Sheepdog is just an anagram of Sep Hodge."

Draw Something in This Space

. . . that will help us understand your childhood.

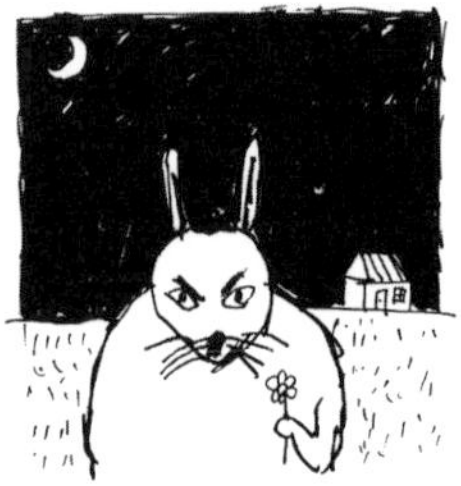

Draw Some Sort of Doodle

. . . using the random lines below as a starting point.

And Now for a Few More Questions . . .

■ *What do you hate drawing?*
Dogs, shadows, bushes, offices, money, scissors, Ancient Egypt, fire, snails, hands, sand, oranges, glass, fish, crowds, heights, enclosed spaces, snakes, flying, meeting new people, blood.

■ *Being as accurate as possible, how many desert island cartoons do you think you've come up with and submitted to* The New Yorker?
About ten.

■ *What's the funniest thing that you witnessed, overheard, or came up with that you couldn't figure out how to use in a cartoon?*
Astronaut dog.

Naming Names

■ *What name might you give to a mild-mannered, middle-aged, bespectacled dental assistant in one of your cartoons?*
First rule of cartooning is never give people names.

■ *Other than Lance, what name would you give to a twenty-eight-year-old entertainment lawyer with a blue-dyed fauxhawk who cycles on weekends?*
Never.

■ *What would be a good name for a new, commercially unviable breakfast cereal?*
"If anything happens, I love you."

■ *Come up with a name for an unpleasant medical procedure.*
Kidney Hypnosis.

■ *If you used a pen name, what would it be?*
Edward Steeed.

Complete the Pie Chart Below

. . . in a way that tells us something about your life or how you think.

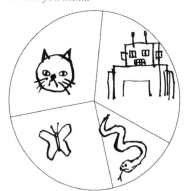

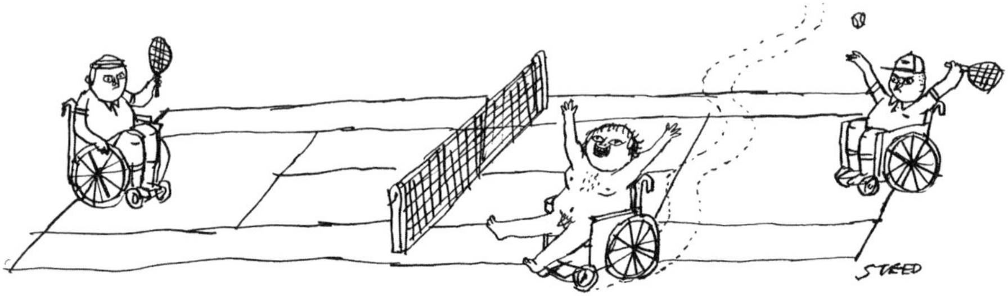
STEED

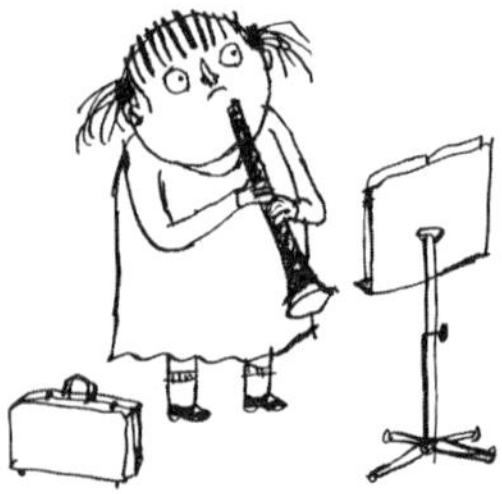

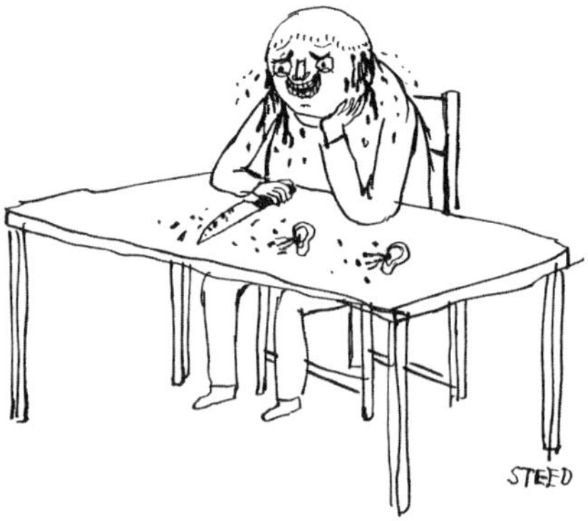
STEED

"Okay. Carry on."

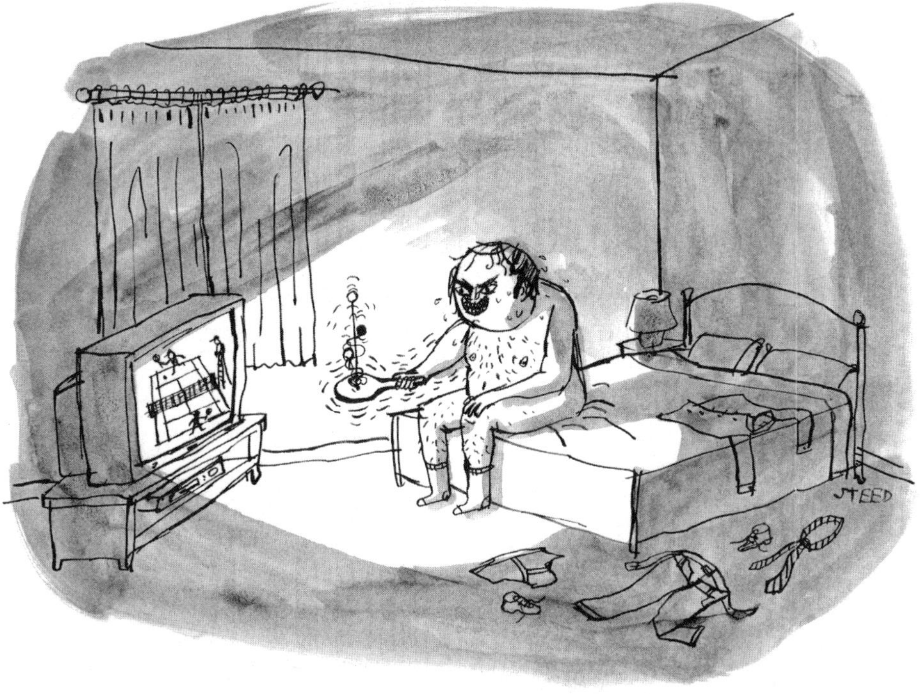
STEED

STEED

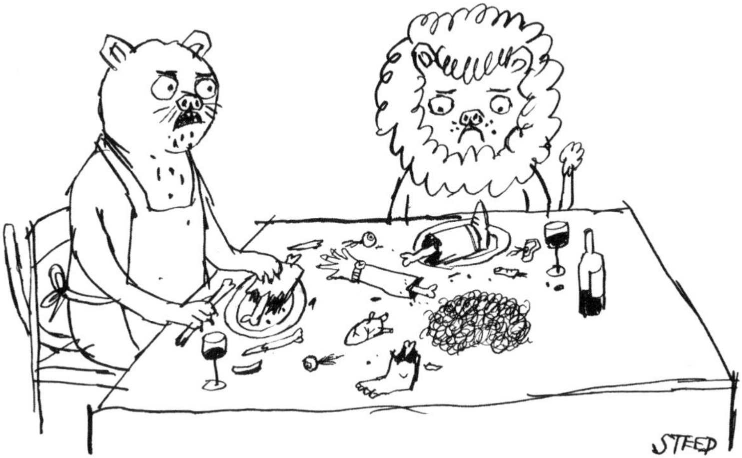
STEED

"What's the matter? I thought you like Art Garfunkel."

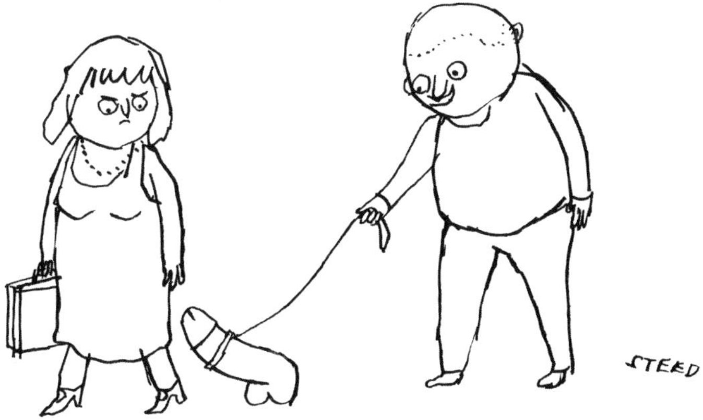
STEED

"Oooh, I think he likes you."

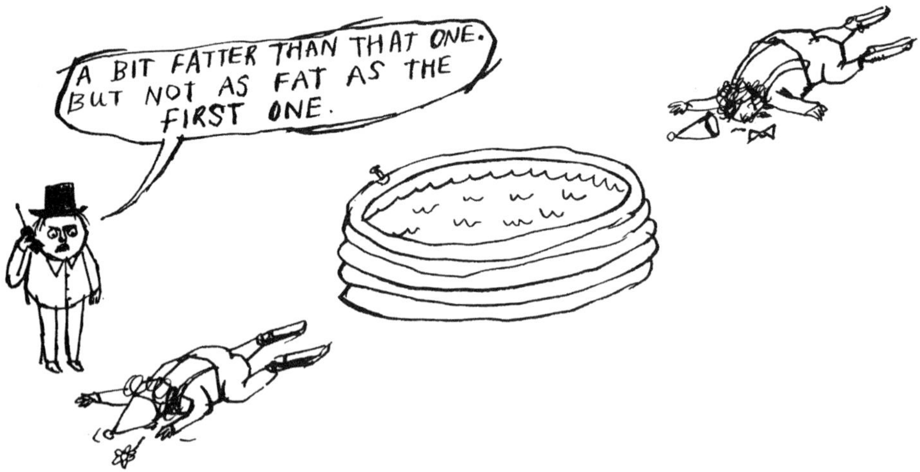
A BIT FATTER THAN THAT ONE. BUT NOT AS FAT AS THE FIRST ONE.

STEED

P. S. Mueller

MUELLER

Frequently Asked Questions

- *Where do you get your ideas?*
  A secret place inside your head.

- *Which comes first, the picture or the caption?*
  The horror! The horror!

- *How'd you get started?*
  I was born in the sea. At first, I just sort of floated around and absorbed sunlight, but after many years I slowly became a witless jellyfish, which was great until I found myself struggling in high school. Then peer pressure got to me, like, big time. Not long after that, I became a changeling mutant thing with a raging appetite for randomly acquired gene fragments to give my DNA some cool racing stripes. Eventually, however, despite my best efforts, I developed bilateral symmetry, eyes, facial hair, and a boyish grin, and then failed horribly in my attempt to master Chinese kick-farming, which gave me cauliflower feet. Perhaps not surprisingly, I was soon taken aboard a strange craft by mambo salad people from space. They were a crunchy race of aruguloids of crouton, which is about all I can remember before the experiments began. I woke up here utterly soaked in vinaigrette. And so, without a clear memory of my captors, I wander the streets of this grim dystopian megalopolis. Is that OK?

Maybe there's a way out of this place. Perhaps my plankton friends will help. In closing, I'd just like to say evolution is a lie, and God was made by the oceans. Thanks.

- *I admire . . .*
  My own boundless capacity for coffee and my wife's patience.

- *How do you deal with rejection?*
  I tend to tell editors that, fine, I'll just take my MacArthur genius grant and go squat in a field somewhere in the former Yugoslavia, goddammit!

- *What are some things that make you laugh and why?*
  The Donald Rumsfeld squint—it's just flat-out comical the way he brings it right to the edge of that crazy old man thing. And cats, always cats—because in the absence of prey, they're quite happy to attack their own little charades.

- *I've got a great idea for a cartoon—wanna hear it?*
  No. I'd rather taste it.

Infrequently Asked Questions

- *Have you mooned or been mooned more often in your life?*
  Mooned much many moons ago.

- *What would make a terrible pizza topping?*
  All those missing bees.

- *What might one expect to find at a really low-budget amusement park?*
  Petting abattoir.

- *What did the shepherd say to the three-legged sheepdog?*
  Where's lambie, you hideous freak?

And Now for a Few More Questions . . .

- *What do you hate drawing?*
  Victims. I can't stand the way their eyes appear to follow you.

- *Being as accurate as possible, how many desert island cartoons do you think you've come up with and submitted to* The New Yorker*?*
  Twenty or so. It's like an illness.

- *What's the funniest thing that you witnessed, overheard, or came up with that you couldn't figure out how to use in a cartoon?*
  Once, when discussing spearfishing, a friend seriously asked about what kind of bait is placed on the point.

Naming Names

- *What name might you give to a mild-mannered, middle-aged, bespectacled dental assistant in one of your cartoons?*
  Doris Bundt.

- *Other than Lance, what name would you give to a twenty-eight-year-old entertainment lawyer with a blue-dyed fauxhawk who cycles on weekends?*
  Matthew Diffee.

- *What would be a good name for a new, commercially unviable breakfast cereal?*
  Floor Chex.

- *Come up with a name for an unpleasant medical procedure.*
  Nastyplasty.

- *If you used a pen name, what would it be?*
  Mr. Pen.

Complete the Pie Chart Below

. . . in a way that tells us something about your life or how you think.

APPLE PIE
CHERRY PIE
BLUEBERRY PIE
WHALE PIE

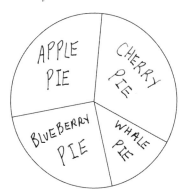

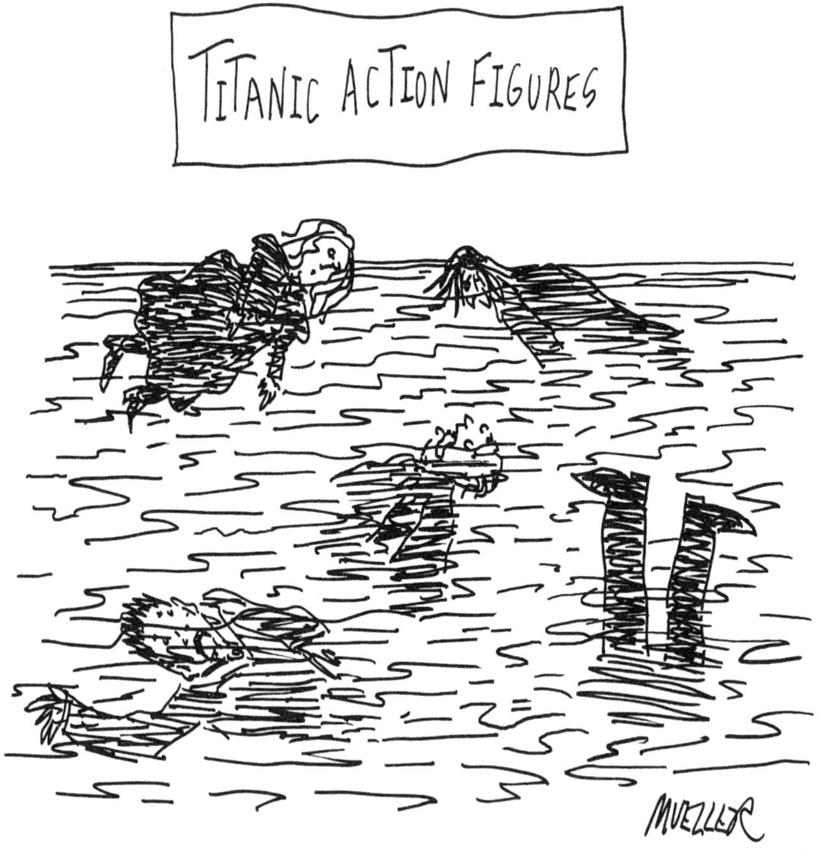
TITANIC ACTION FIGURES
MUELLER

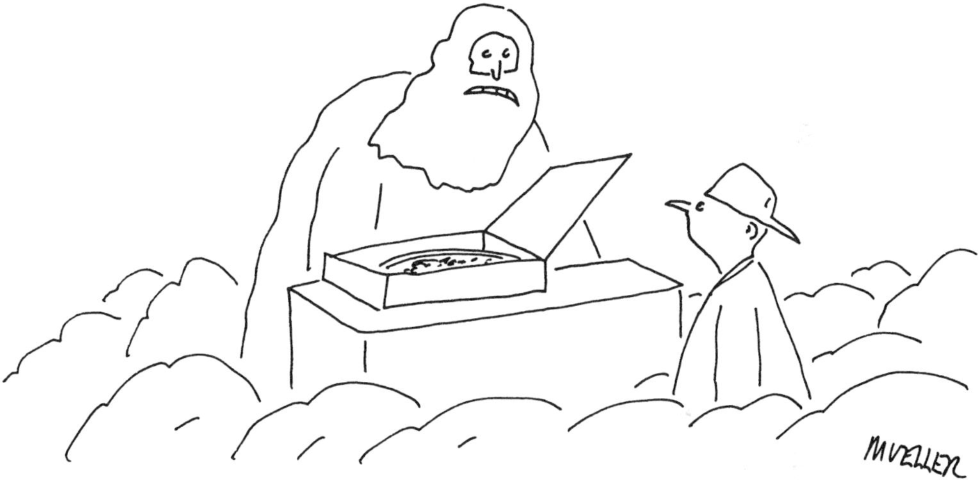
MUELLER

"It's got pineapple on it. You'll have to go to hell."

"I can't talk right now—I'm about to do something really stupid."

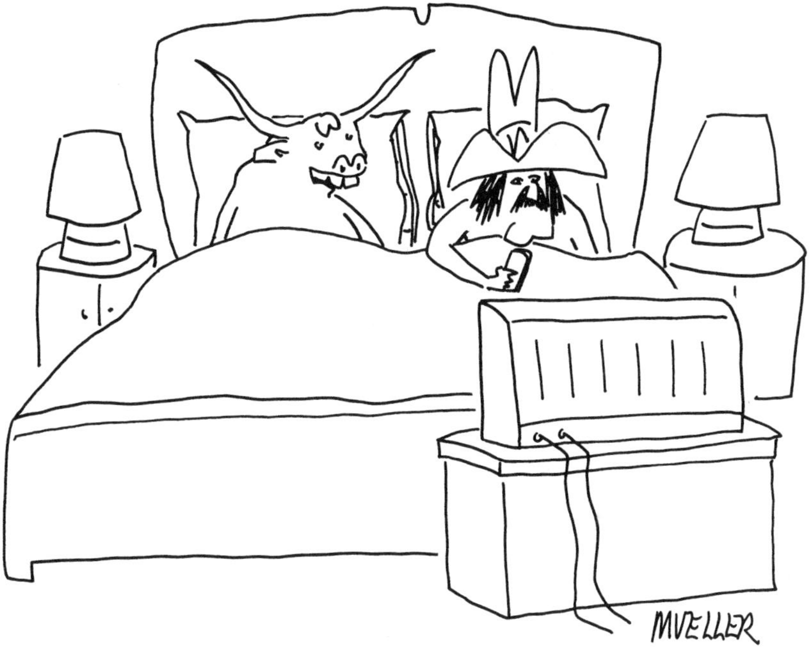
MUELLER

"Fast forward to the part where you herd me."

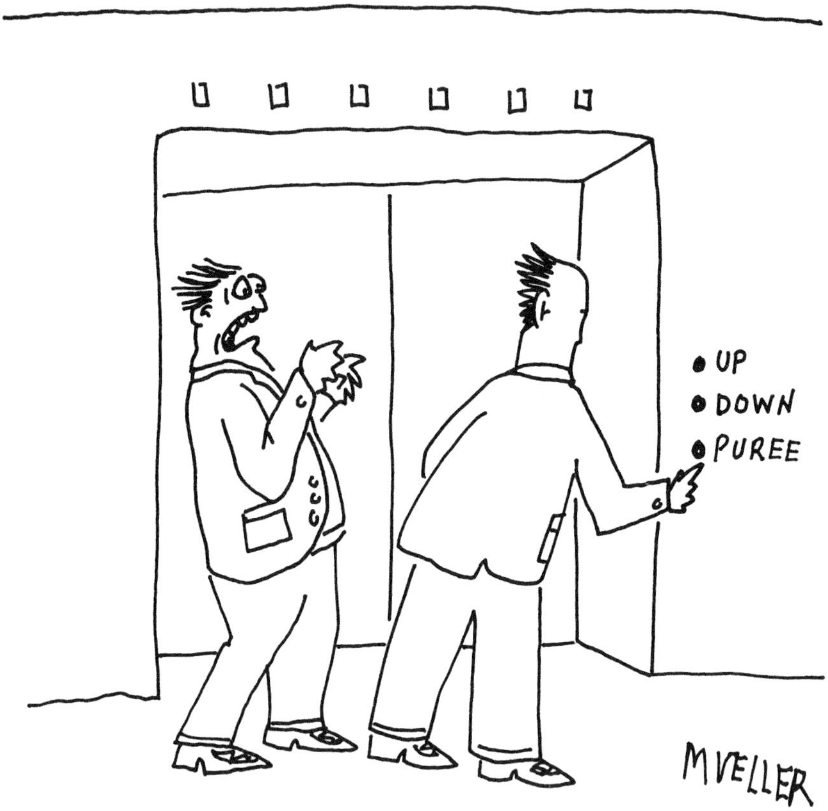
UP
DOWN
PUREE
MUELLER

CRACK HOE

MUELLER

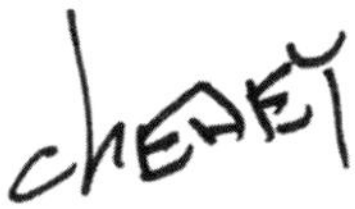
CHENEY

Tom Cheney

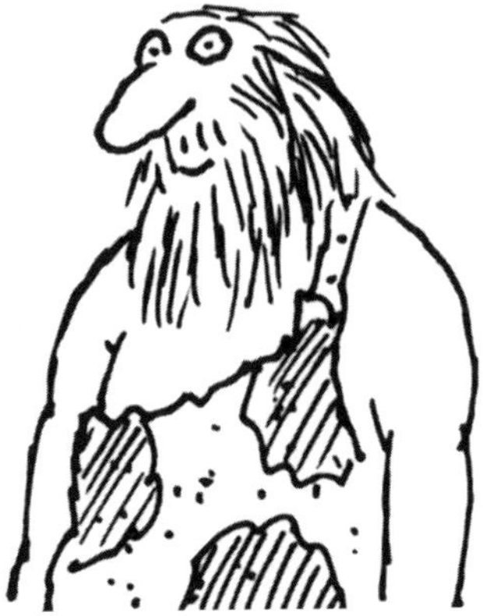

Frequently Asked Questions

- *Where do you get your ideas?*
  The produce section of the supermarket, but only if they're fresh.

- *Which comes first, the picture or the caption?*
  The picture, unless I overhear a couple of conservatives talking.

- *How'd you get started?*
  I got started the way all cartoonists do . . . one batch of submissions after another until I had enough rejection slips to construct a small studio of my own.

- *I admire . . .*
  Lenny Bruce, George Carlin, and Richard Pryor.

- *How do you deal with rejection?*
  I regard it as the norm. Selling work is the exception. Even after thirty years in this business, I still think of each cartoon sale as a miracle.

- *What are some things that make you laugh and why?*
  People who take themselves very seriously—it seems the only thing they have going for them is their own importance, and that, in and of itself, is hysterical.

- *I've got a great idea for a cartoon—wanna hear it?*
  Yes, but only if you're willing to bet one thousand dollars that it's never been done before.

Infrequently Asked Questions

- *Have you mooned or been mooned more often in your life?*
  The mooner, but only in church.

- *What would make a terrible pizza topping?*
  Lake Erie.

- *What might one expect to find at a really low-budget amusement park?*
  The Bobbing for Piranha tub.

- *What did the shepherd say to the three-legged sheepdog?*
  Here, Tripod, c'mere, boy!

Draw Something in This Space

. . . that will help us understand your childhood.

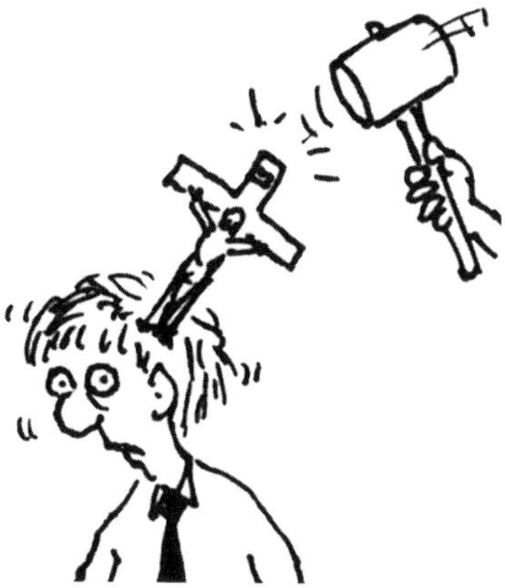

And Now for a Few More Questions . . .

- *What do you hate drawing?*
  Trees, badgers, baby elephants, marbles, and nude Eskimos.

- *Being as accurate as possible, how many desert island cartoons do you think you've come up with and submitted to* The New Yorker*?*
  Two, maybe three . . . oh, alright, about fifty.

- *What's the funniest thing that you witnessed, overheard, or came up with that you couldn't figure out how to use in a cartoon?*
  Watching an intoxicated man trying to find the coin return on a parking meter.

Naming Names

- *What name might you give to a mild-mannered, middle-aged, bespectacled dental assistant in one of your cartoons?*
  Yolanda Flench.

- *Other than Lance, what name would you give to a twenty-eight-year-old entertainment lawyer with a blue-dyed fauxhawk who cycles on weekends?*
  Laird Bodine.

- *What would be a good name for a new, commercially unviable breakfast cereal?*
  Anchovy Puffs.

- *Come up with a name for an unpleasant medical procedure.*
  A colonoscopic tonsillectomy.

- *If you used a pen name, what would it be?*
  Dixon Ticonderoga.

Complete the Pie Chart Below

. . . in a way that tells us something about your life or how you think.

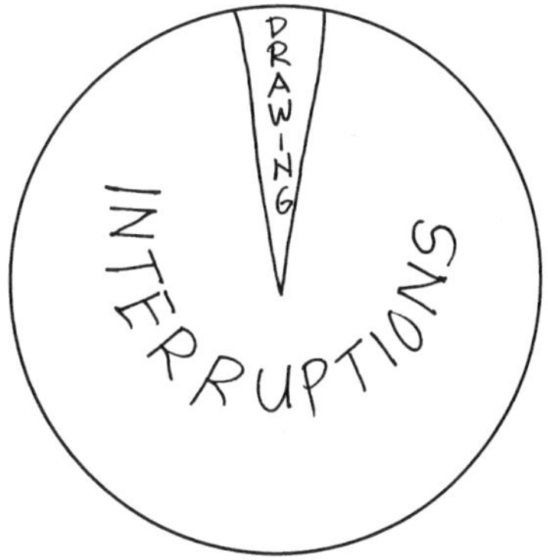
DRAWING
INTERRUPTIONS

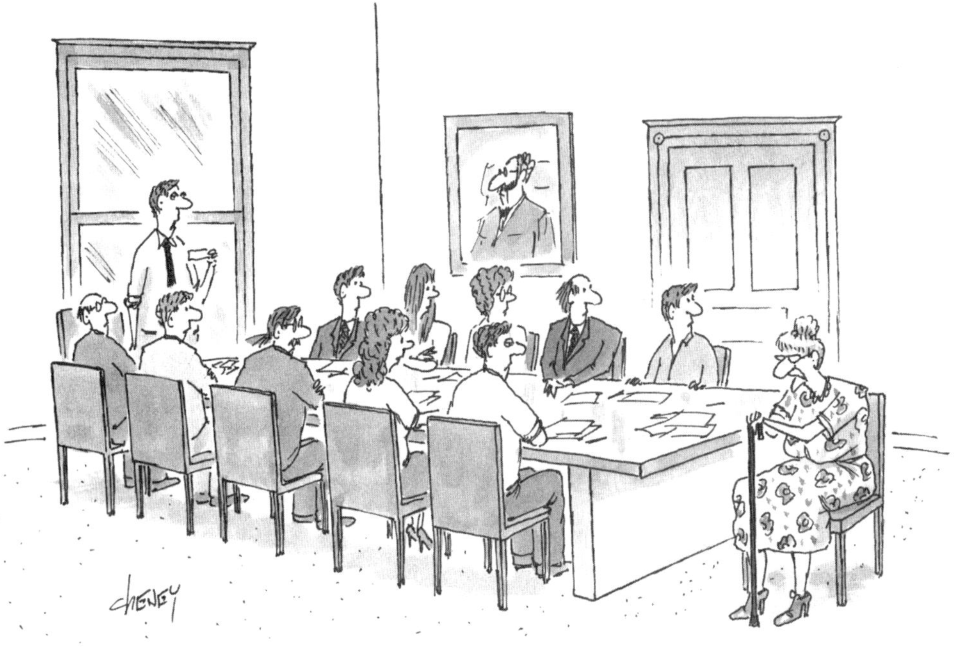
CHENEY

"We're going to be here awhile, folks—
I count eleven 'not guilty's' and one 'fry the bastard.'"

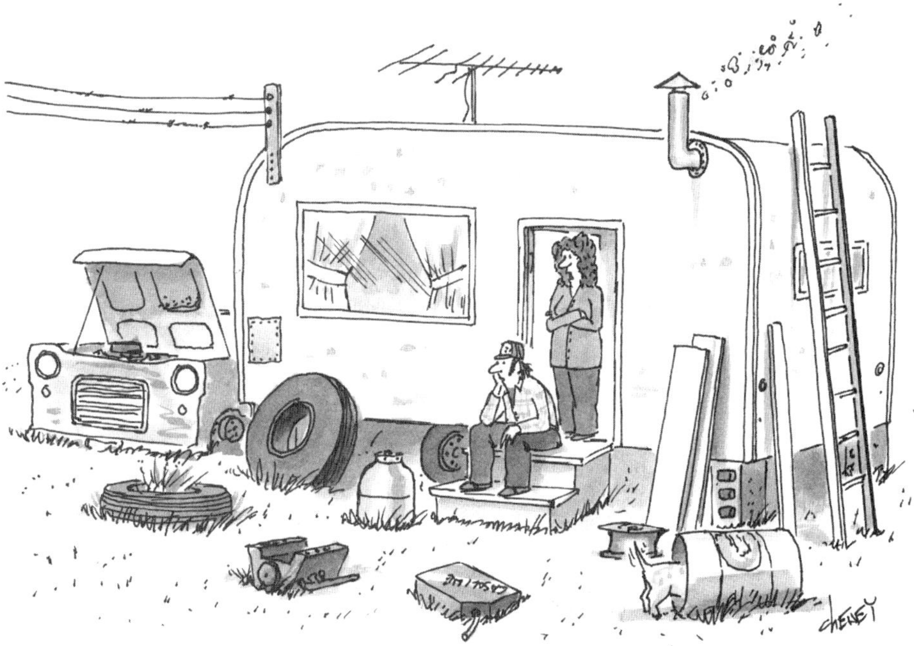
CHENEY

"What do you say we just kick back and let things slide for a while?"

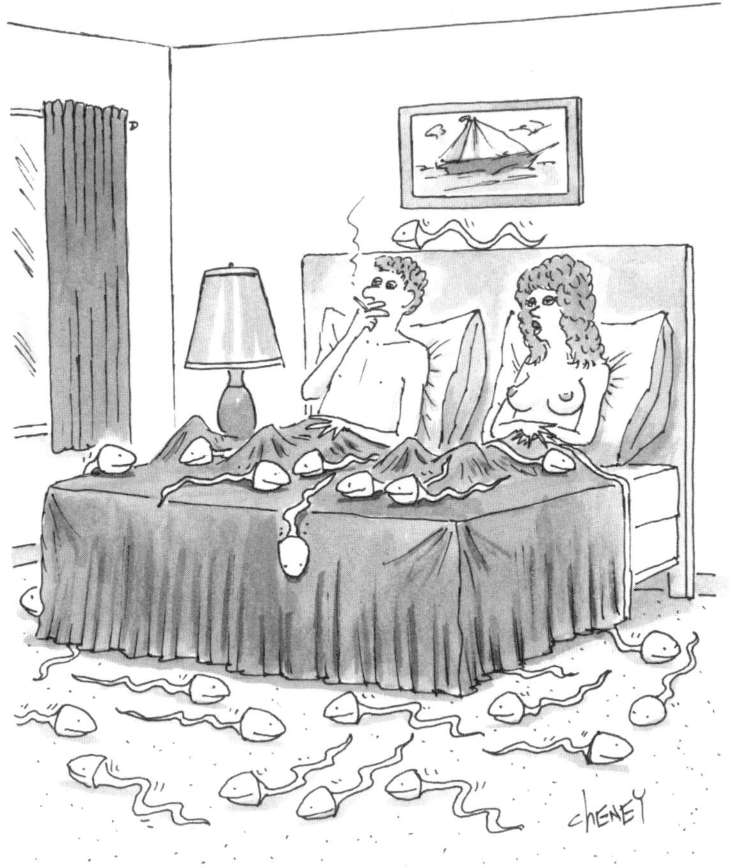
cheney

"So, how long have you been working at the plutonium plant?"

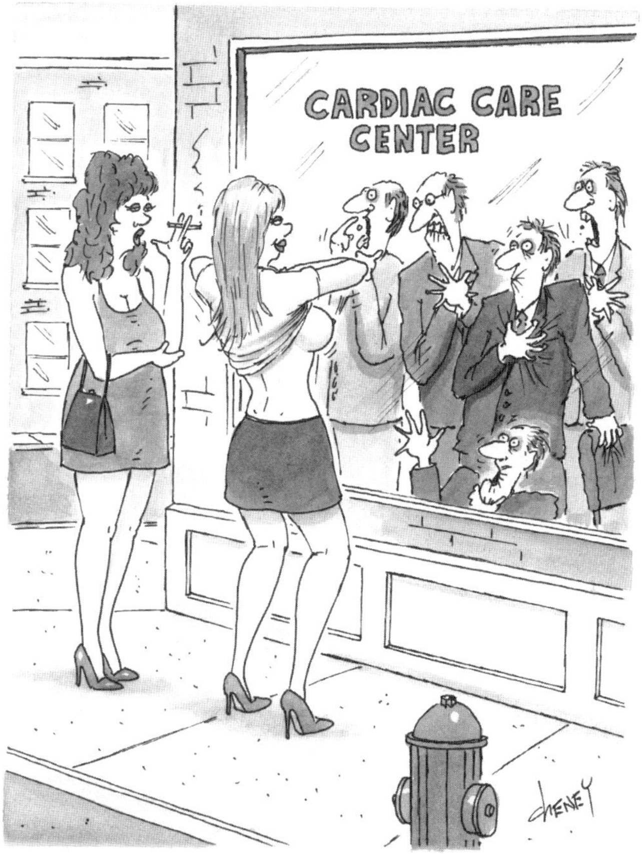
CARDIAC CARE
CENTER
CHENEY

"You're one sick puppy, Nadine."

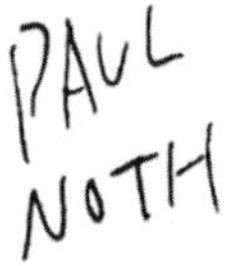
PAUL
NOTH

Paul Noth

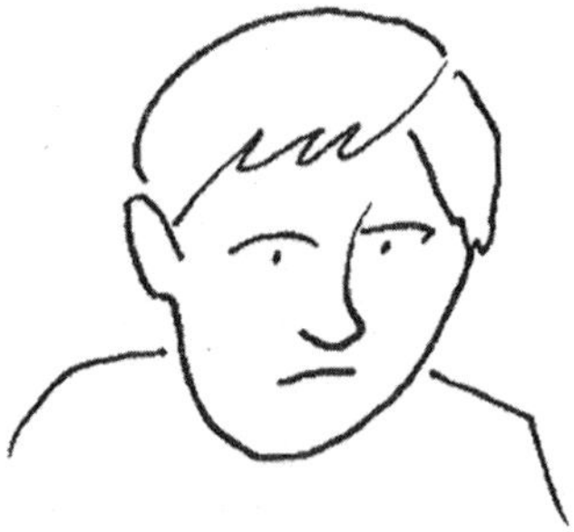

Frequently Asked Questions

- *Where do you get your ideas?*
  From a magical place called Boredom.

- *Which comes first, the picture or the caption?*
  1. Mental image/idea.
  2. Written caption (if necessary).
  3. Drawing.

- *How'd you get started?*
  Sketchin' for nickels on the old Bert Levy Circuit.

- *I admire . . .*
  See self-portrait.

- *How do you deal with rejection?*
  Constantly.

- *What are some things that make you laugh and why?*
  My wife, Parnell—the funniester person in the world—Noths, Thiels, the best and worst cartoon, P. G. Wodehouse, Chuck Jones and Michael Maltese, Jack Handey, W. C. Fields, Woody Allen, Marx Brothers, etc.

- *I've got a great idea for a cartoon—wanna hear it?*
  How did you get into my basement?

Infrequently Asked Questions

- *Have you mooned or been mooned more often in your life?*
  I guess "been mooned." No, wait . . . hold on a sec. . . . Okay, make that "mooned."

- *What would make a terrible pizza topping?*
  Mike Wallace.

- *What might one expect to find at a really low-budget amusement park?*
  The "Tilt-O-Merle."

Draw Some Sort of Doodle

. . . using the random lines below as a starting point.

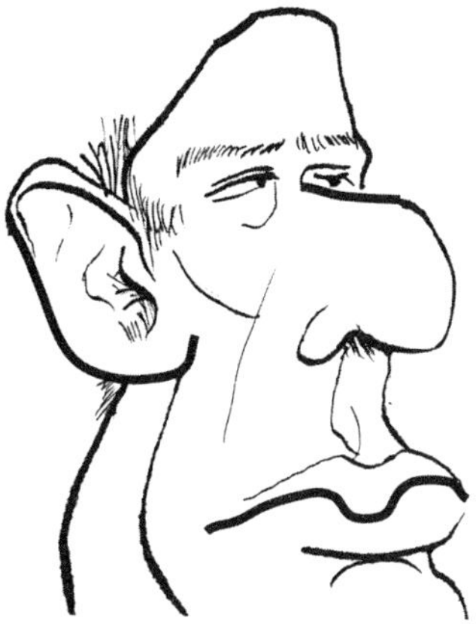

And Now for a Few More Questions . . .

- *What do you hate drawing?*

  WORDS and LETTERING

- *Being as accurate as possible, how many desert island cartoons do you think you've come up with and submitted to* The New Yorker*?*

  Five.

- *What's the funniest thing that you witnessed, overheard, or came up with that you couldn't figure out how to use in a cartoon?*

  That time I was stranded on a desert island.

Naming Names

- *What name might you give to a mild-mannered, middle-aged, bespectacled dental assistant in one of your cartoons?*

  Jenkins.

- *Other than Lance, what name would you give to a twenty-eight-year-old entertainment lawyer with a blue-dyed fauxhawk who cycles on weekends?*

  Pierce.

- *What would be a good name for a new, commercially unviable breakfast cereal?*

  Swollen Bub-O's.

- *Come up with a name for an unpleasant medical procedure.*

  Swollen-Bubo-Lance-Pierce.

- *If you used a pen name, what would it be?*

  Jenkins.

Complete the Pie Chart Below

. . . in a way that tells us something about your life or how you think.

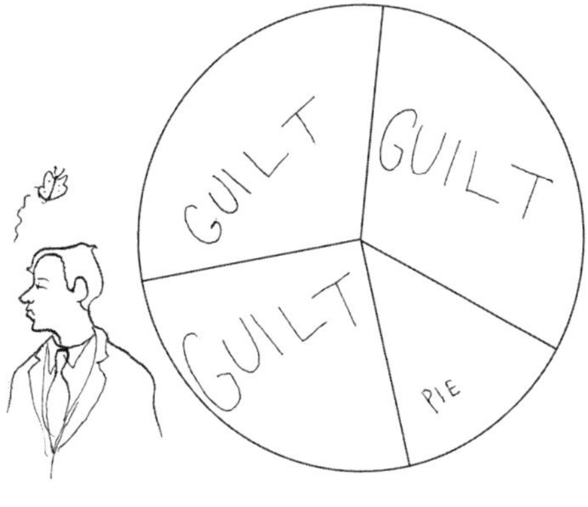
GUILT
GUILT
GUILT
PIE

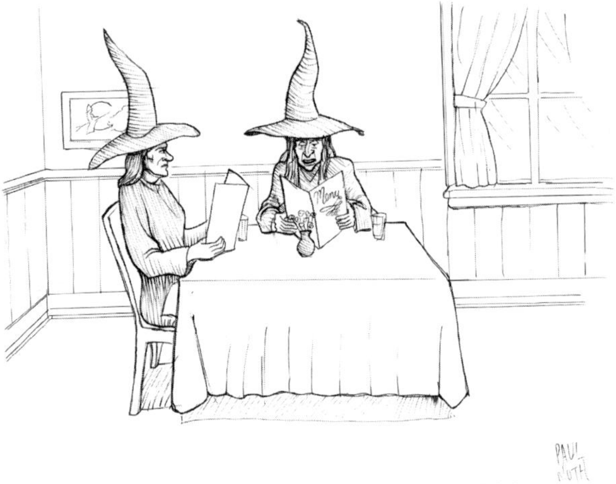
Menu
PAUL NOTH

"I'm thinking about having a child."

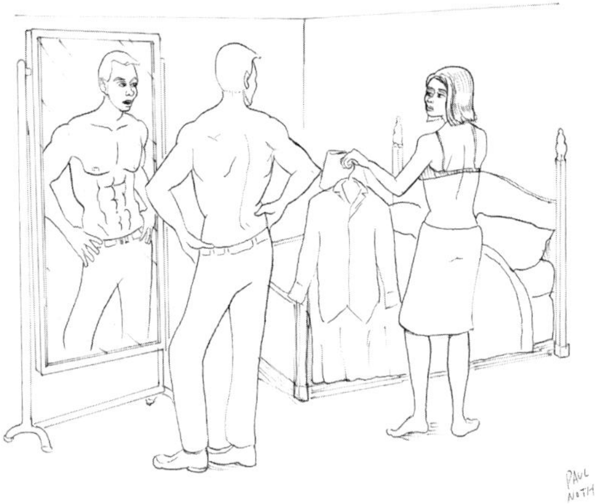
PAUL NOTH

"Do these abs make me look gay?"

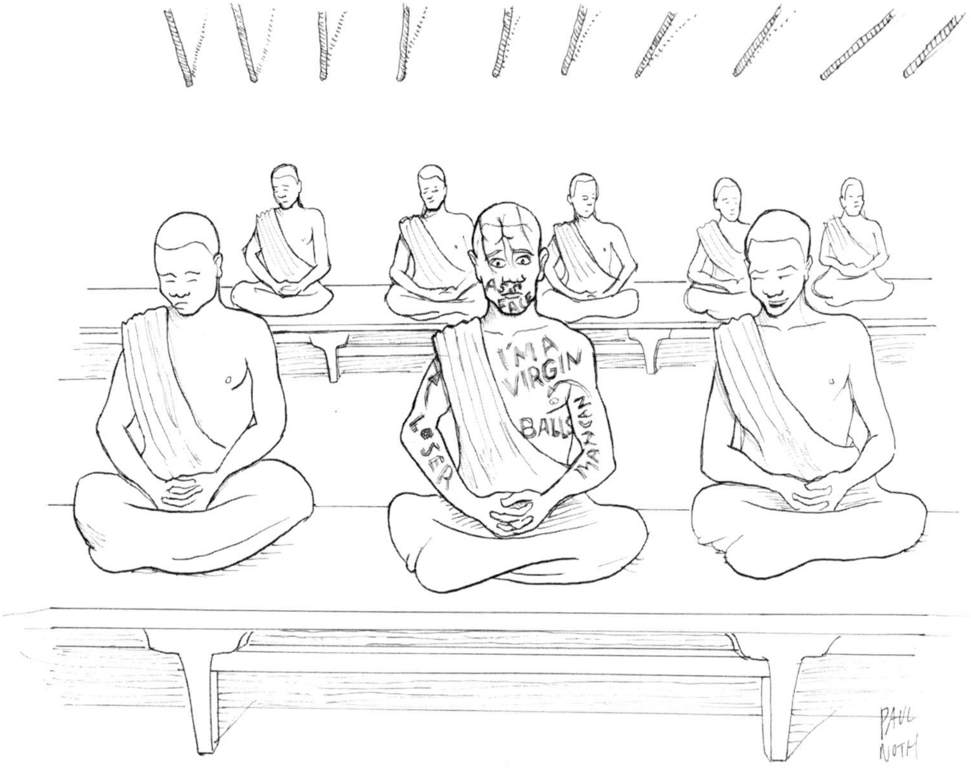
I'M A
VIRGIN
BALLS
LOSER
PAUL NOTH

"Dude, you totally passed out."

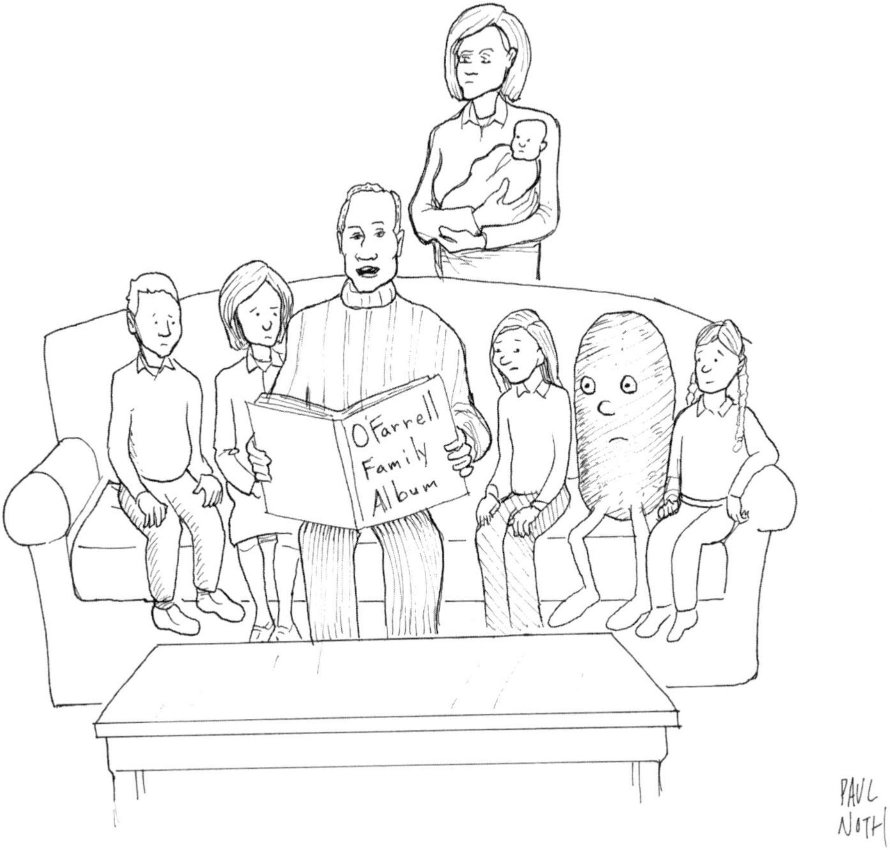
O'Farrell
Family
Album
PAUL
NOTH

"So, kids, you should all be thankful we don't live during a potato famine. Especially you, Jimmy."

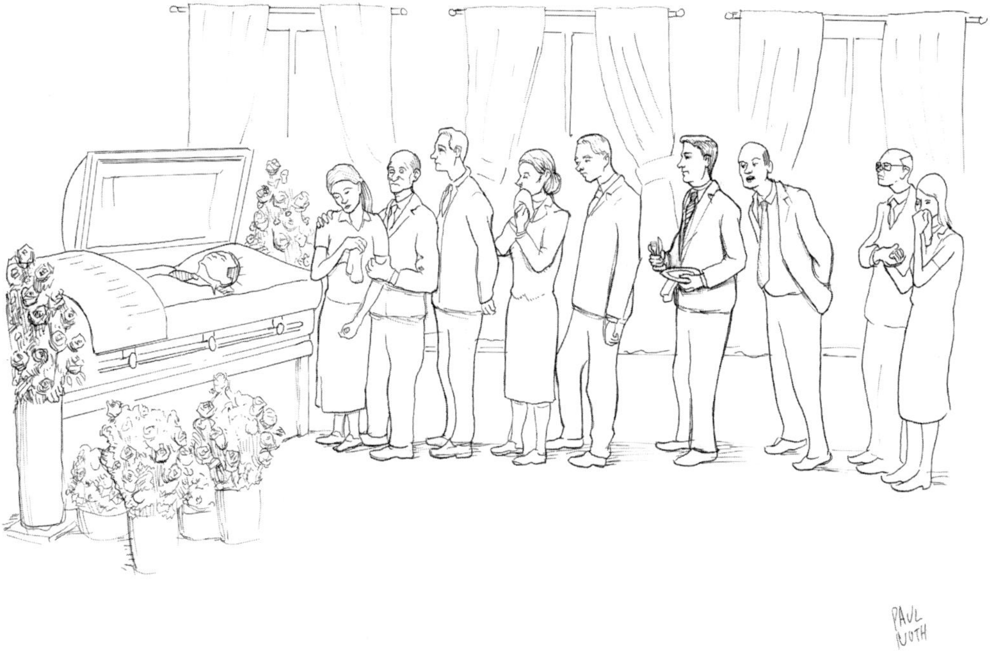
PAUL NOTH

"Wrong line, buddy."

Lars

Lars Kenseth

Frequently Asked Questions

- *Where do you get your ideas?*
  I get them from a guy named Idea Steve who sells cartoons under a bridge near the docks. He sells "other things" too, but I'm married. I see Navied down there sometimes.

- *Which comes first, the picture or the caption?*
  The caption usually comes first. Sometimes, if I'm really out of ideas, I'll just draw something and hope I get a caption. Then I just sit there and try to wonder.

- *How'd you get started?*
  My dad introduced me to the likes of Charles Addams and Sam Gross when I was very young. I would spend all day poring over cartoons with wide-eyed enthusiasm and think, "I am so much better than these clowns."

- *I admire . . .*
  Matt Diffee. . . . If the price is right.

- *How do you deal with rejection?*
  Scotch and late-night email screeds.

- *What are some things that make you laugh and why?*
  I don't know if anything's funnier than a gambling addict who's hit rock bottom. The out turned pockets, the sobbing, the rough stubble. Anyway, my dad is the funniest guy I know.

Infrequently Asked Questions

- *Have you mooned or been mooned more often in your life?*
  I don't think I've ever mooned or been mooned in my life!! Wow. Honestly, I don't know if that's a good thing.

- *What would make a terrible pizza topping?*
  J. K. Simmons.

- *What might one expect to find at a really low-budget amusement park?*
  Your seventh-grade science teacher at the levers of the Tilt-A-Whirl and in the depths of despair.

- *What did the shepherd say to the three-legged sheepdog?*
  I do.

Draw Something in This Space

. . . that will help us understand your childhood.

POTATOES
FRIEND
FLYER!

And Now for a Few More Questions . . .

- *What do you hate drawing?*
  Skinny people. My people are all fat oval pegs, and when I veer too far outside of that, nobody's happy.

- *Being as accurate as possible, how many desert island cartoons do you think you've come up with and submitted to* The New Yorker*?*
  Eleven.

- *What's the funniest thing that you witnessed, overheard, or came up with that you couldn't figure out how to use in a cartoon?*
  The First Punic War.

Naming Names

- *What name might you give to a mild-mannered, middle-aged, bespectacled dental assistant in one of your cartoons?*
  Gail Rathbone.

- *Other than Lance, what name would you give to a twenty-eight-year-old entertainment lawyer with a blue-dyed fauxhawk who cycles on weekends?*
  Tanner.

- *What would be a good name for a new, commercially unviable breakfast cereal?*
  The Lovely Bones.

- *Come up with a name for an unpleasant medical procedure.*
  Langston-Killabrew Elimination Procedure.

- *If you used a pen name, what would it be?*
  Glenn Close.

Complete the Pie Chart Below

. . . in a way that tells us something about your life or how you think.

PIZZA
WINE
POLITICS
PAUL GIAMATTI

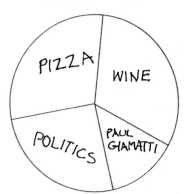

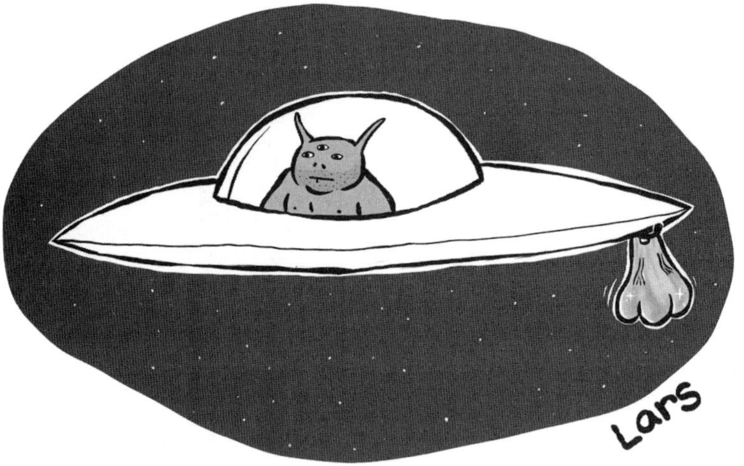
Lars

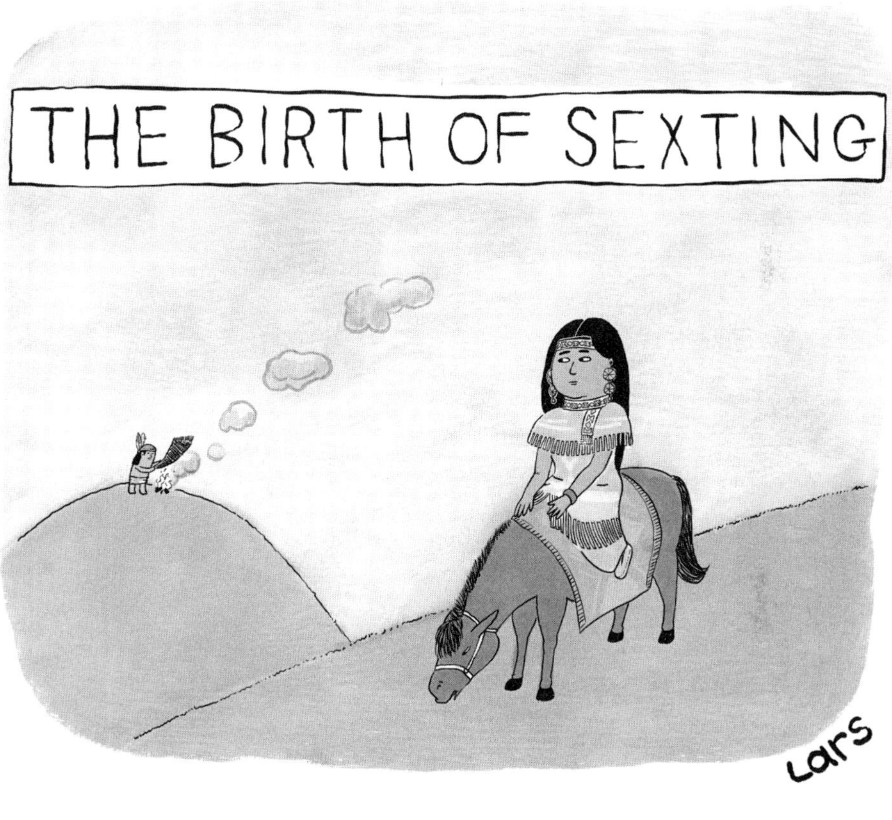
THE BIRTH OF SEXTING
Lars

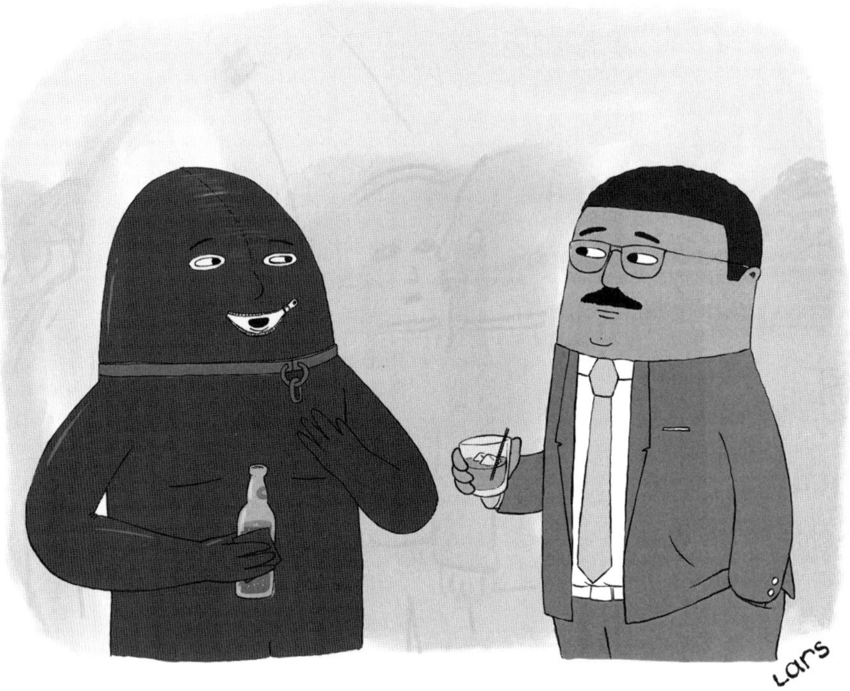
Lars

"No way! I'm also into stocks and bonds!"

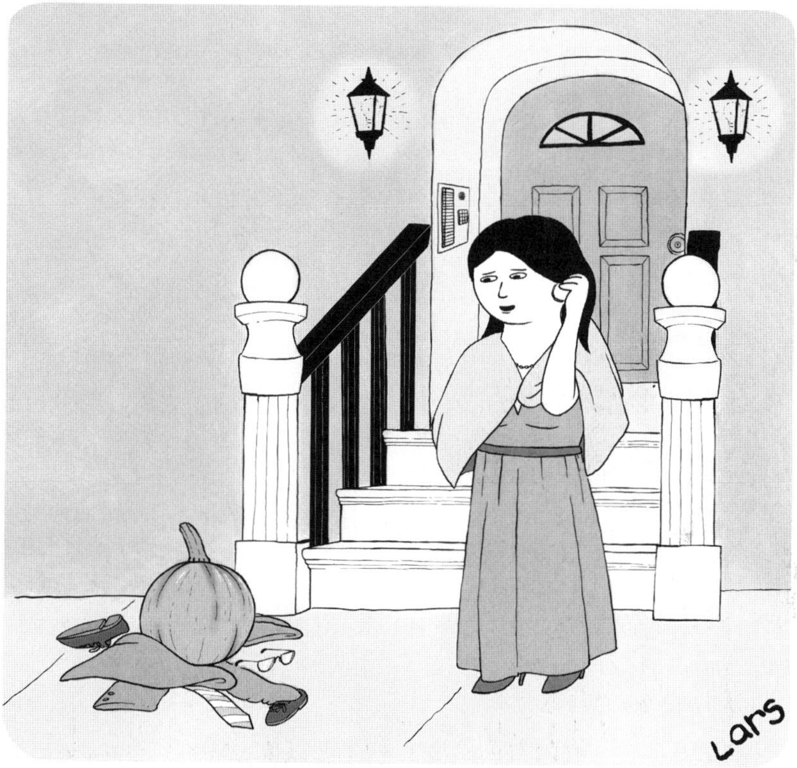
Lars

"That late already? Heh, wow . . . you can still come up if you want . . ."

S.GROSS

PLAYING RIGHT FIELD
IN THE DIRT YARD IN
THE BRONX.

Sam Gross

Frequently Asked Questions

- *Where do you get your ideas?*
  funnycartoons@autocafé.com.

- *Which comes first, the picture or the caption?*
  The agony.

- *How'd you get started?*
  I have a button at the base of my spine.

- *I admire . . .*
  Lou Myers and Hap Kliban. They were working at a level that I'm trying to attain.

- *How do you deal with rejection?*
  It doesn't bother me at all.

- *What are some things that make you laugh and why?*
  Pretty much everything and I don't know why, and I don't want to know why.

- *I've got a great idea for a cartoon—wanna hear it?*
  No, but I think Diffee has a need to.

Infrequently Asked Questions

- *Have you mooned or been mooned more often in your life?*
  I was once mooned by a starlet if that is at all possible.

- *What would make a terrible pizza topping?*
  Anything alive.

- *What might one expect to find at a really low-budget amusement park?*
  The Tunnel of Onan.

- *What did the shepherd say to the three-legged sheepdog?*
  A large erection will keep you from toppling over.

And Now for a Few More Questions . . .

- *What do you hate drawing?*
  Ten pins and horses. I've never done a cartoon of a horse bowling.

■ *Being as accurate as possible, how many desert island cartoons do you think you've come up with and submitted to* The New Yorker?

All of my gags are desert island gags. Those that are bought are redrawn by the staff at *The New Yorker* so that they take place somewhere else.

■ *What's the funniest thing that you witnessed, overheard, or came up with that you couldn't figure out how to use in a cartoon?*

It involved a naked eighty-three-year-old diabetic grandmother, and I can't go into any more detail.

Draw Something in This Space

. . . that will help us understand your childhood.

FIRECRACKER

DOG TURDS

Naming Names

■ *What name might you give to a mild-mannered, middle-aged, bespectacled dental assistant in one of your cartoons?*

Fiona.

■ *Other than Lance, what name would you give to a twenty-eight-year-old entertainment lawyer with a blue-dyed fauxhawk who cycles on weekends?*

Fiona.

■ *What would be a good name for a new, commercially unviable breakfast cereal?*

Sugarturds.

■ *Come up with a name for an unpleasant medical procedure.*

Endopancreatic lobar probe.

■ *If you used a pen name, what would it be?*

Mont Blanc.

Complete the Pie Chart Below

. . . in a way that tells us something about your life or how you think.

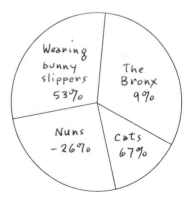

Wearing bunny slippers 53%

The Bronx 9%

Nuns −26%

Cats 67%

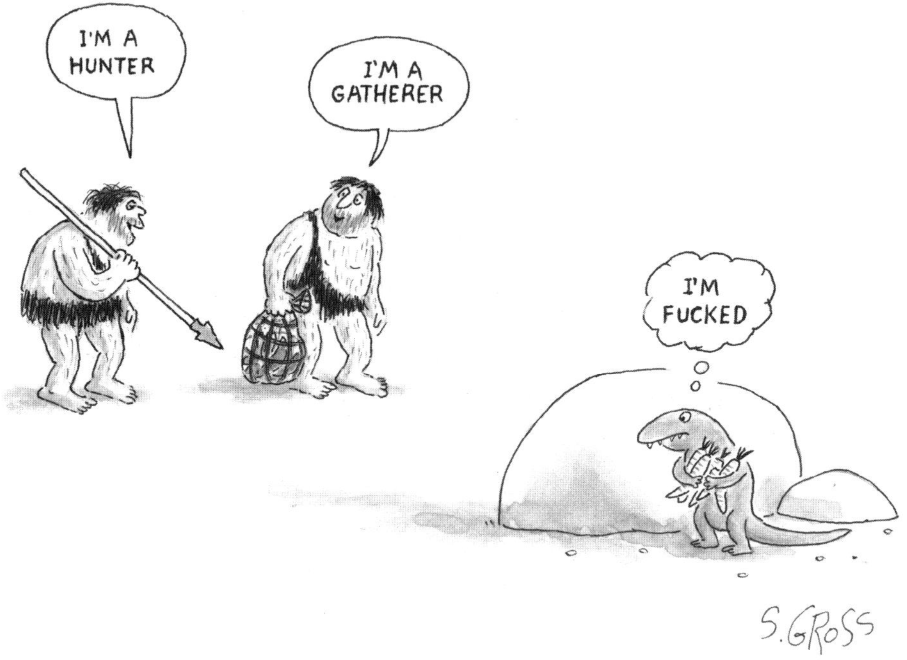
I'M A HUNTER
I'M A GATHERER
I'M FUCKED
S. GROSS

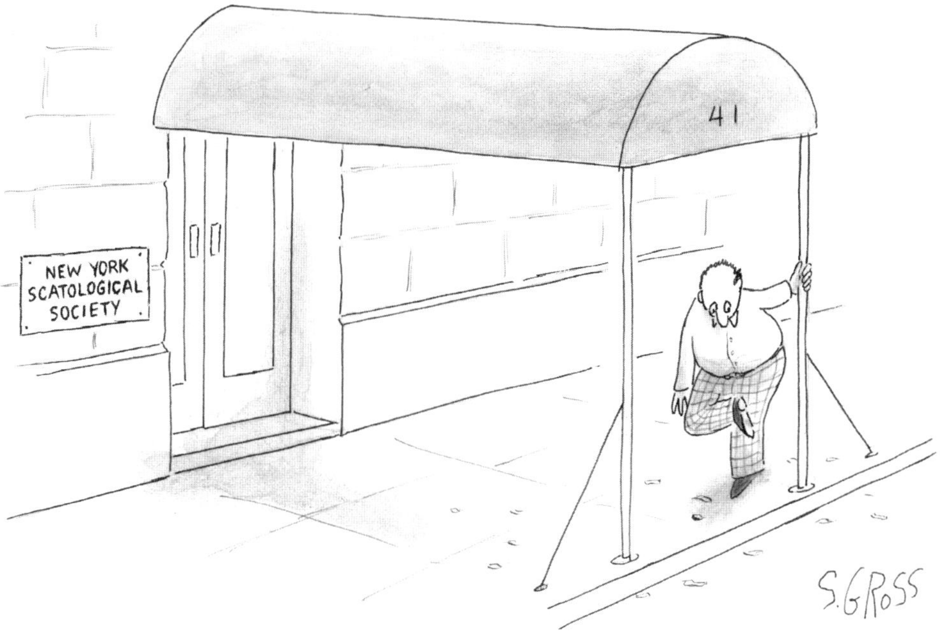
41
NEW YORK
SCATOLOGICAL
SOCIETY
S.GROSS

"*We've already blamed it on the Jews.*"

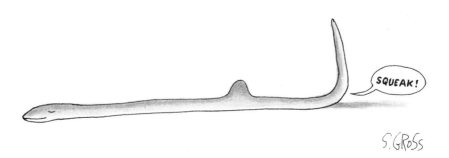

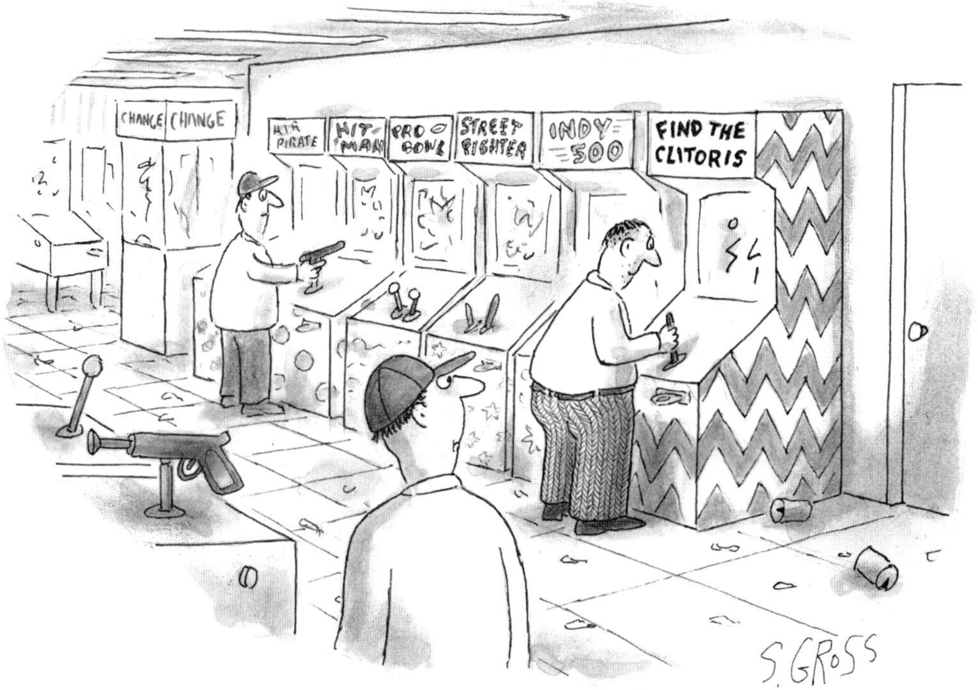
CHANGE
CHANGE
AIR PIRATE
HIT MAN
PRO BOWL
STREET FIGHTER
INDY 500
FIND THE CLITORIS
S. GROSS

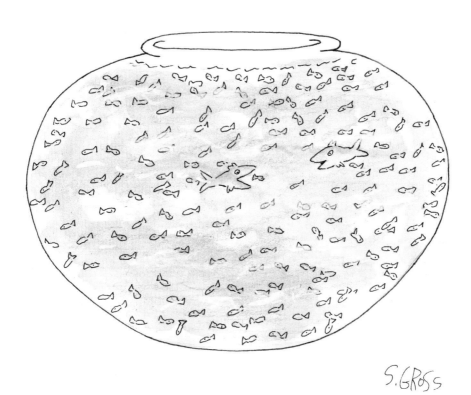

"If I had the abortion we wouldn't be eating so good."

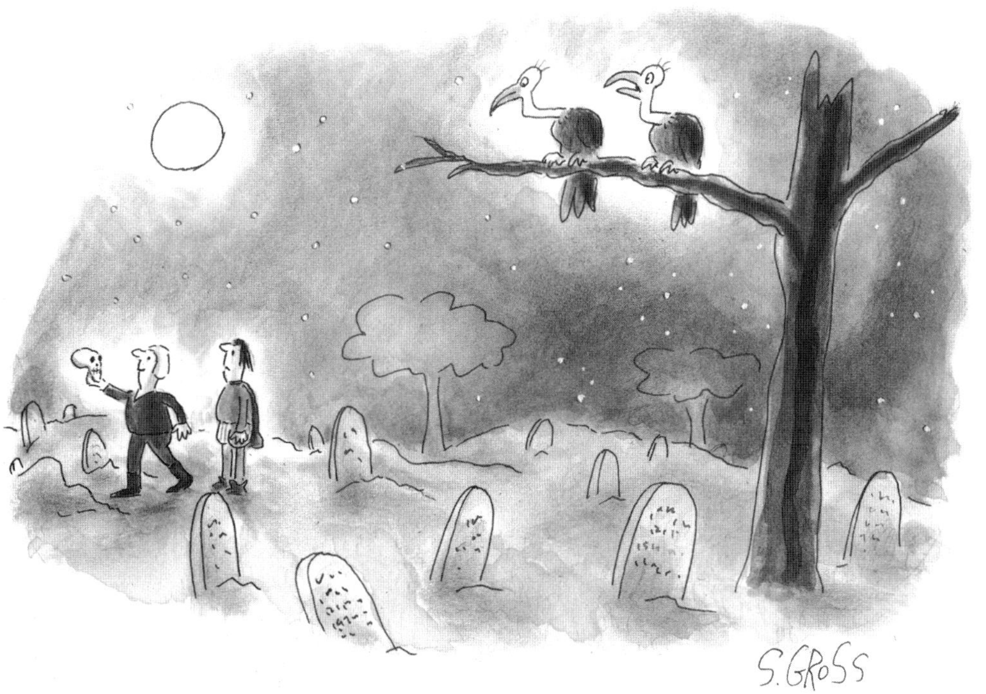
S. GROSS

"I knew Yorick also. He gave me diarrhea."

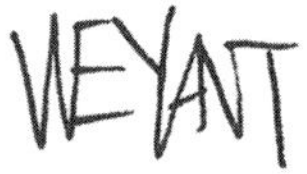

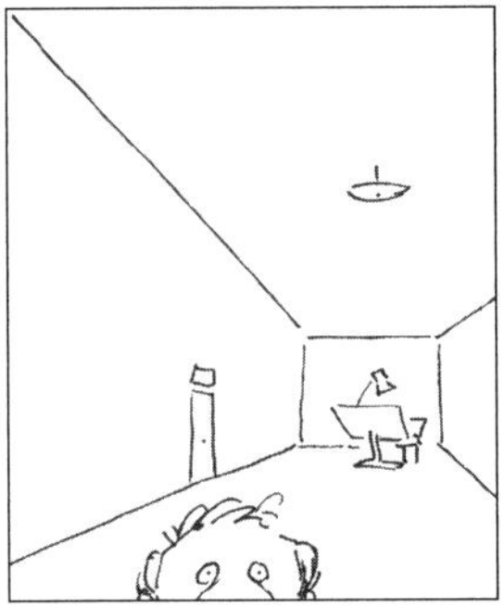

Christopher Weyant

Frequently Asked Questions

- *Where do you get your ideas?*
  Deep in the heart of New Jersey, buried in an old abandoned mine there lies a trunk full of gags. Unfortunately, all about desert islands.

- *Which comes first, the picture or the caption?*
  The egg—wait—no, chicken.

- *How'd you get started?*
  Usually with a cup of coffee.

- *I admire . . .*
  In the cartoon world, I was raised on the perverse brilliance of Sam Gross and Gahan Wilson. Limitless imaginations. Bob Weber is stunning—I've learned so much from his lyrical line.

- *How do you deal with rejection?*
  I take a long *shvitz* in a seven-foot-long tub filled with scotch. Single malt if I feel particularly wounded.

- *What are some things that make you laugh and why?*
  Human relationships. That's all there is when you boil it down. Husband and wife, diner and waiter, ventriloquist and dummy, lifeguard and drowning man, dog and cat, and so on. Relationships are never equal, always in conflict, and therefore, forever funny. But ventriloquist and dummy is my favorite by far. . . .

- *I've got a great idea for a cartoon—wanna hear it?*
  That's the first three minutes of every cocktail party I've ever been to.

Draw Something in This Space

. . . that will help us understand your childhood.

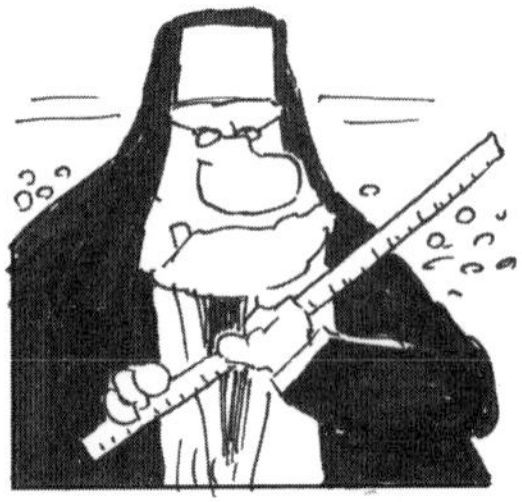

Infrequently Asked Questions

- *Have you mooned or been mooned more often in your life?*
  I proudly refuse to write a Venus or Uranus joke here.

- *What would make a terrible pizza topping?*
  Cheese.

- *What might one expect to find at a really low-budget amusement park?*
  Most of my family. We're carny proud.

- *What did the shepherd say to the three-legged sheepdog?*
  Sit. Stay. Fall over.

And Now for a Few More Questions . . .

- *What do you hate drawing?*
  The shattered hopes and dreams of a generation. That, and walnuts.

- *Being as accurate as possible, how many desert island cartoons do you think you've come up with and submitted to* The New Yorker*?*
  Zero. Although strangely, some were published under my name.

- *What's the funniest thing that you witnessed, overheard, or came up with that you couldn't figure out how to use in a cartoon?*
  Once, there was this guy and he did this thing at this place, and it was a riot! You can't make that stuff up! Good times.

Naming Names

- *What name might you give to a mild-mannered, middle-aged, bespectacled dental assistant in one of your cartoons?*
  Phil McCavities.

- *Other than Lance, what name would you give to a twenty-eight-year-old entertainment lawyer with a blue-dyed fauxhawk who cycles on weekends?*
  Nancy.

- *What would be a good name for a new, commercially unviable breakfast cereal?*
  Hemorrhoids—now with Lil' Marshmallows!

- *Come up with a name for an unpleasant medical procedure.*
  Transnasalshmeckelectomy, with a twist.

- *If you used a pen name, what would it be?*
  Max Kensington or Karl Merriweather would be my nom de 'toon.

Complete the Pie Chart Below

. . . in a way that tells us something about your life or how you think.

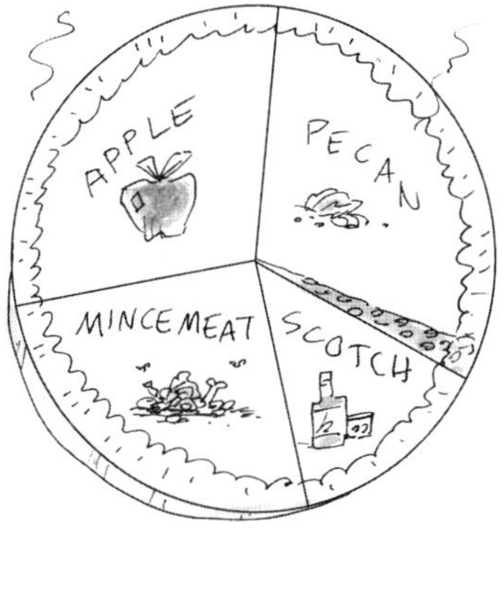
APPLE
PECAN
MINCEMEAT
SCOTCH

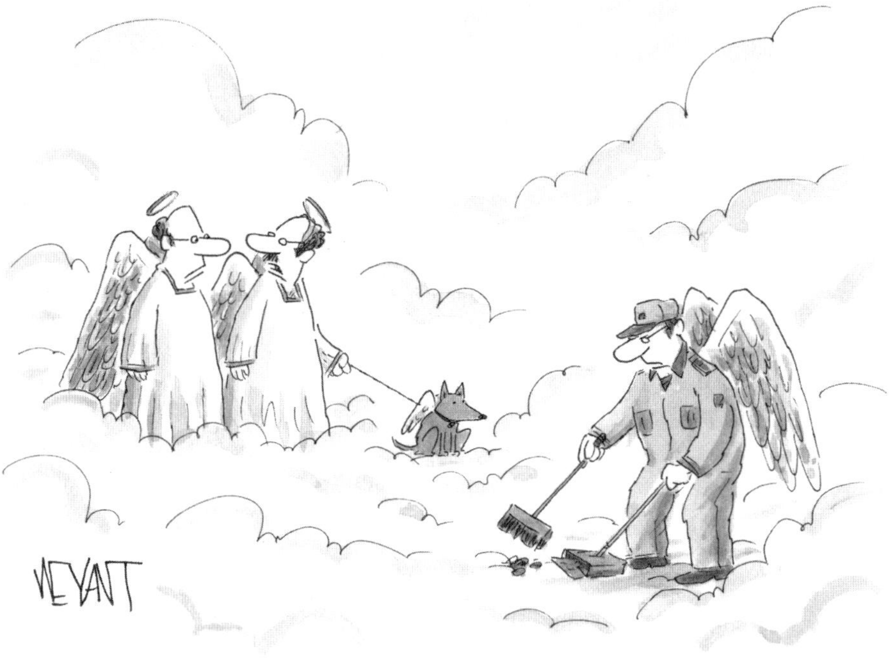
WEYANT

"Atheist."

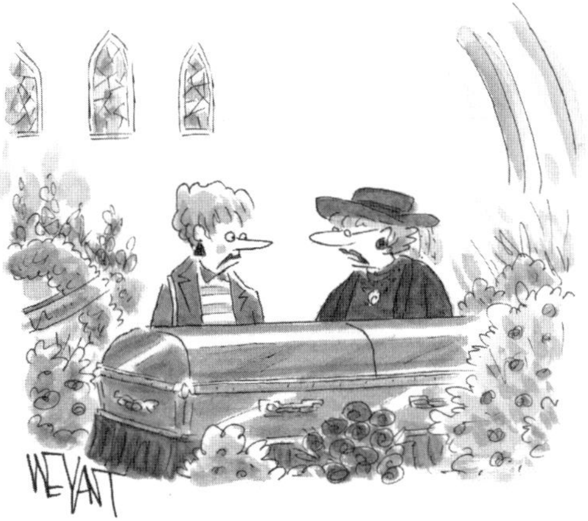
WEYANT

"It would have been an open casket, but he overdosed on Viagra."

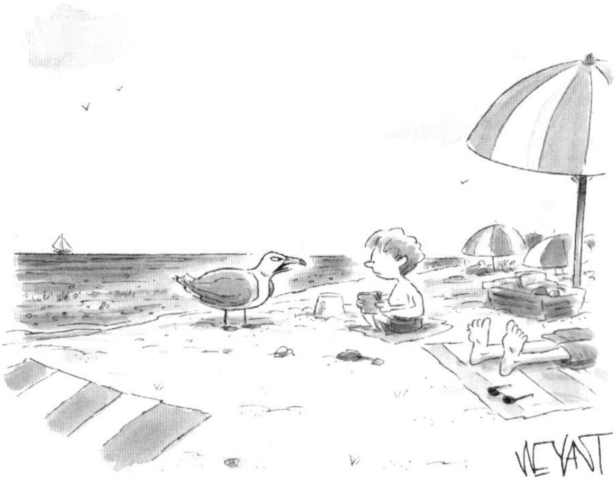
WEYANT

"Hand over the sandwich or I'll crap on your parents."

"Mostly, I just miss his hand."

"I told you I'm not into any kinky stuff."

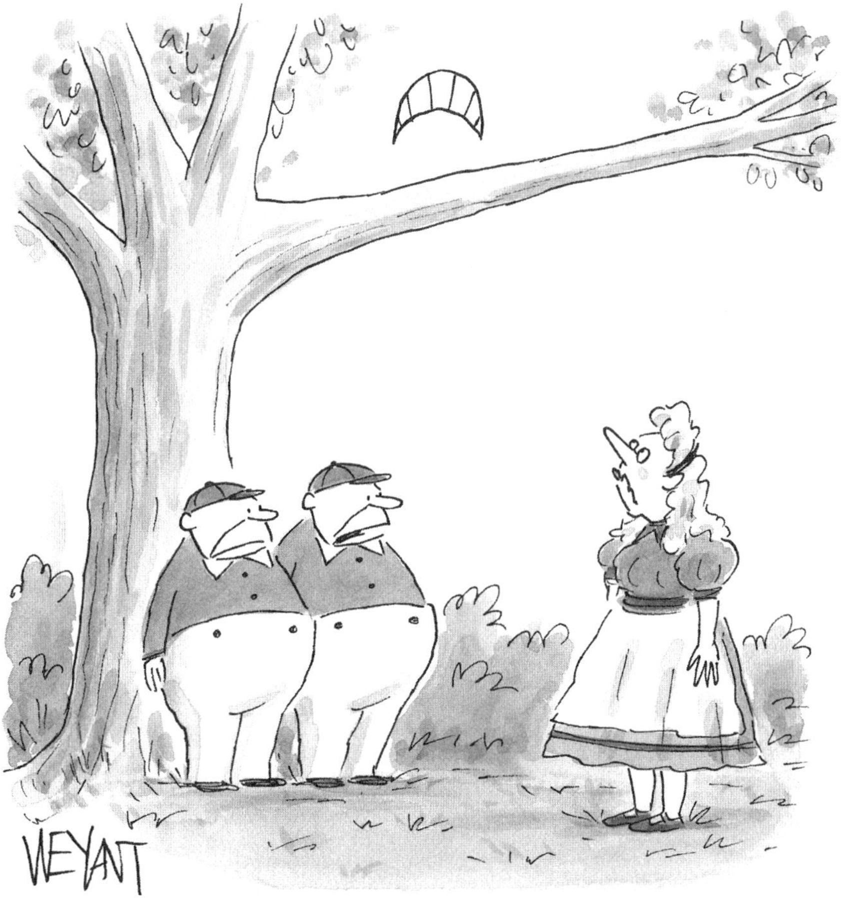
WEYANT

"We had him neutered."

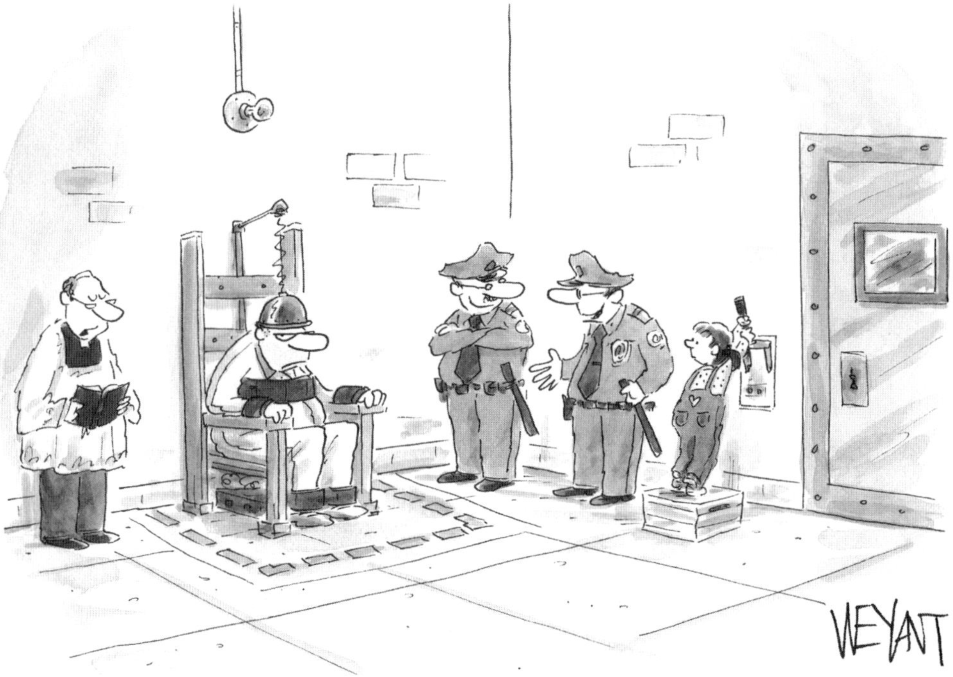
WEYANT

"I've got to admit, Bring Your Daughter to Work Day really adds a touch of home to the workplace."

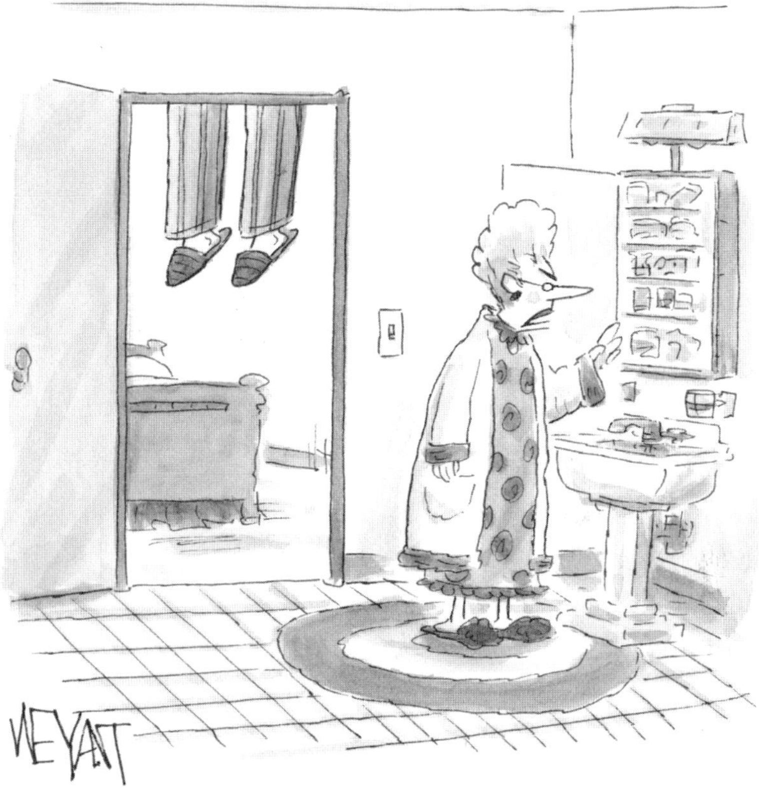
WEYANT

"Richard, did you use all of the dental floss?"

······················· ACKNOWLEDGMENTS ·······················

A book is sorta like a freight train—one of those old-timey ones. Someone has to draw the plans and consult a map; someone has to build trestle bridges over rivers and blast tunnels through mountains; someone has to lay the track, connect all the cars, grease the wheels, collect tickets, check the pocket watch, shovel coal; and someone has to toot the horn. The horn-tooting was my job, and all the rest was done by the following fine folks:

Tanya Erlach, David Kuhn, Billy Kingsland, Arlie Johansen, and the crew at Workman Publishing, including Liz Davis, Peggy Gannon, Janet Vicario, Sue Macleod, and Peter Workman, who all had a hand in the previous iteration of this book. Sarah Curley, Beth Levy, and Galen Smith, who helped to revise and update this version. And my editor, Megan Nicolay, who's been here for it all. Thanks also to Bob Mankoff, David Remnick, Emma Allen, and especially the cartoonists themselves who came up with all the material, old and new, that you see in here. If you see any of these people out anywhere, buy them something nice.

COPYRIGHT INFORMATION